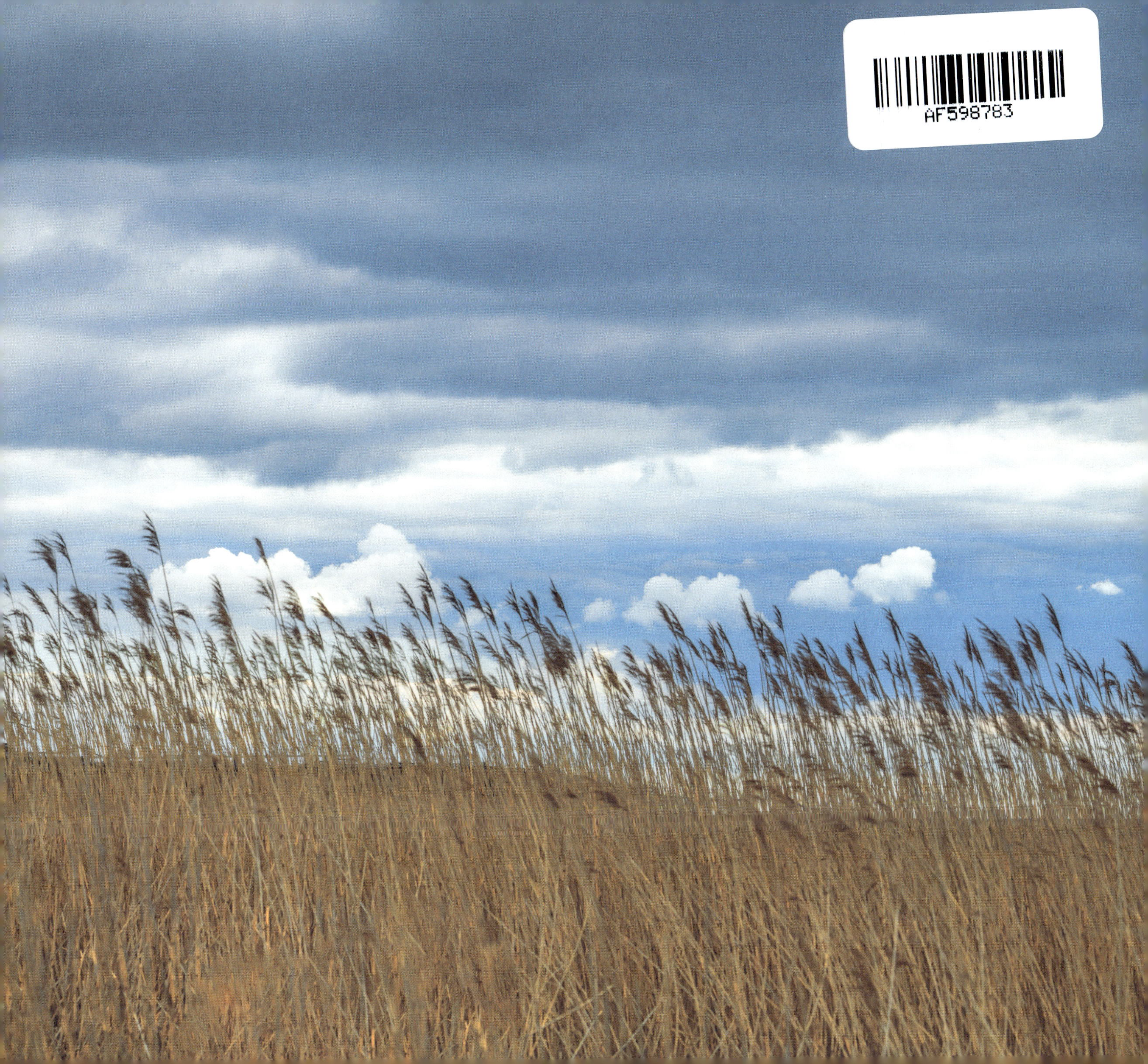

DAVID SKERNICK

BACK ROADS *of New England*

CONNECTICUT, RHODE ISLAND, MASSACHUSETTS, MAINE, NEW HAMPSHIRE, AND VERMONT

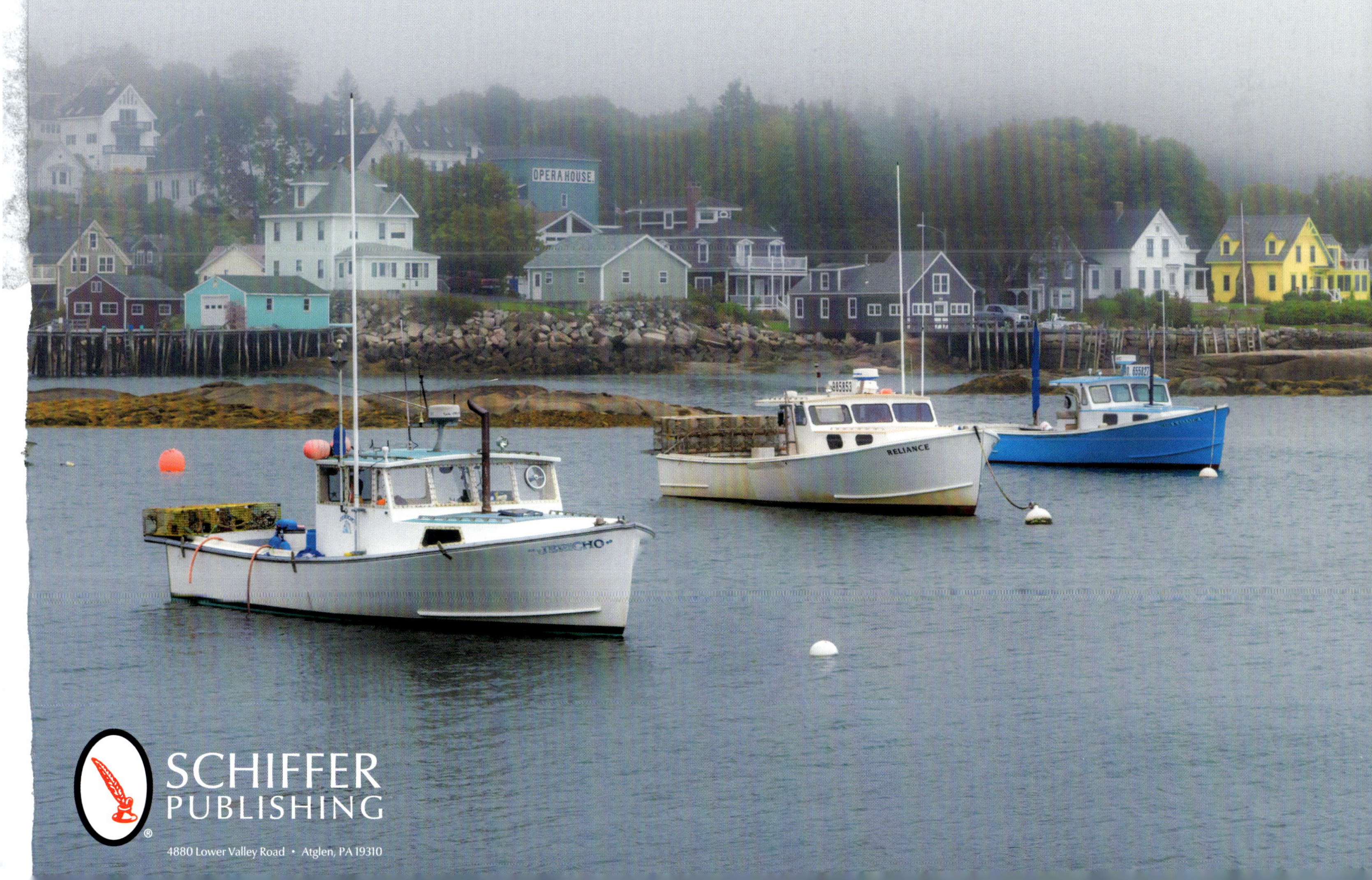

SCHIFFER PUBLISHING

4880 Lower Valley Road • Atglen, PA 19310

Other Schiffer Books by the Author:

Back Roads of Northern California,
ISBN 978-0-7643-5762-6

Back Roads of Southern California,
ISBN 978-0-7643-5763-3

Back Roads of the Southwest,
ISBN 978-0-7643-5858-6

Back Roads of the Great Plains,
ISBN 978-0-7643-6186-9

Back Roads of the Pacific Northwest,
ISBN 978-0-7643-6290-3

Back Roads of the Midwest,
ISBN 978-0-7643-6483-9

How Did You Get That Shot?,
ISBN 978-0-7643-5728-2

Easy Astrophotography,
ISBN 978-0-7643-6684-0

Library of Congress Control Number: 2024931521

Edited by Ian Robertson
Type set in Proxima Nova

ISBN: 978-0-7643-6826-4
Printed in China

Published by Schiffer Publishing, Ltd.
4880 Lower Valley Road
Atglen, PA 19310
Phone: (610) 593-1777; Fax: (610) 593-2002
Email: info@schifferbooks.com
Web: www.schifferbooks.com

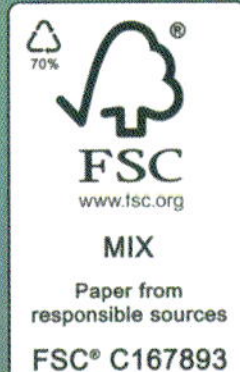

New England has a harsh climate, a barren soil, a rough and stormy coast, and yet we love it, even with a love passing that of dwellers in more favored regions.

—Henry Cabot Lodge

INTRODUCTION

Autumn in New England. Who has never heard about that? It seems to be synonymous with "fall colors." I travel and photograph mostly in the fall and spring. Spring flowers and fall colors are like spice to a photographer; they flavor the landscape. A mundane field can be transported into a fairyland; a single tree can become a composition on fire. You bet I came to New England in the fall. It isn't the only season or the only subject of this book, but yeah, it's there. It would not be fair for me to try to define a region by only showing what it looks like two or three weeks out of a year, but fall in New England is bigger than time.

The northeastern corner of the United States is known for a few other things; for example, have you ever had a clam cake? They are a little more like fritters than cakes—deep-fried doughy things with clams inside. I know I didn't make that sound so good, but they are amazing! New England is full of paradoxes like that. The weather is terrible, but rain, snow, and fog are sort of like secret weapons to us camera jockeys; everything looks better wet, or frosted with snow! There are some sand beaches, but much of the coast is rocky and treacherous, creating staggering waves and spectacular beauty. Did you know that Maine has more shoreline miles than California?

Even the people are paradoxical. Reserved and quiet, yet welcoming and incredibly generous. When I asked if I could photograph the inside of Norm's Diner in Groton, Connecticut, the owner said no because the grill was in use and didn't look pristine. Then she called me back over and said I could come back after they closed. So yeah, she and her brother hung around after closing to give me the time to take the photo in this book. I met people like that all over New England.

My books are not meant to be exhaustive collections of photographs from each region. They are more a collection of places and things I see as I drive along. I travel 50,000 miles or so every year along the back roads of the United States. Cities and freeways hold little interest for me. I call this getting lost on "gray roads."

As I crisscross the back roads of this amazing country, I find little gems and prizes everywhere. If you are looking for your favorite spot or road, I may not have found it yet. I will keep looking, and you are, of course, welcome to contact me and make suggestions. I would love to hear from you. Lots of my favorite places were found when I asked someone at a gas station or restaurant, "What's good to see around here?"

Most of my photographs reveal another kind of freedom: panoramic photographs. As a photographer, I was trained in the art of seeing things through the confined dimensions of a 35 mm piece of film—approximately 3:2, slightly wider than tall. As all photographers have done, I have worked within these boundaries, using wide-angle lenses to capture more of the scene than would otherwise be possible, but the resulting distortion of distance and perspective never felt quite right. I found myself secretly envious of painters, who could select any shape of canvas on which to create art. When I found panoramic photography, I realized I had discovered my unrestrained canvas. Panorama photographs are carefully crafted from multiple photographs that are combined to form one large image. With panoramas I can photograph without traditional framing limitations. This is immensely satisfying for me, since I feel that panoramas are best able to convey what you would have seen had you been standing there beside me when I took the picture.

Our ride today will start in Connecticut. From there we'll go to Rhode Island and Massachusetts, before heading up to Maine. Driving southwest through New Hampshire and Vermont will get us all the way around New England. Come on—we'll stop for clam cakes along the way!

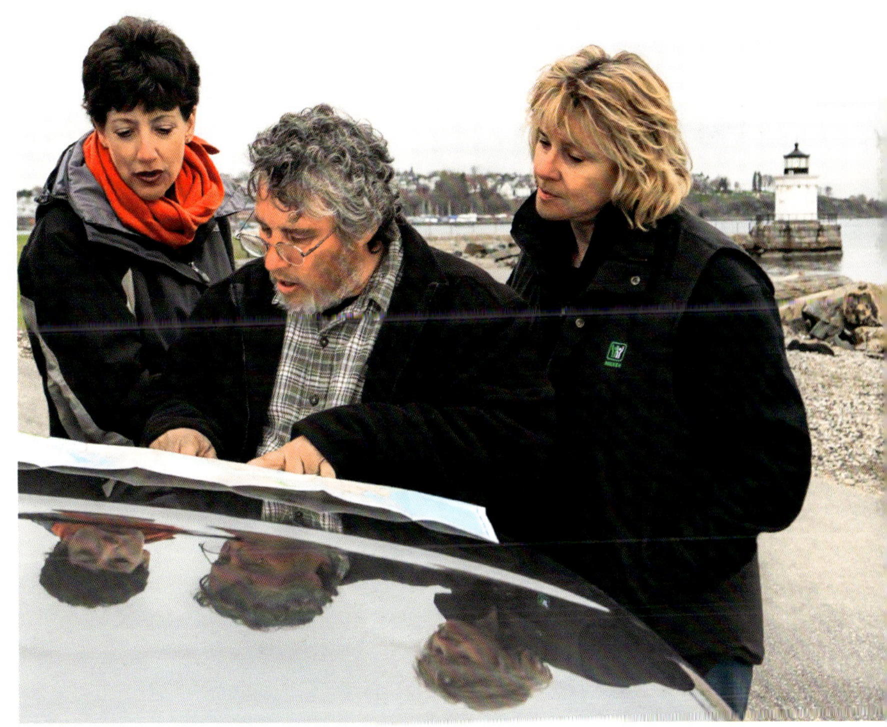

Photo by Carol Zulman

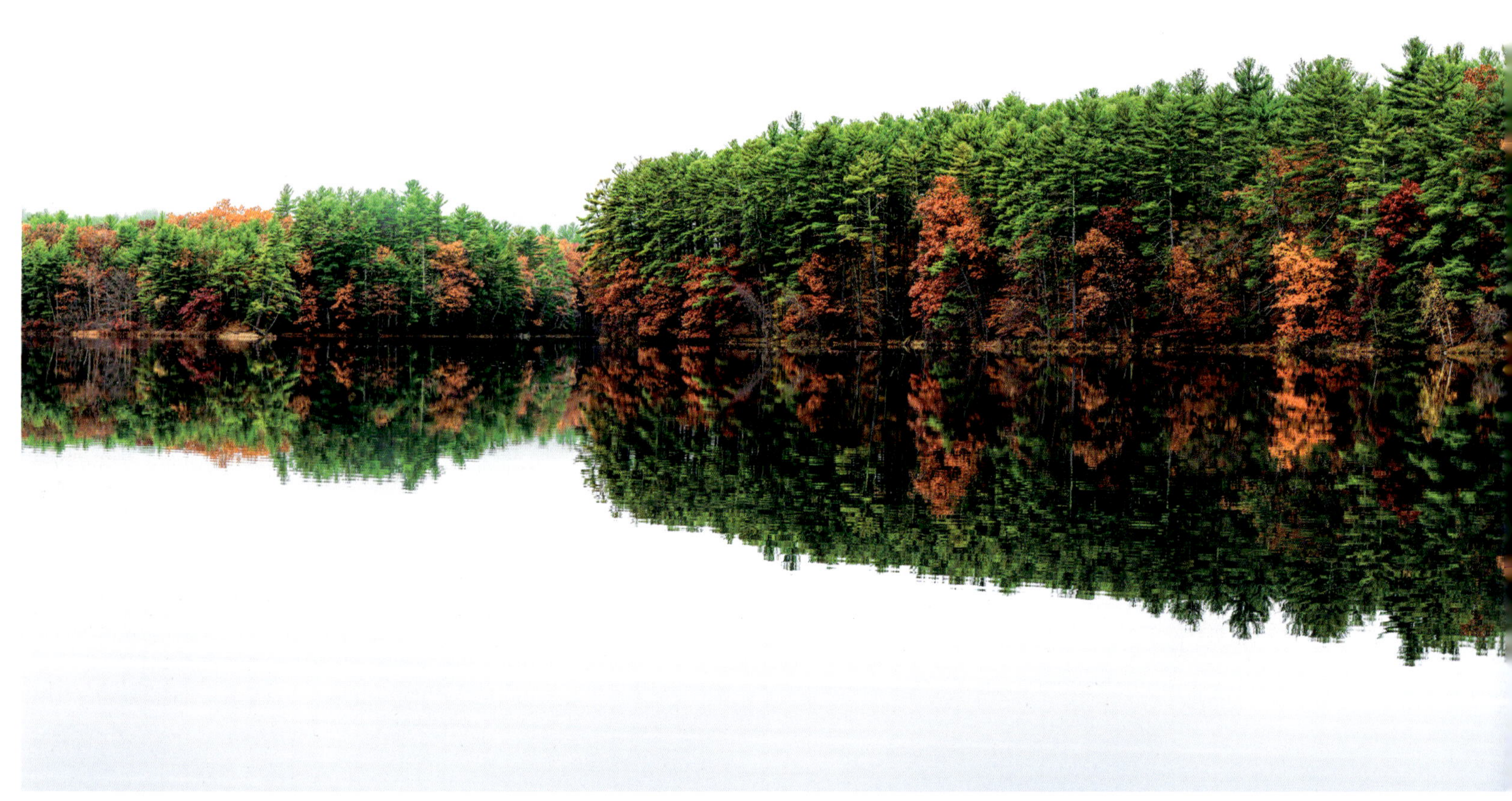

Lake McDonough, Connecticut

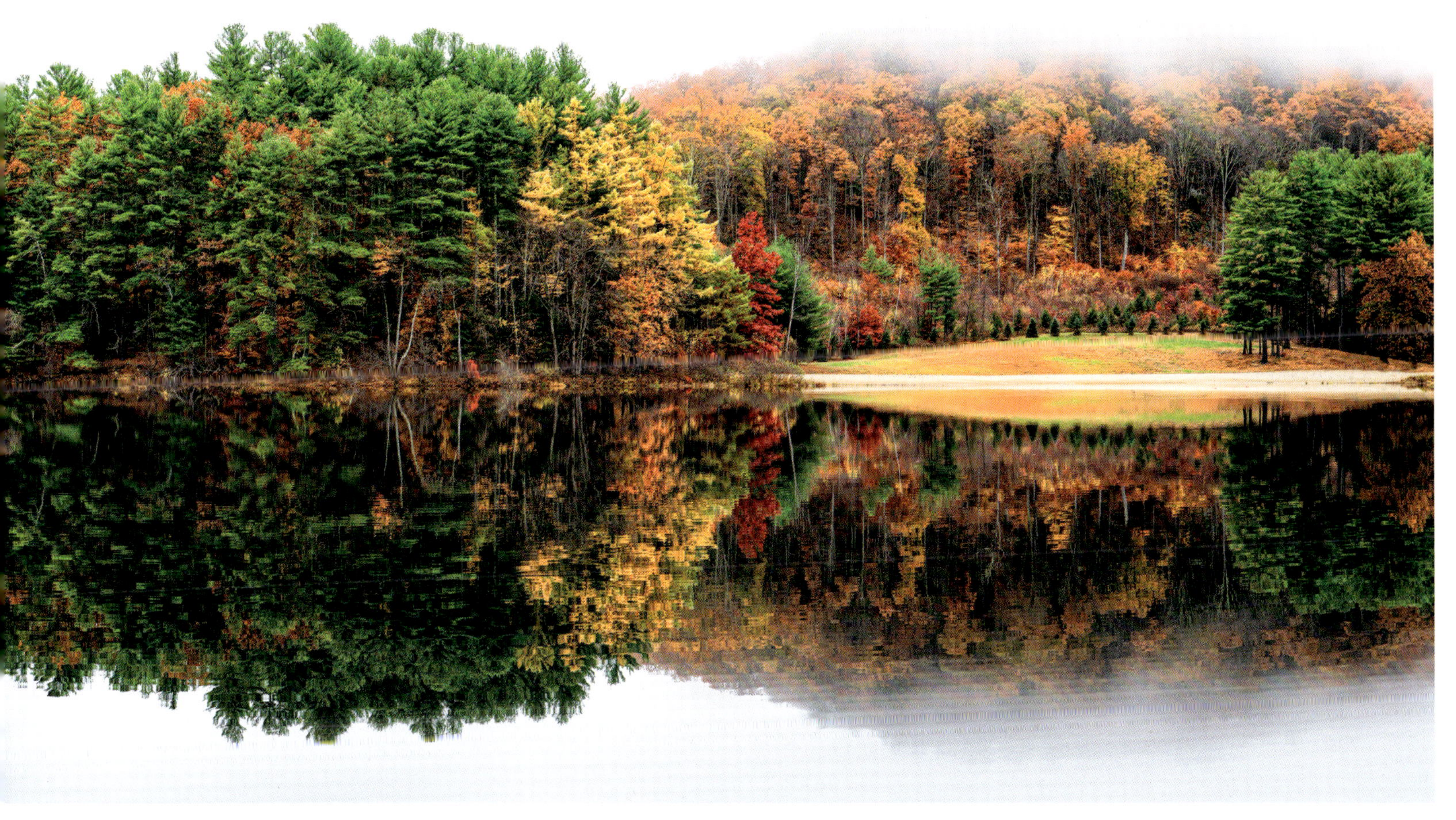

I came around a corner and found this reflection. I was so happy, I was laughing out loud as I got my gear out to take the photo.

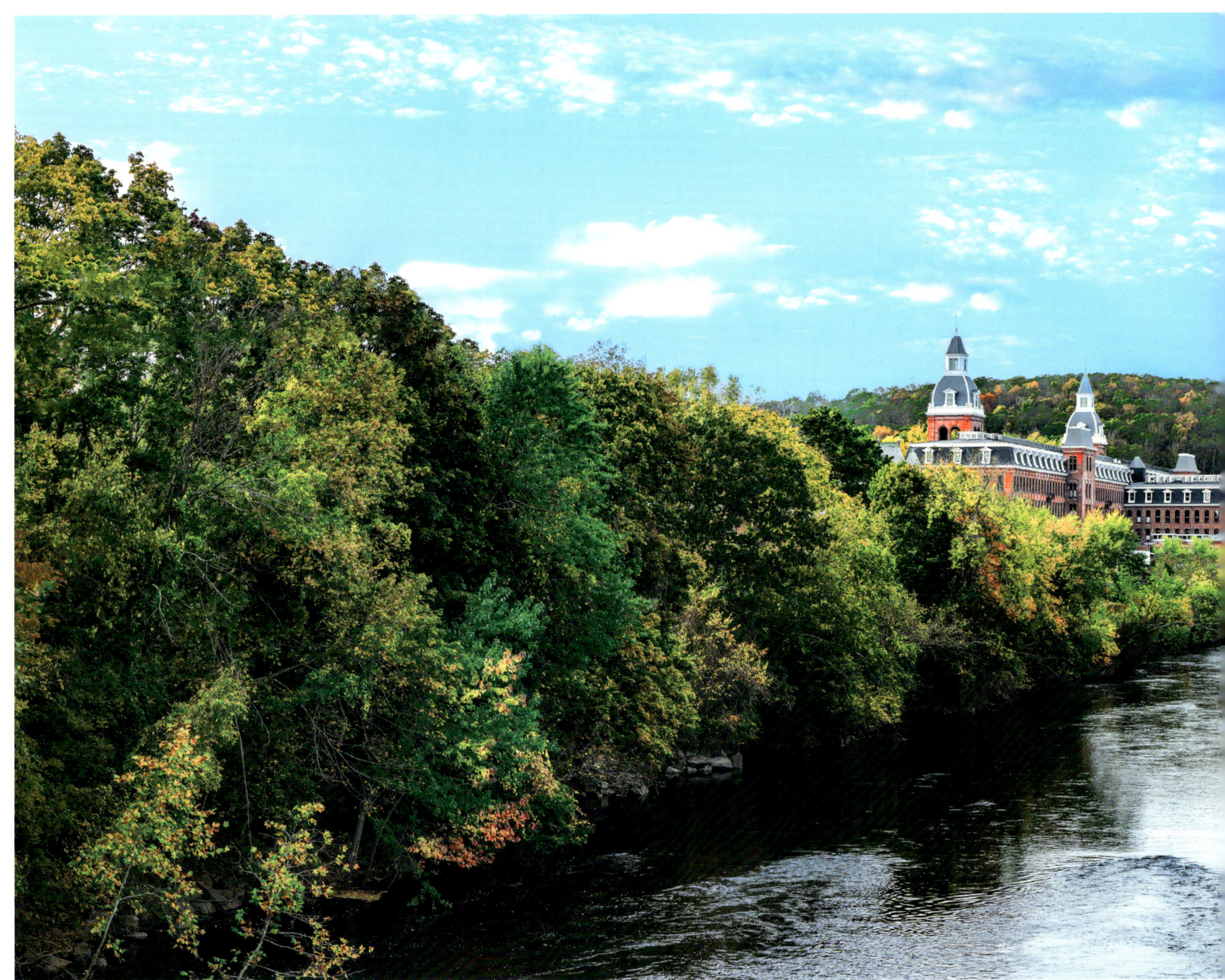

Taftville, Connecticut, and Shetucket River

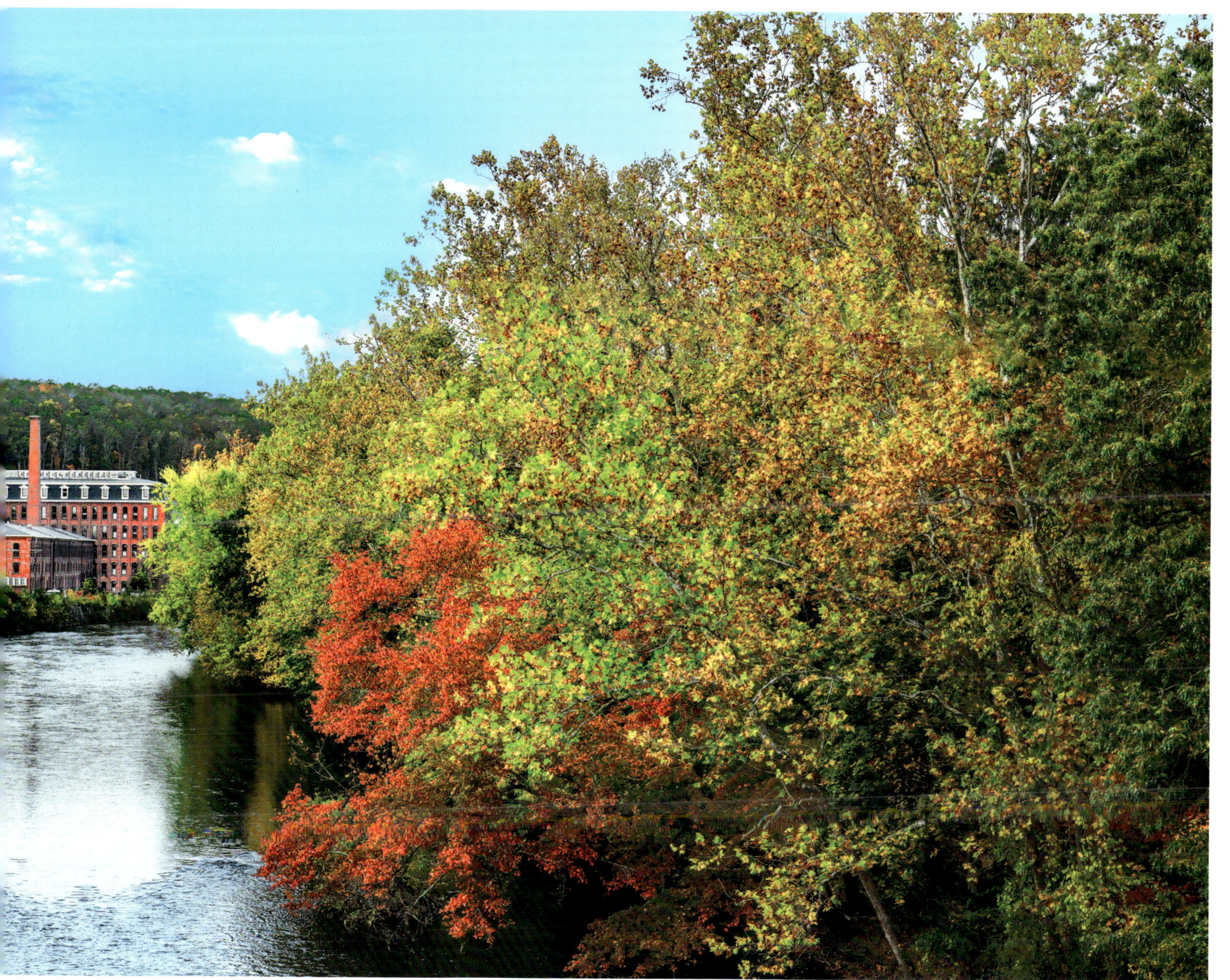

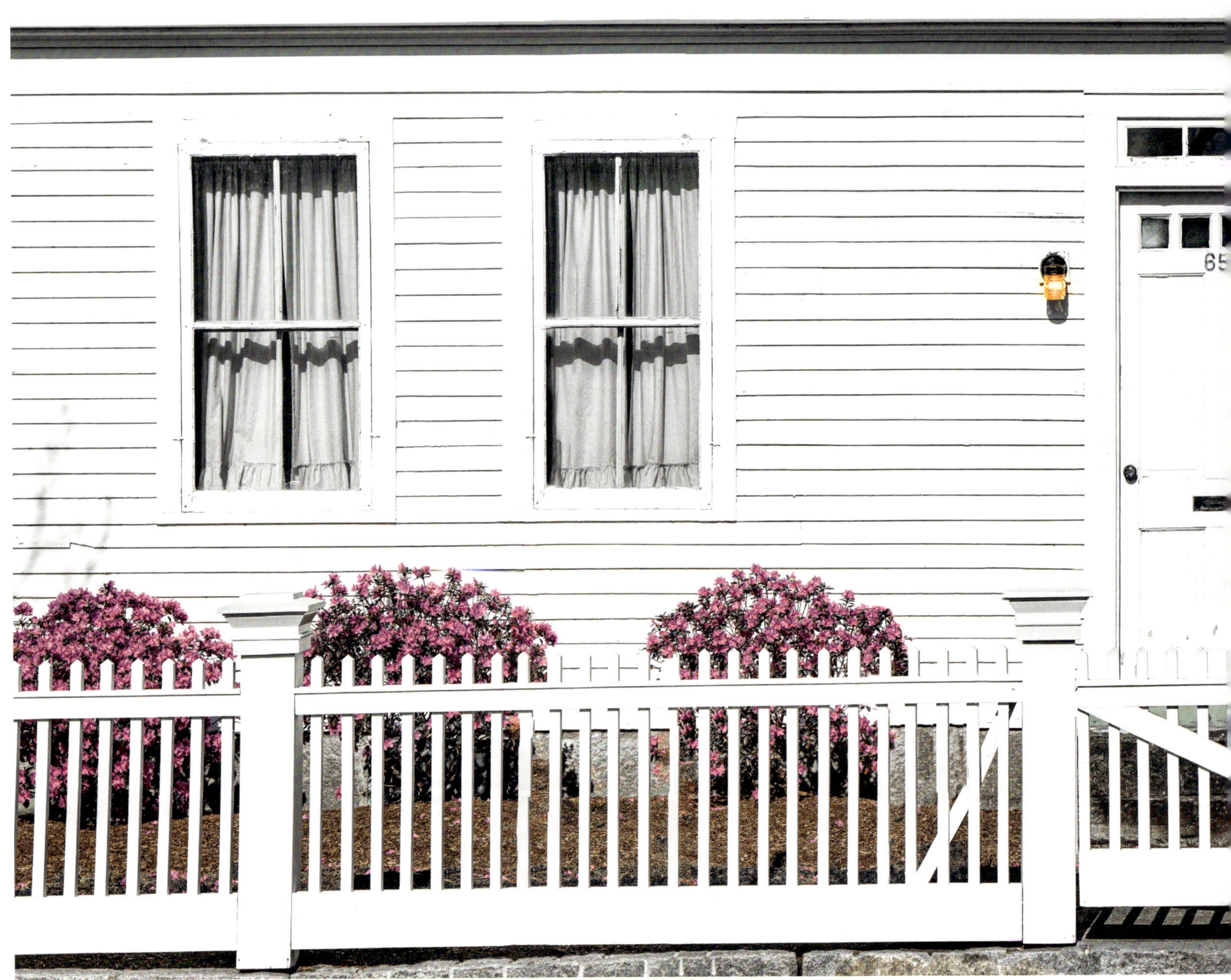

Number 65 with azalea bushes, Connecticut

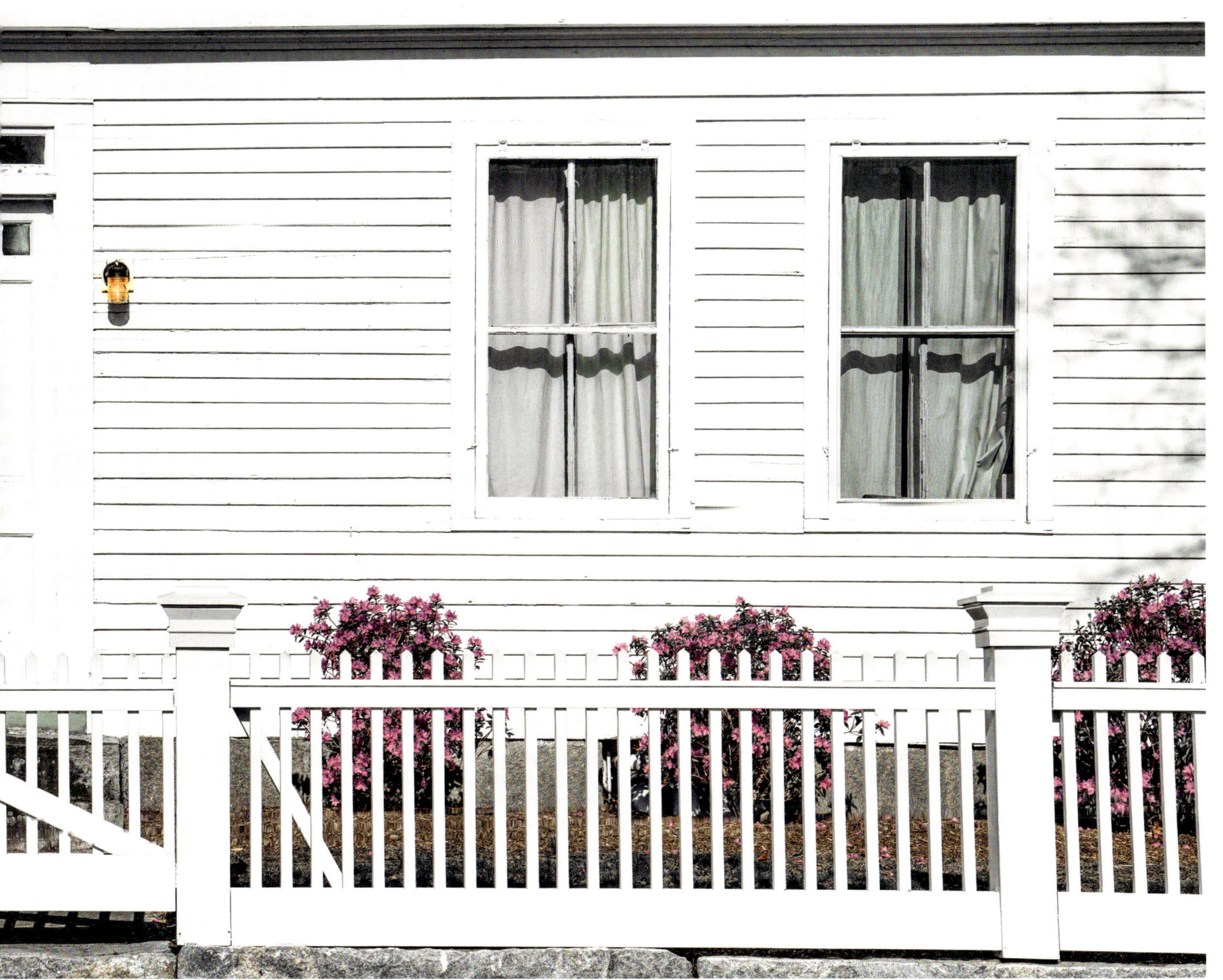

I had to come back three times to get this in the right light and without parked cars or traffic.

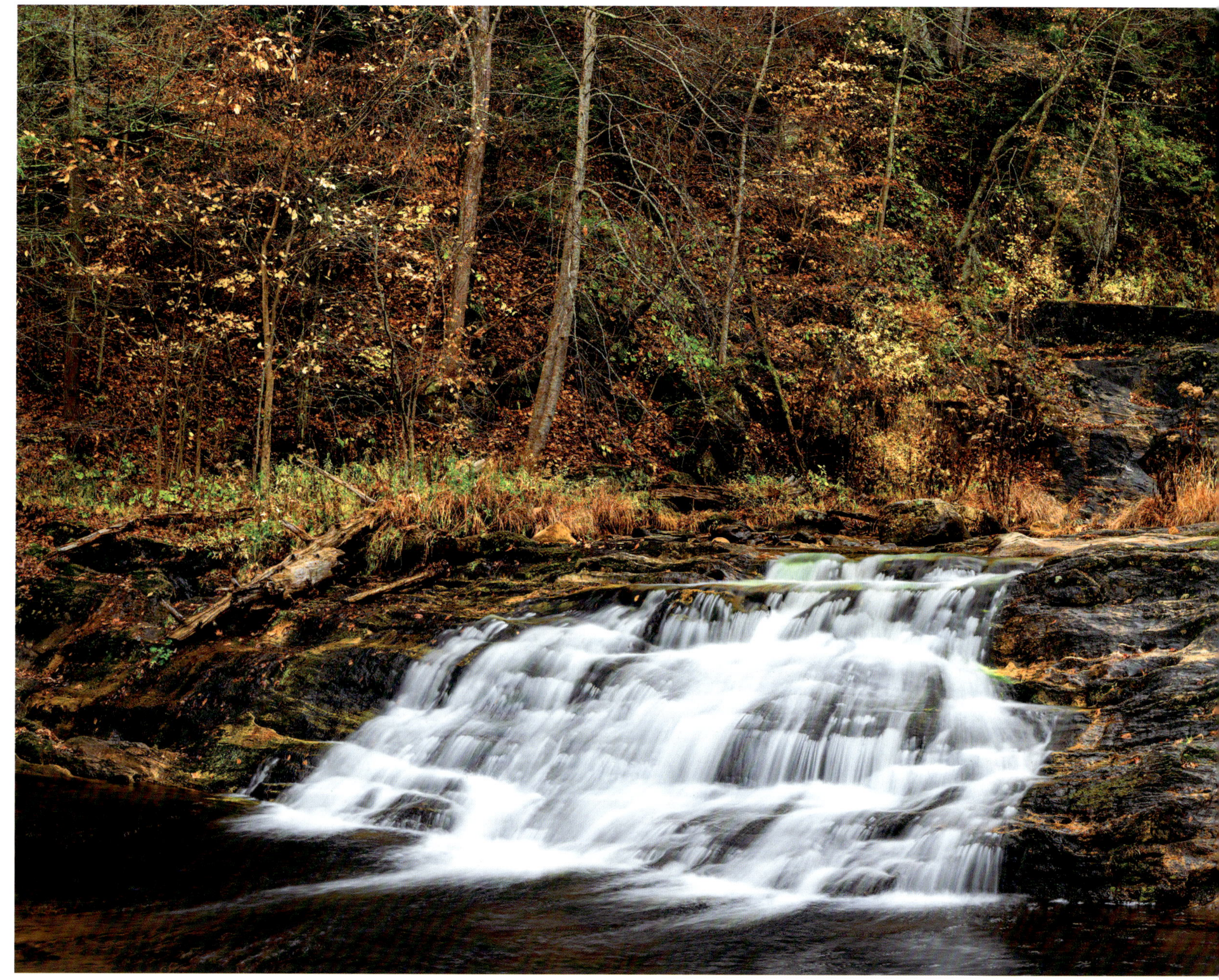

Kent Falls, Connecticut

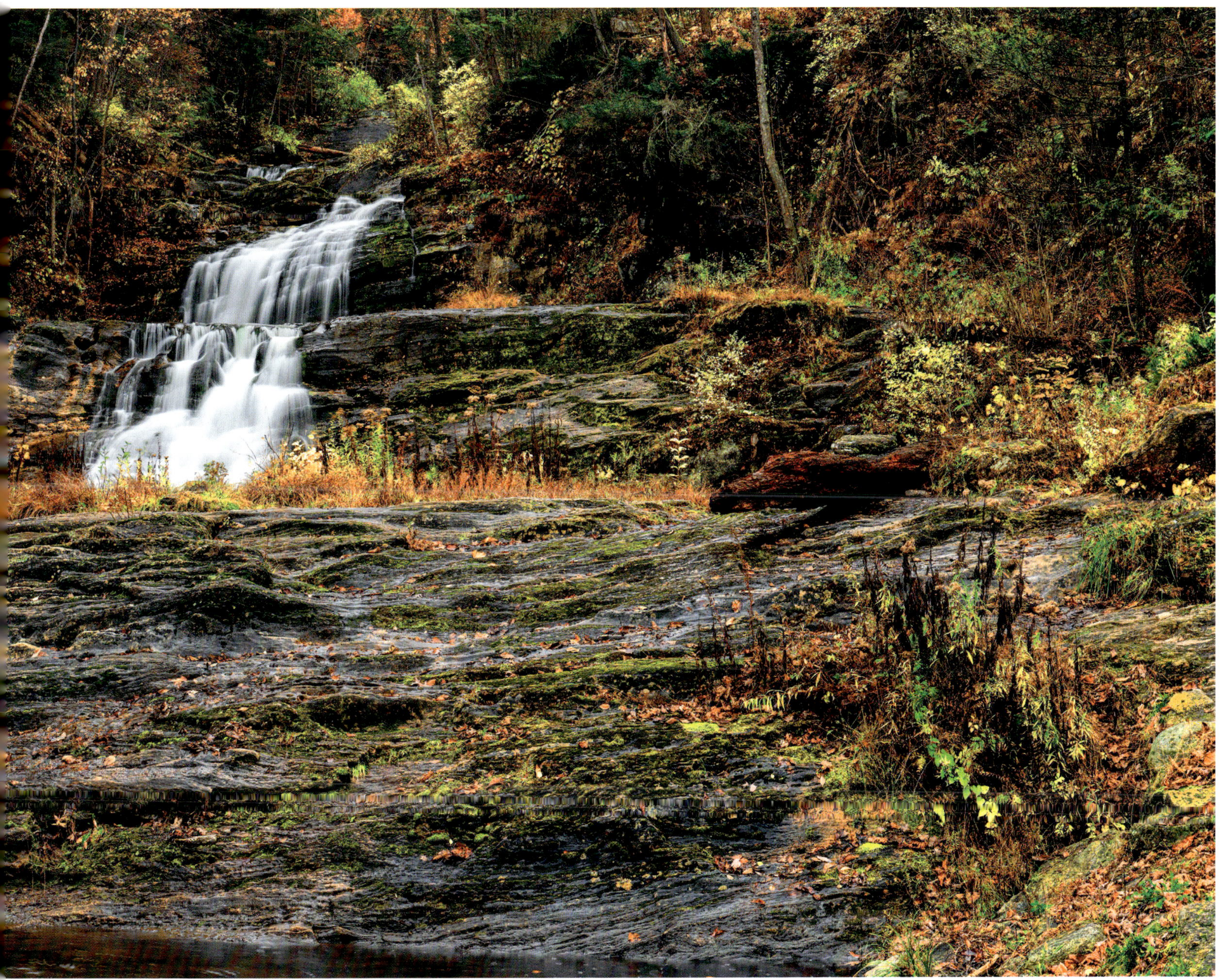

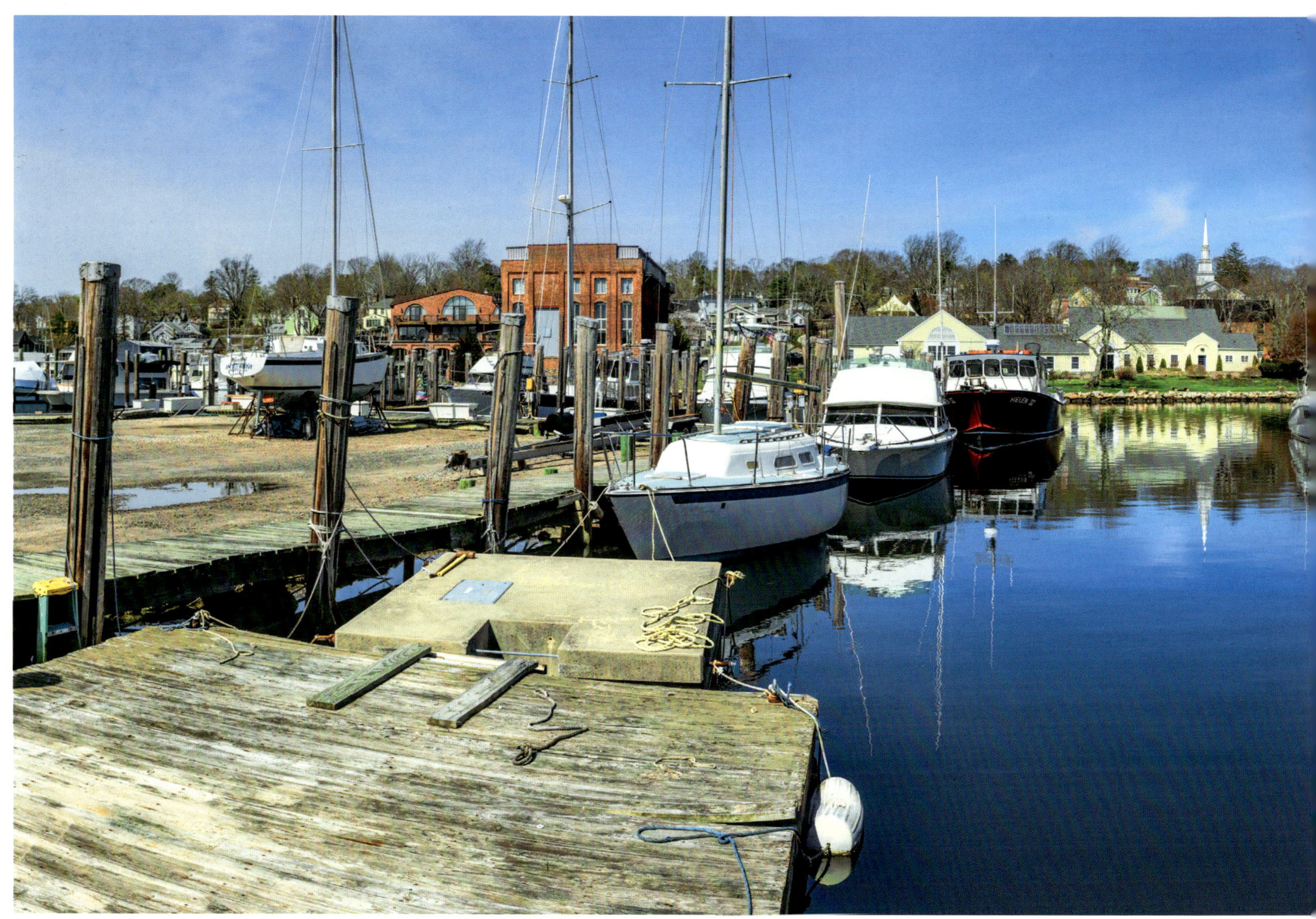

The *Marianne*, Mystic Seaport, Connecticut

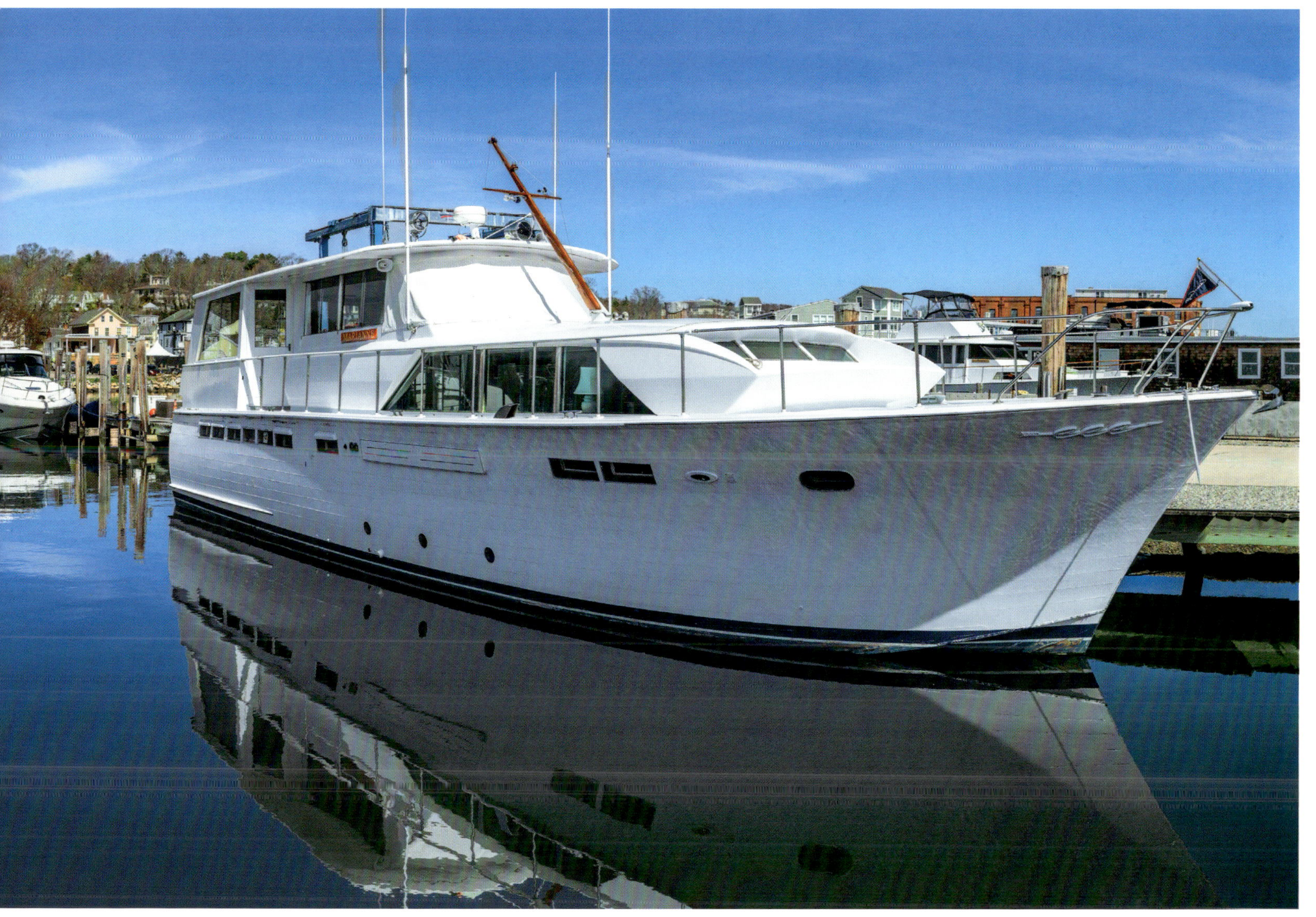

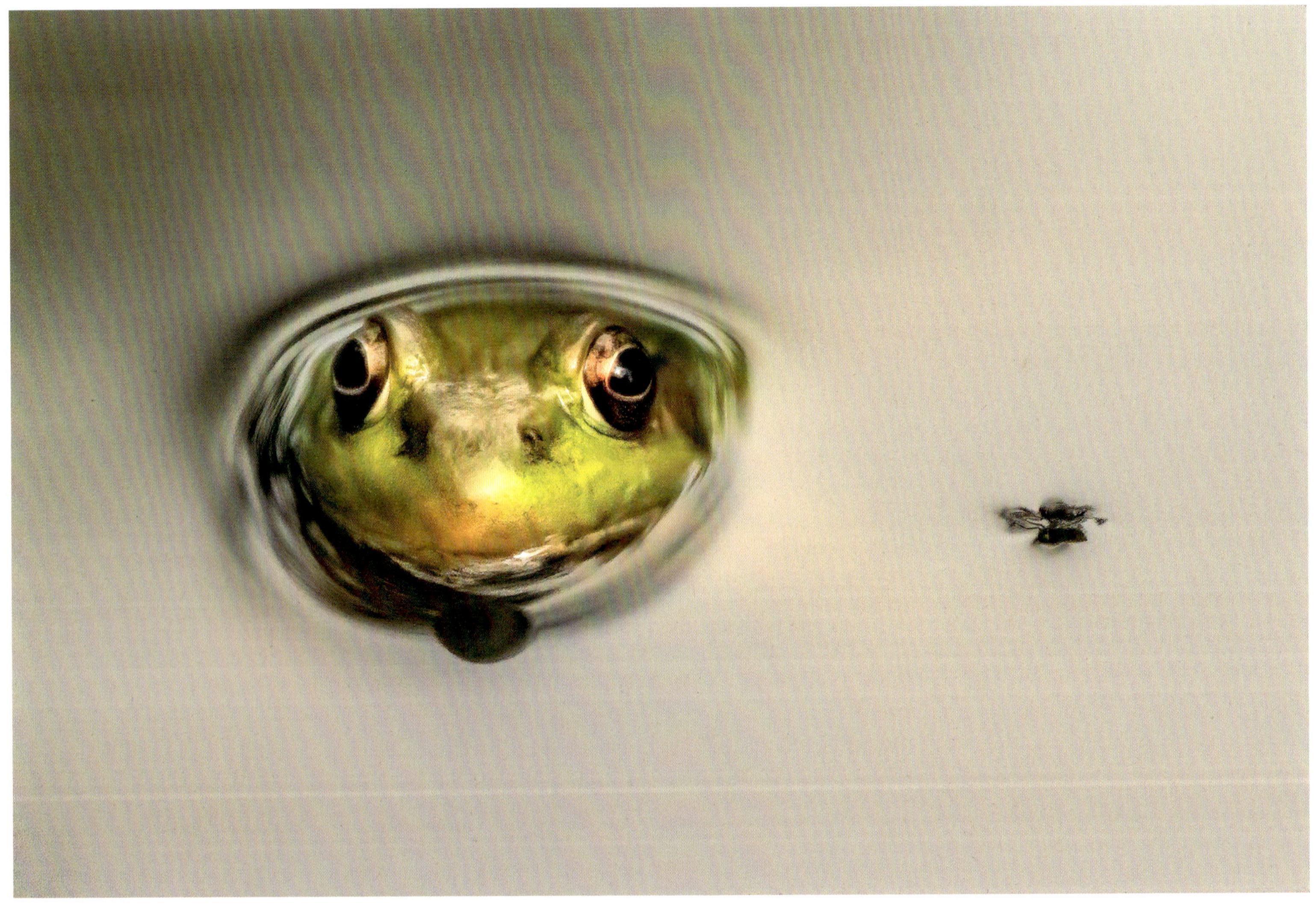

New England bullfrog

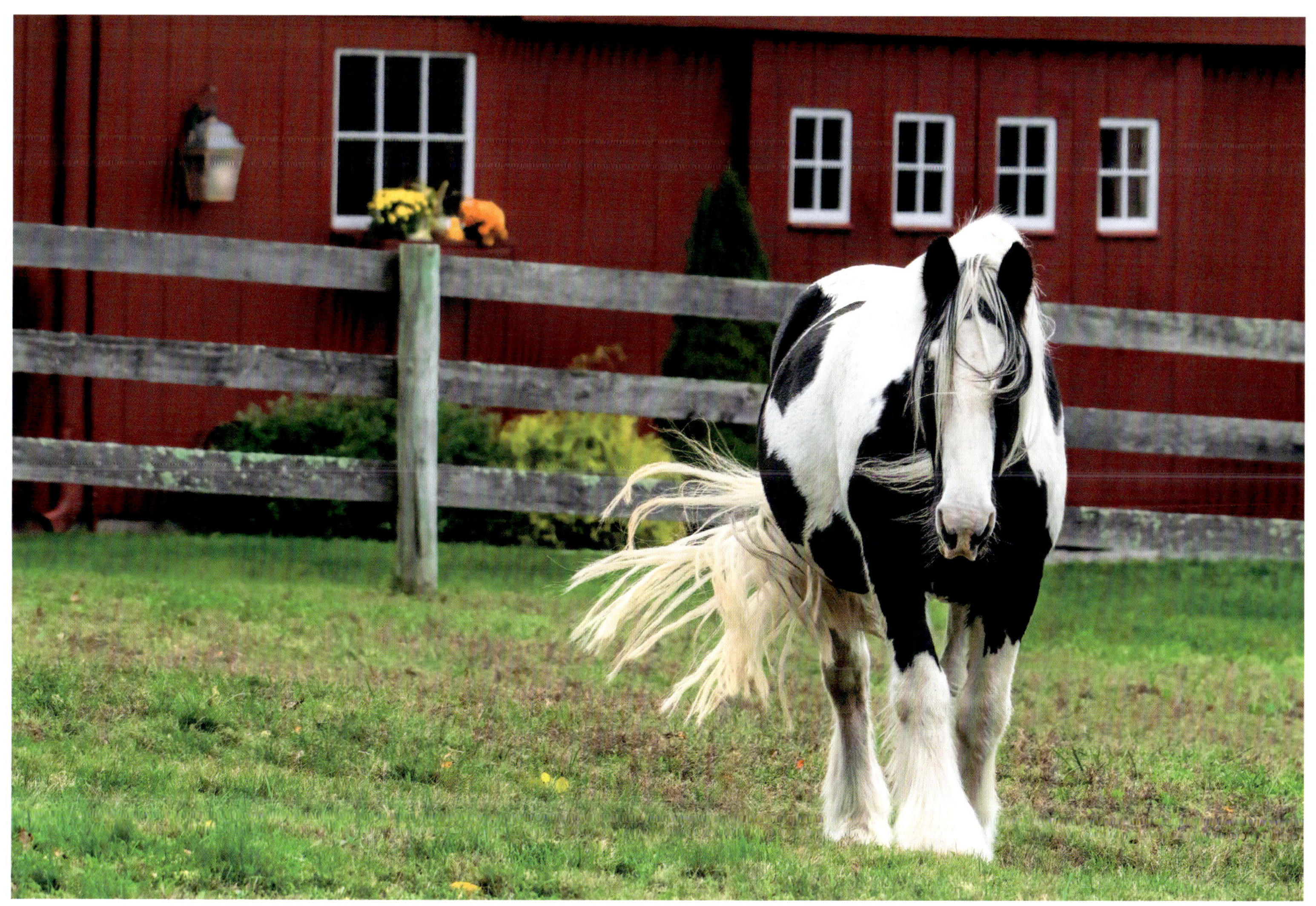

Gypsy Woods horses, Connecticut

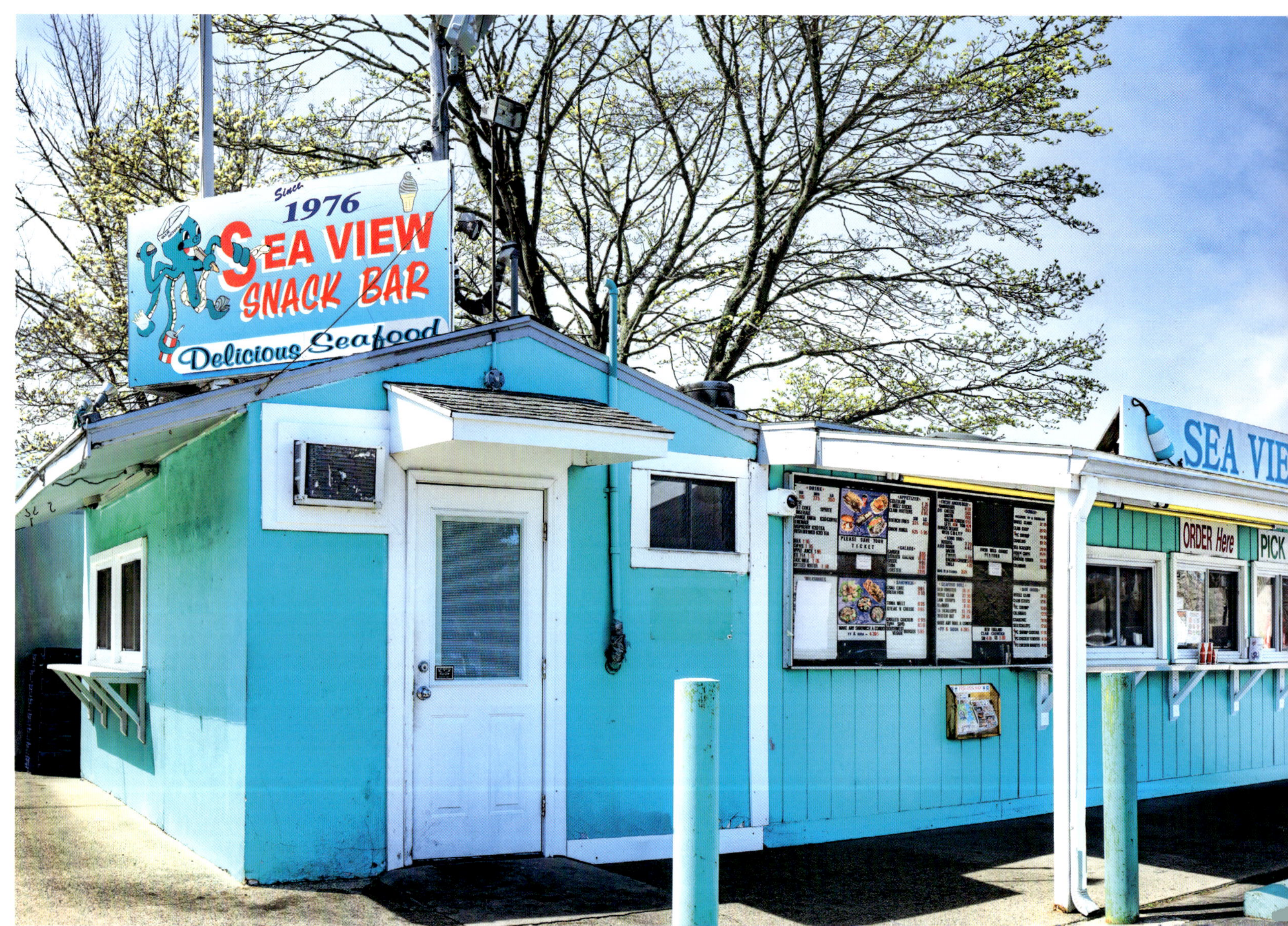

Sea View Snack Bar, Mystic, Connecticut

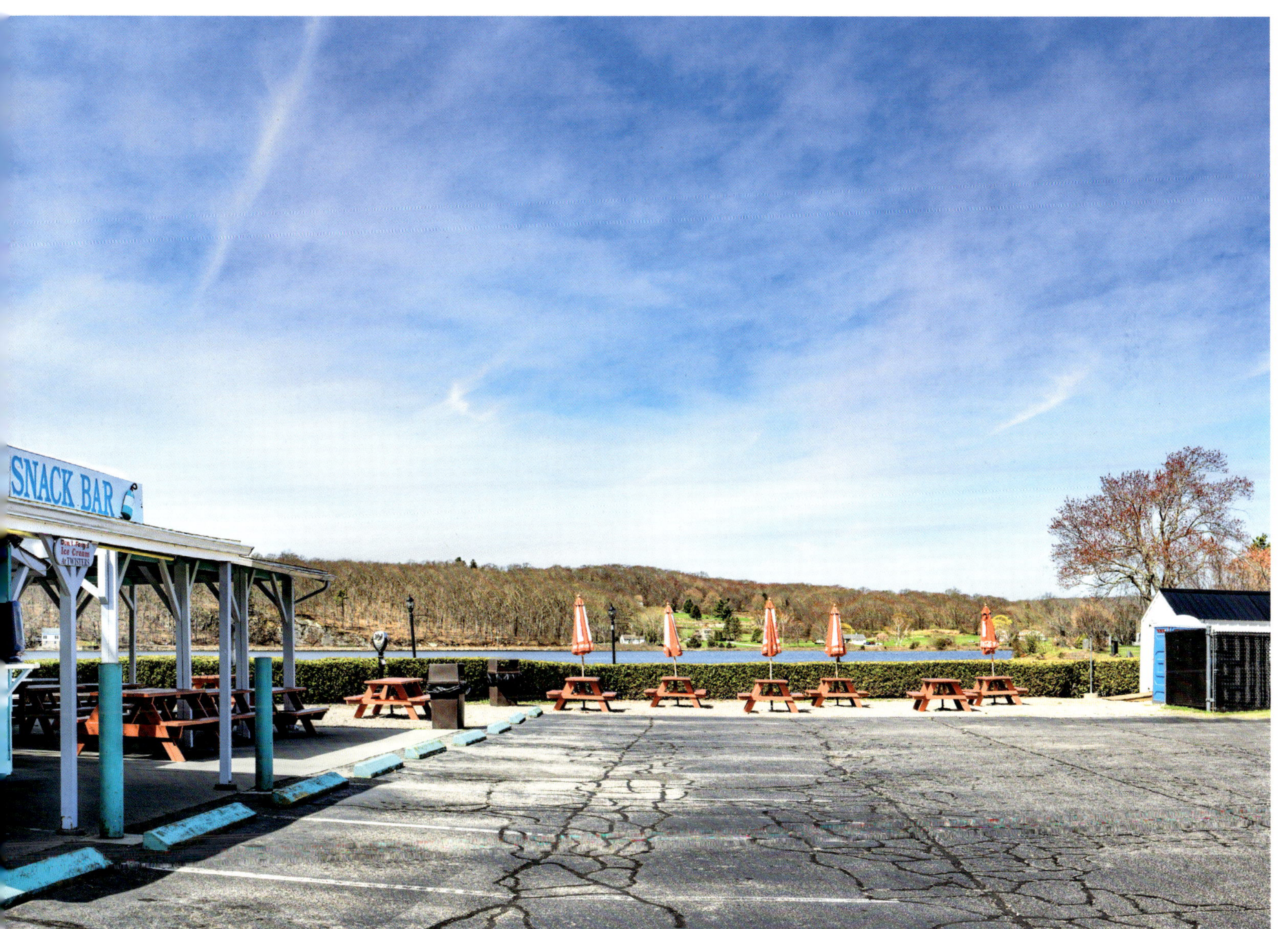

I came back after they opened and had a great lobster roll. In Connecticut, that's just lobster and melted butter on a roll. In Maine they make a lobster salad with mayonnaise. Either way is perfect.

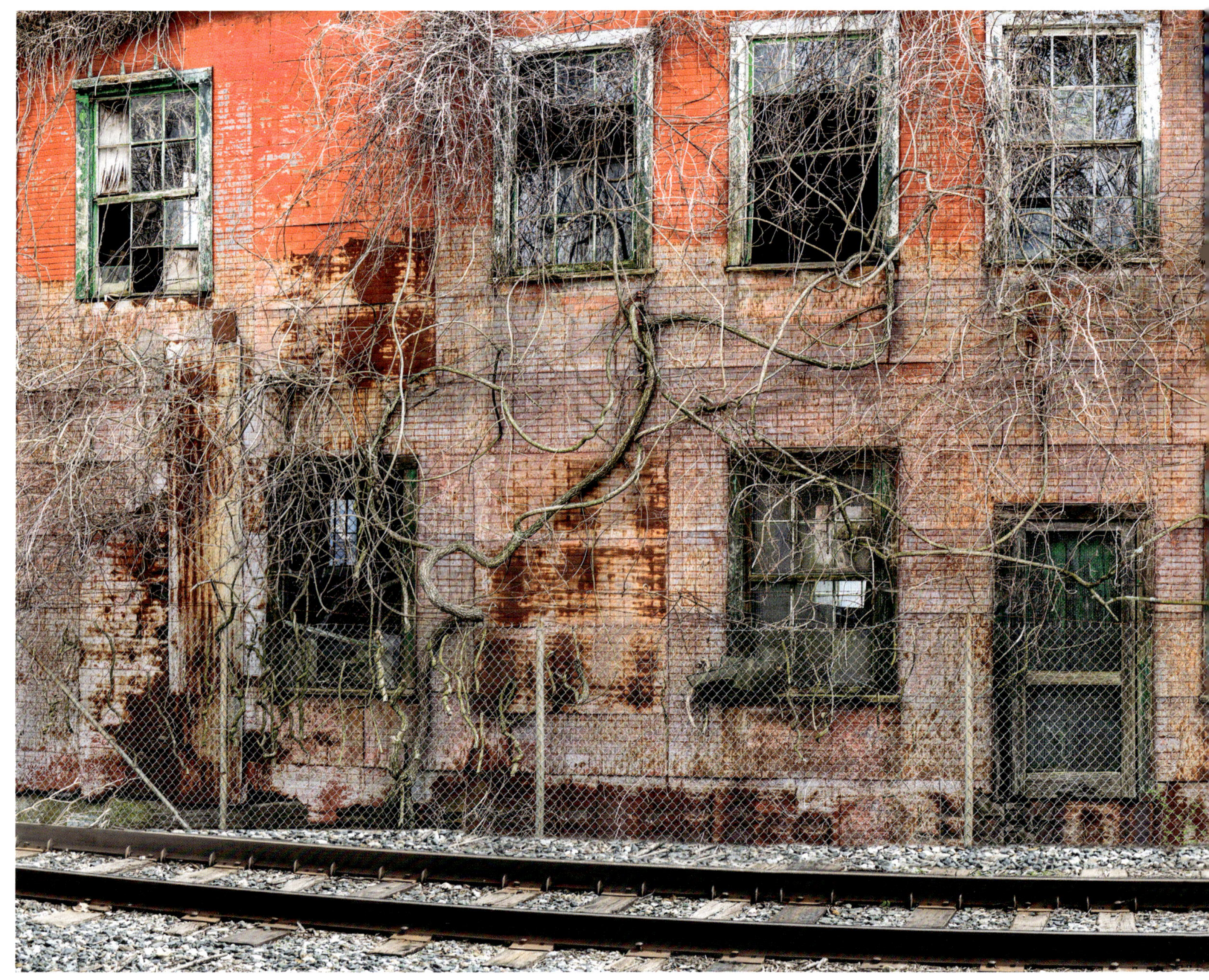

50 Farnsworth Street, New London, Connecticut

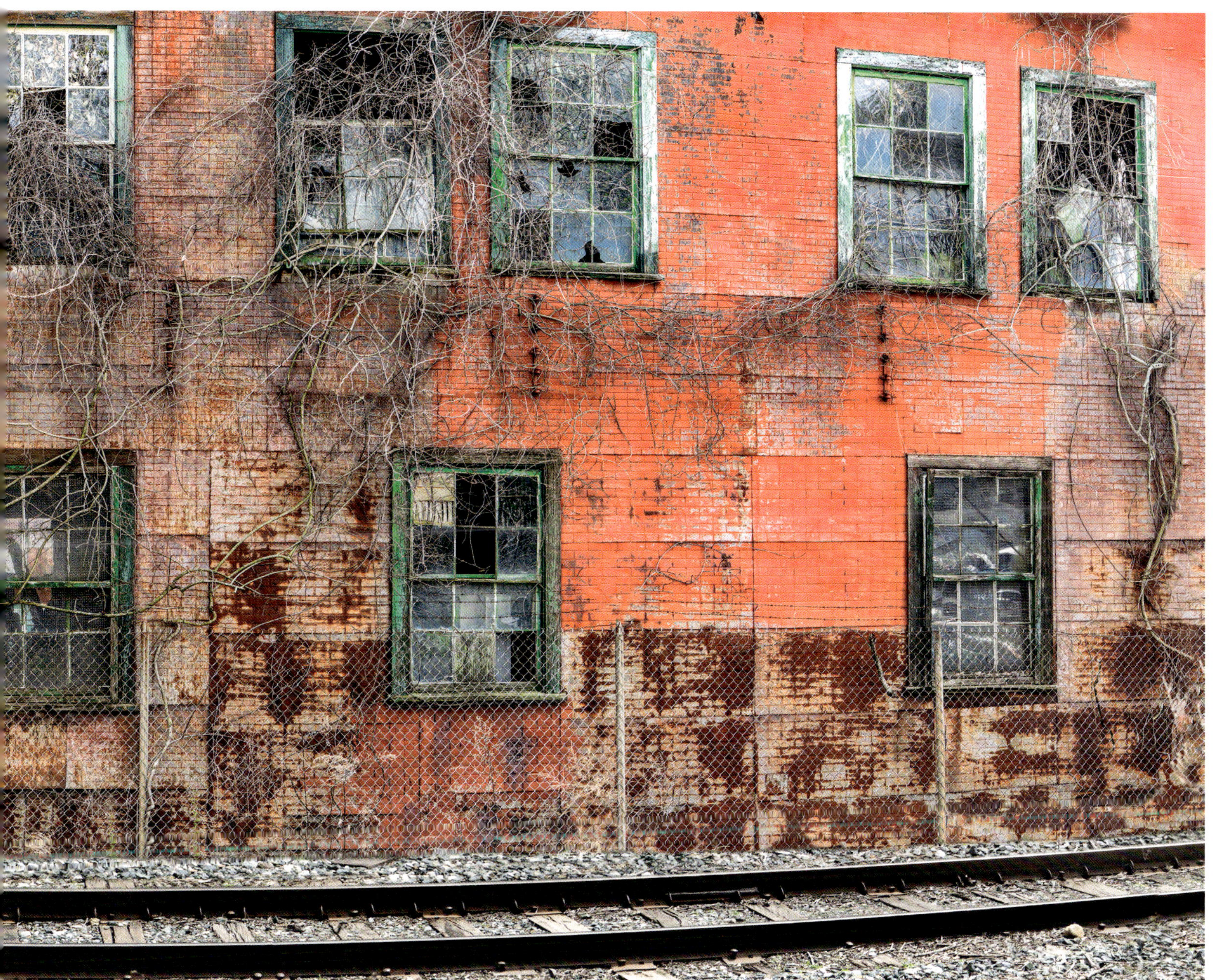

I love when nature reclaims architecture.

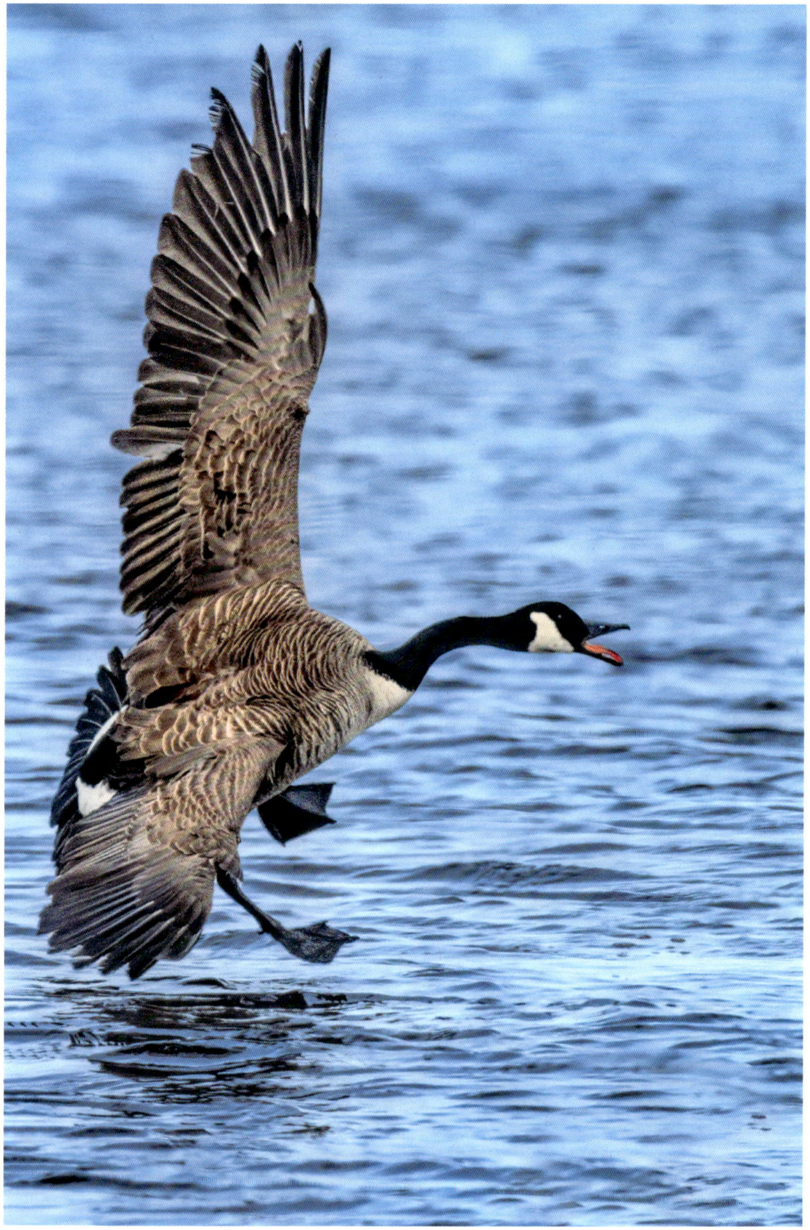

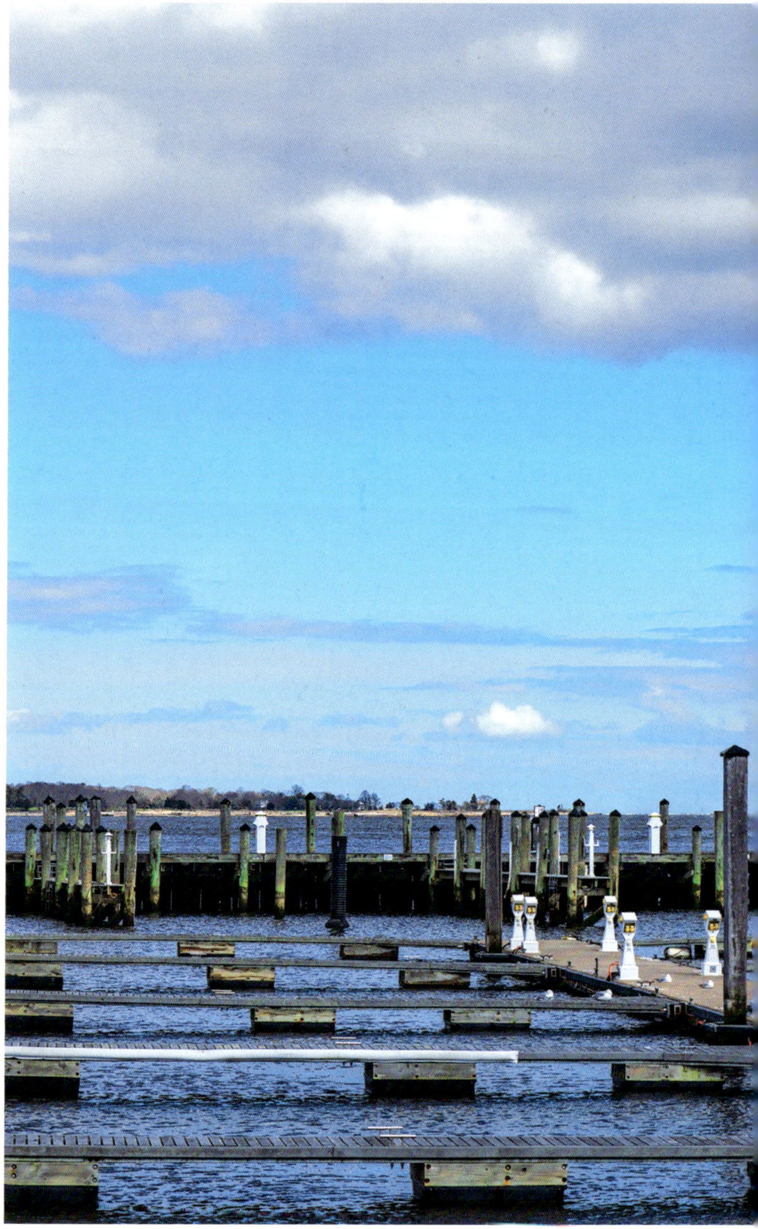

Canada goose on the Connecticut coast

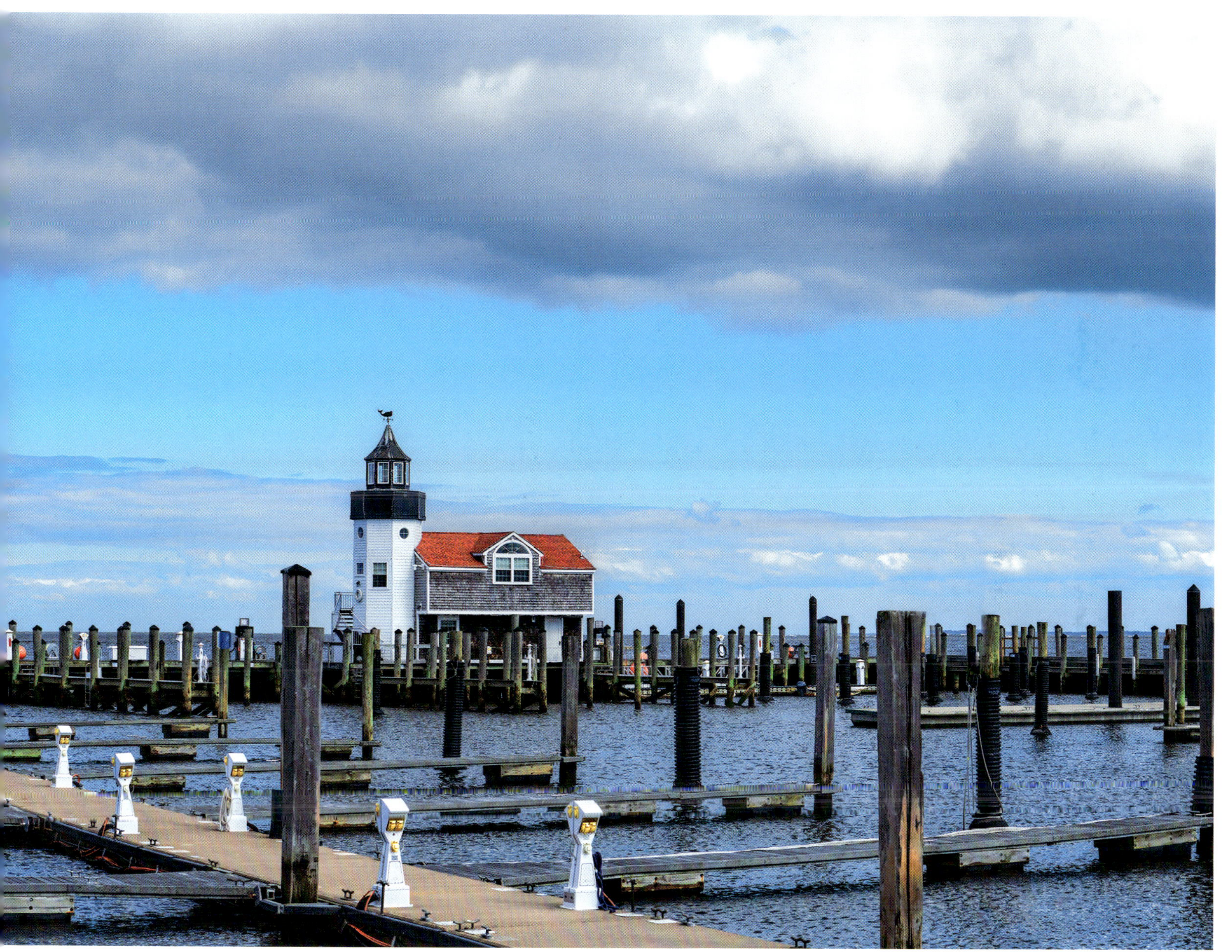

Old Saybrook Point Lighthouse, Connecticut

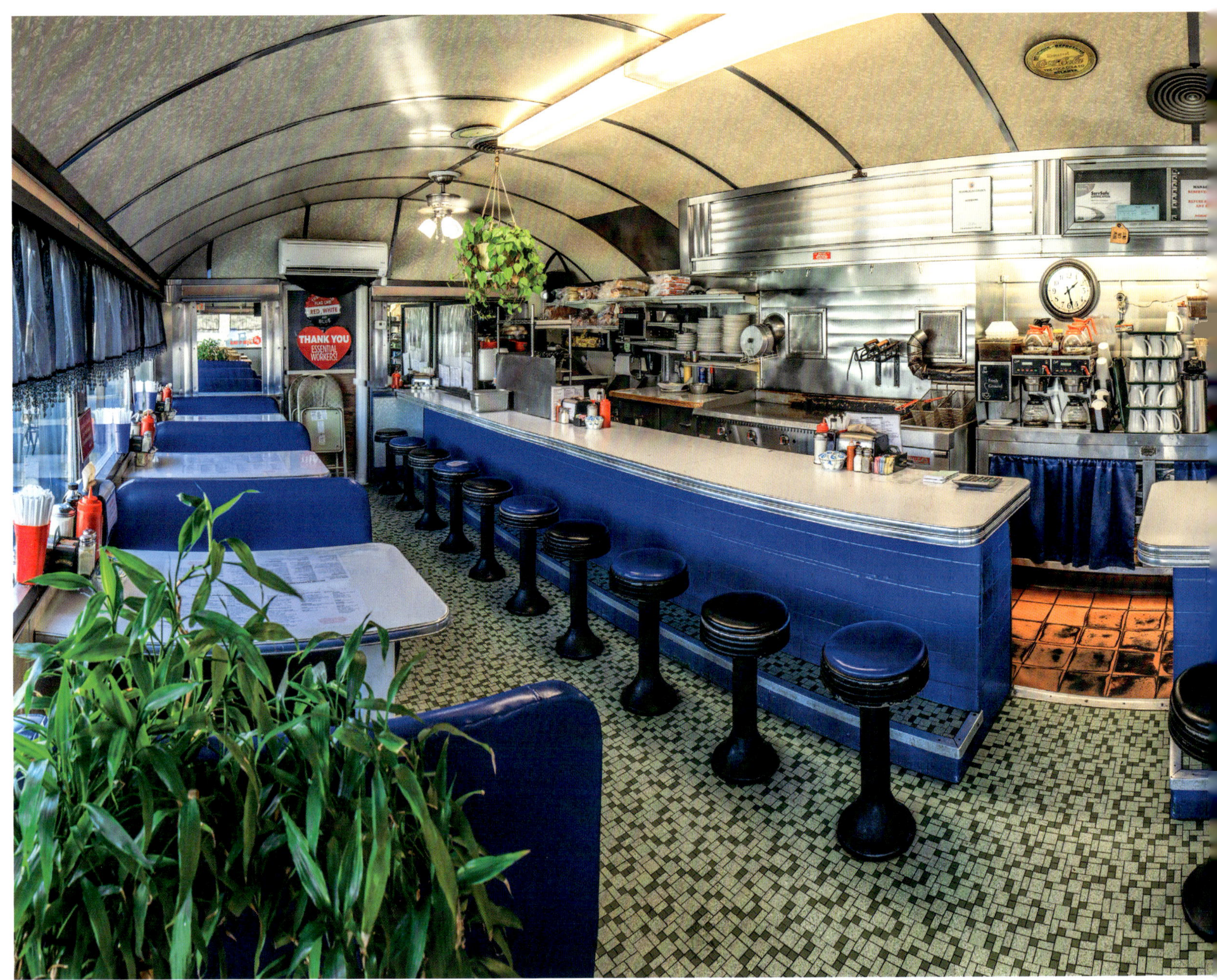

Nor's Diner, Groton, Connecticut

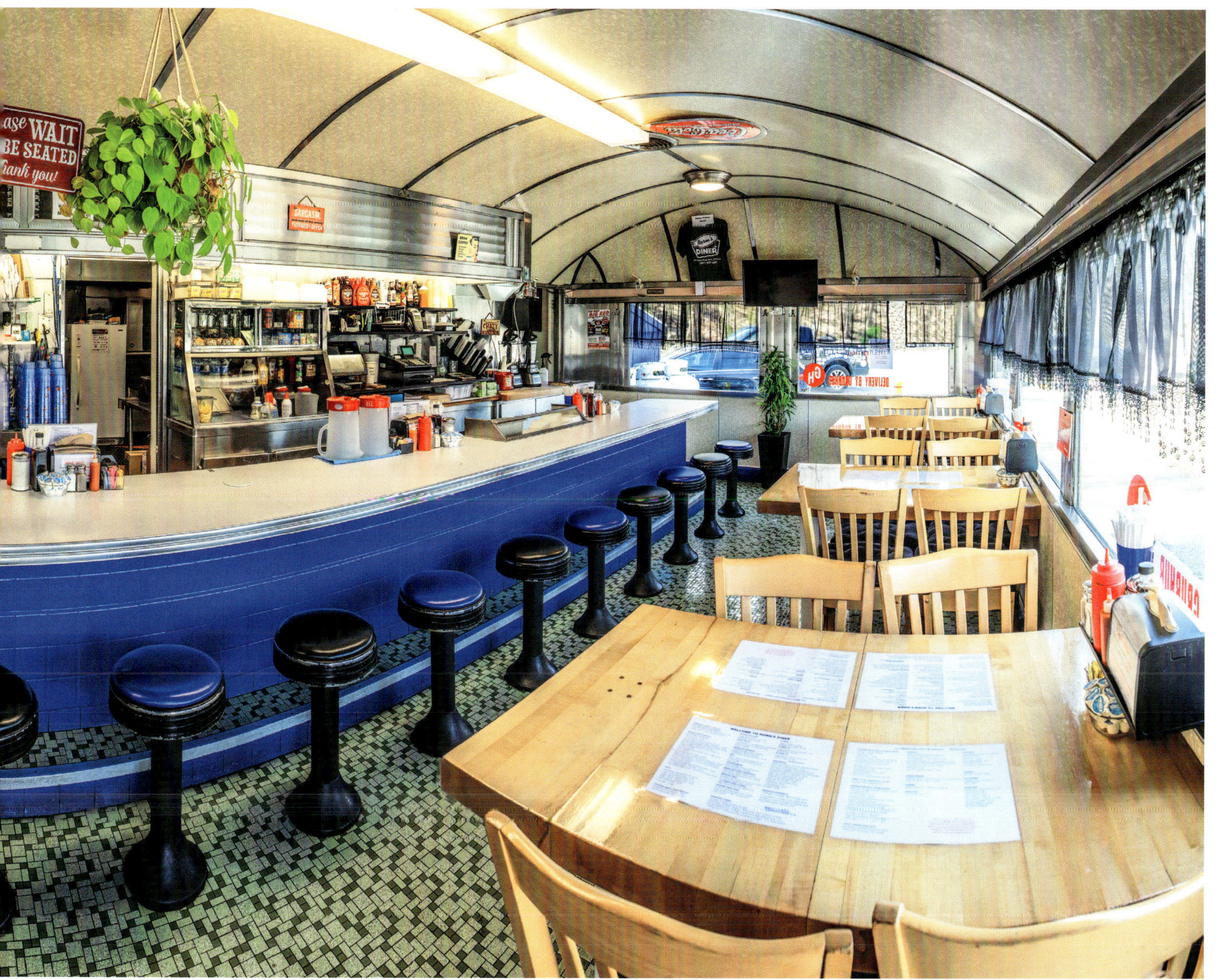

Thank you, Kerystal and Steven, for letting me in after closing, taking down the chairs, and the great breakfast (earlier)!

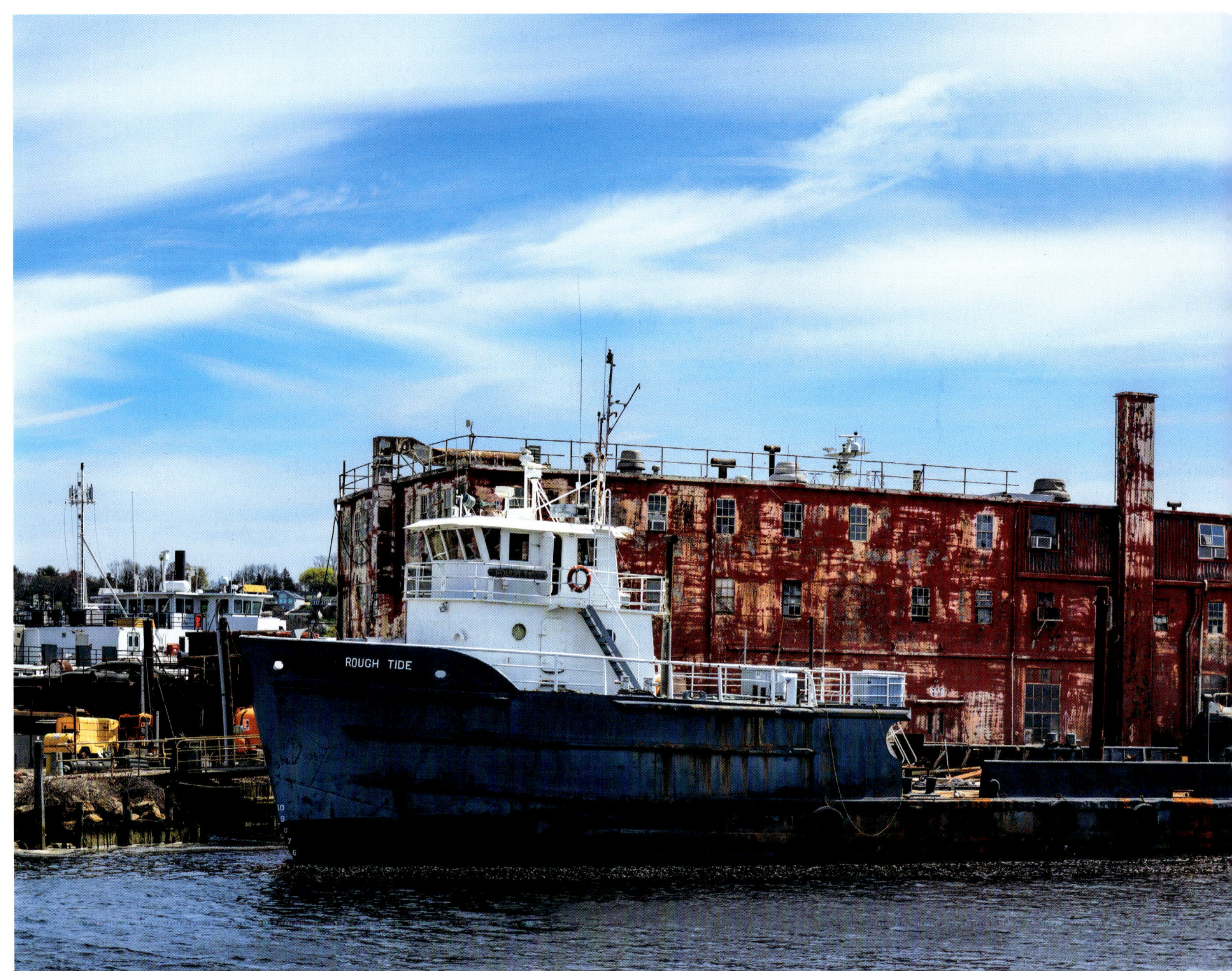

The Rough Tide, Thames Shipyards, New London, Connecticut

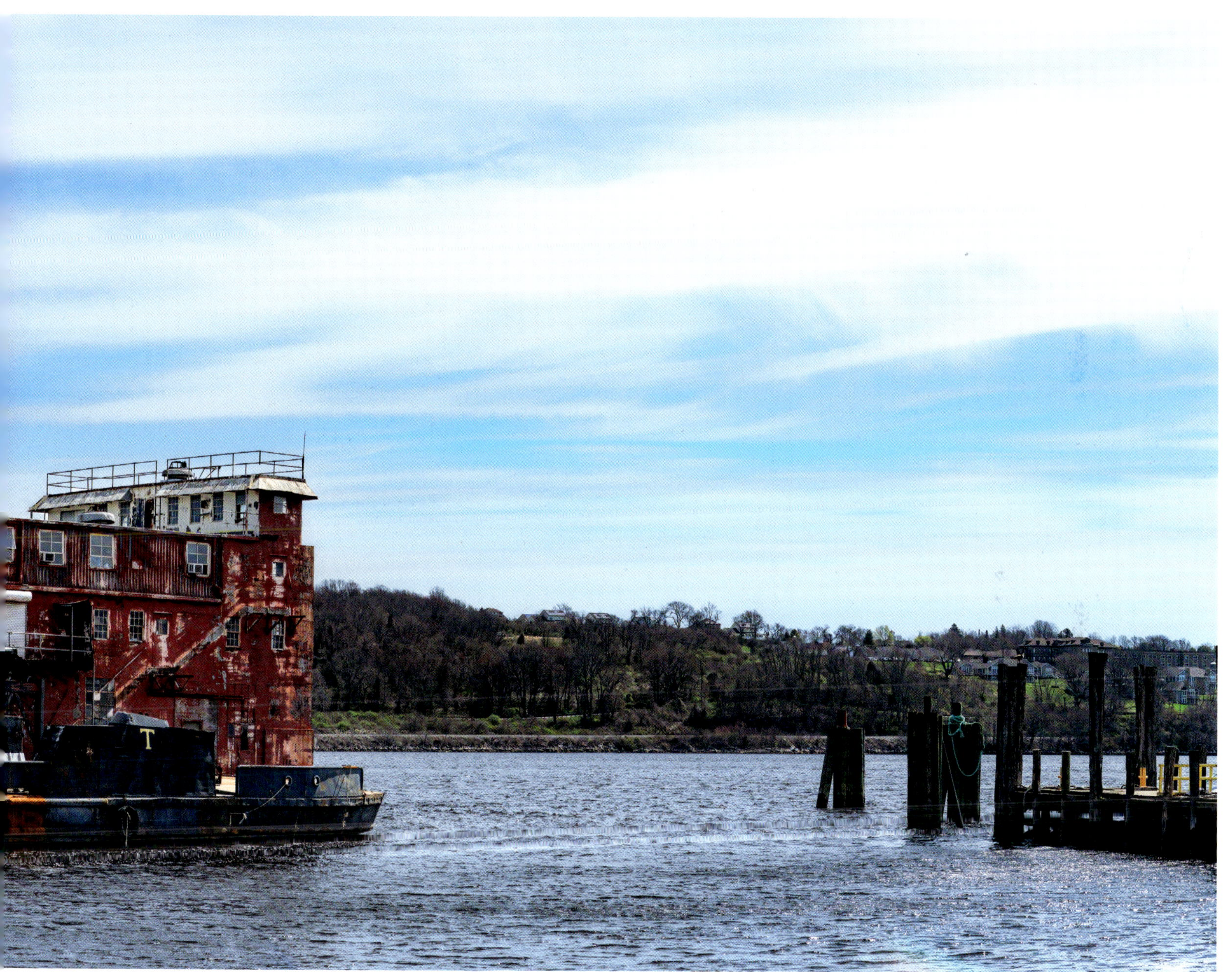

I had to beg permission from the guard at the gate to let me in to take this photo. I had to shoot fast as he stood next to me sort of tapping his foot.

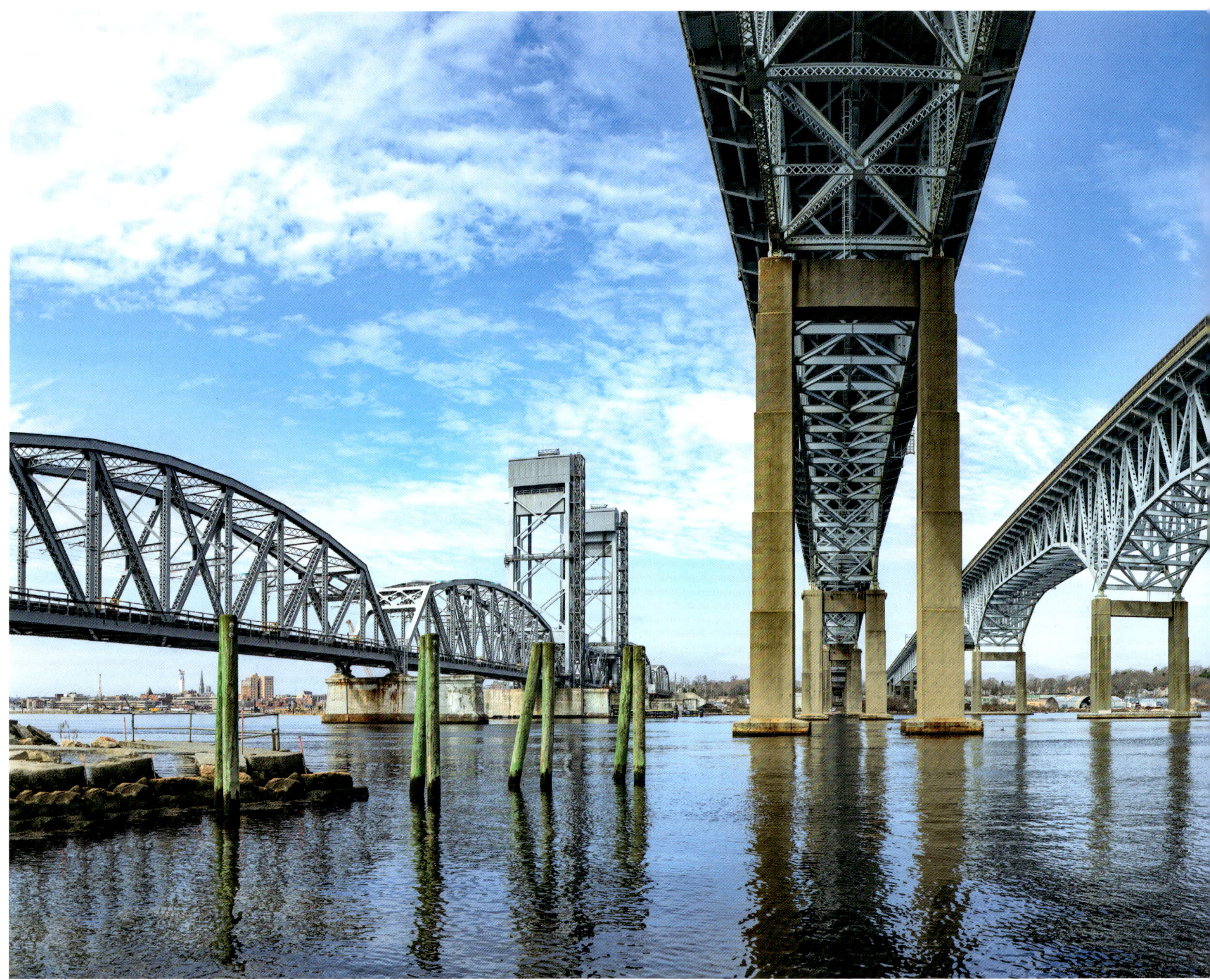

Gold Star Bridge over the Thames River, Connecticut

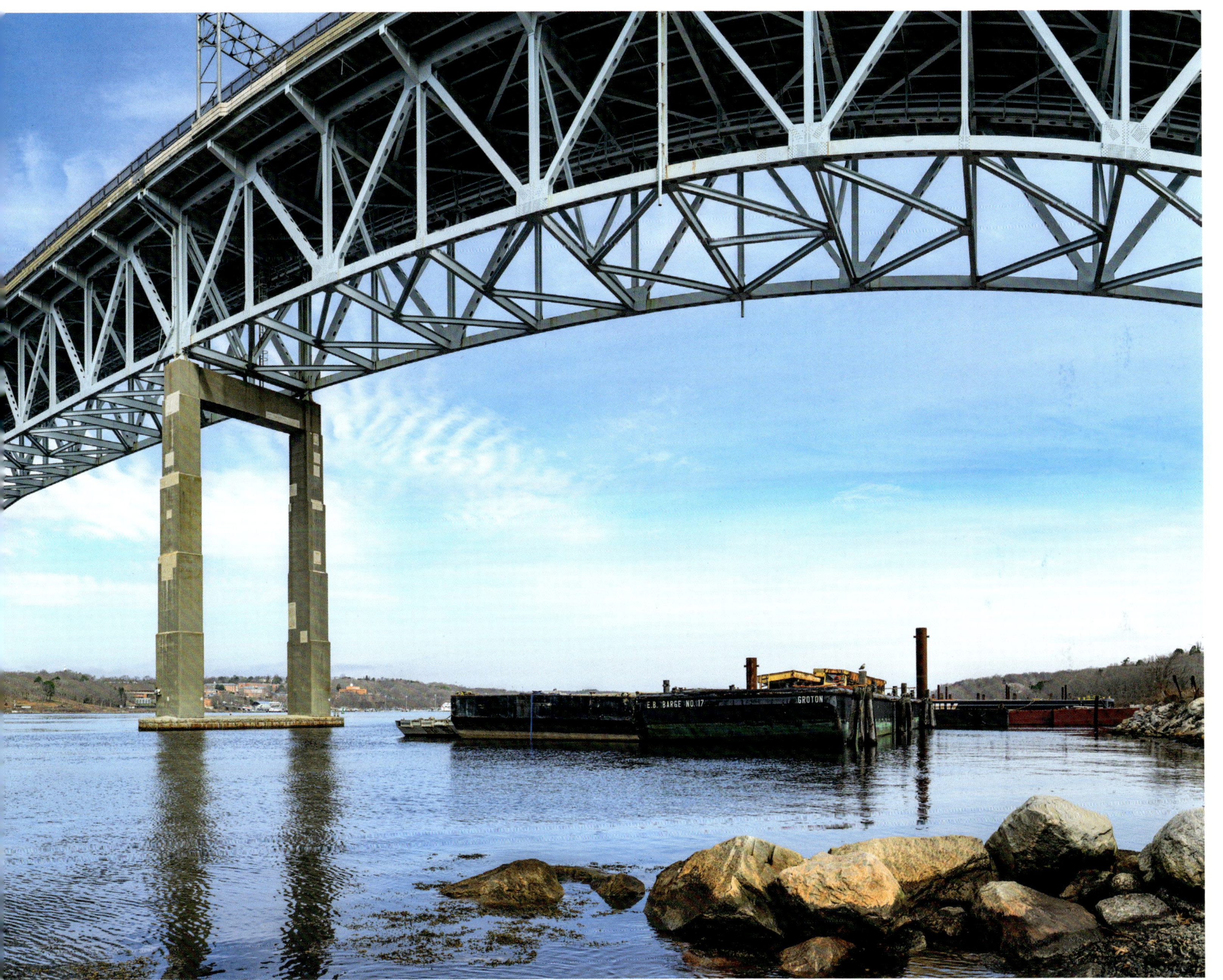

The bridges above carry the north and south lanes of Interstate 95 and US Route 1.

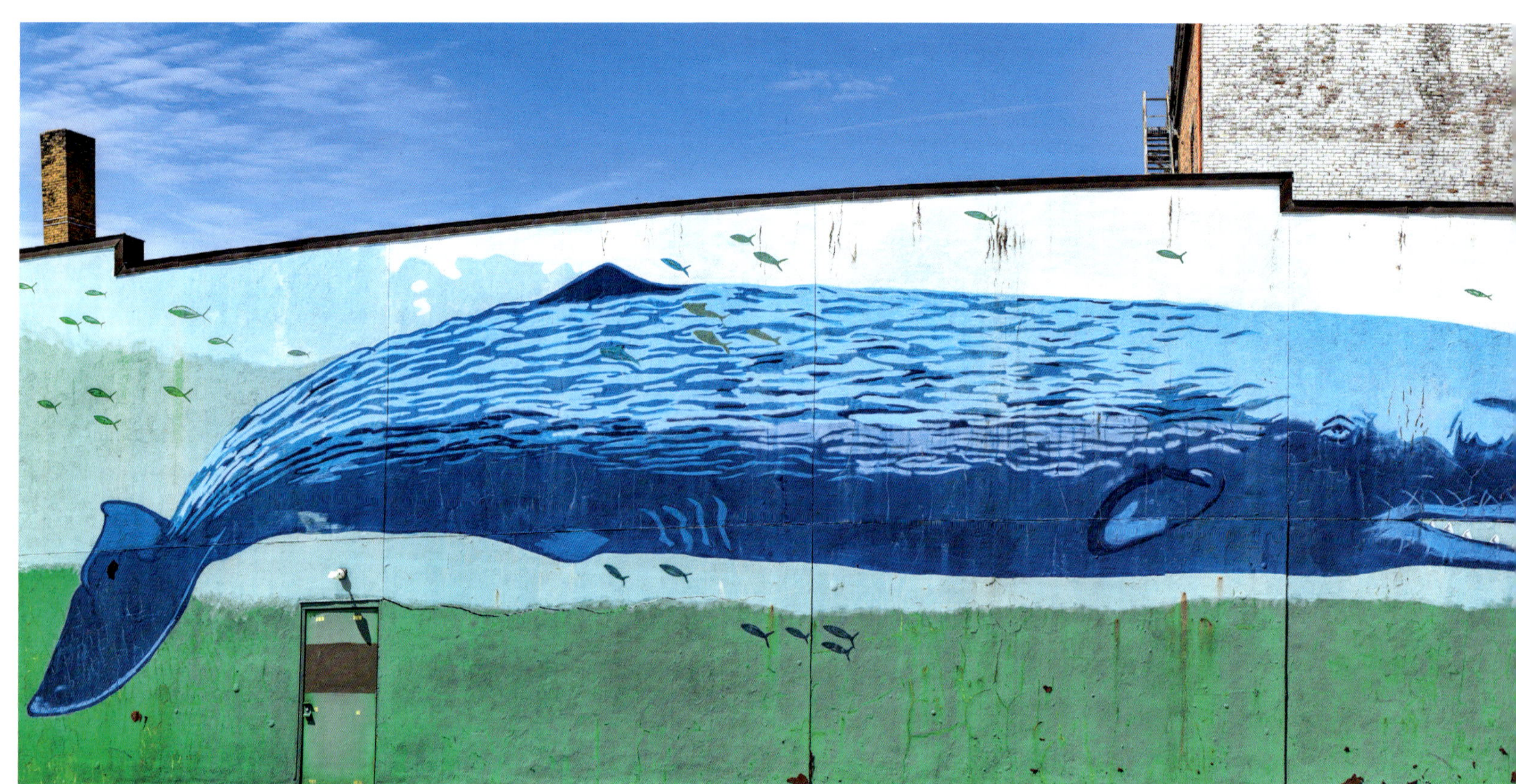

Eugene O'Neill Drive, New London, Connecticut

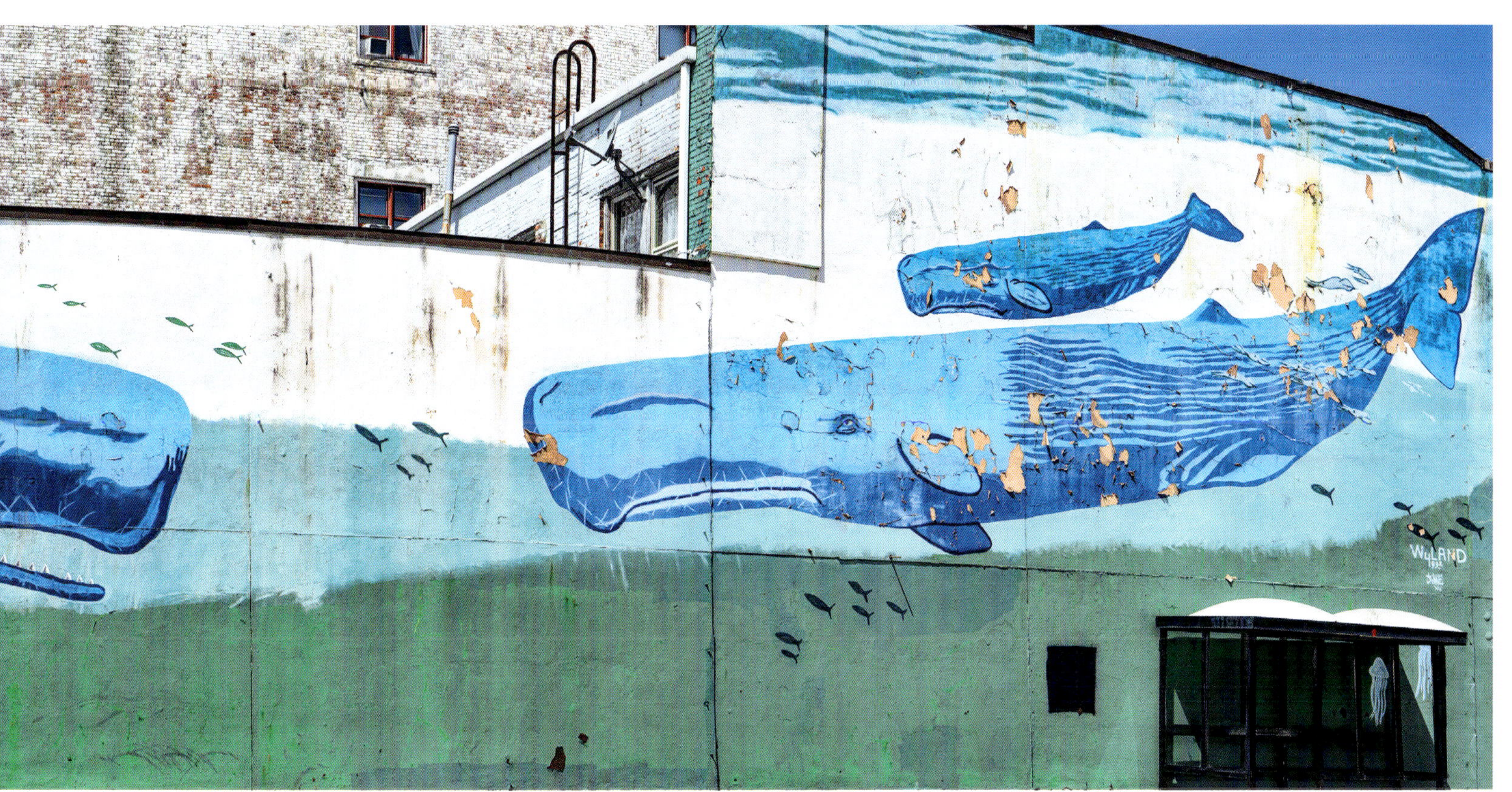

Painting by Wyland

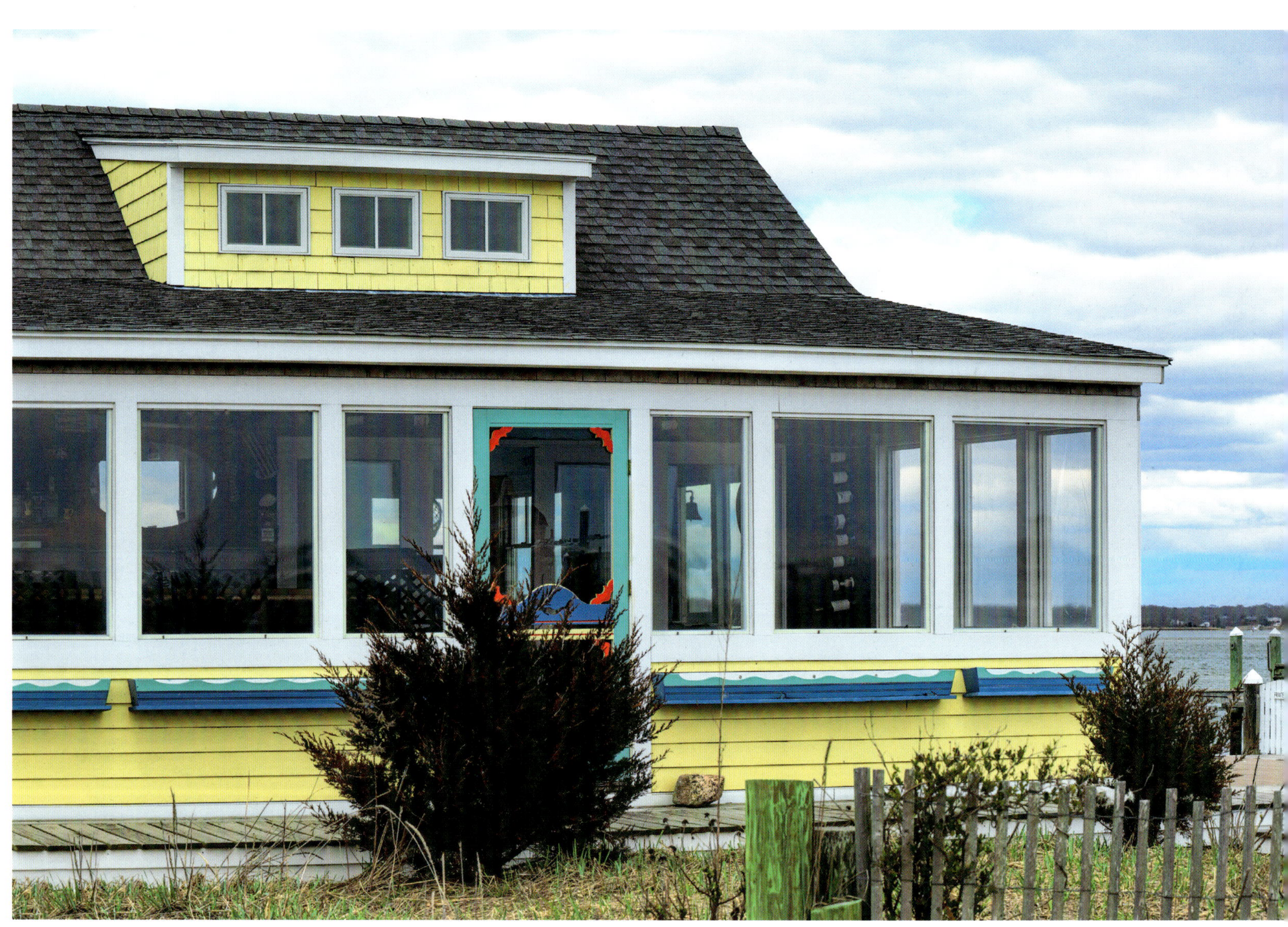

Beach house, Snug Harbor, Jerusalem, Rhode Island

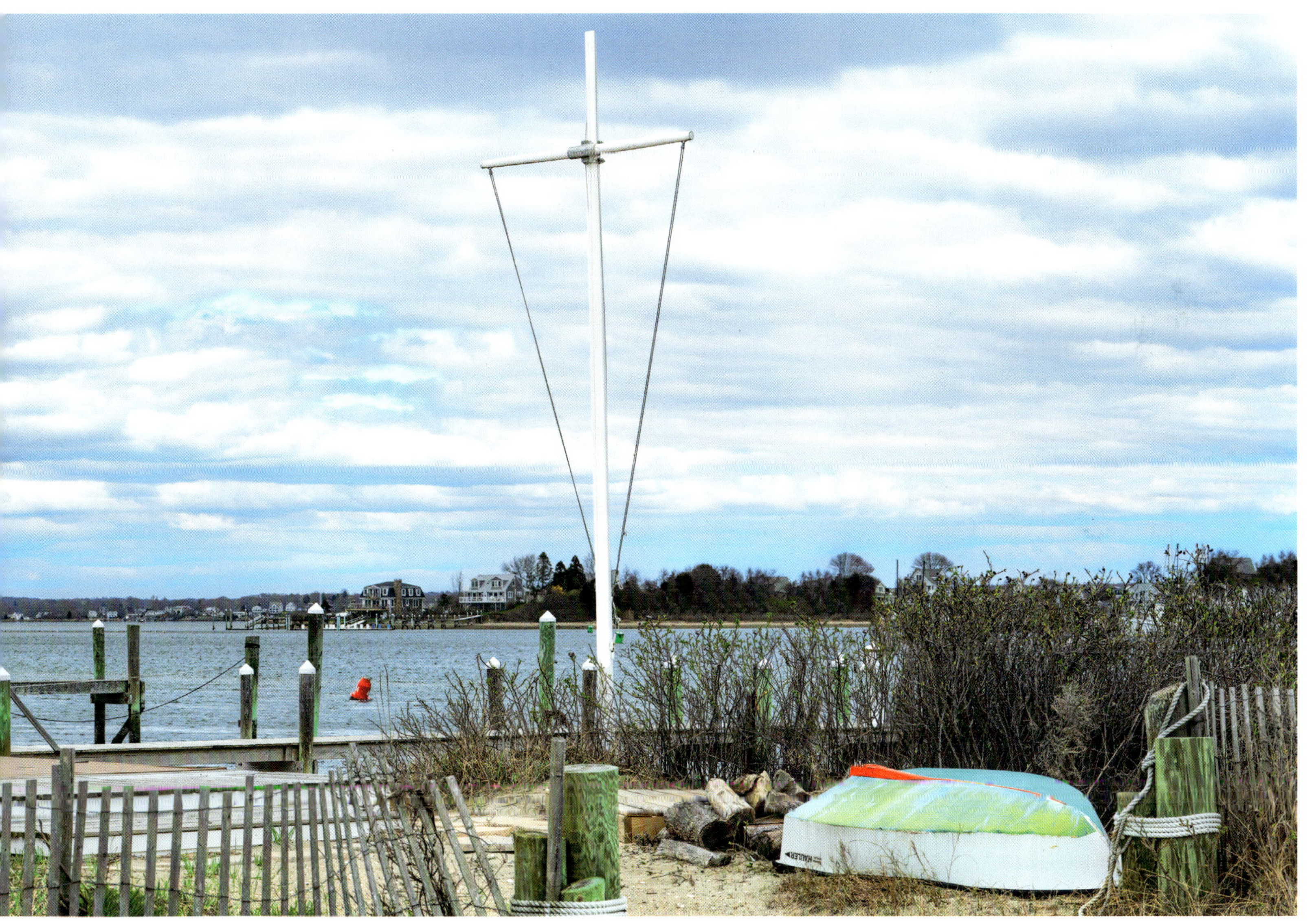

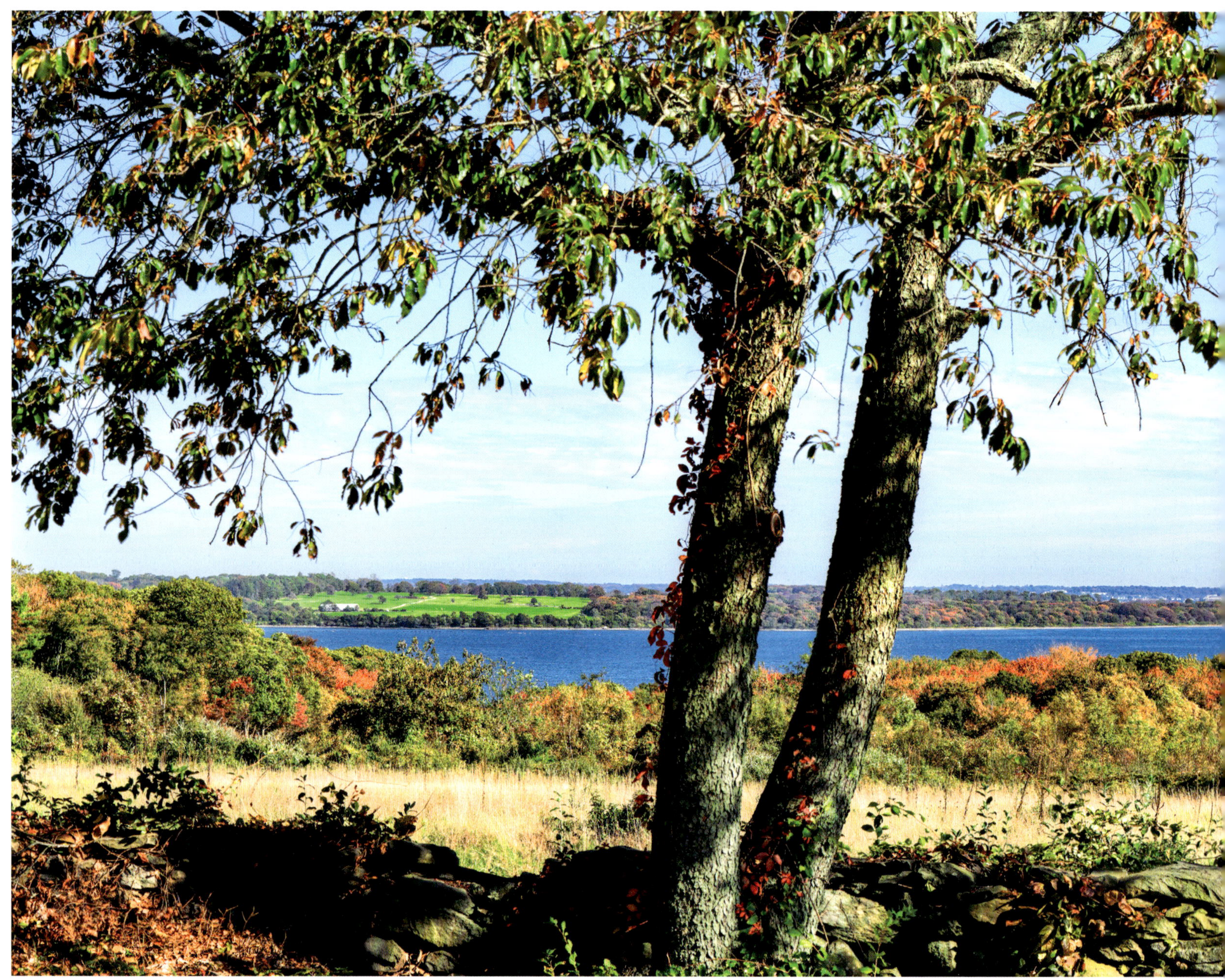

Claiborne Pell Newport Bridge and Rhode Island Sound

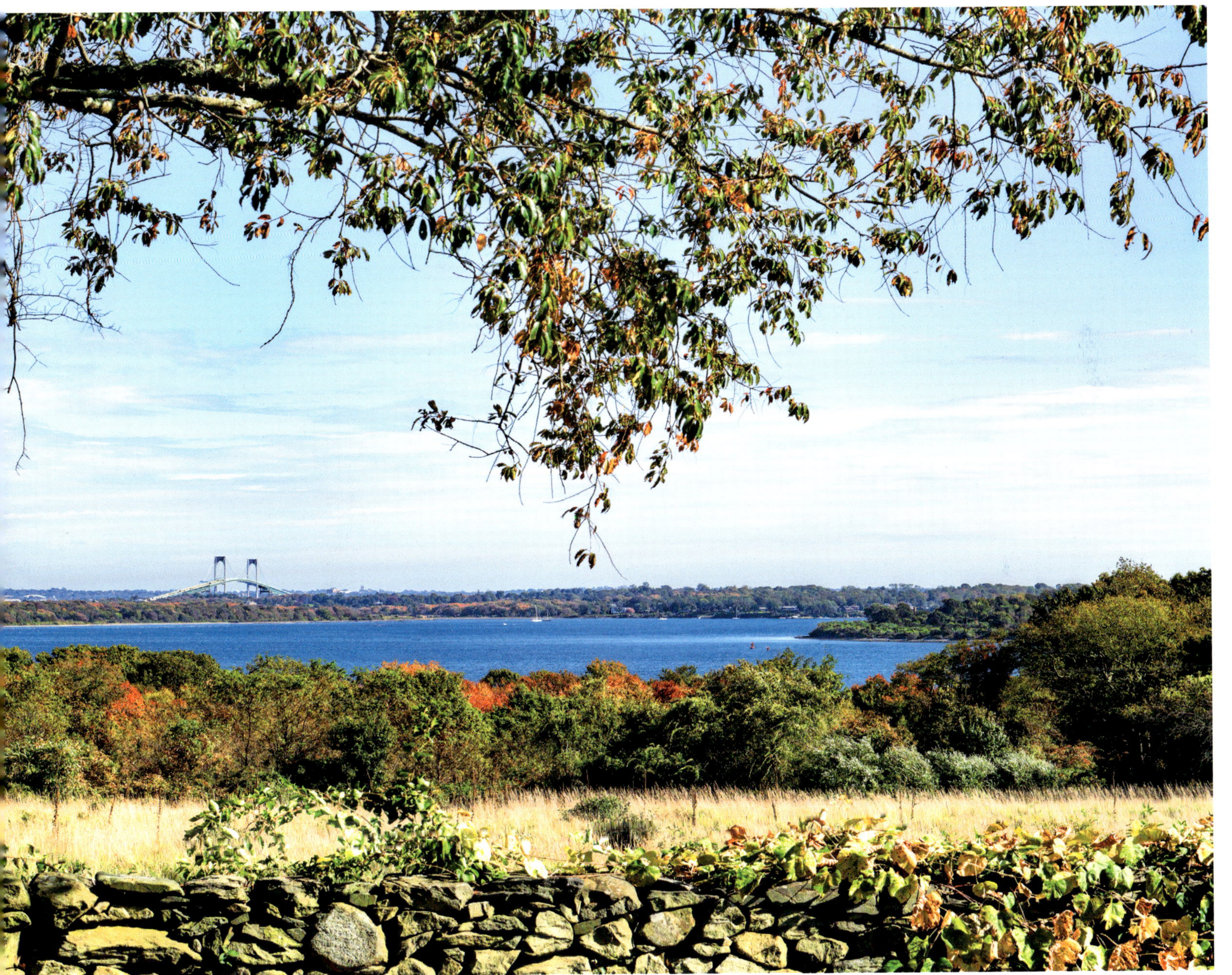

The bridge spans the East Passage of Narragansett Bay.

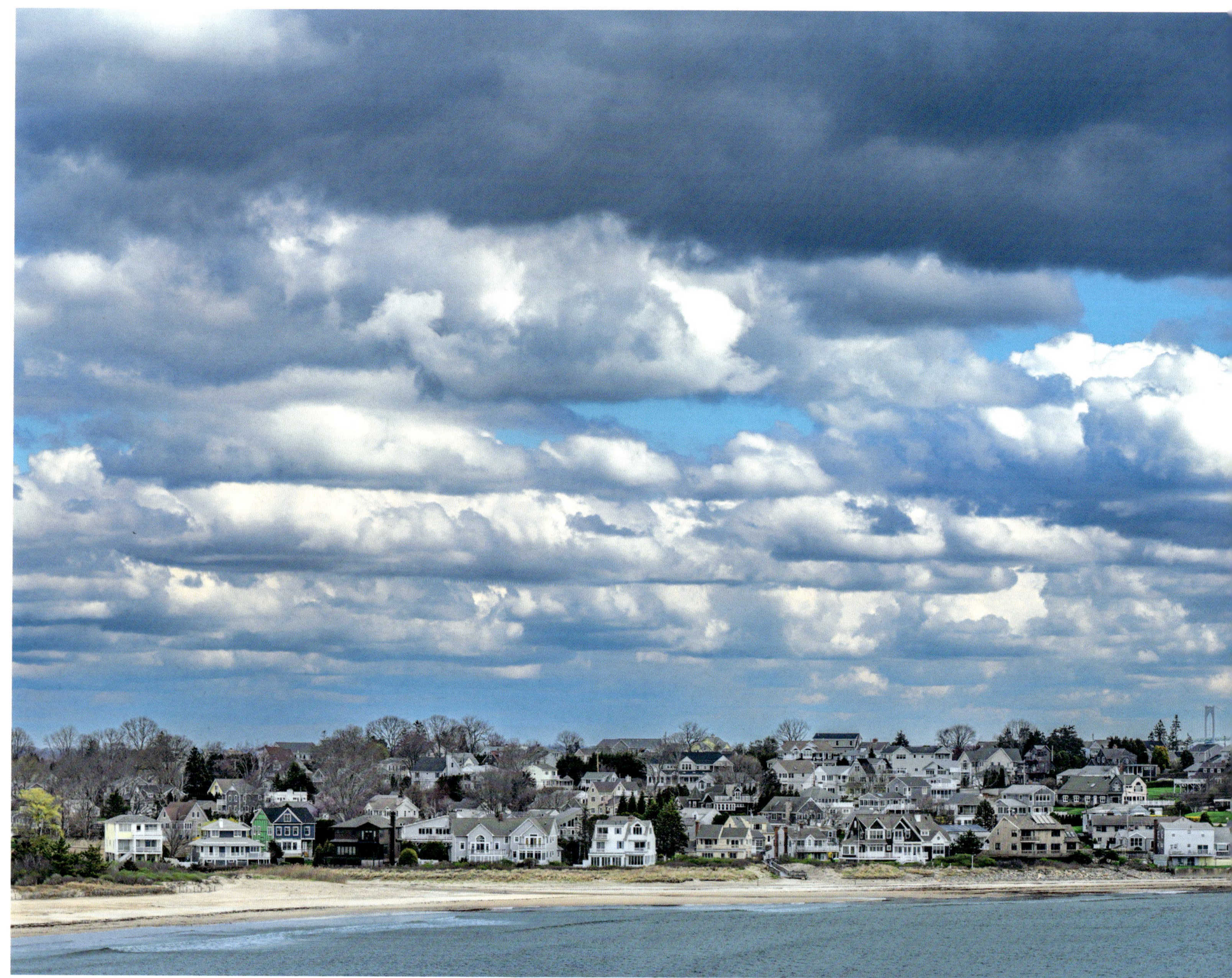

Bonnet Shores across Wesquage Pond, Rhode Island

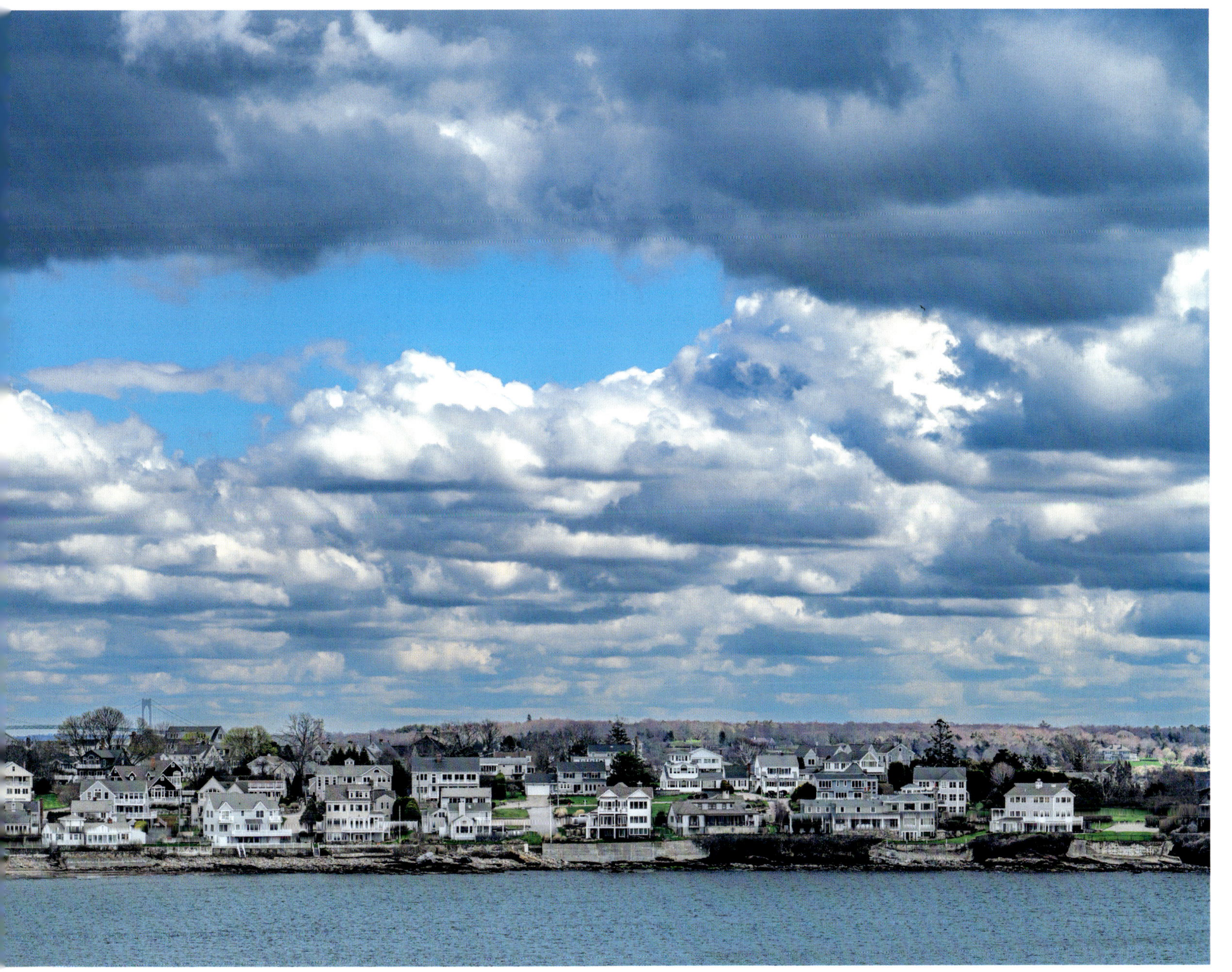

That's the Claiborne Pell Newport Bridge again in the background.

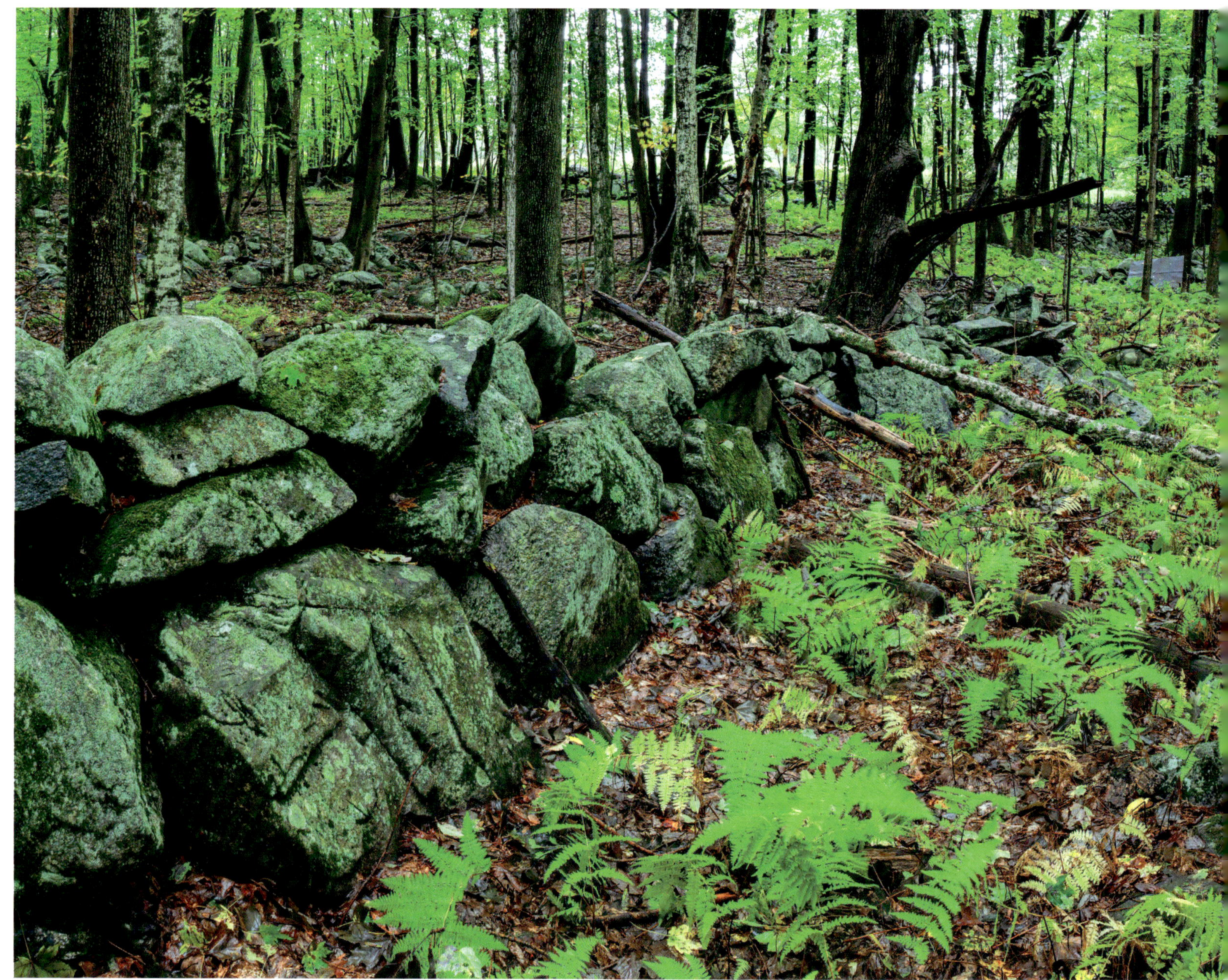

Old New England rock walls, Rhode Island State Highway 14

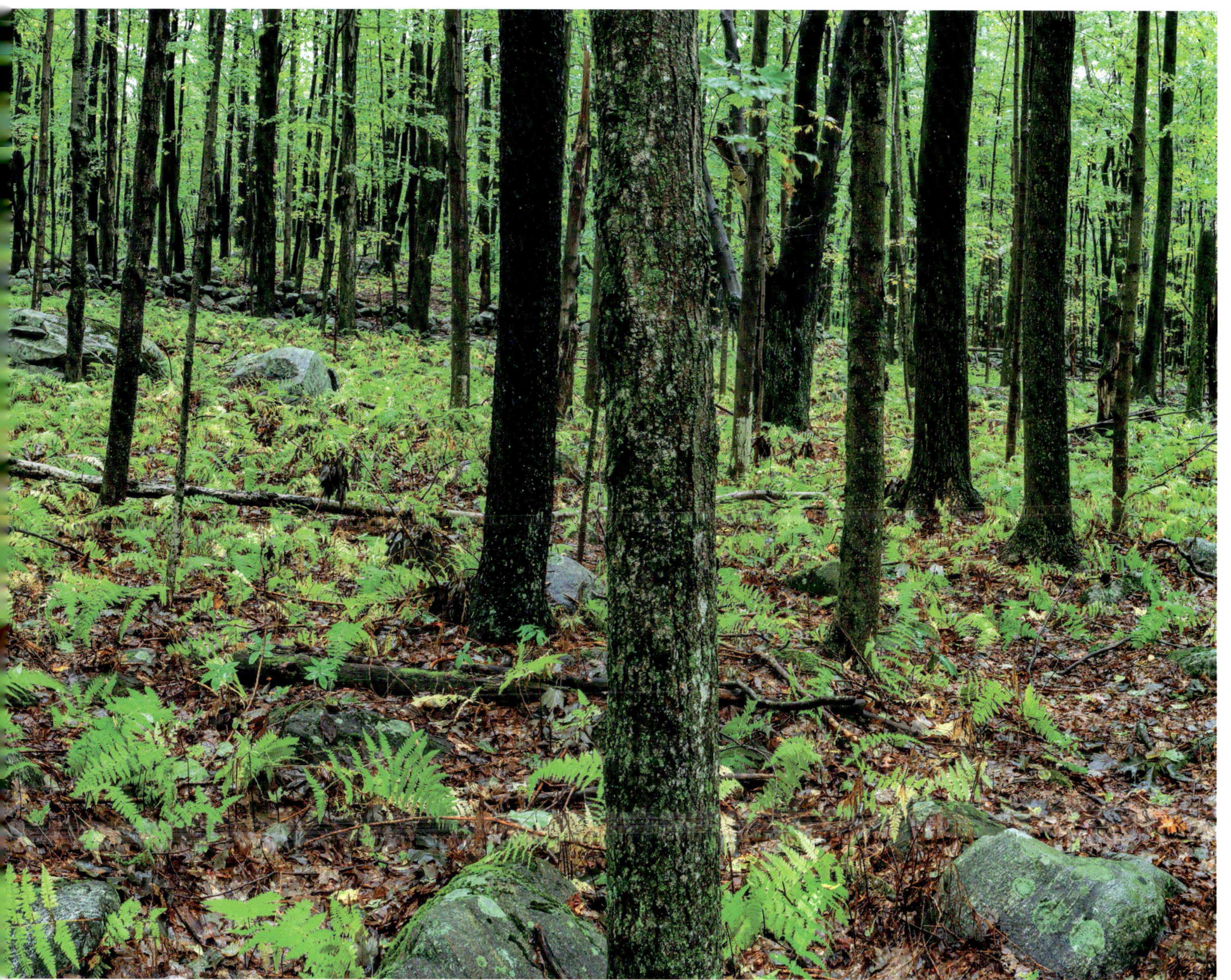

I found this in the woods. It could be more than 200 years old, or maybe it was built last Tuesday. You just never know in New England.

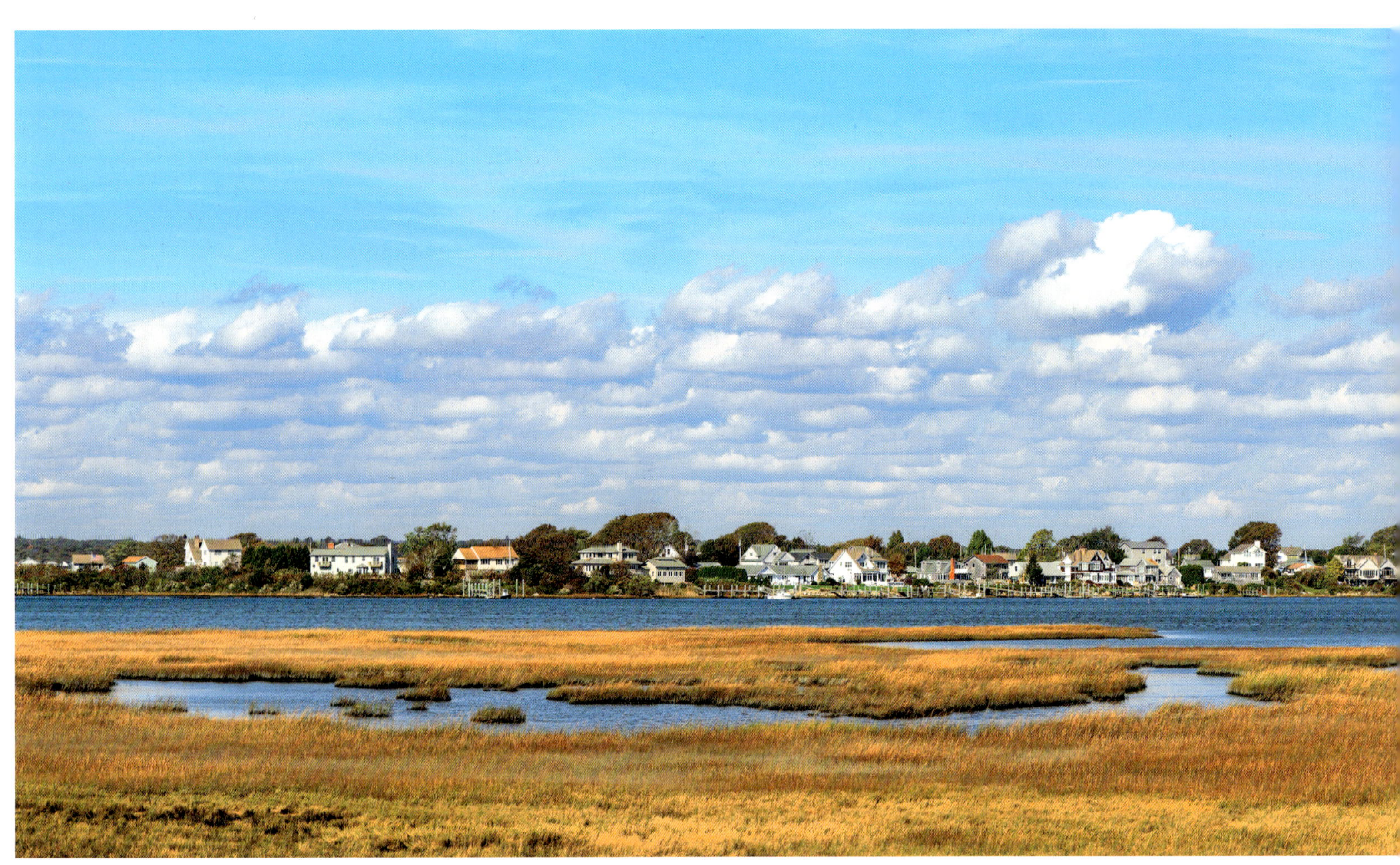

Narragansett, Rhode Island, across Point Judith Pond

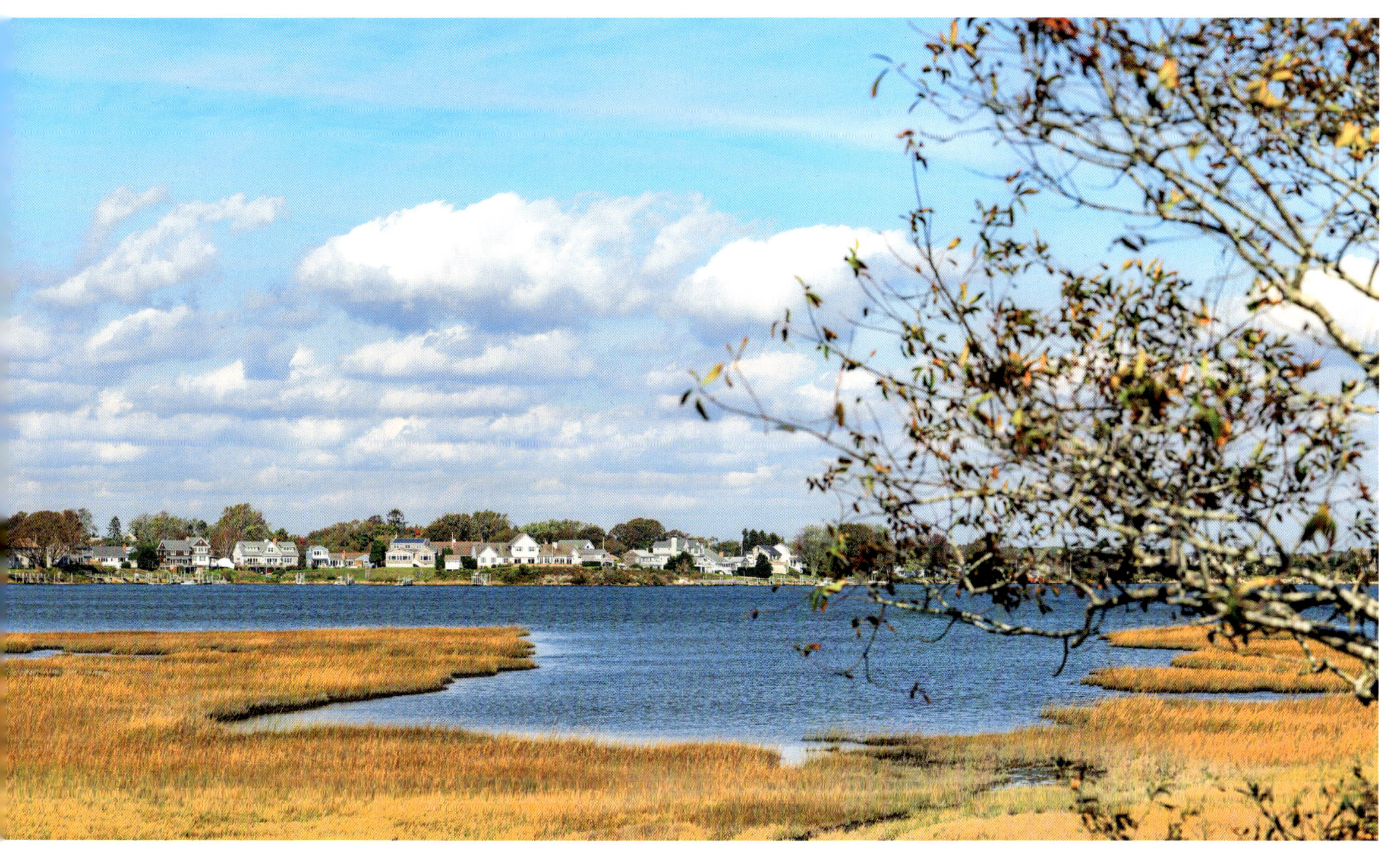

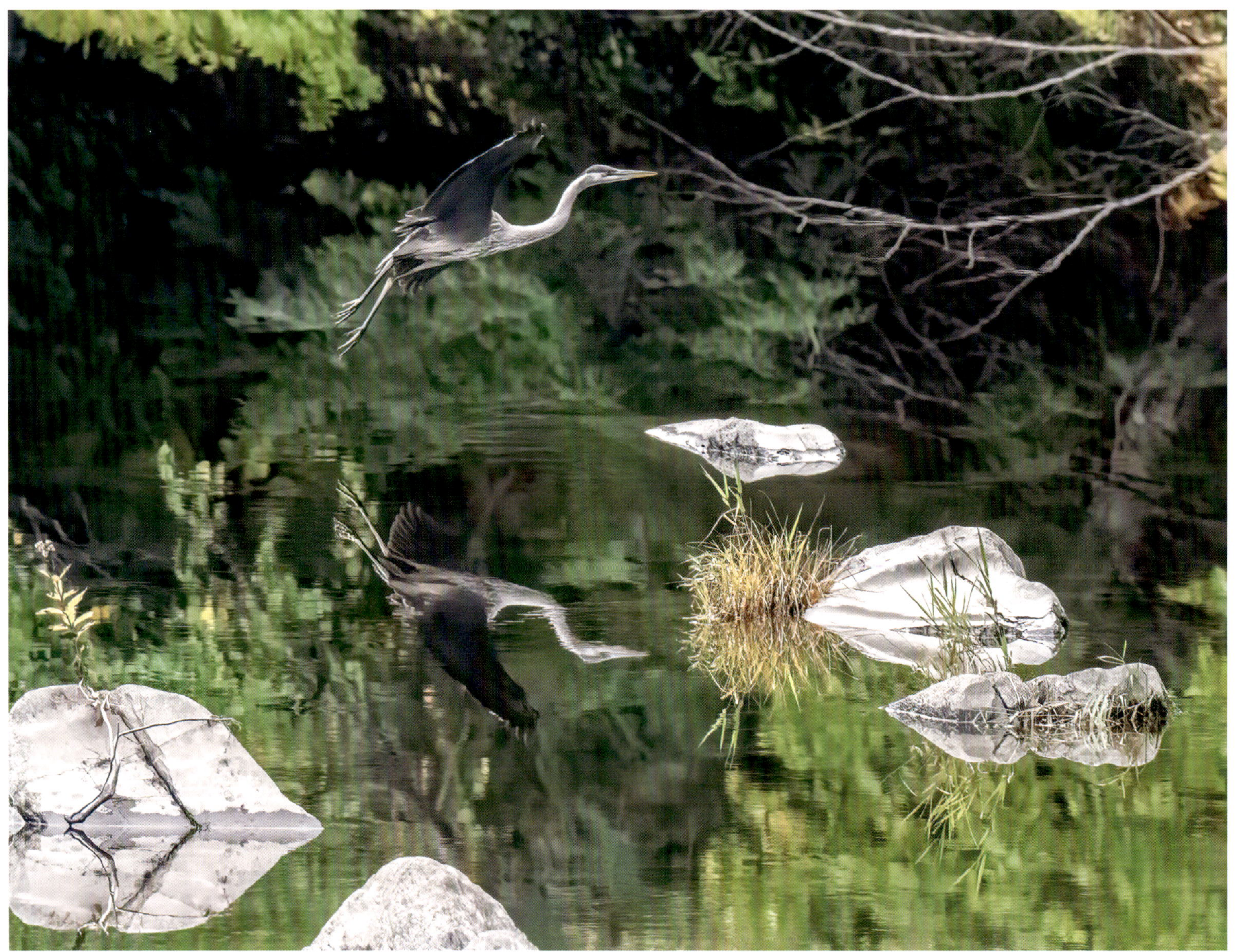

Great blue heron, Long Pond, Rhode Island

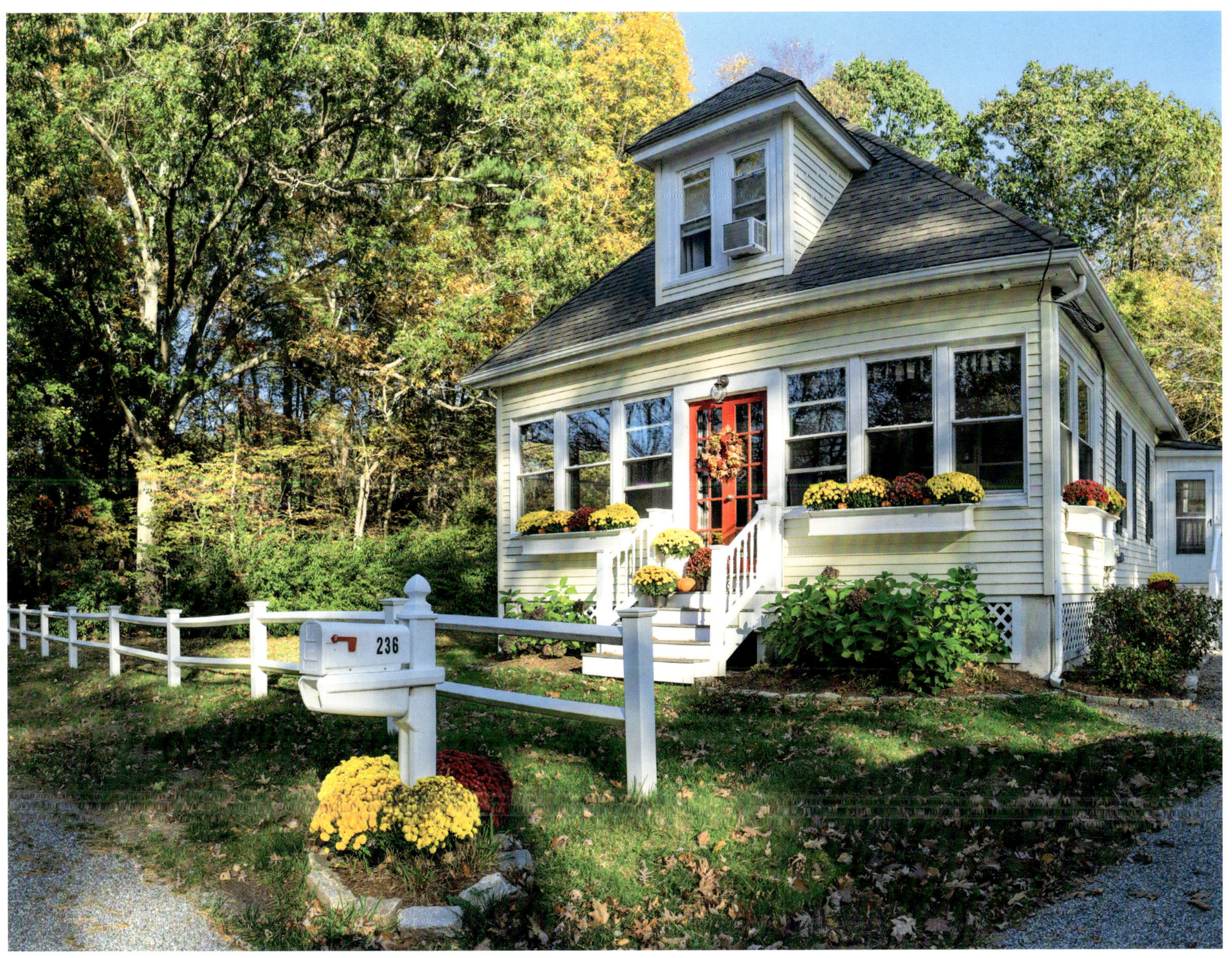

Perfect house, Rhode Island

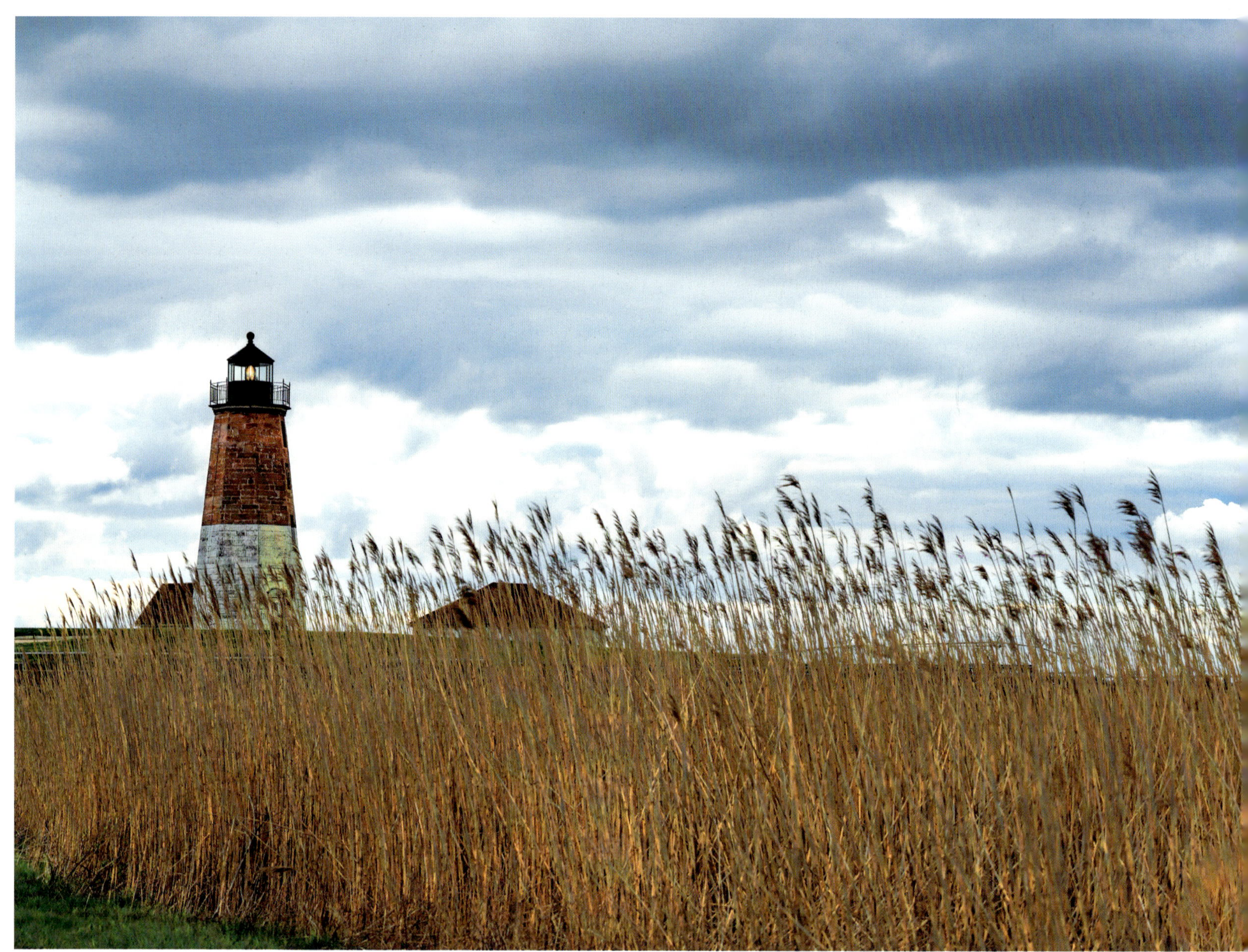

Point Judith Lighthouse, Rhode Island

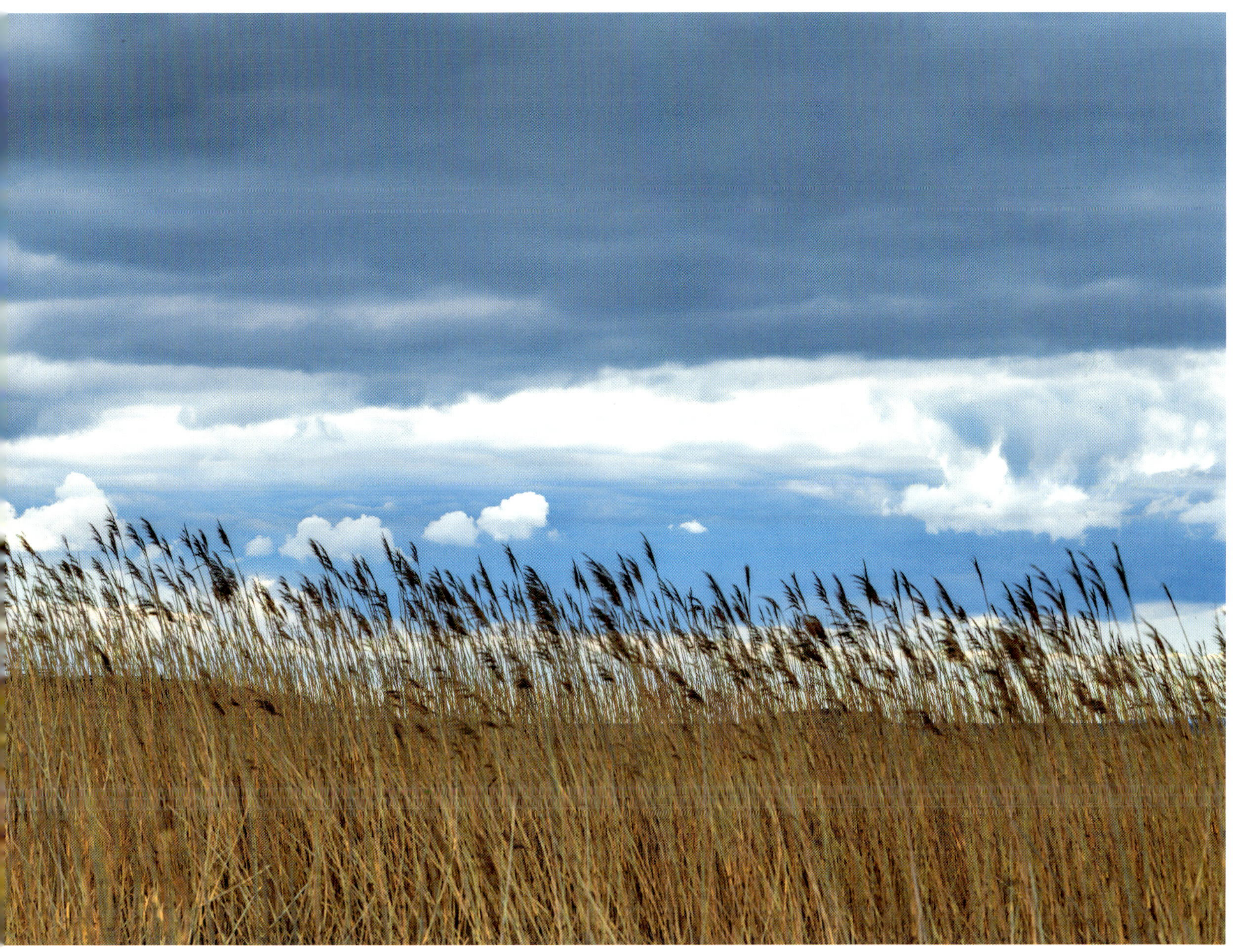

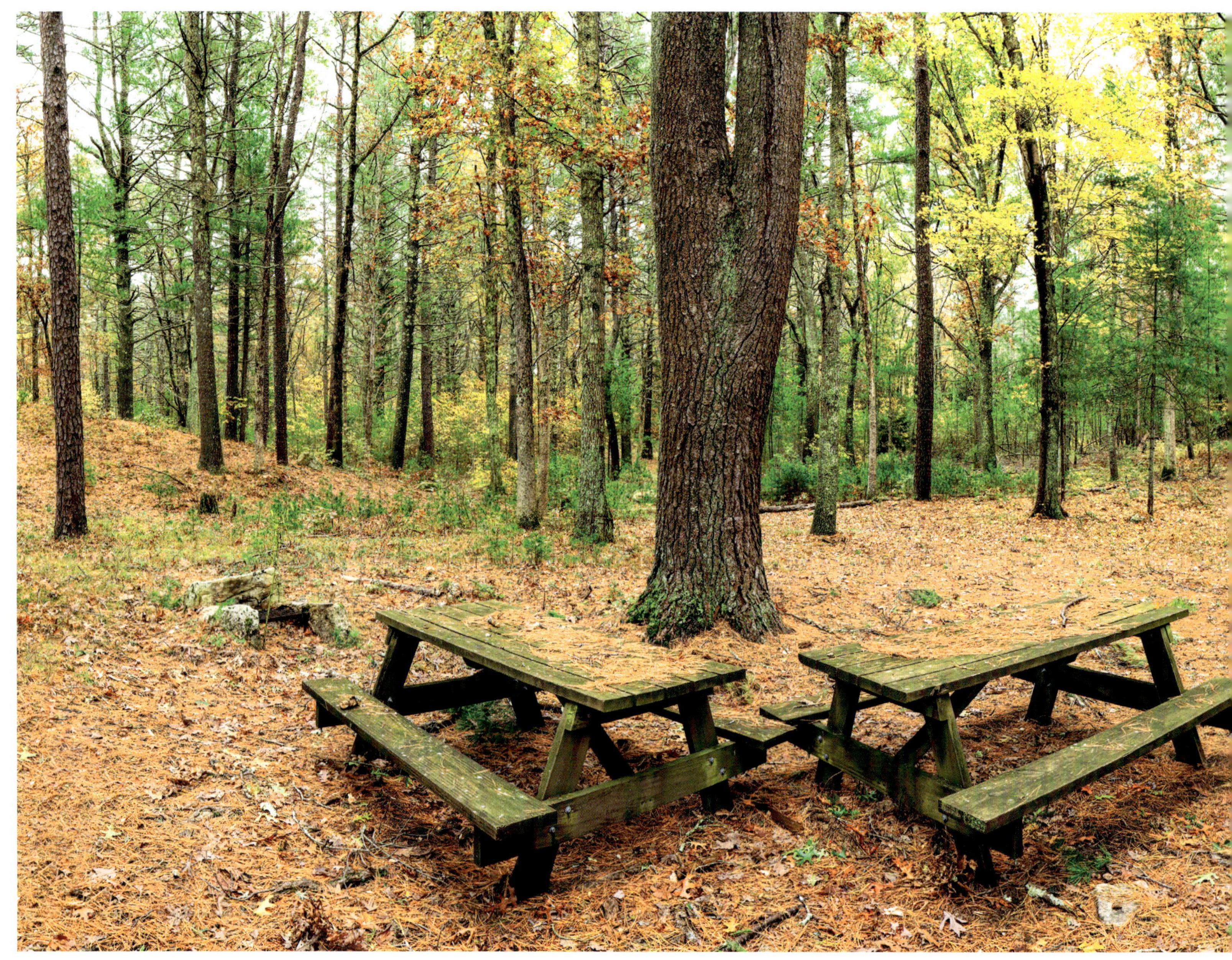

Picnic spot, Pulaski State Park, Rhode Island

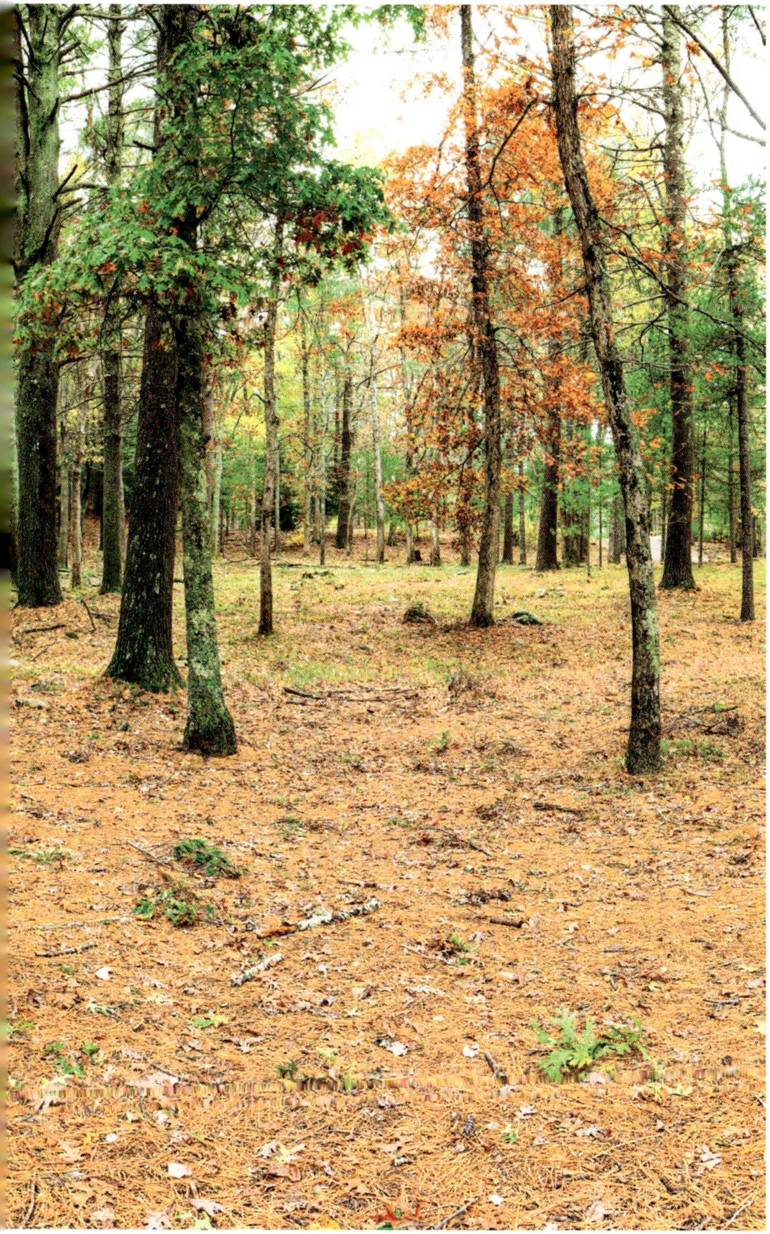

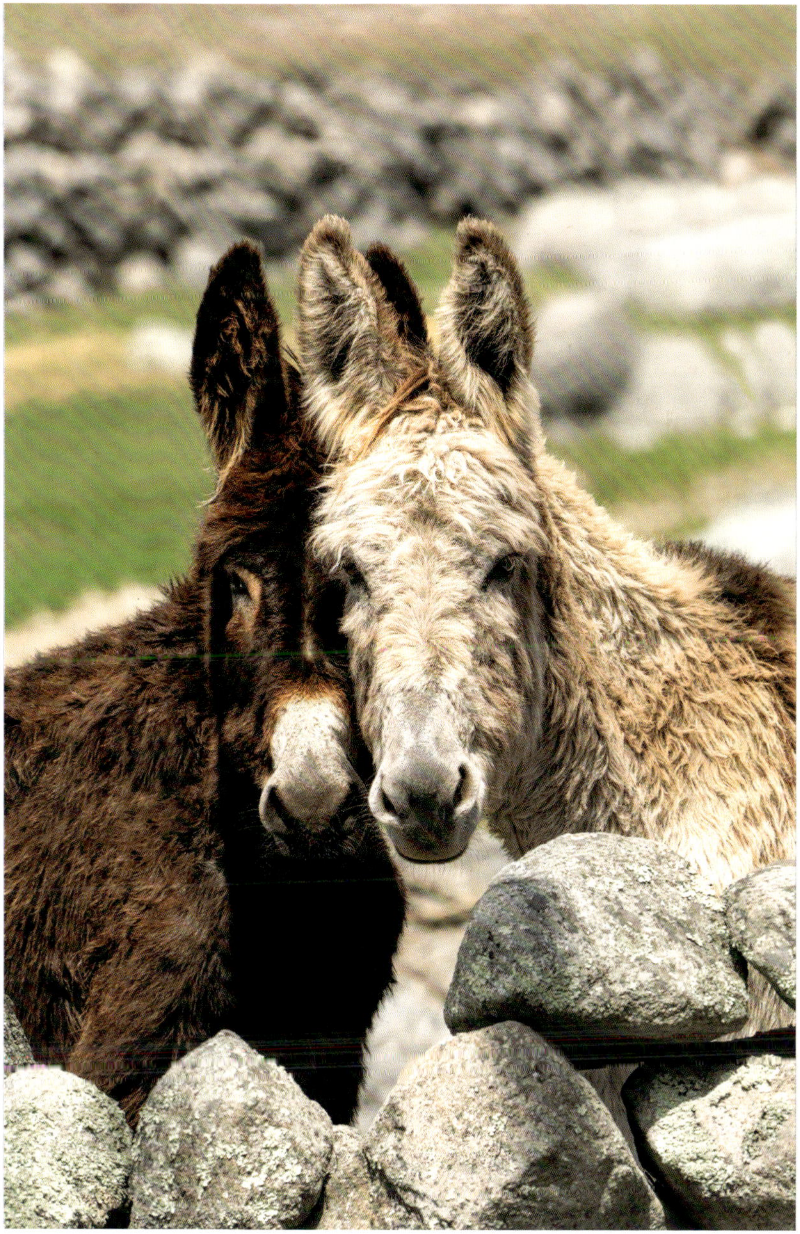

Donkey buddies on a Rhode Island farm

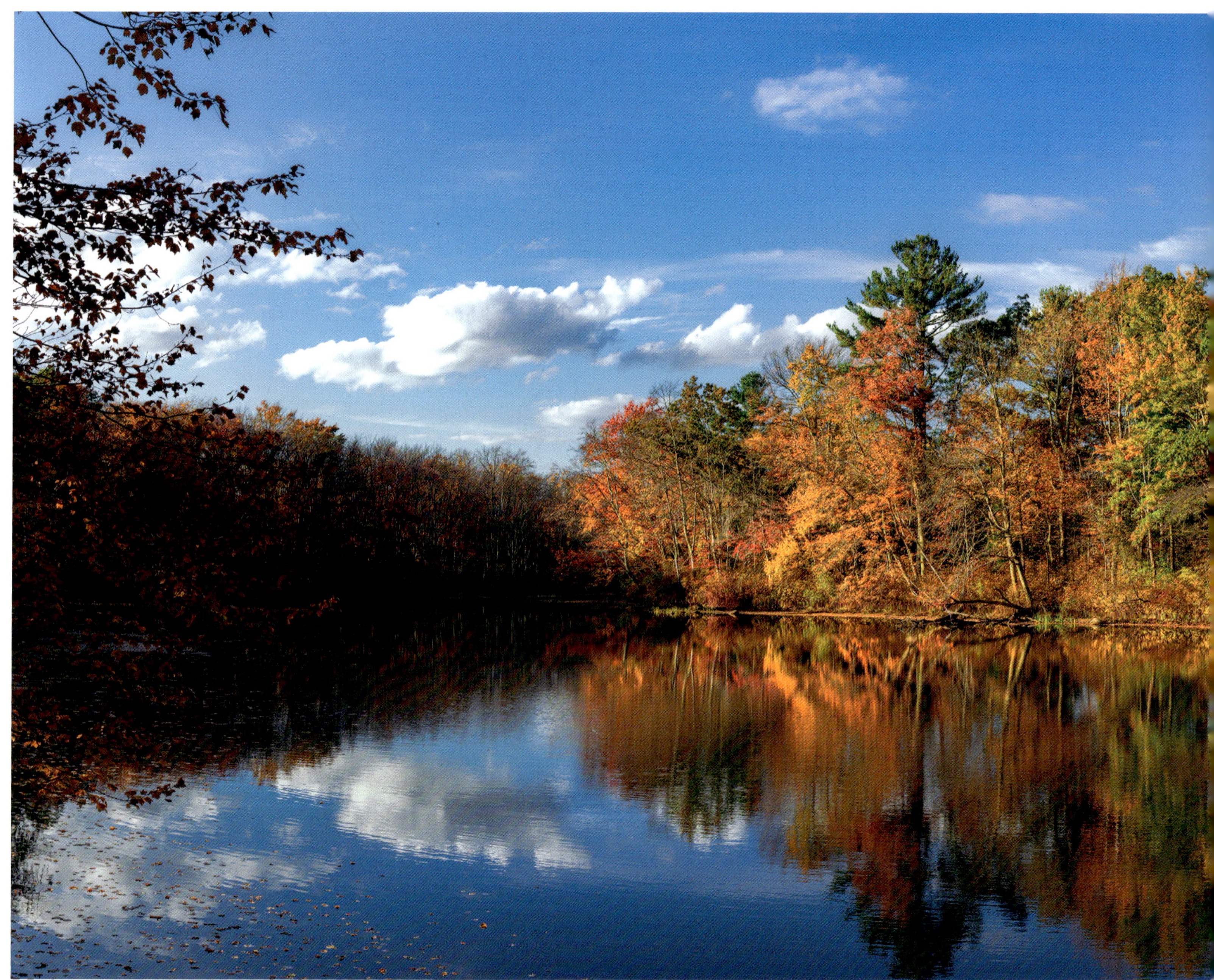

White Mill Pond, Rhode Island

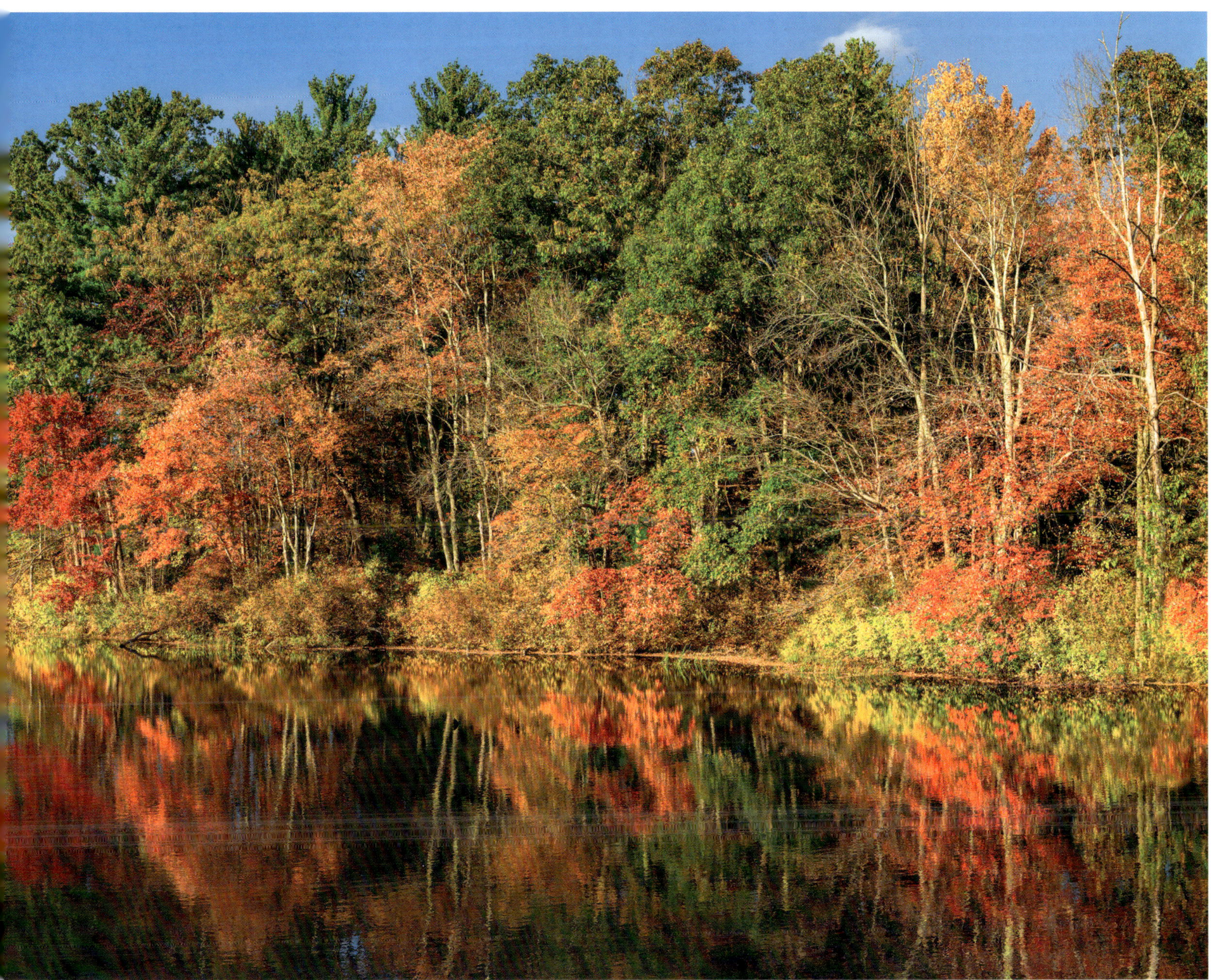

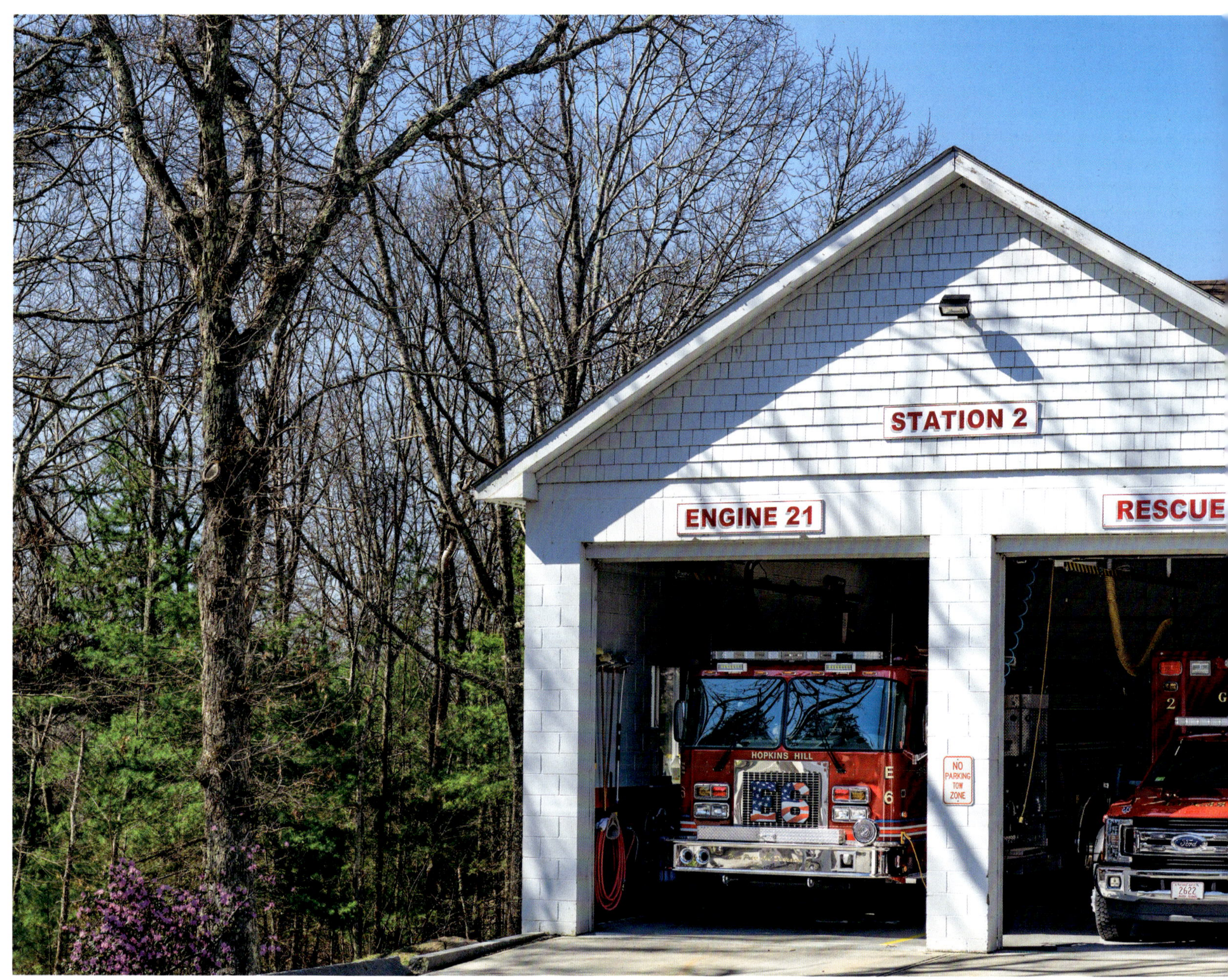

West Greenwich Fire and Rescue, Rhode Island

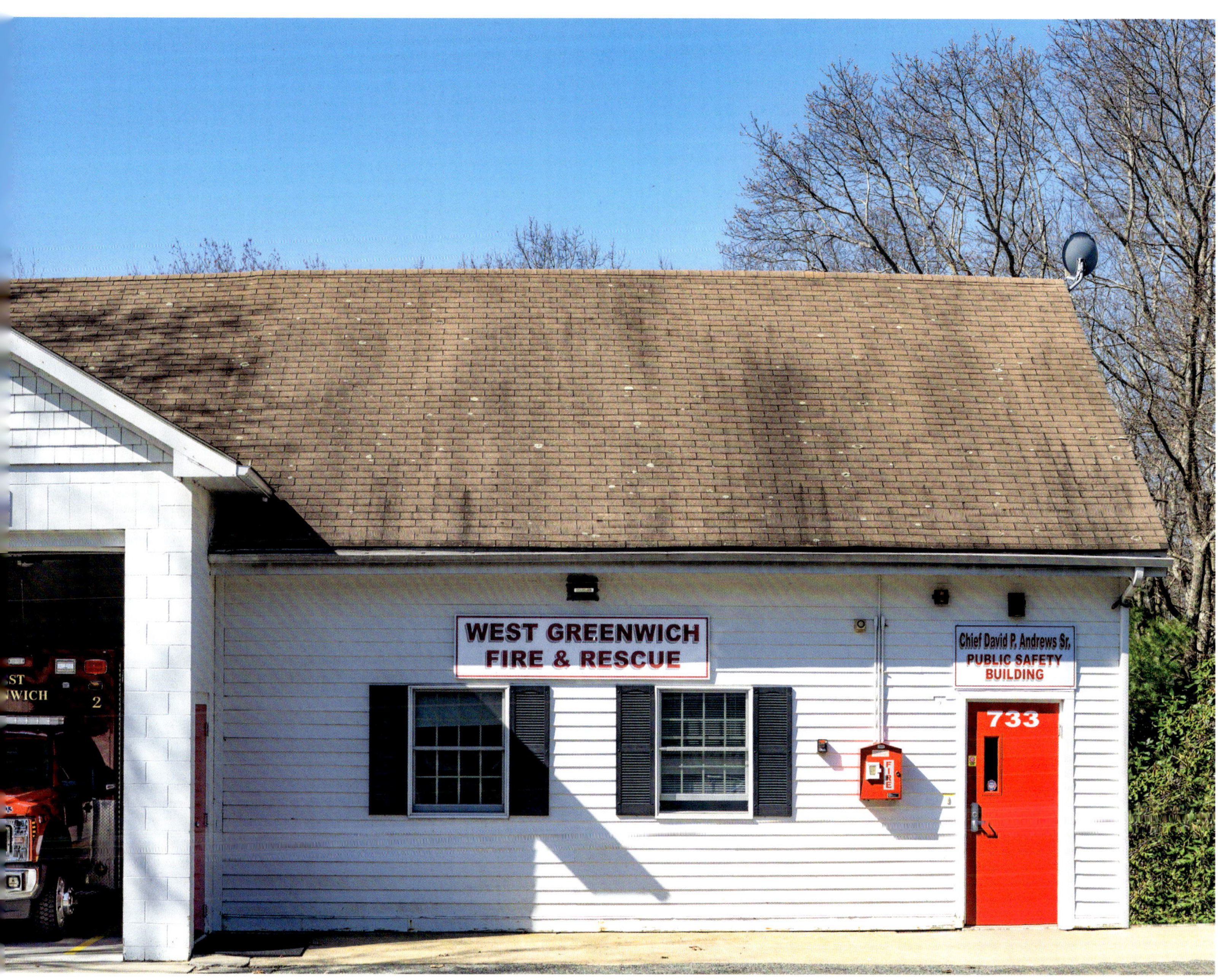

I knocked on the door to ask permission to shoot this fire station, and the answer was "Have at it!" I liked that!

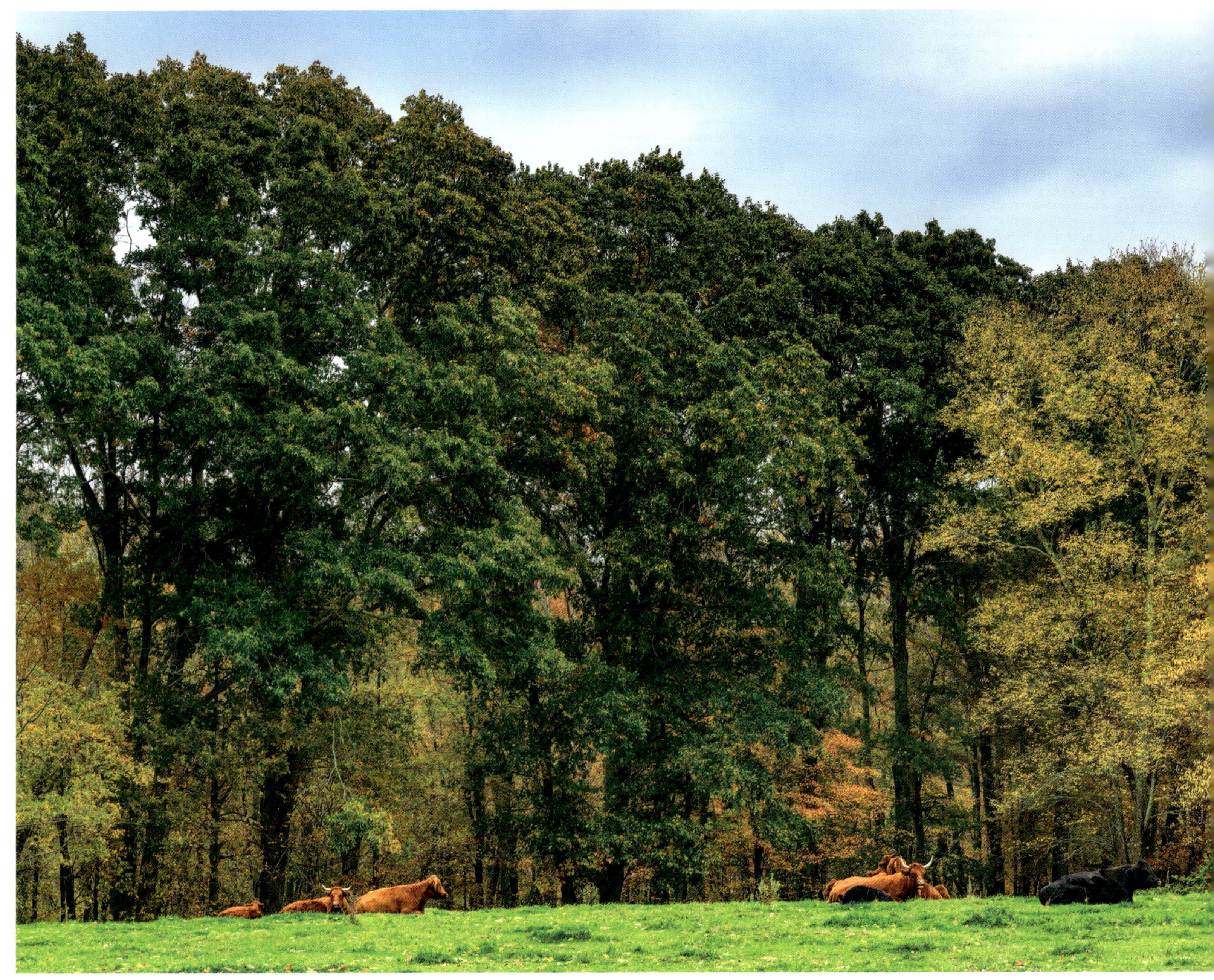

Cattle on North Road, Foster, Rhode Island

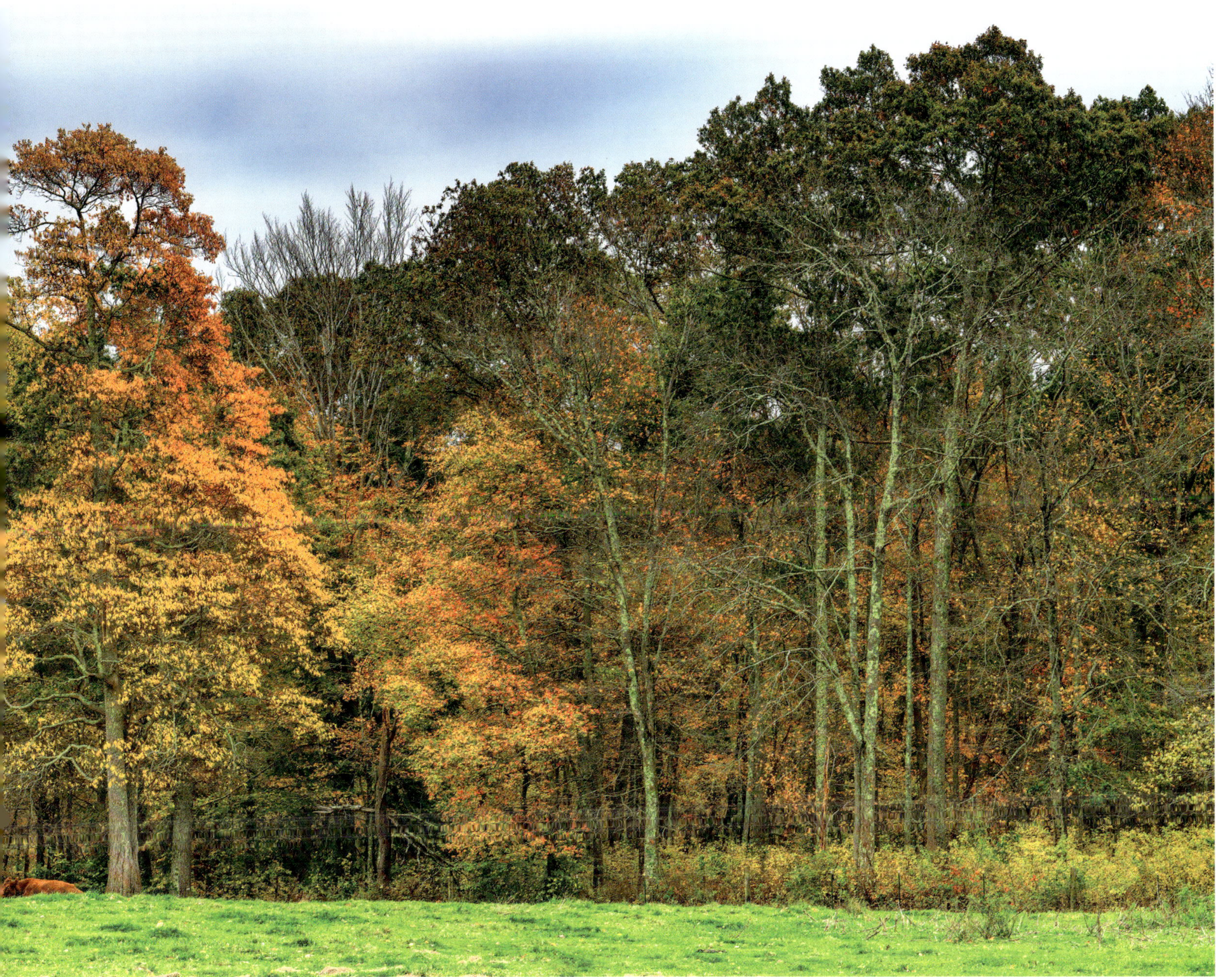

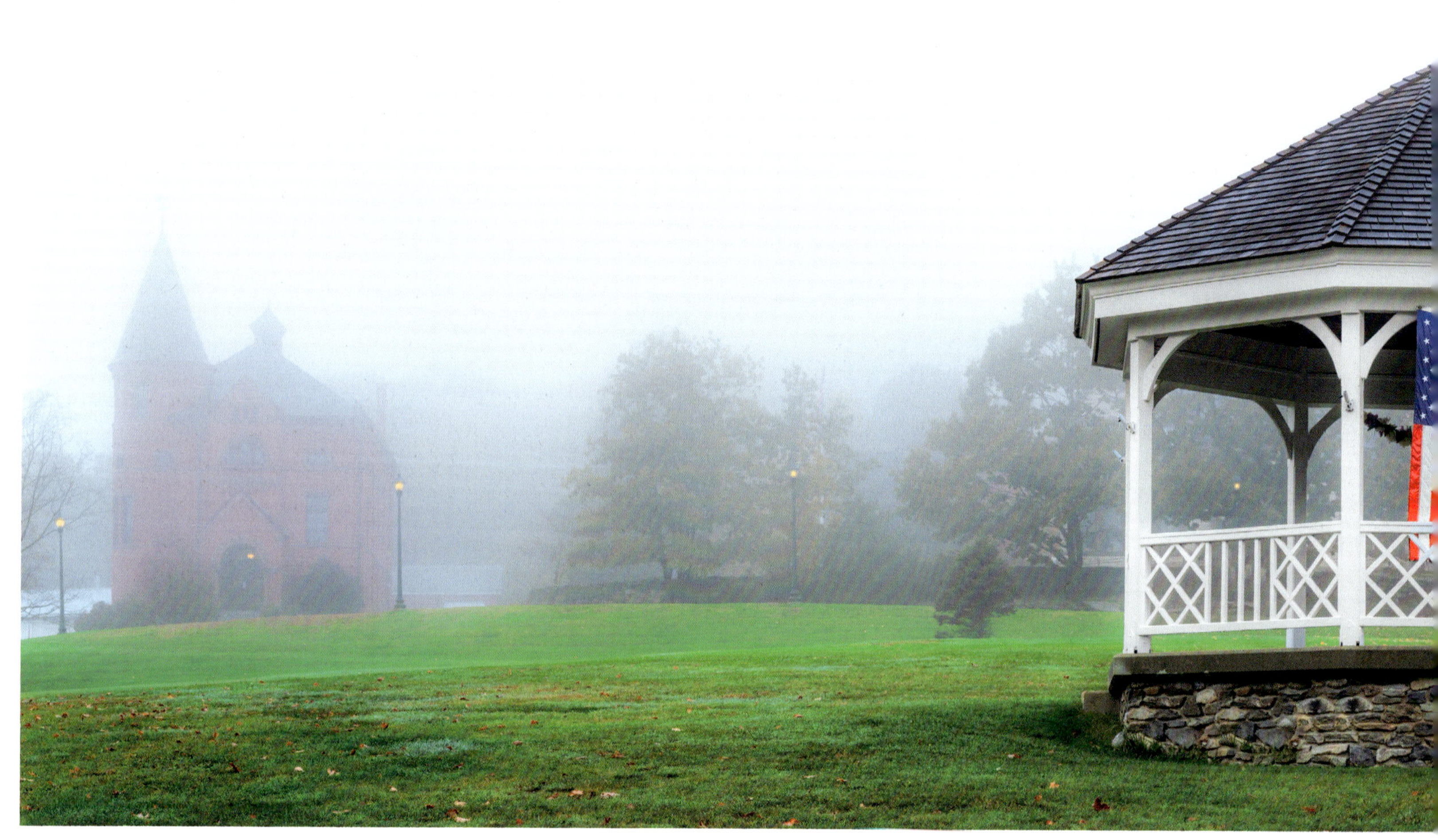

Town Square, Princeton, Massachusetts

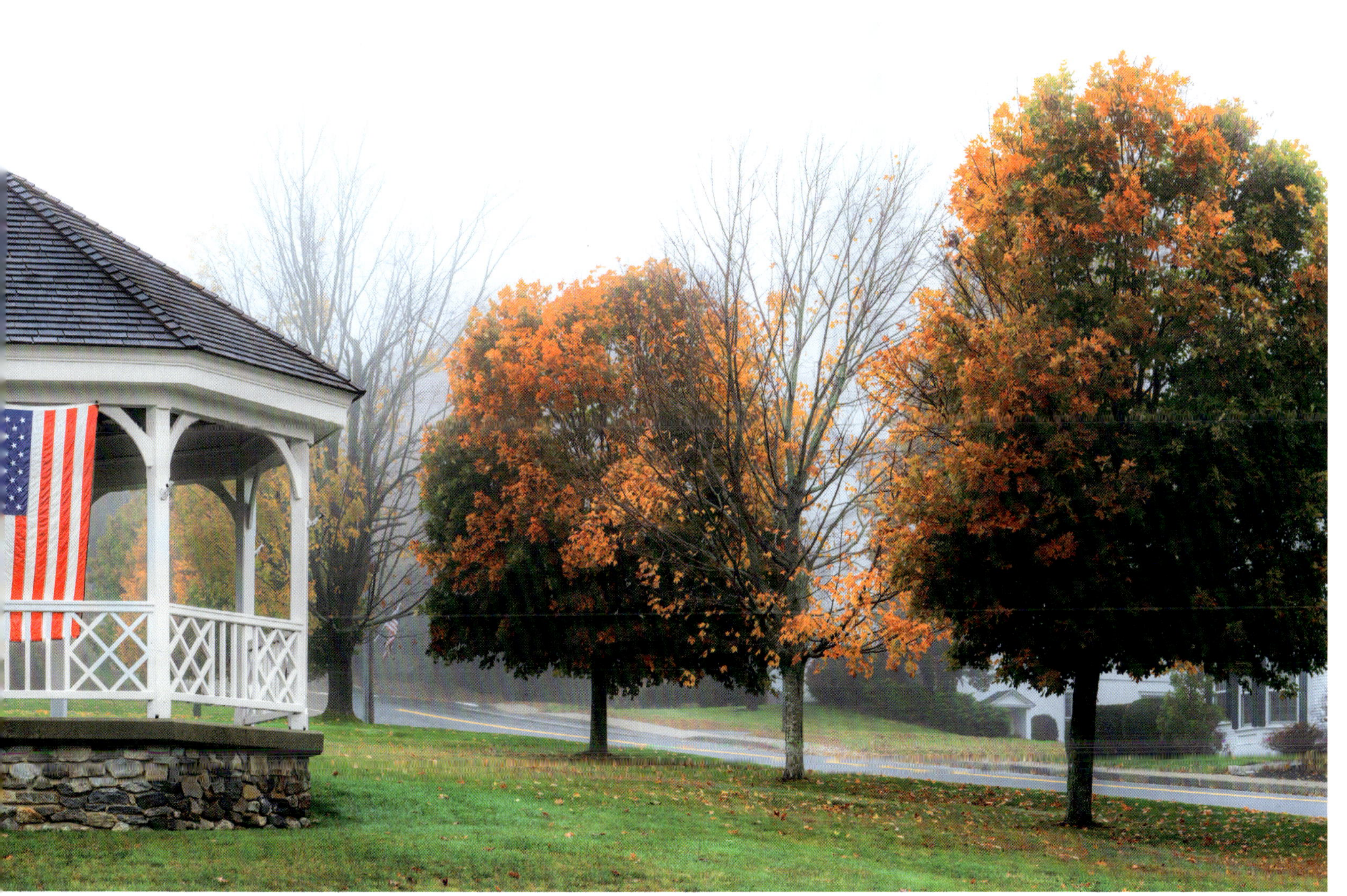

I saw lots of gazebos in town squares all over New England. This one, at this time, was just what I was hoping for.

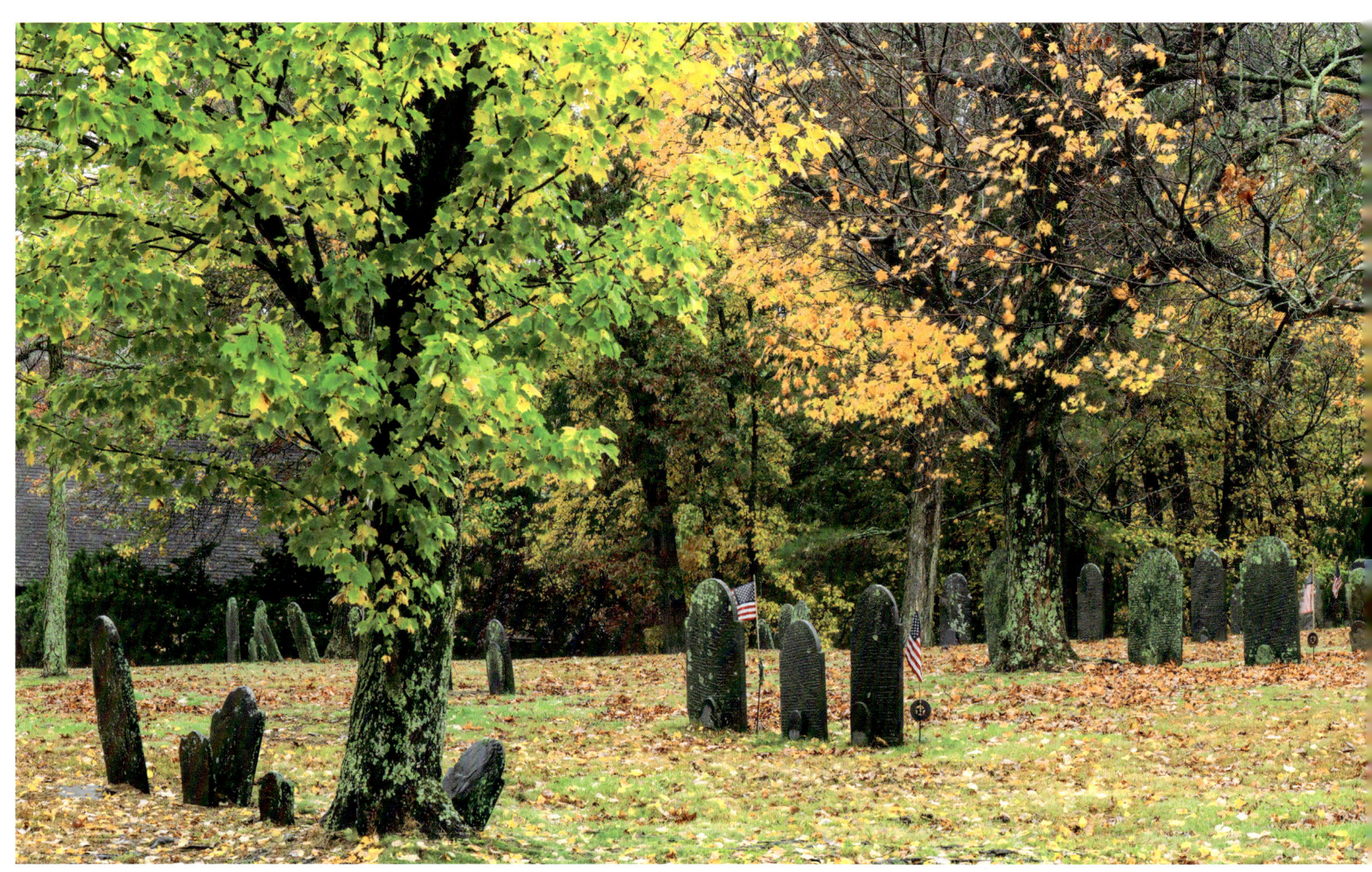

Cemetery, Holden, Massachusetts

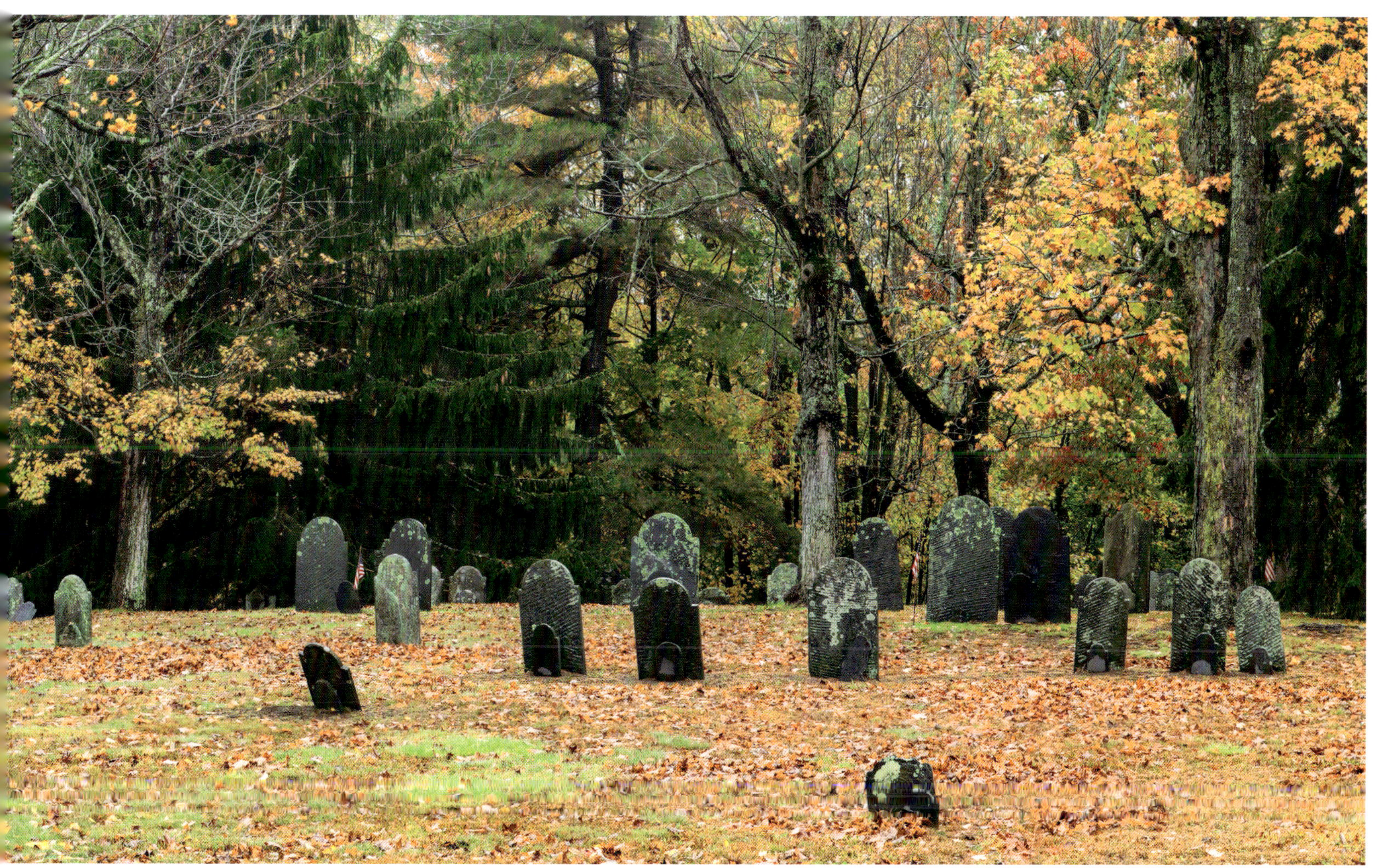

I found graves here from well before the Revolutionary War.

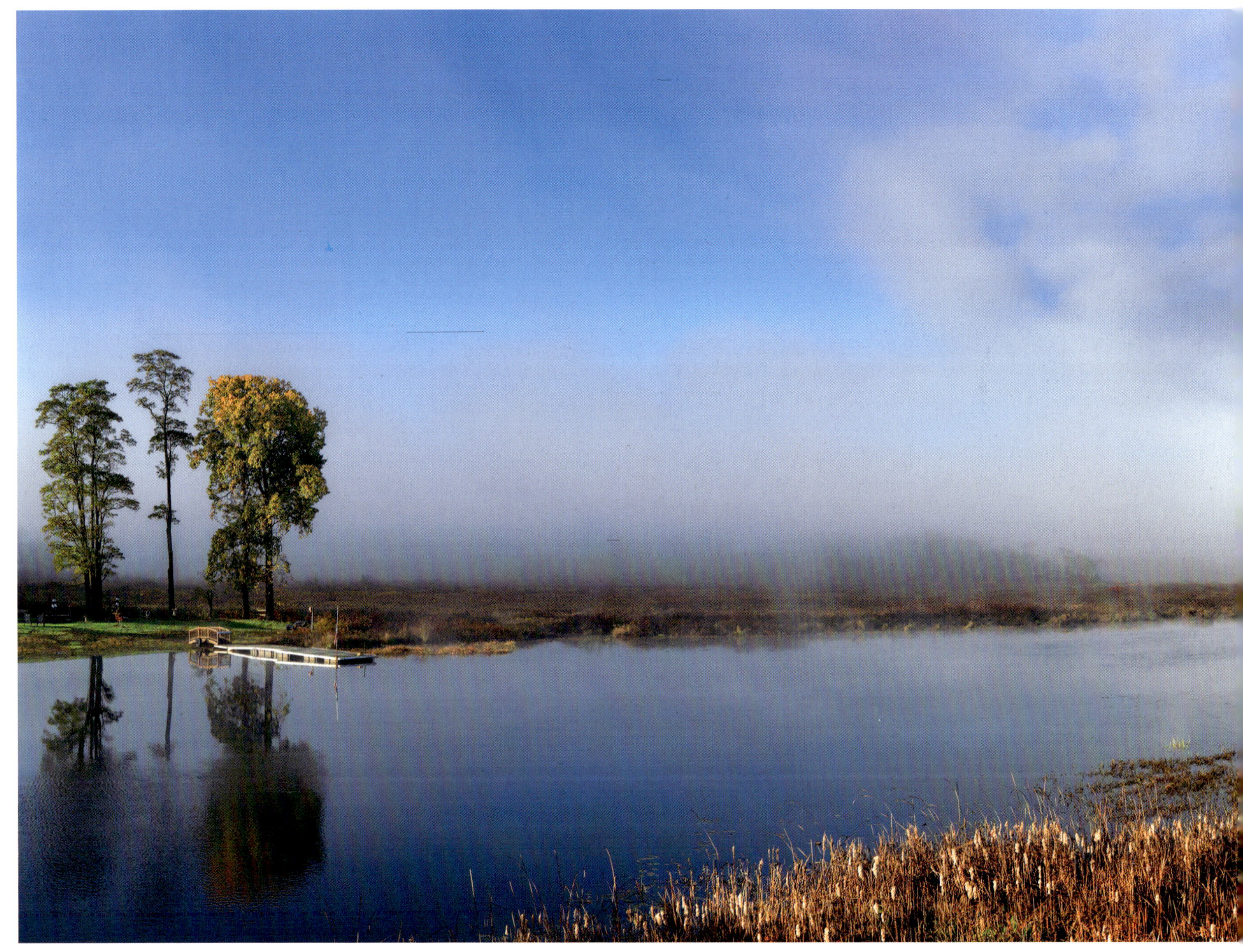

Quaboag River crossing, Massachusetts

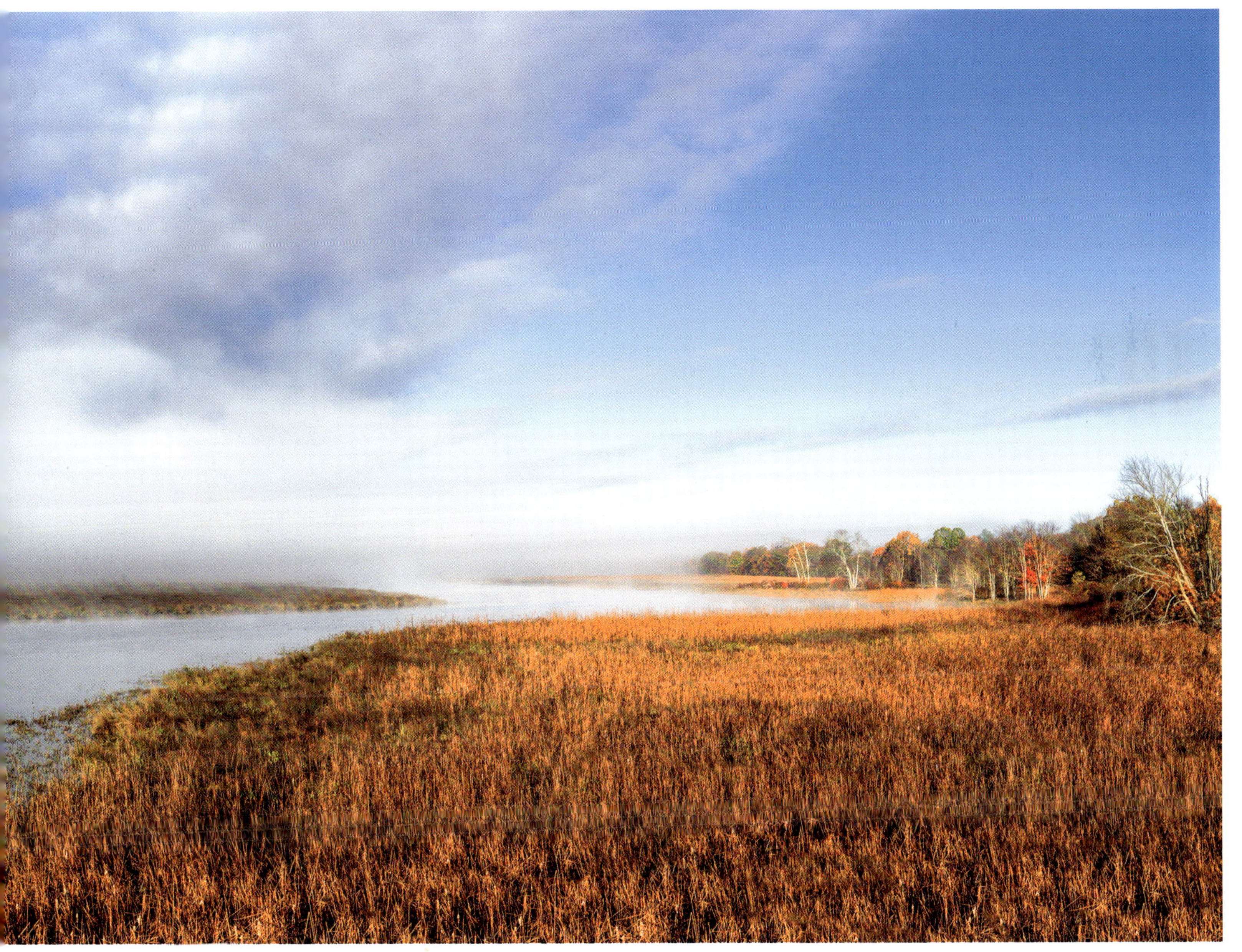

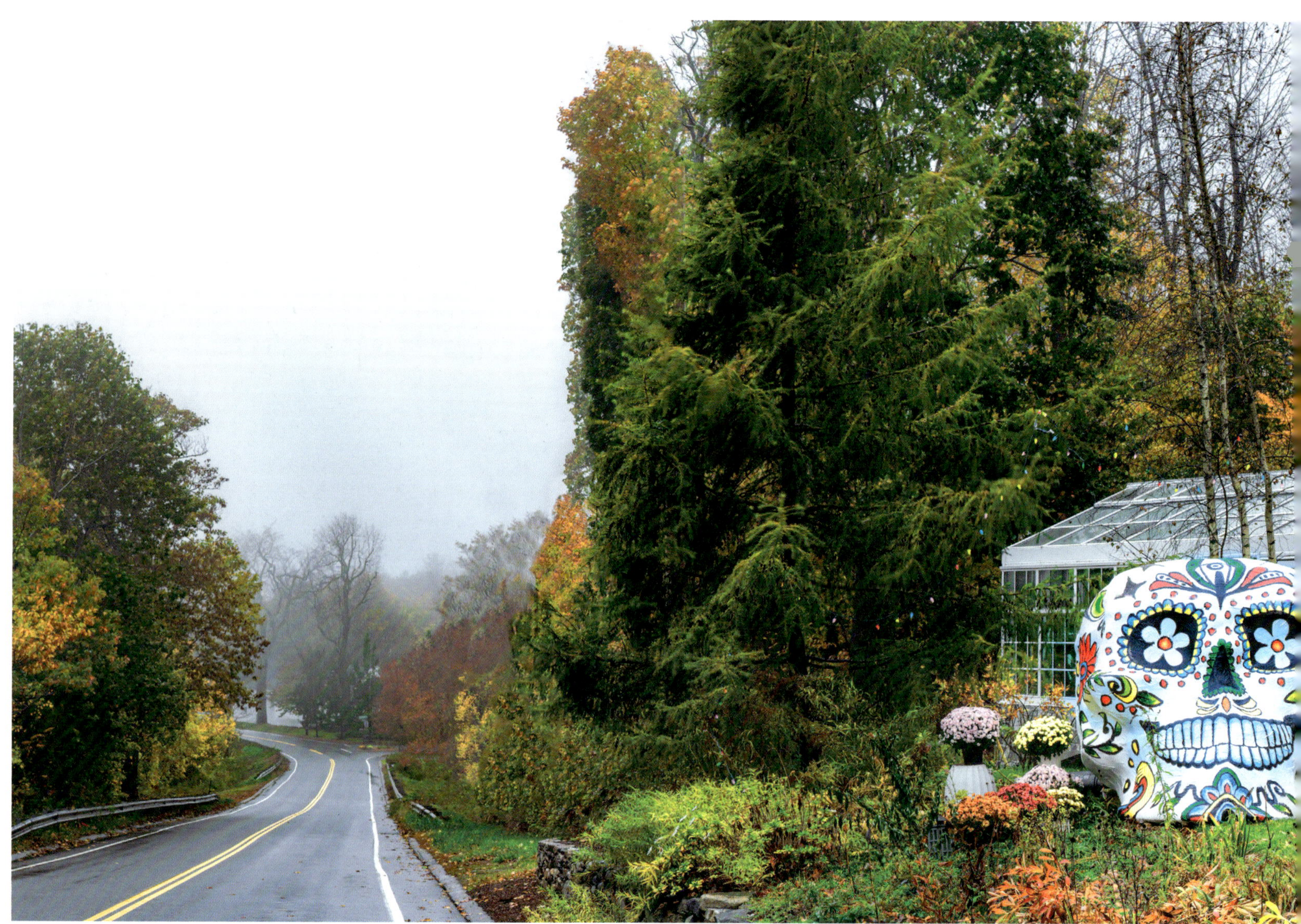

Day of the Dead display, Hubbartston Road, Massachusetts

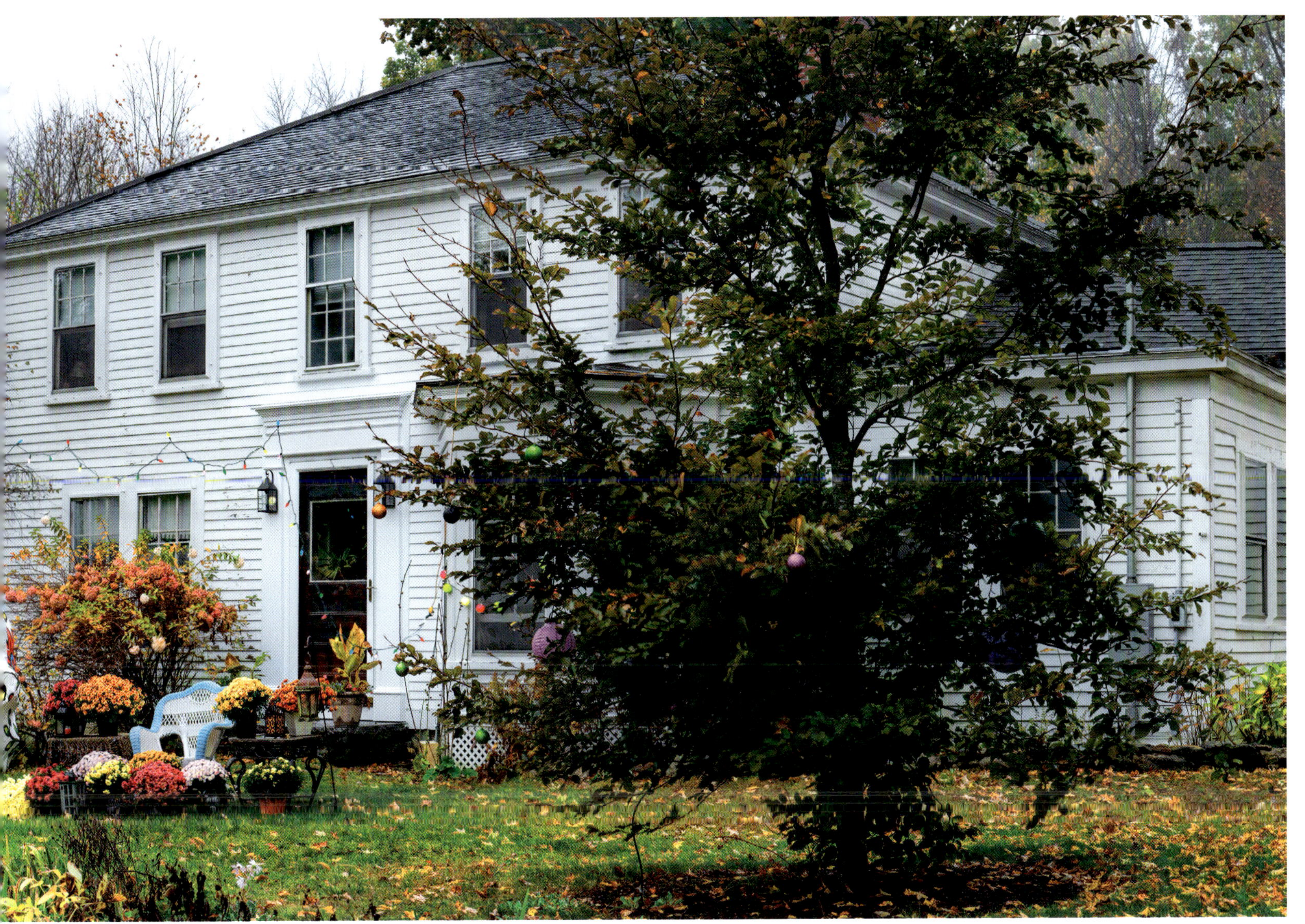

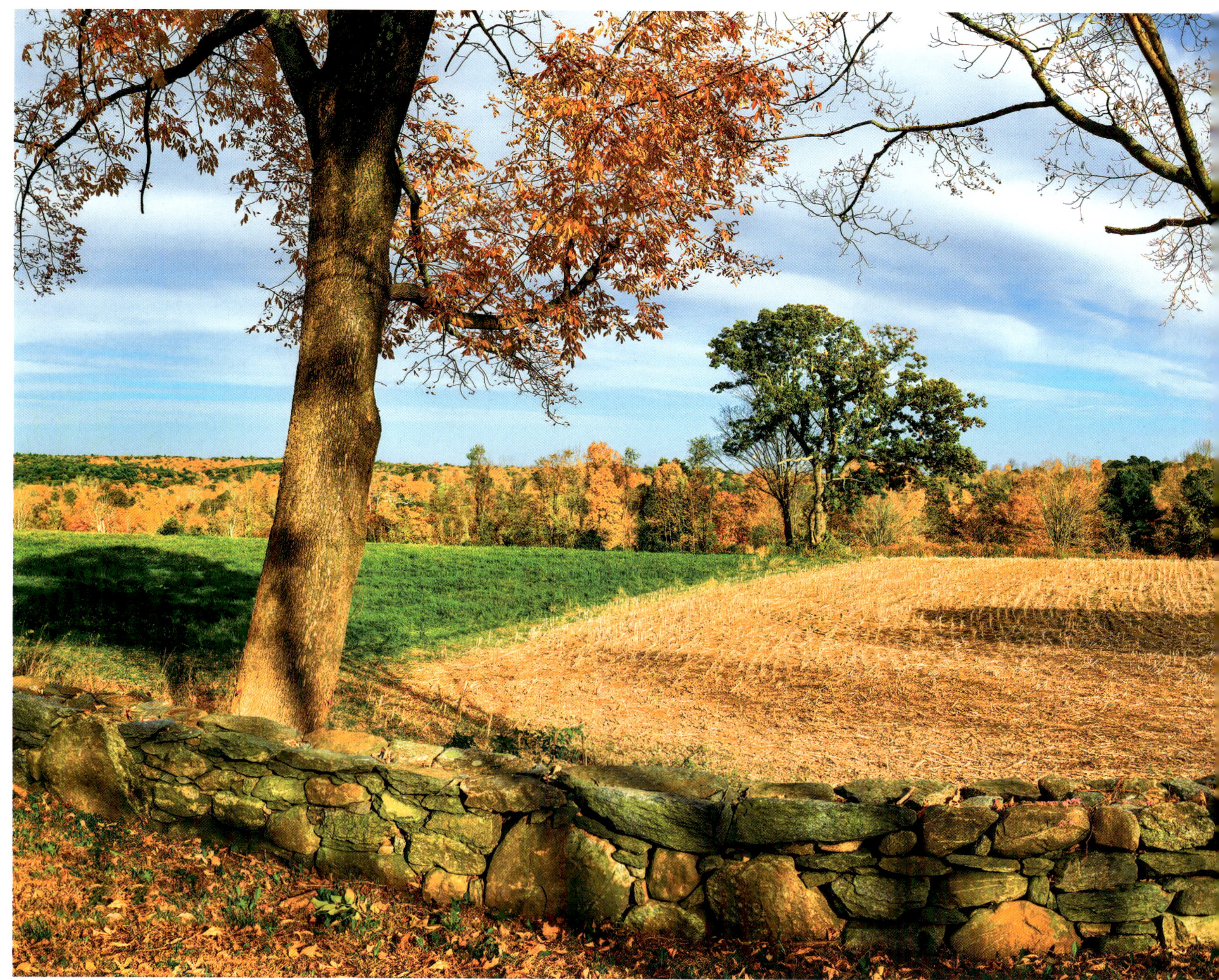

Lone tree, Gilbertville, Massachusetts

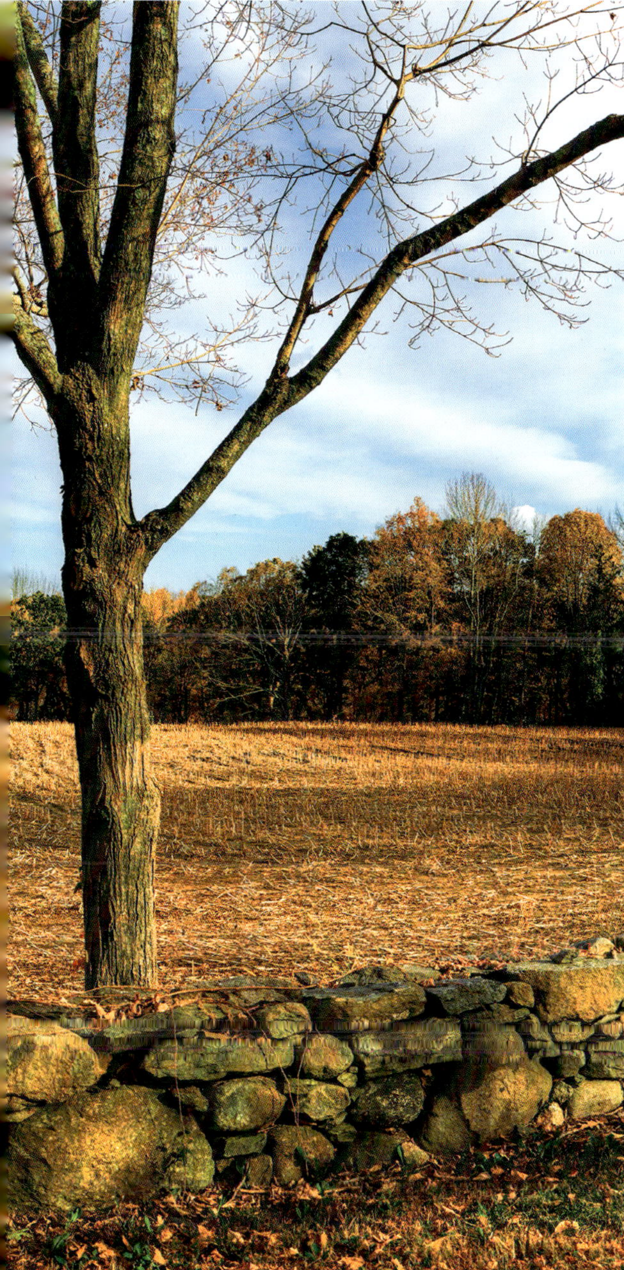

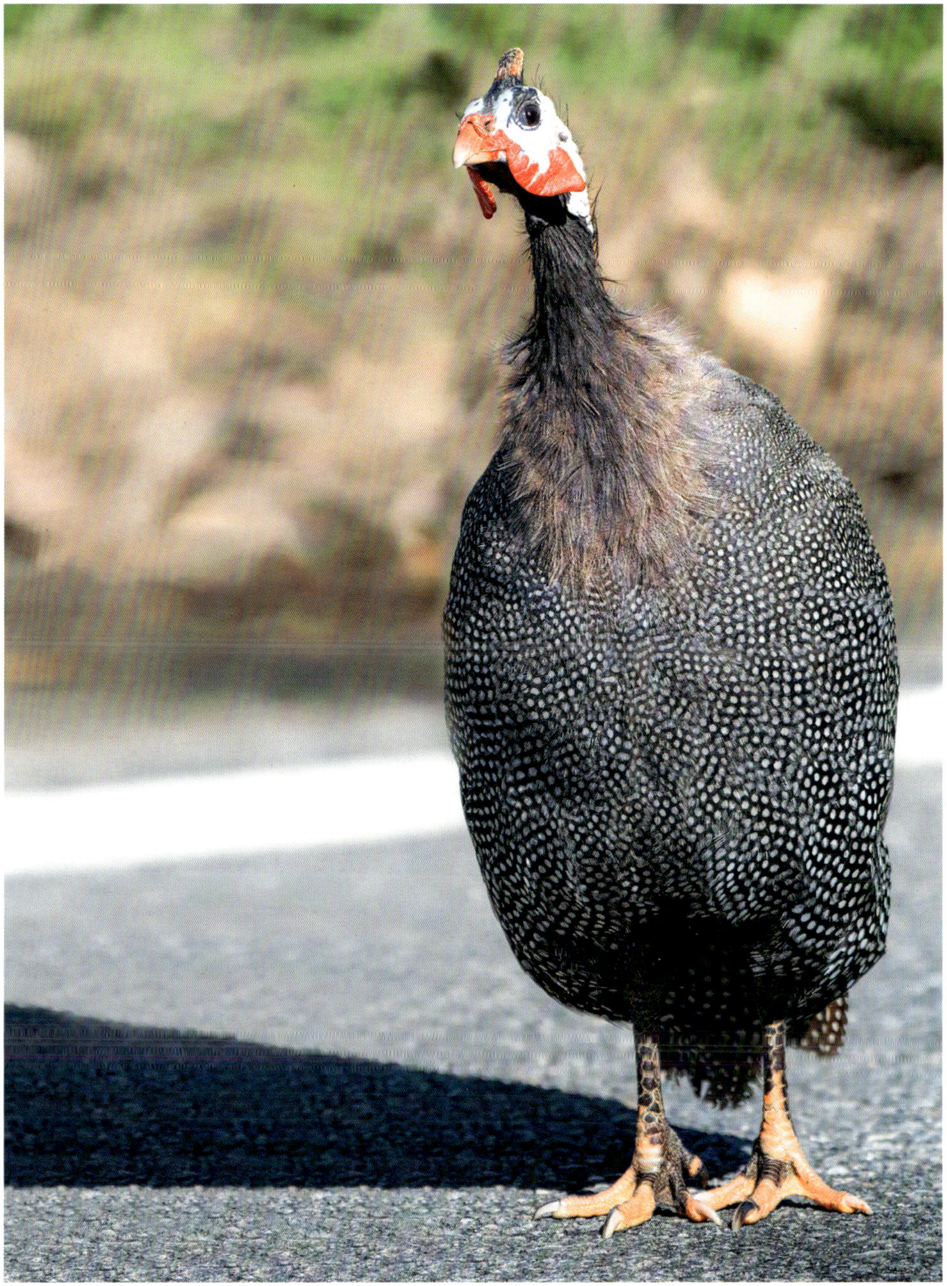

Guinea fowl crossing Massachusetts country road

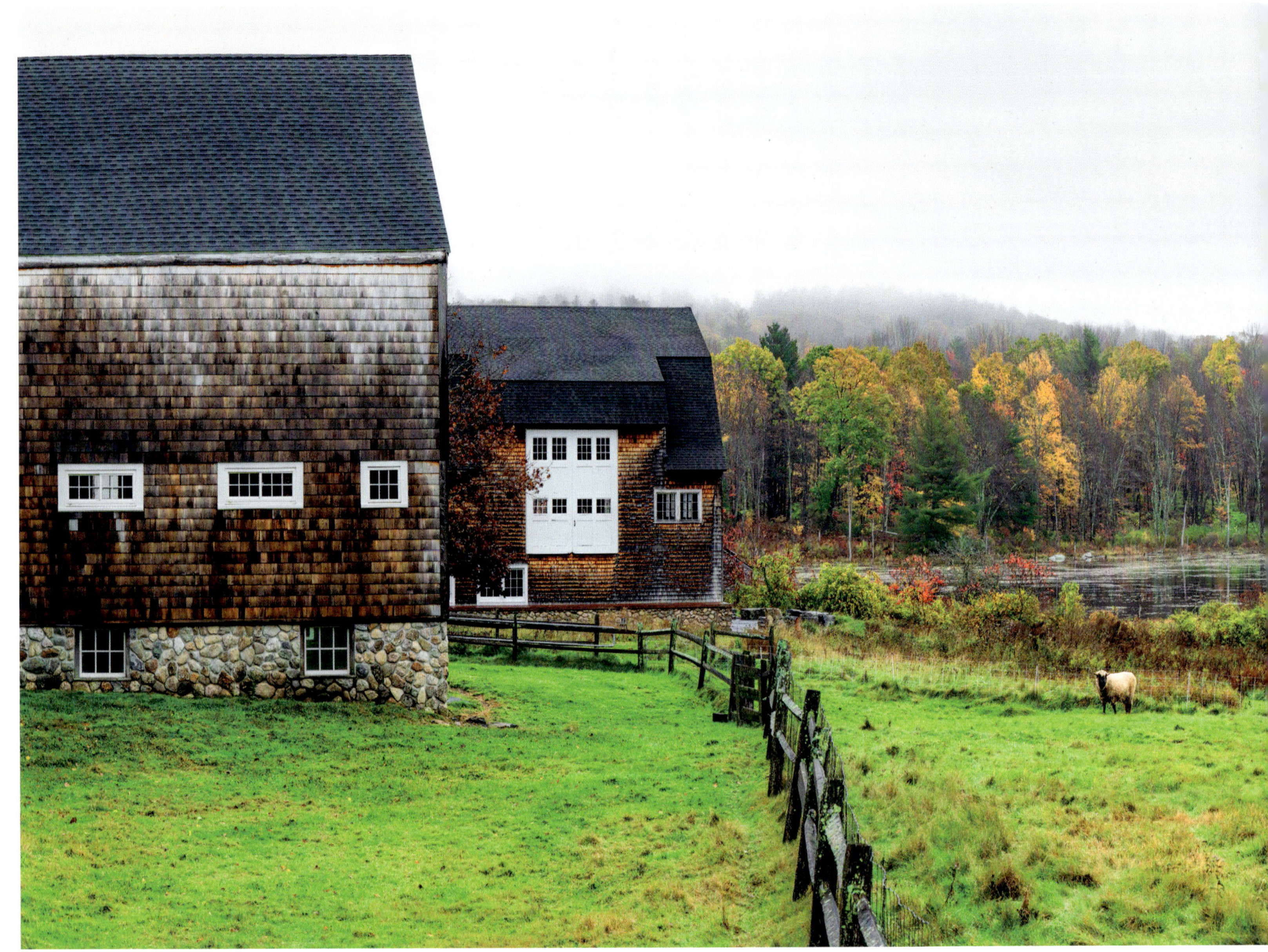

Goodnow Farm, Massachusetts

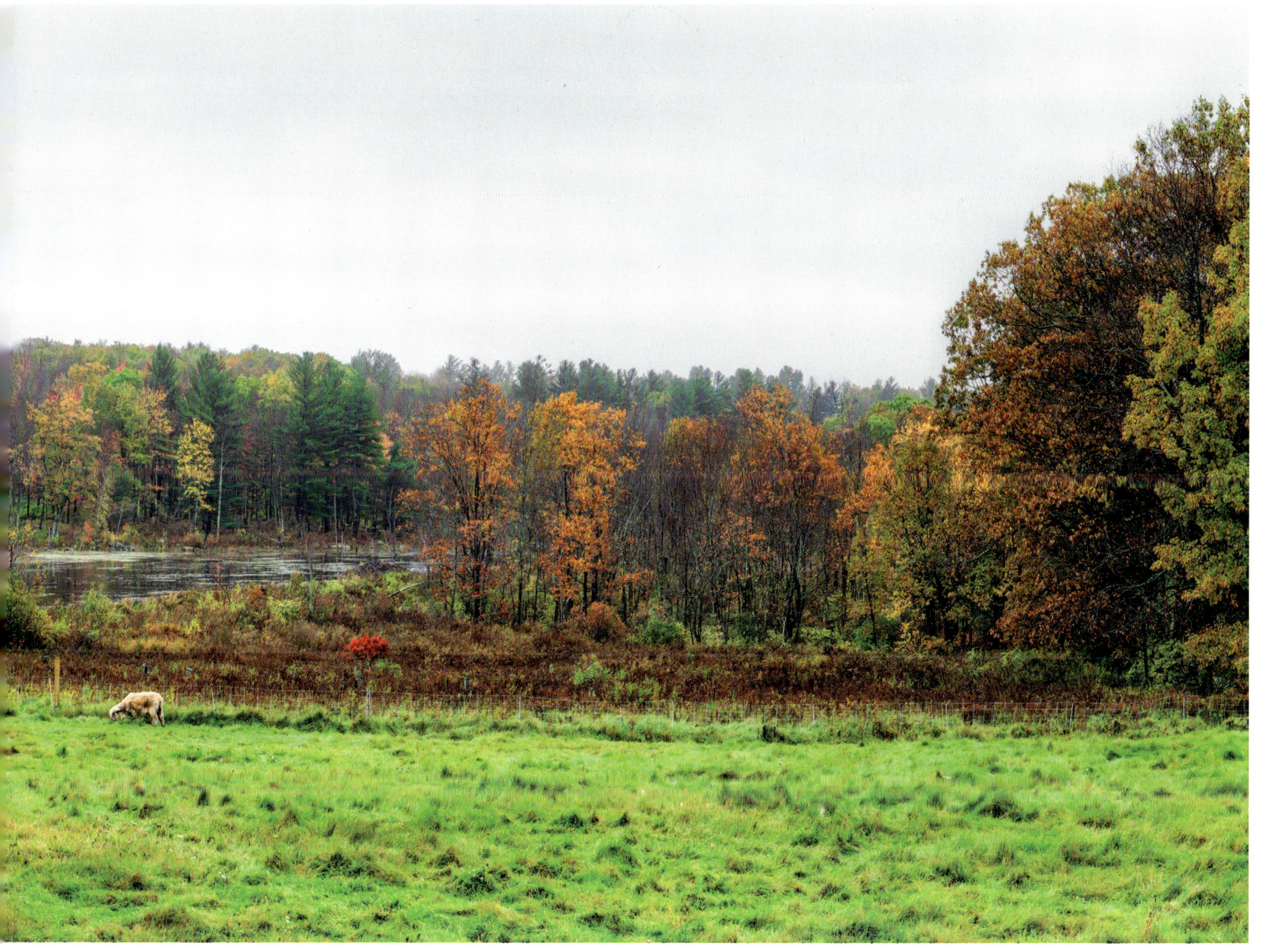

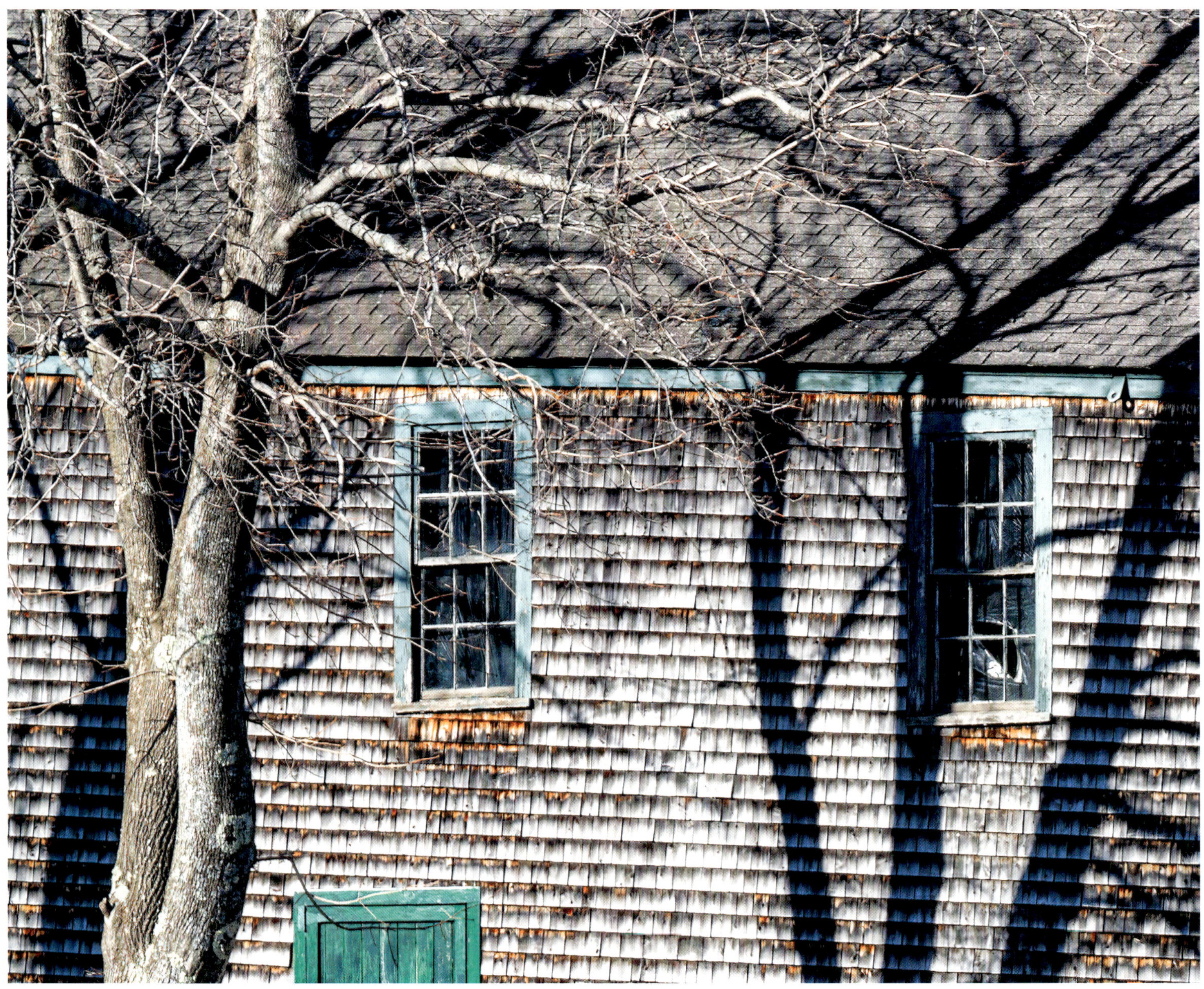

House near Salem, Massachusetts

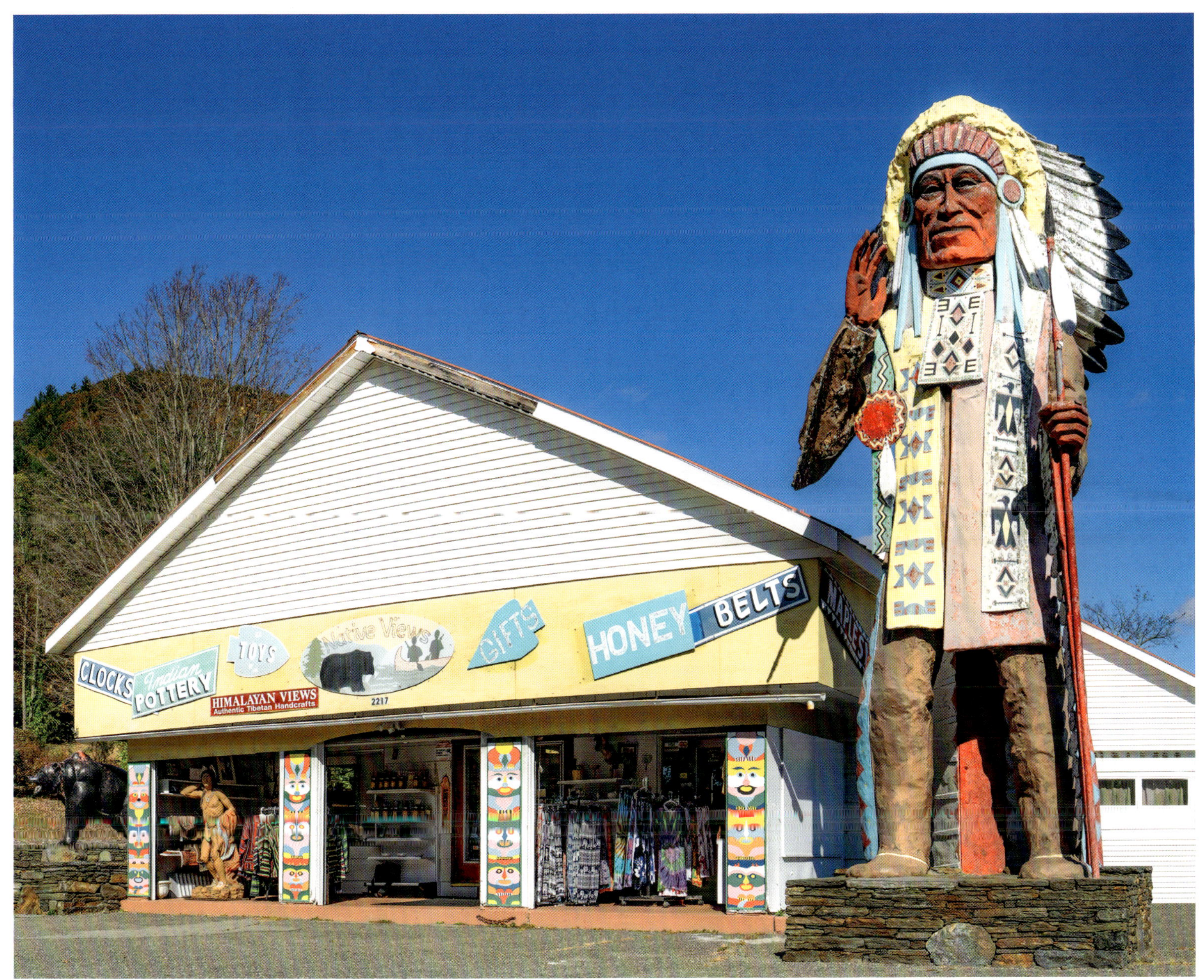

Shelburne Falls, Massachusetts

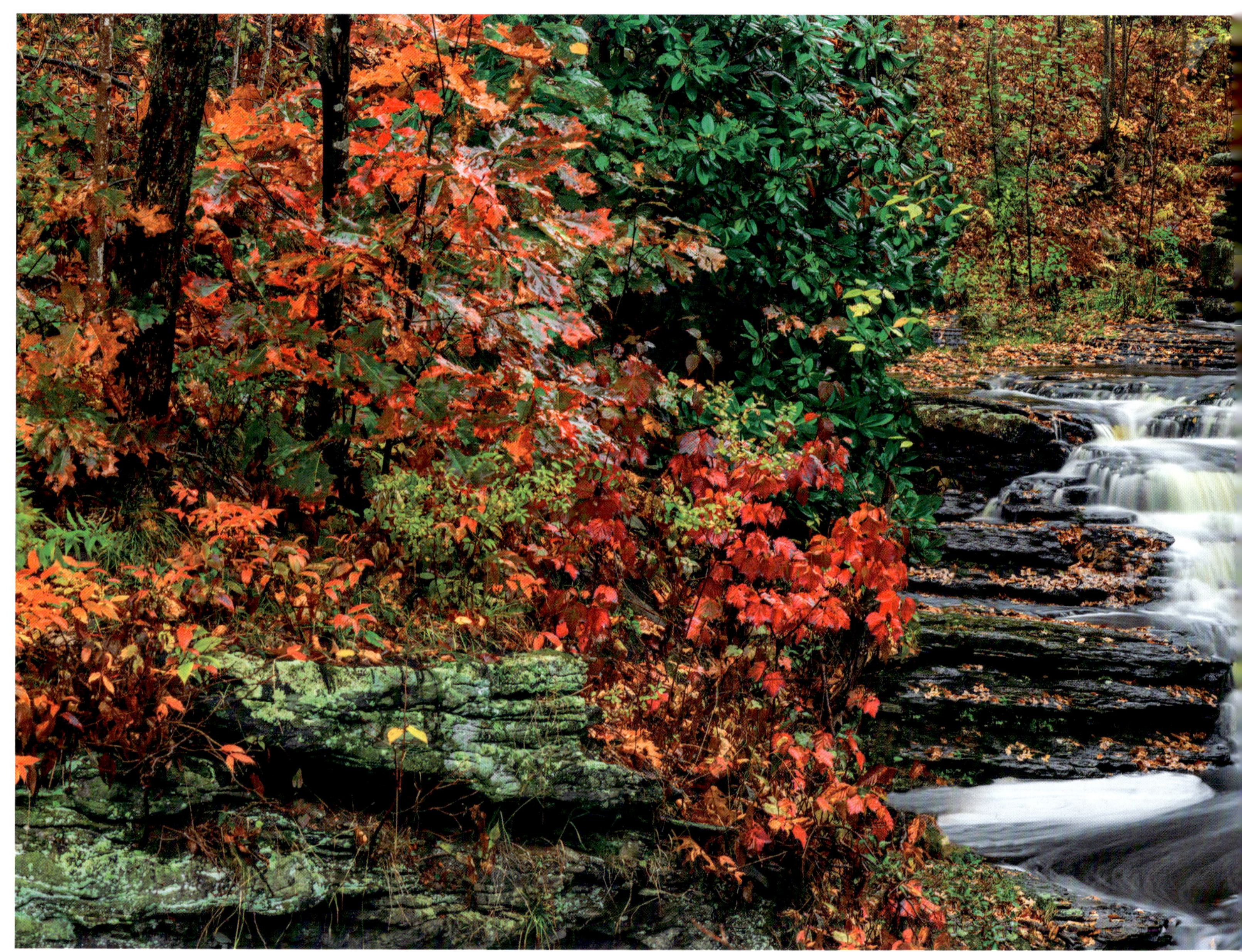

Major Willard Moore Memorial Park, Paxton, Massachusetts

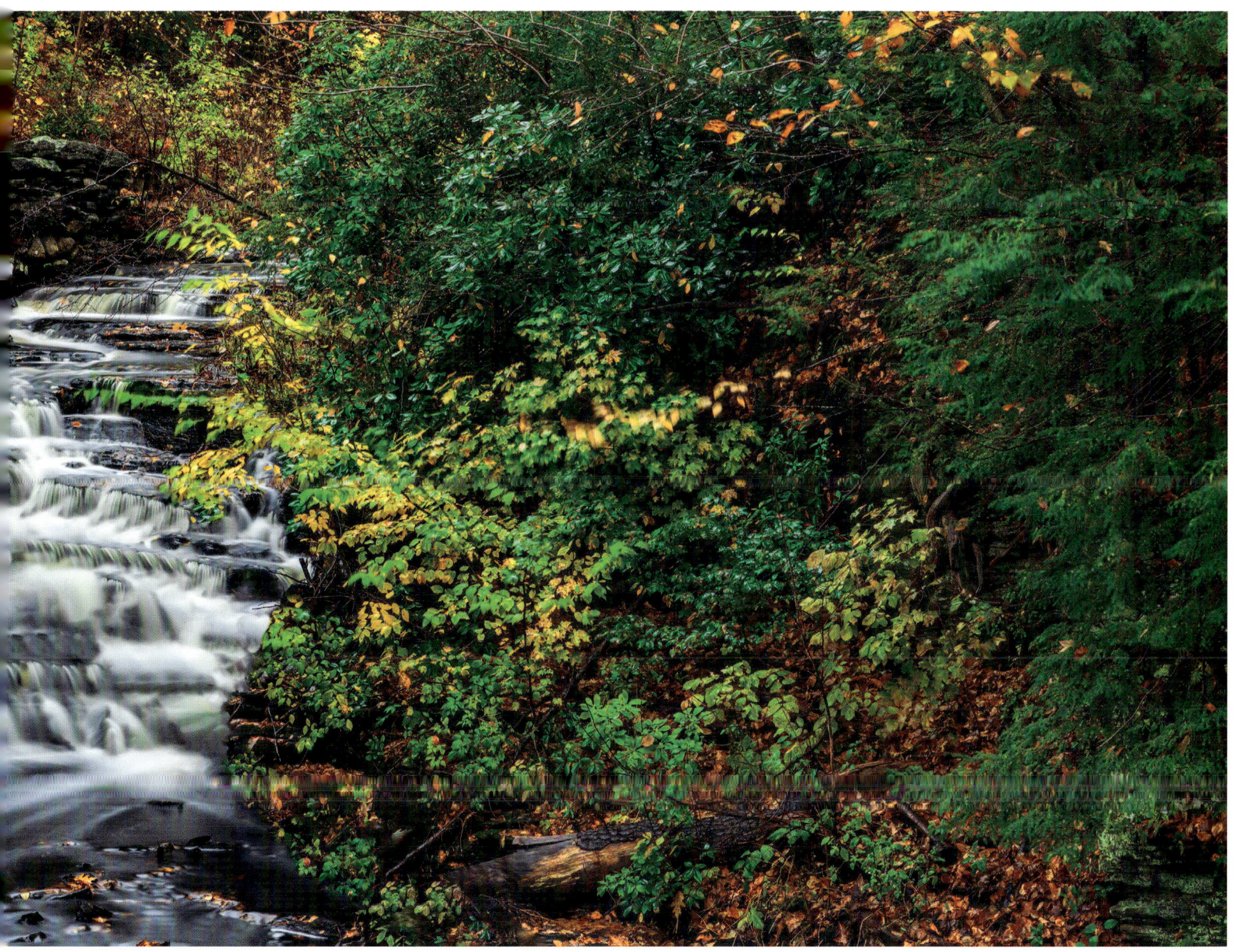

Willard Moore was born in 1743. He was killed at Bunker Hill on June 17, 1775, where he served as major of Doolittle's Massachusetts Regiment.

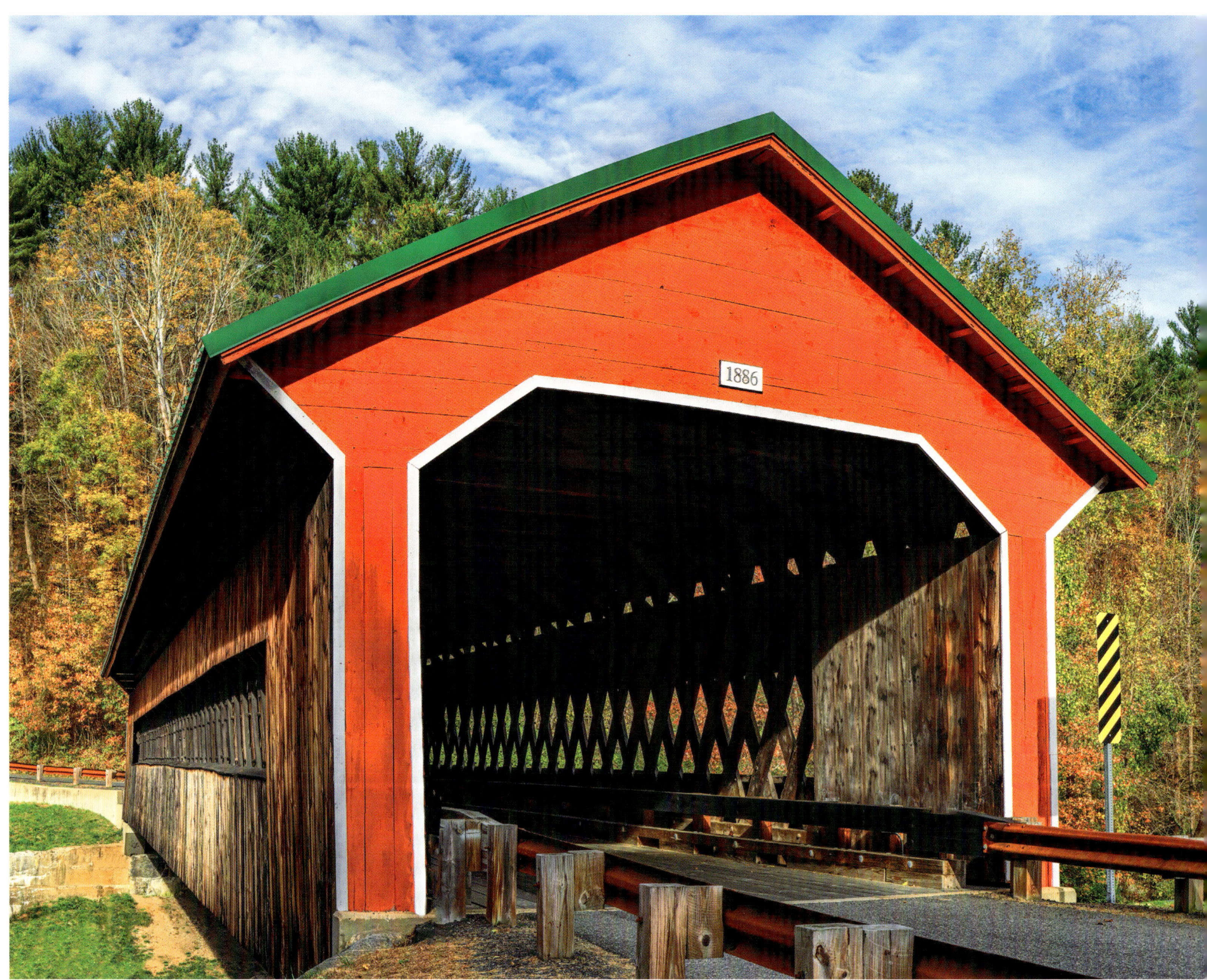

Gilbertville Bridge, Massachusetts, 1886

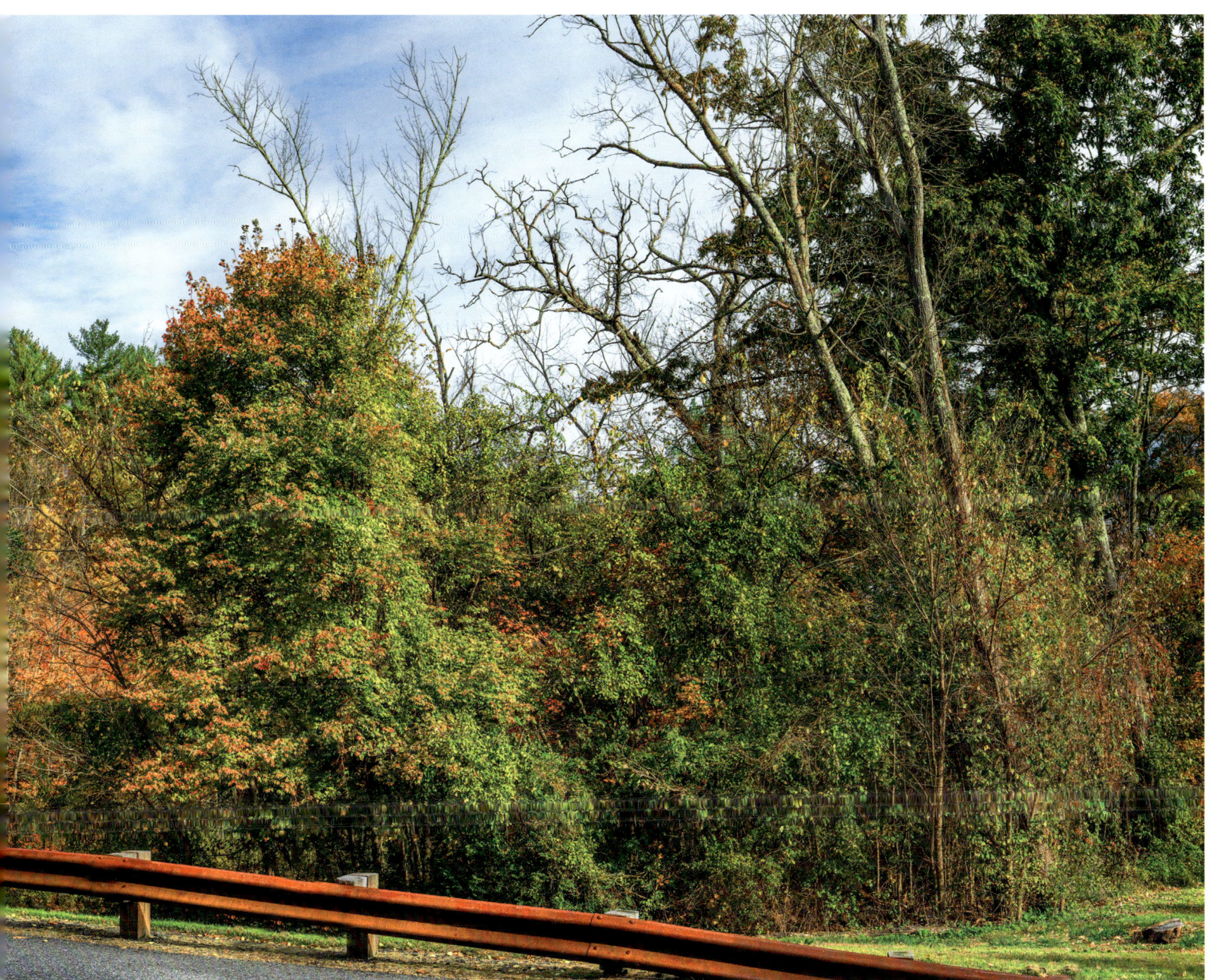

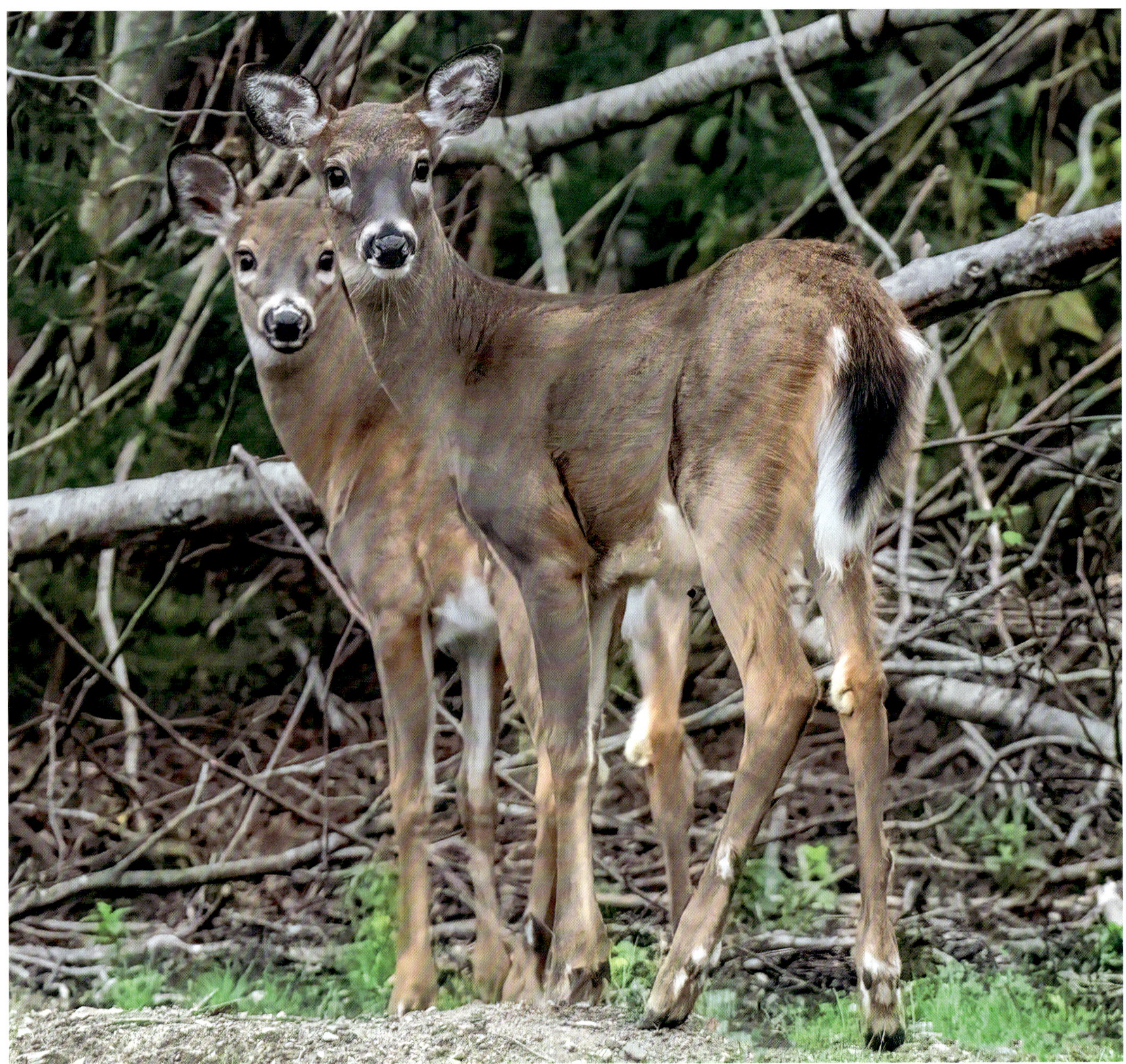

Sweet, curious New England deer

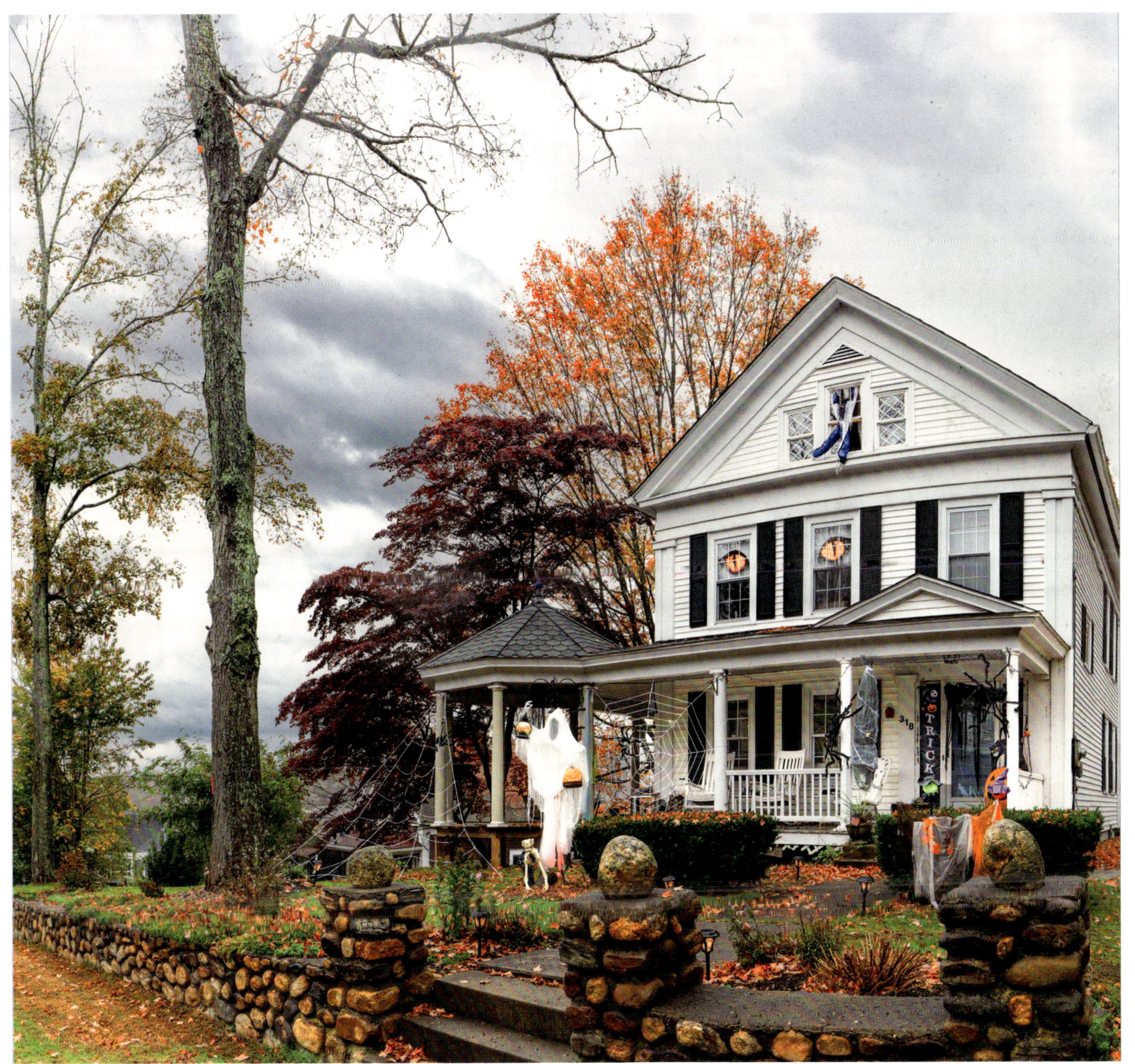

Halloween week in Massachusetts

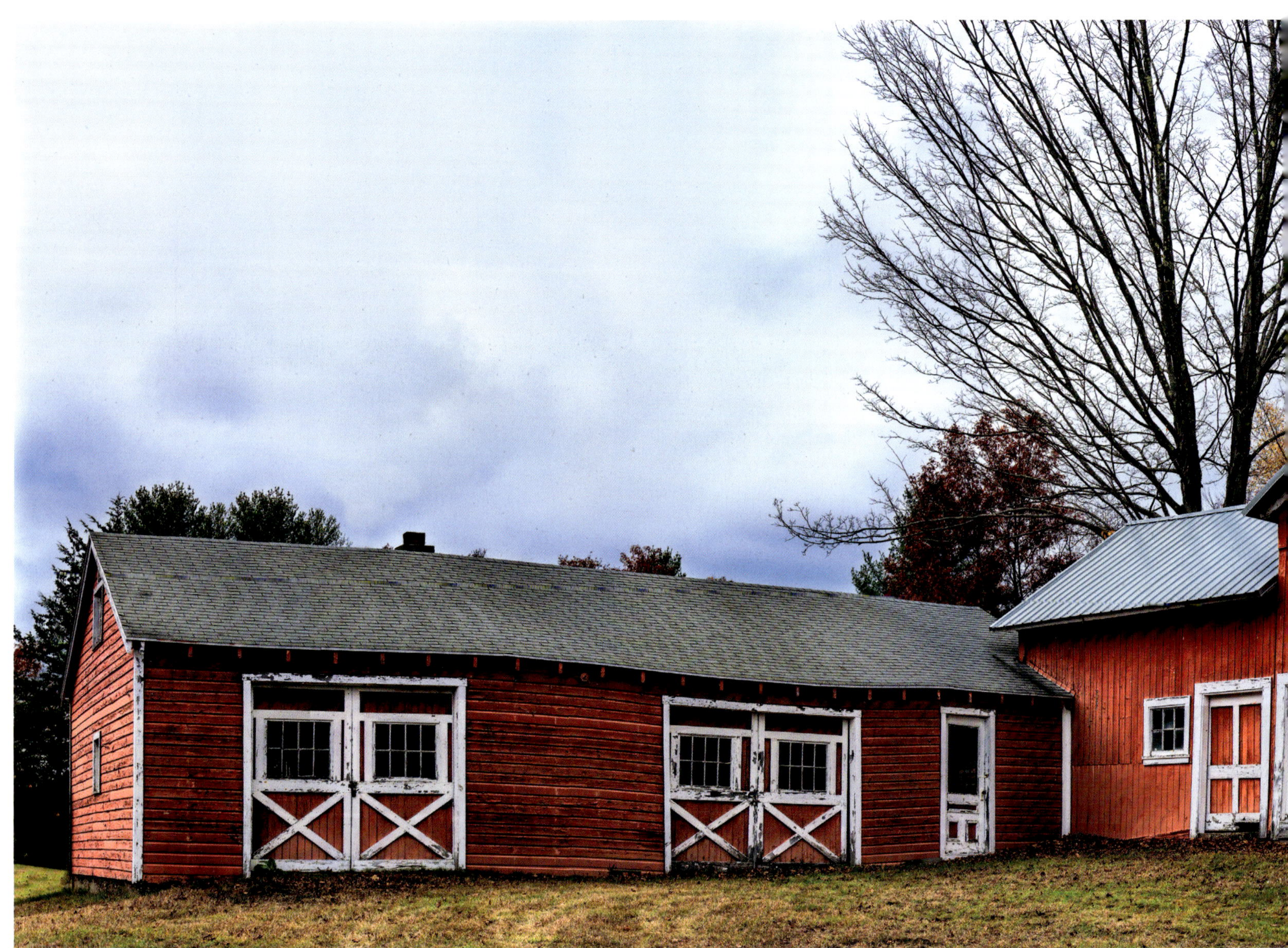

Barn near Granby, Massachusetts

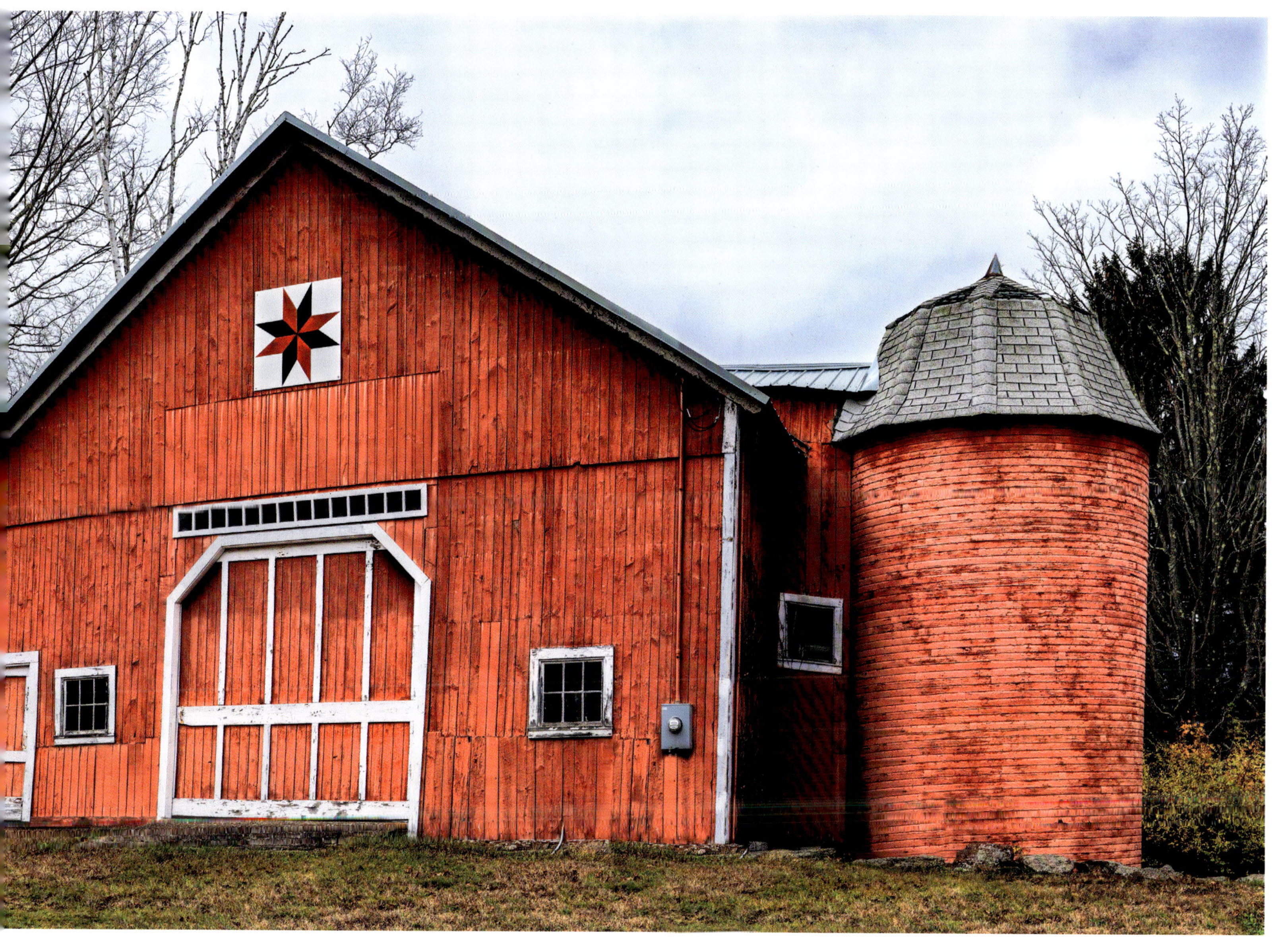

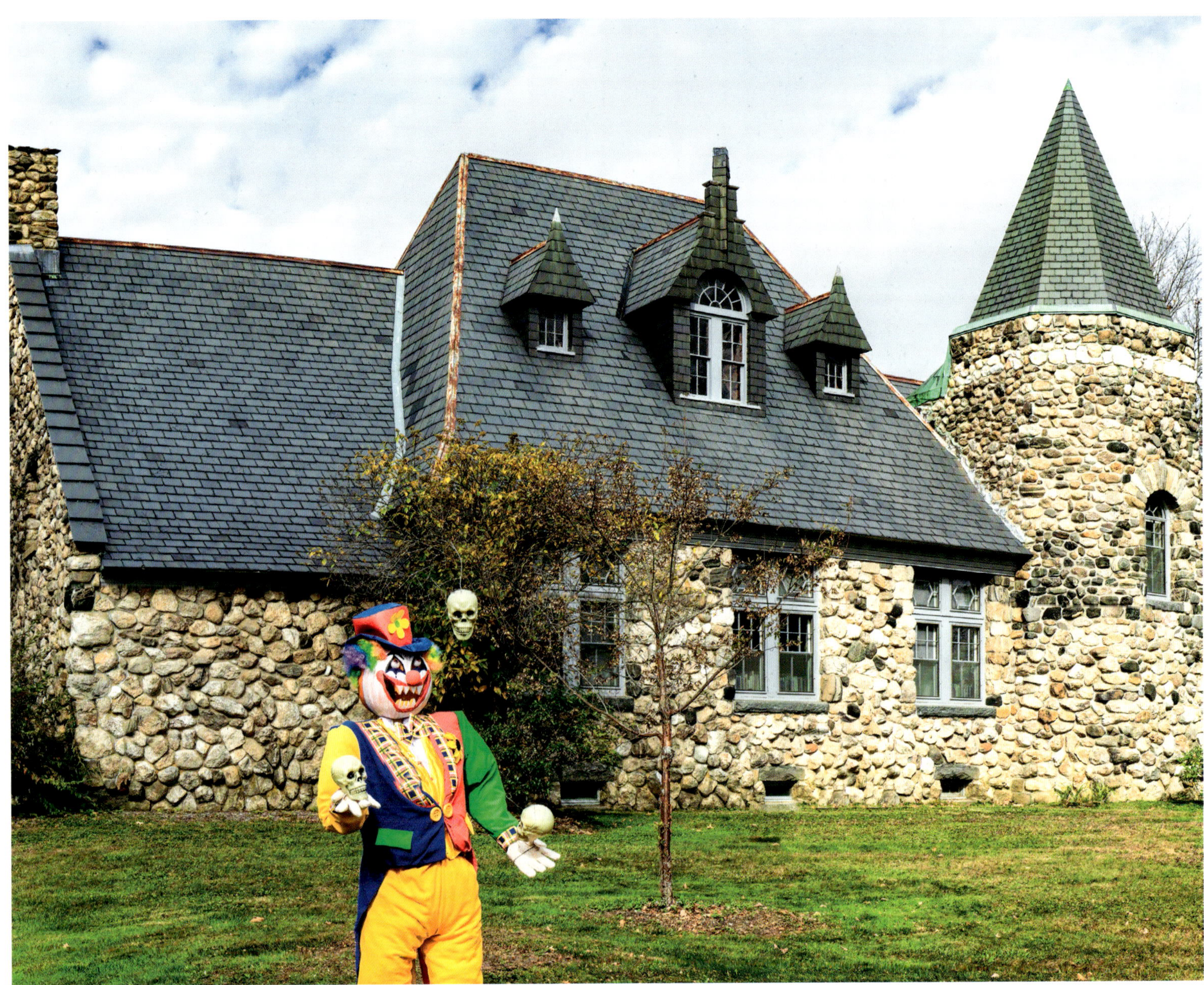

Petersham Memorial Library, Massachusetts, 1890

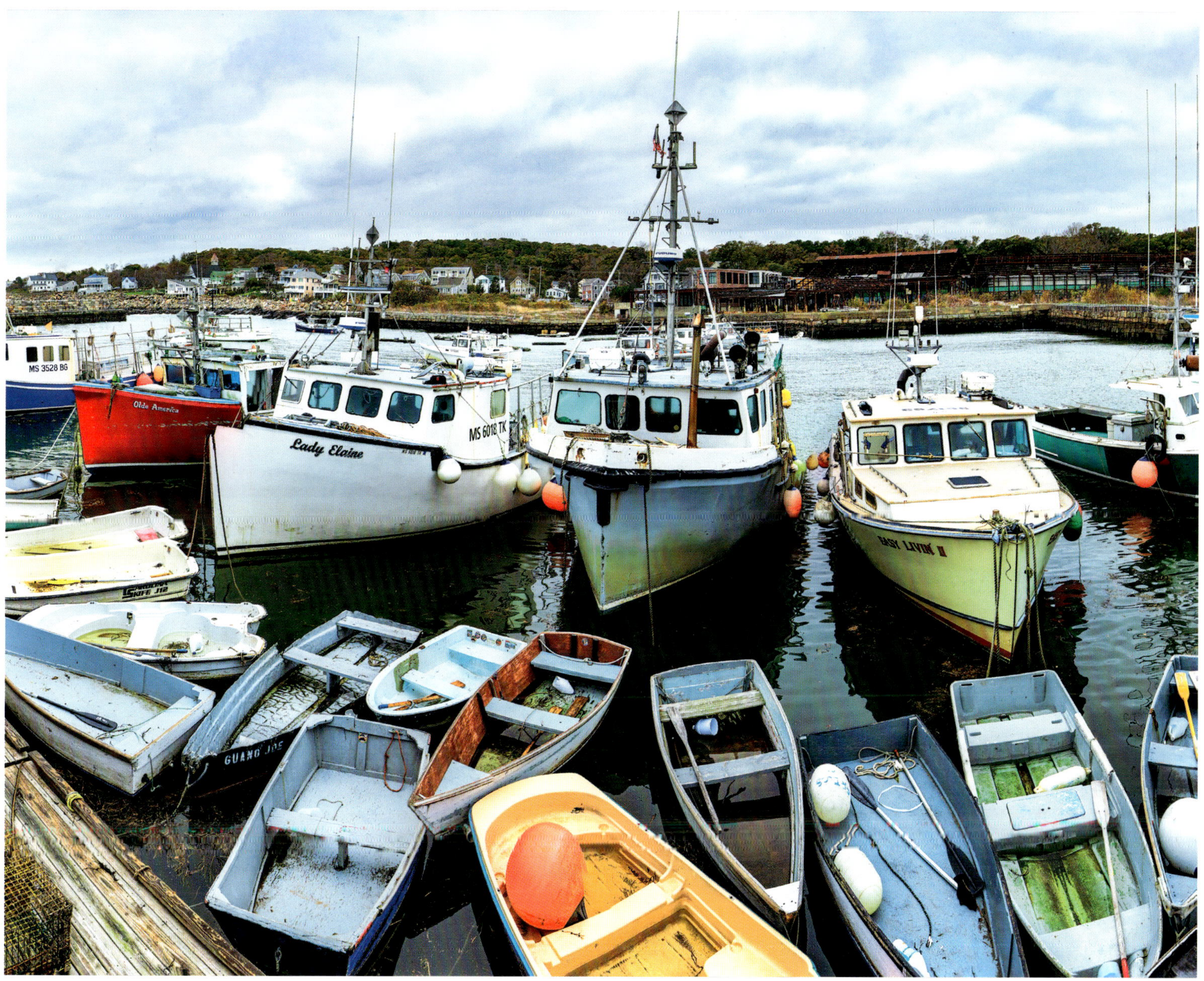

Rockport, Massachusetts

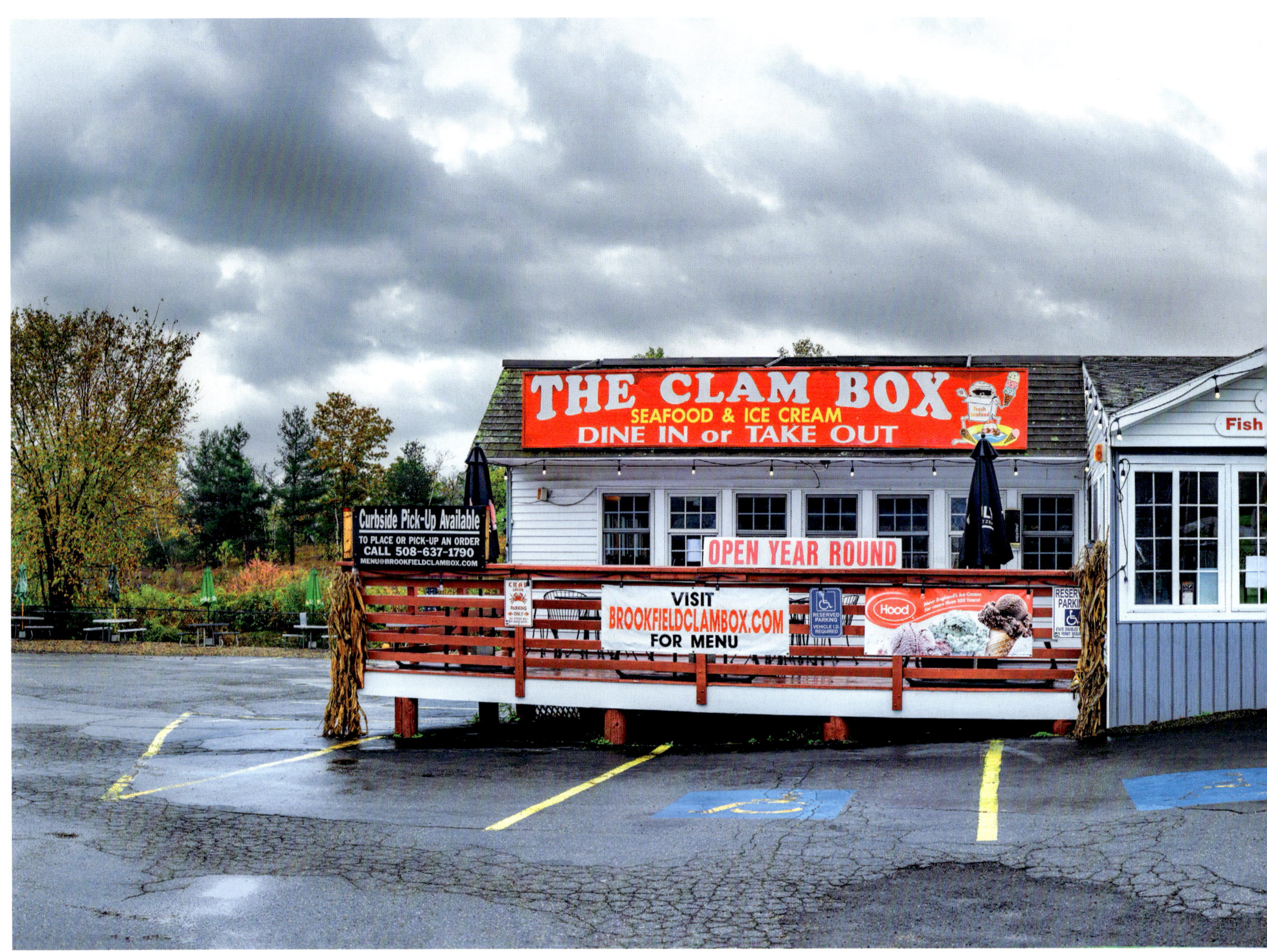

The Clam Box, Brookfield, Massachusetts

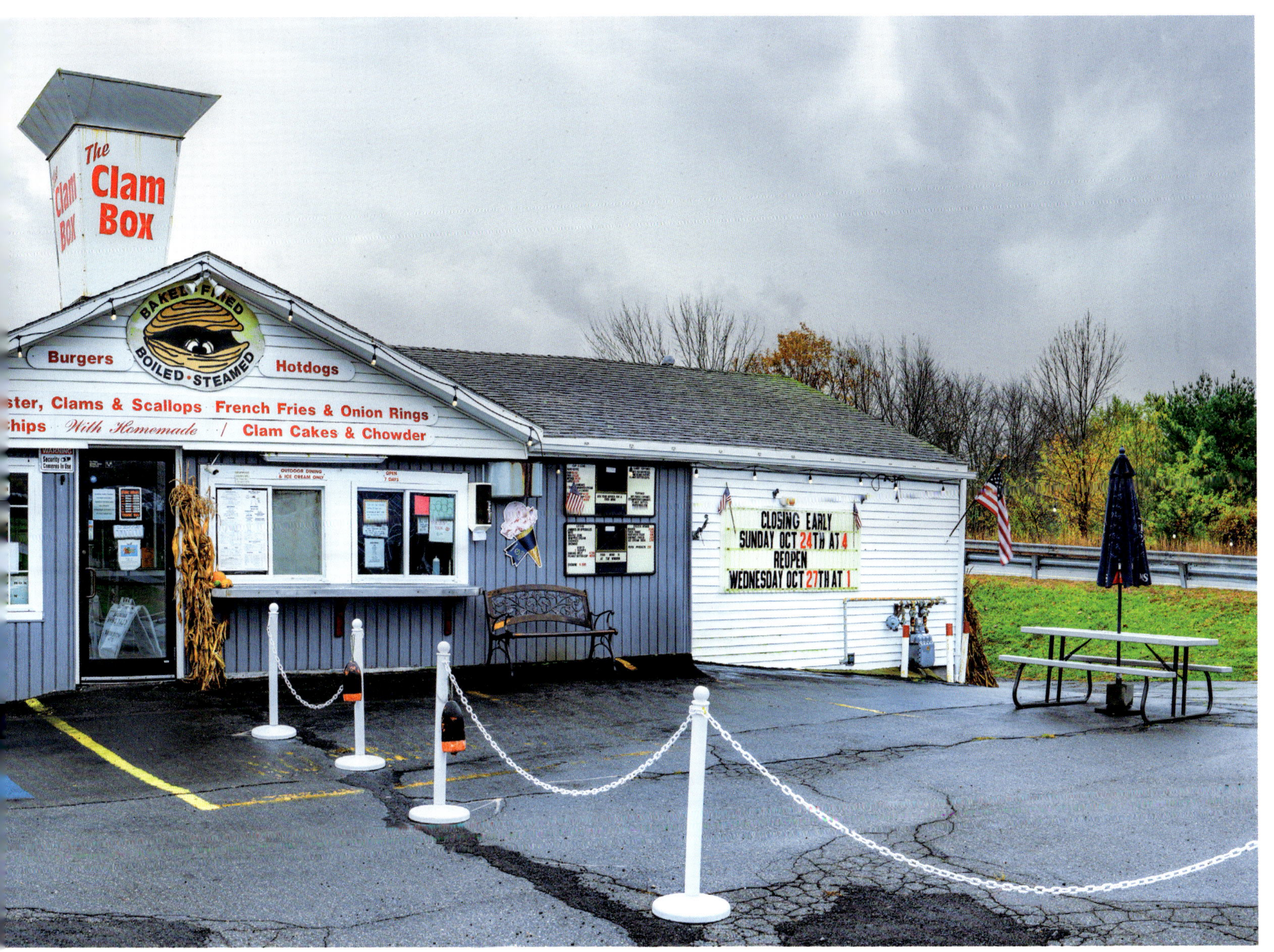

I came back later to have my first-ever clam cake. It is the one by which every other clam cake will be measured. Yup, I'm hooked.

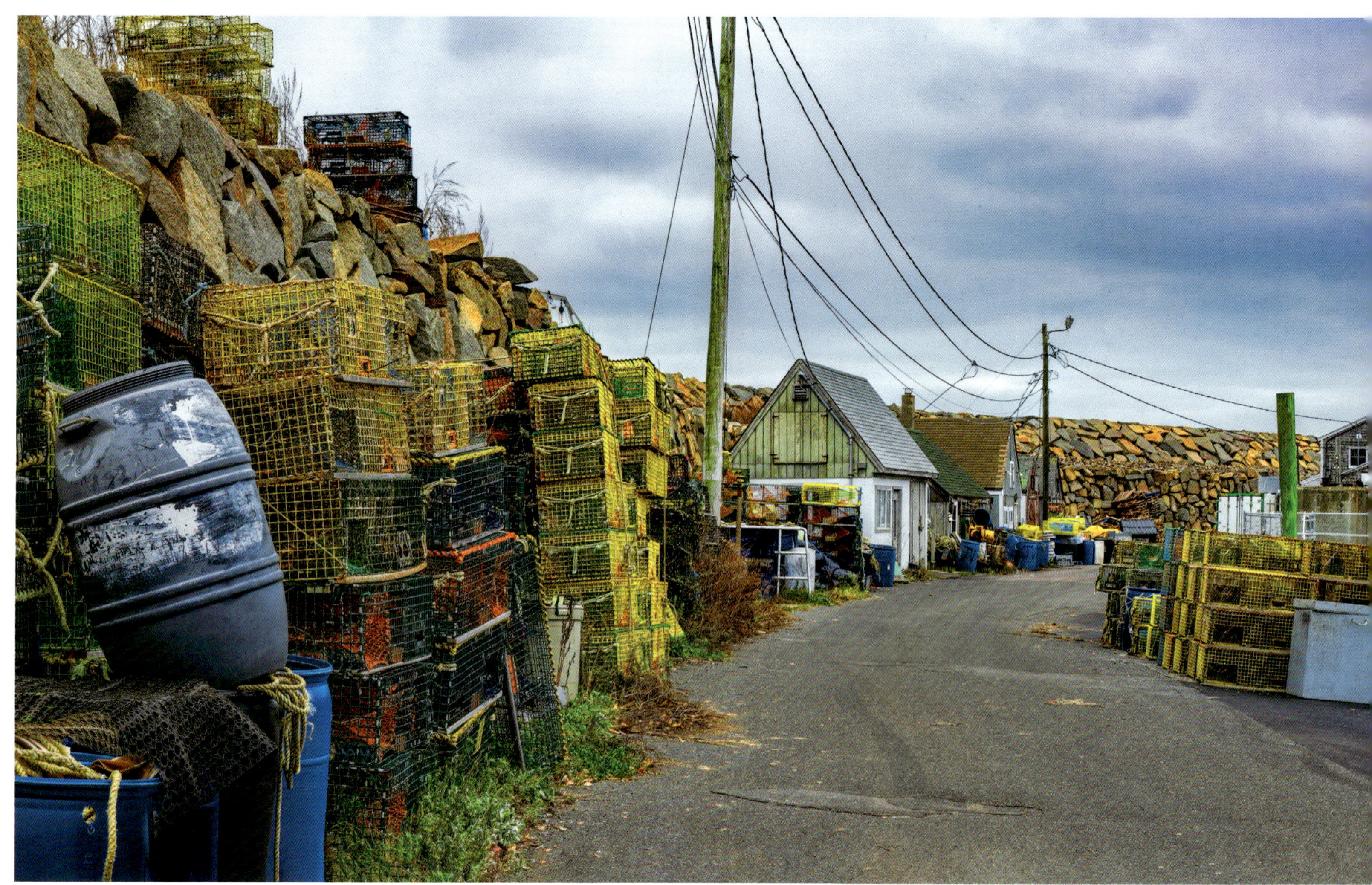

Pigeon Cove, Rockport, Massachusetts

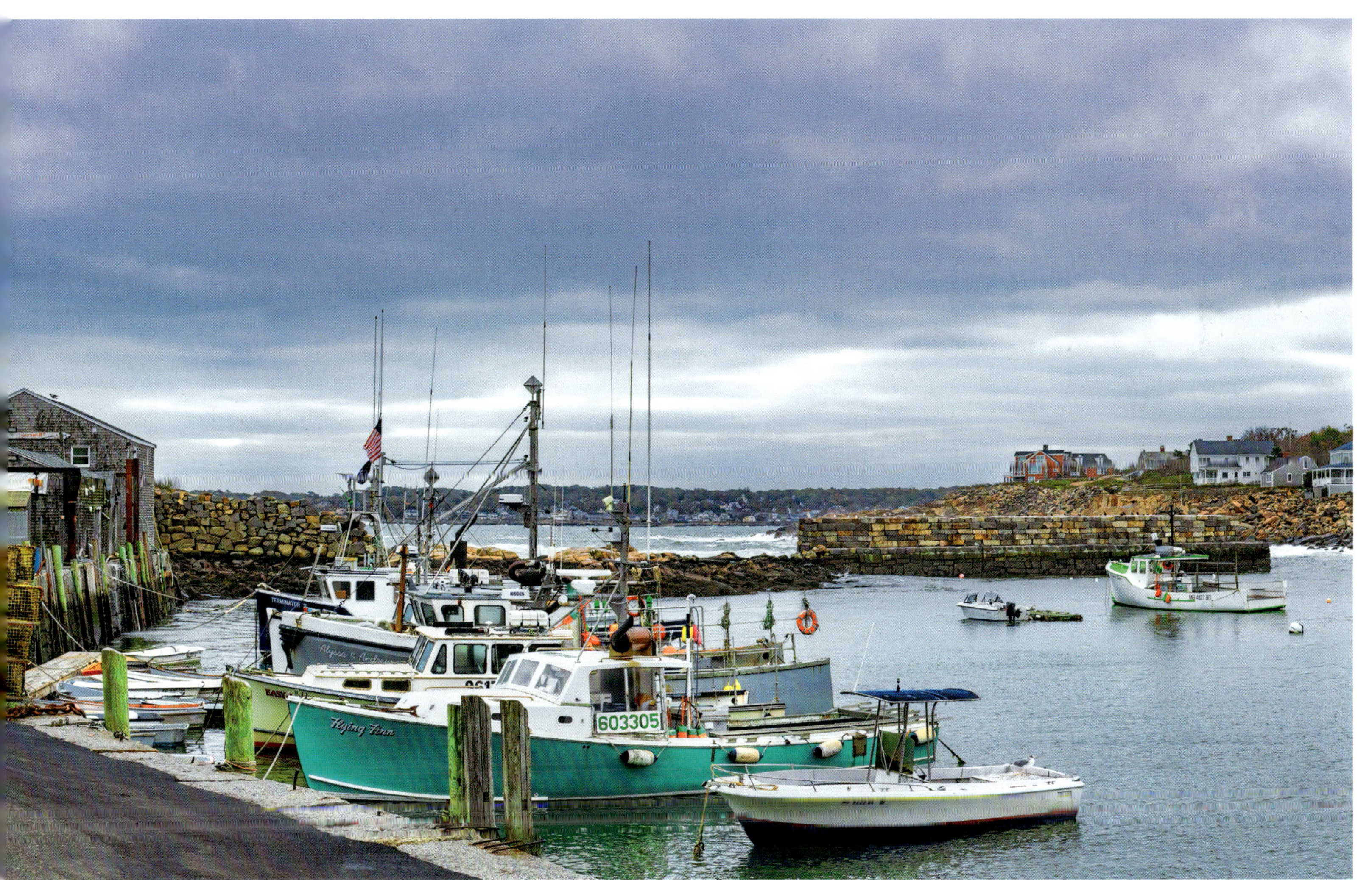

Yes, this is where I shot Bob the Truck for this book, but I like this composition from farther back too.

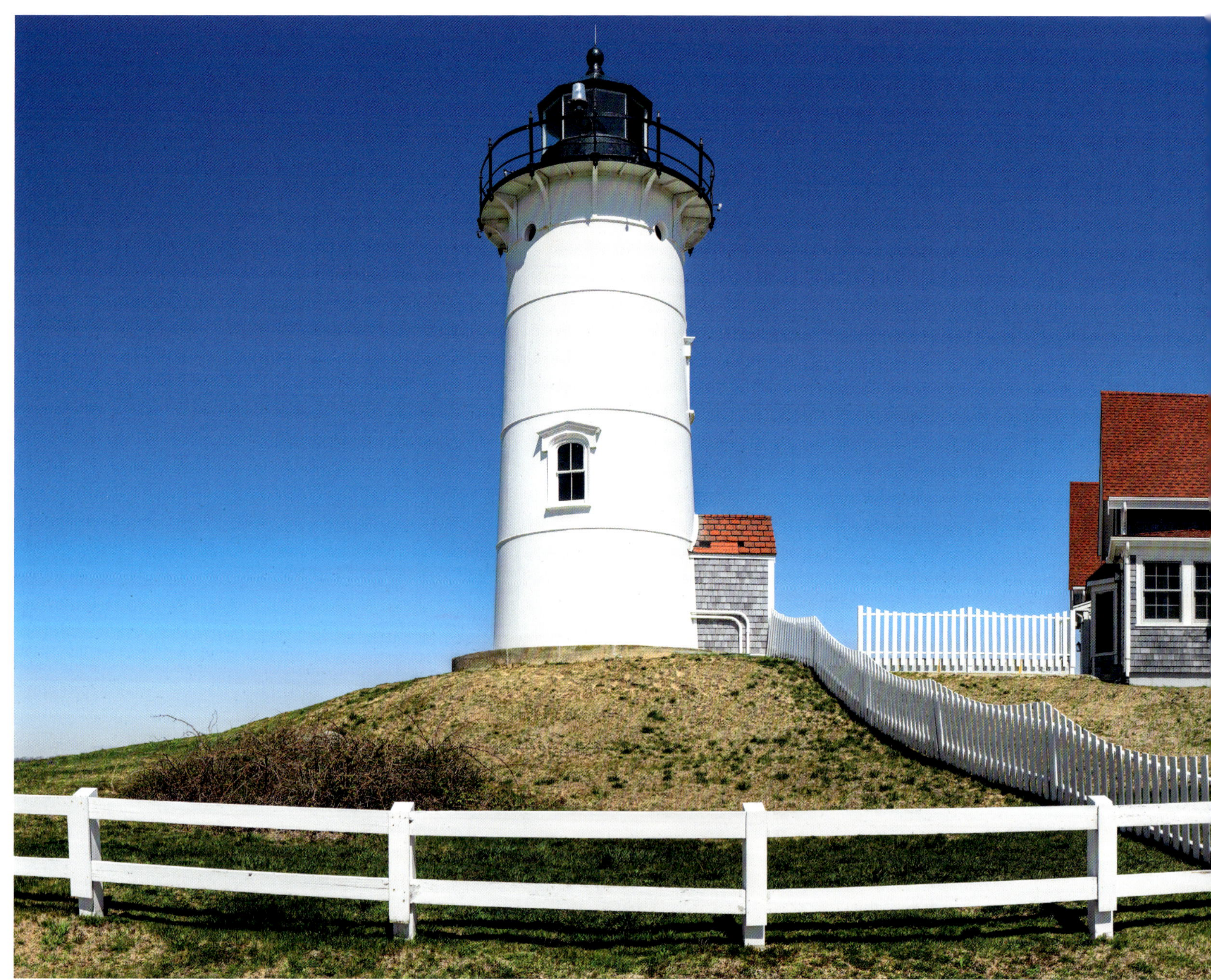

Nobska Lighthouse, Woods Hole, Cape Cod, Massachusetts

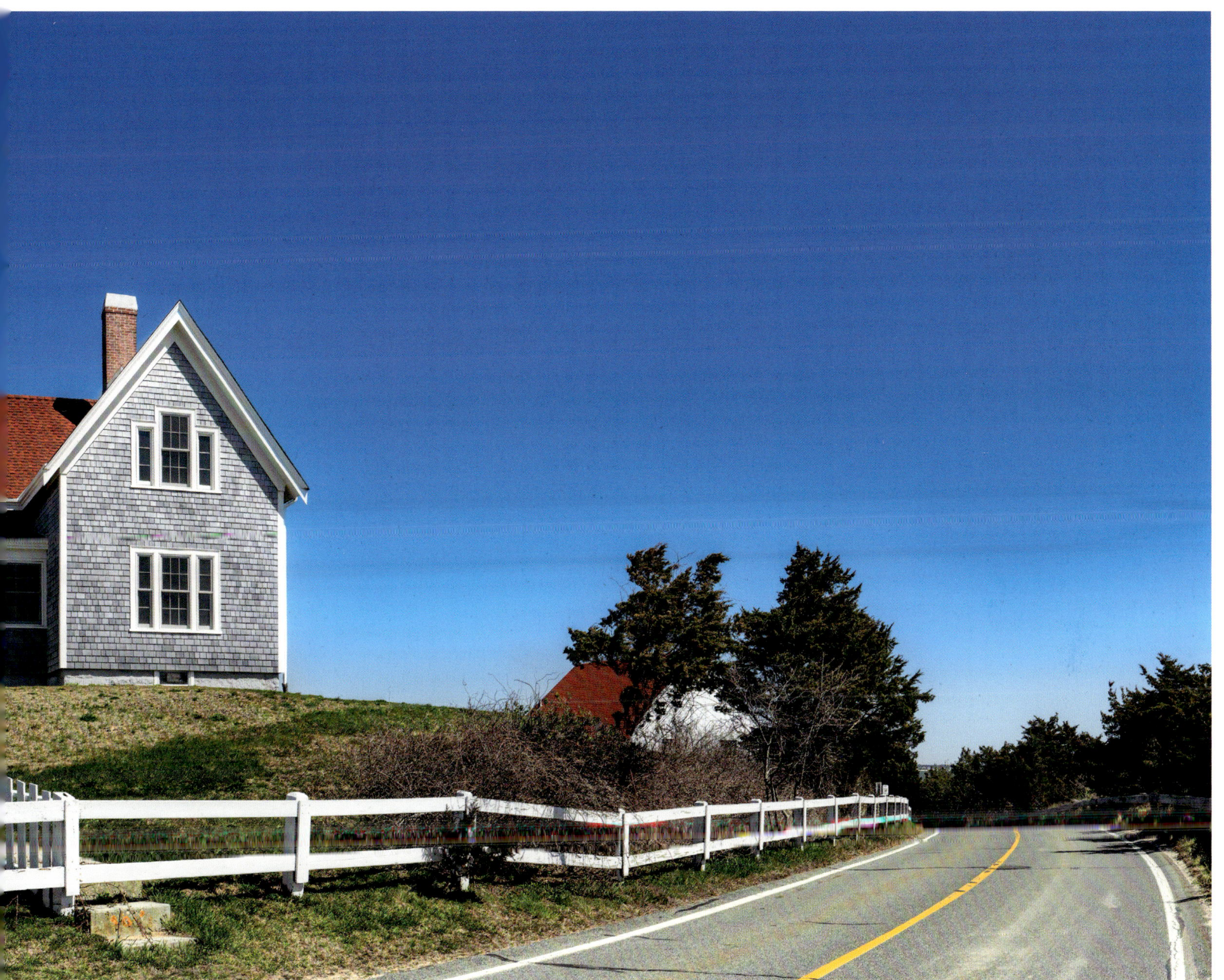

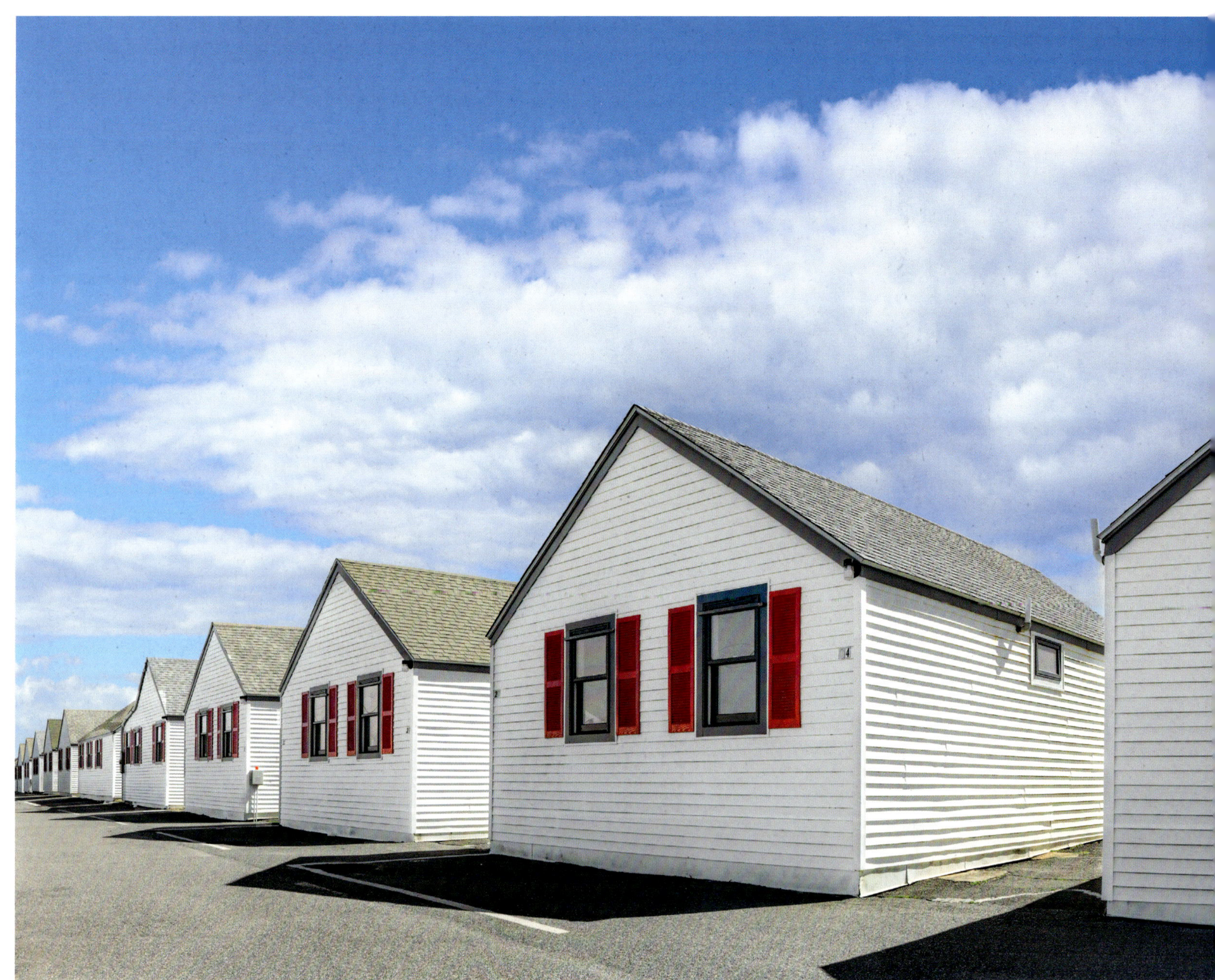

Summer cabins, North Truro, Cape Cod, Massachusetts

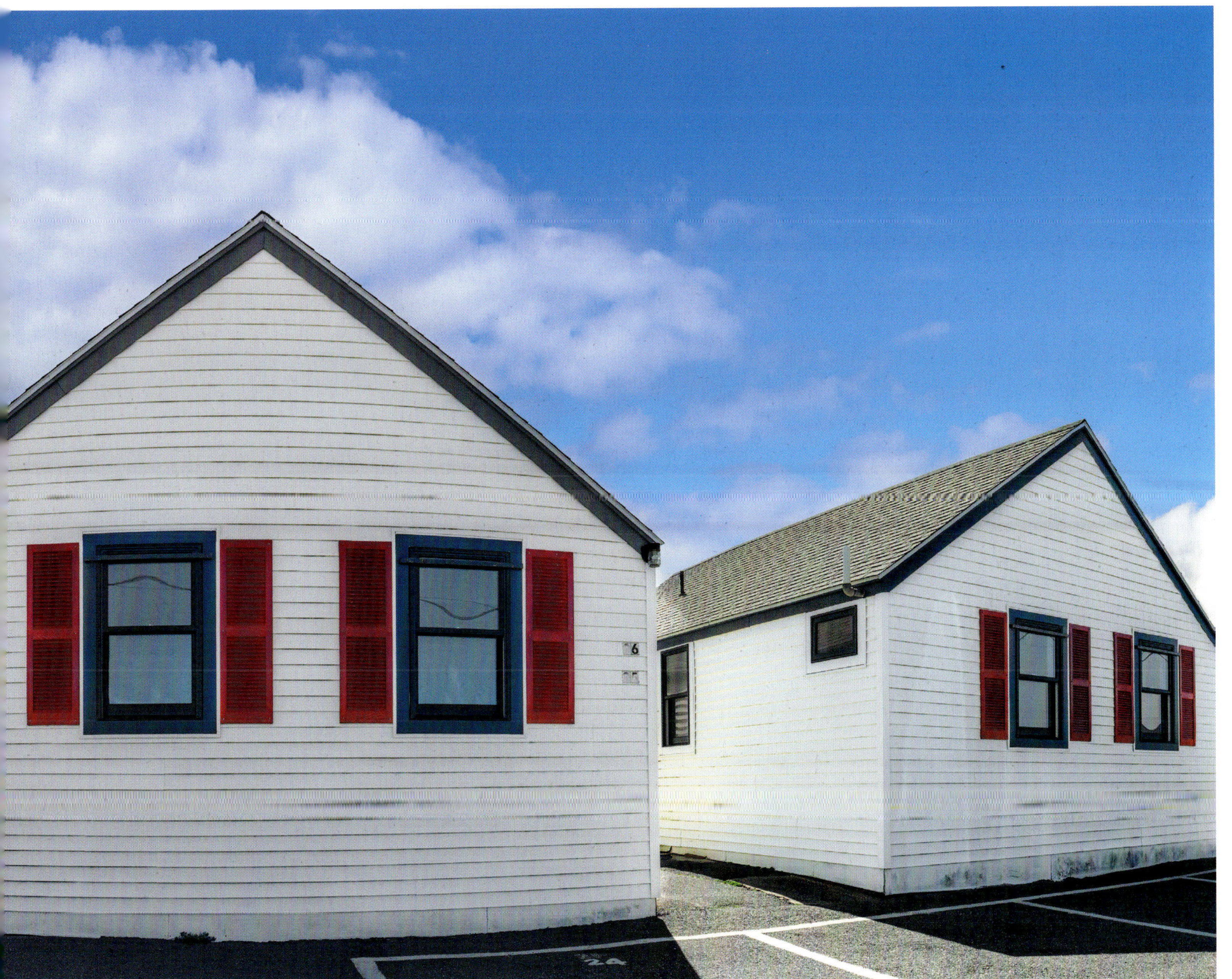
6

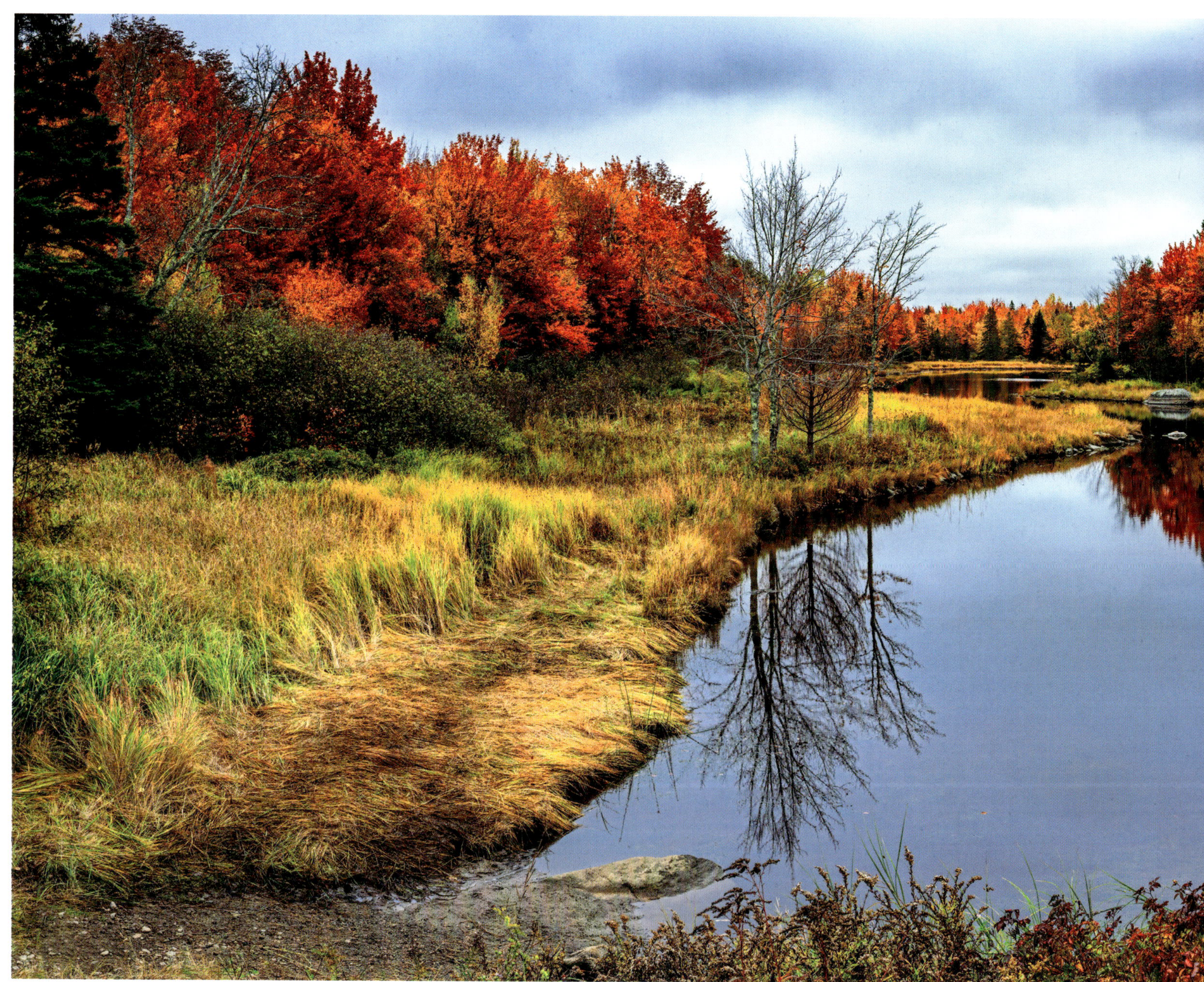

Bracy Cove, Maine

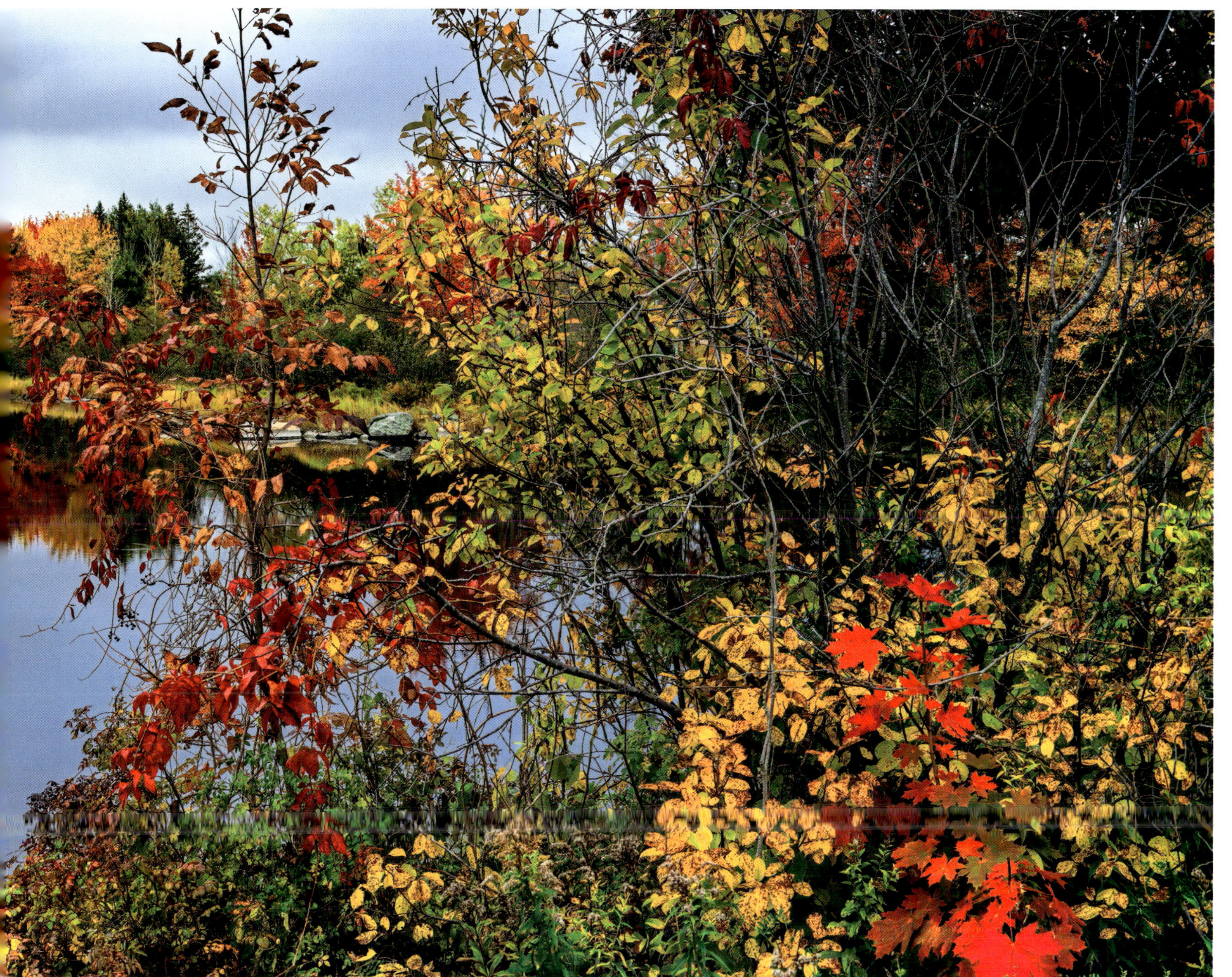

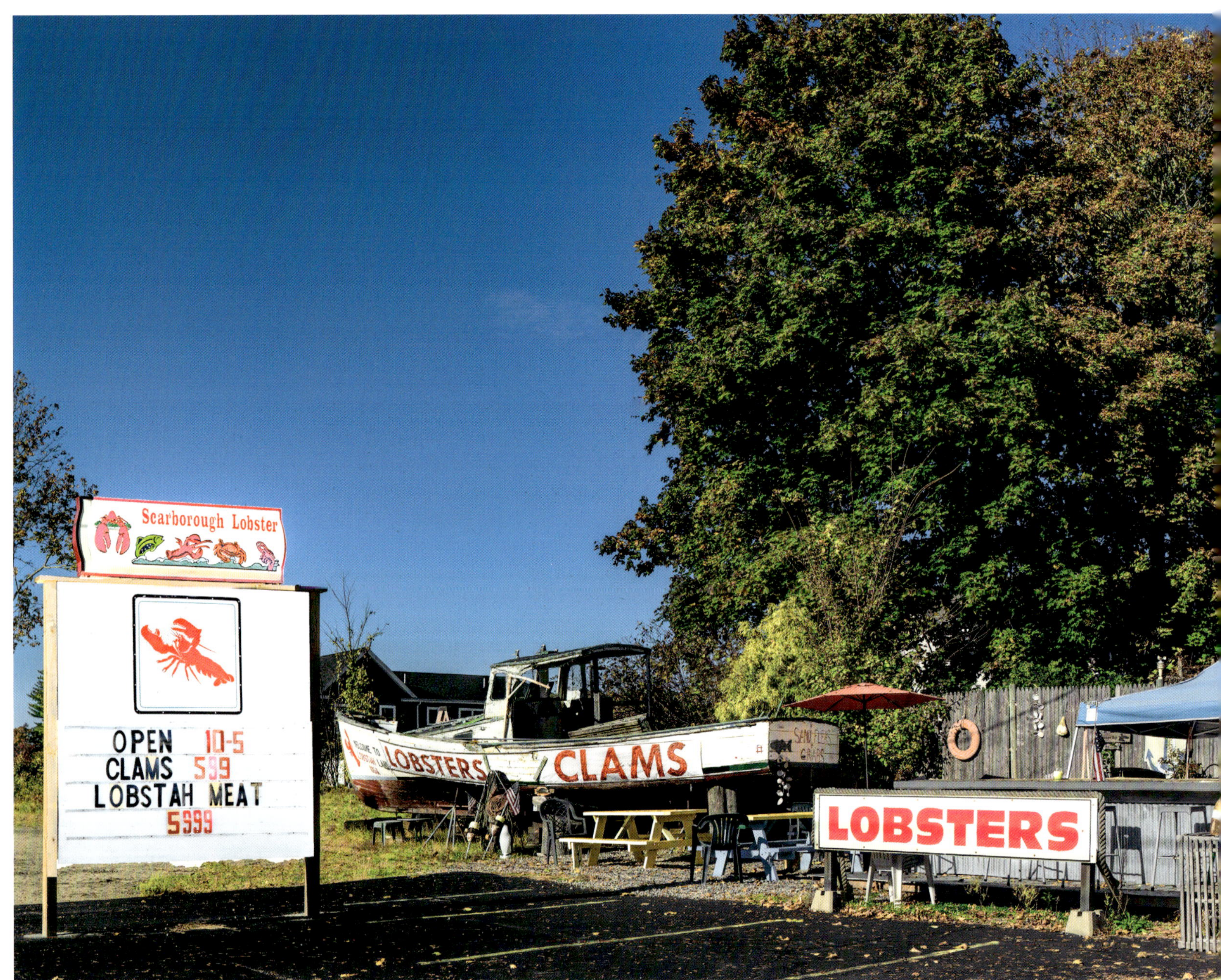

Scarborough Lobster, Maine

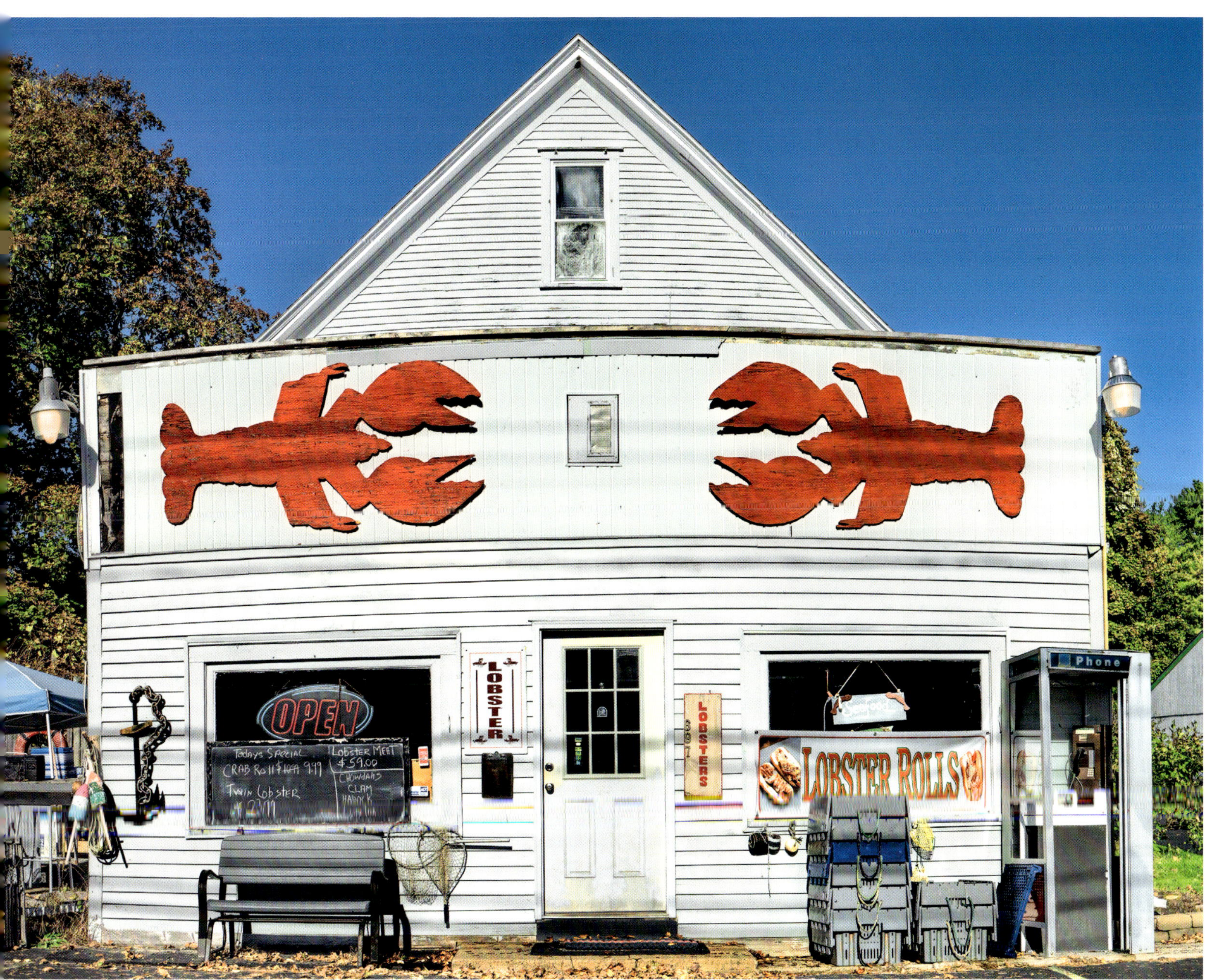

Amazing lobster rolls!

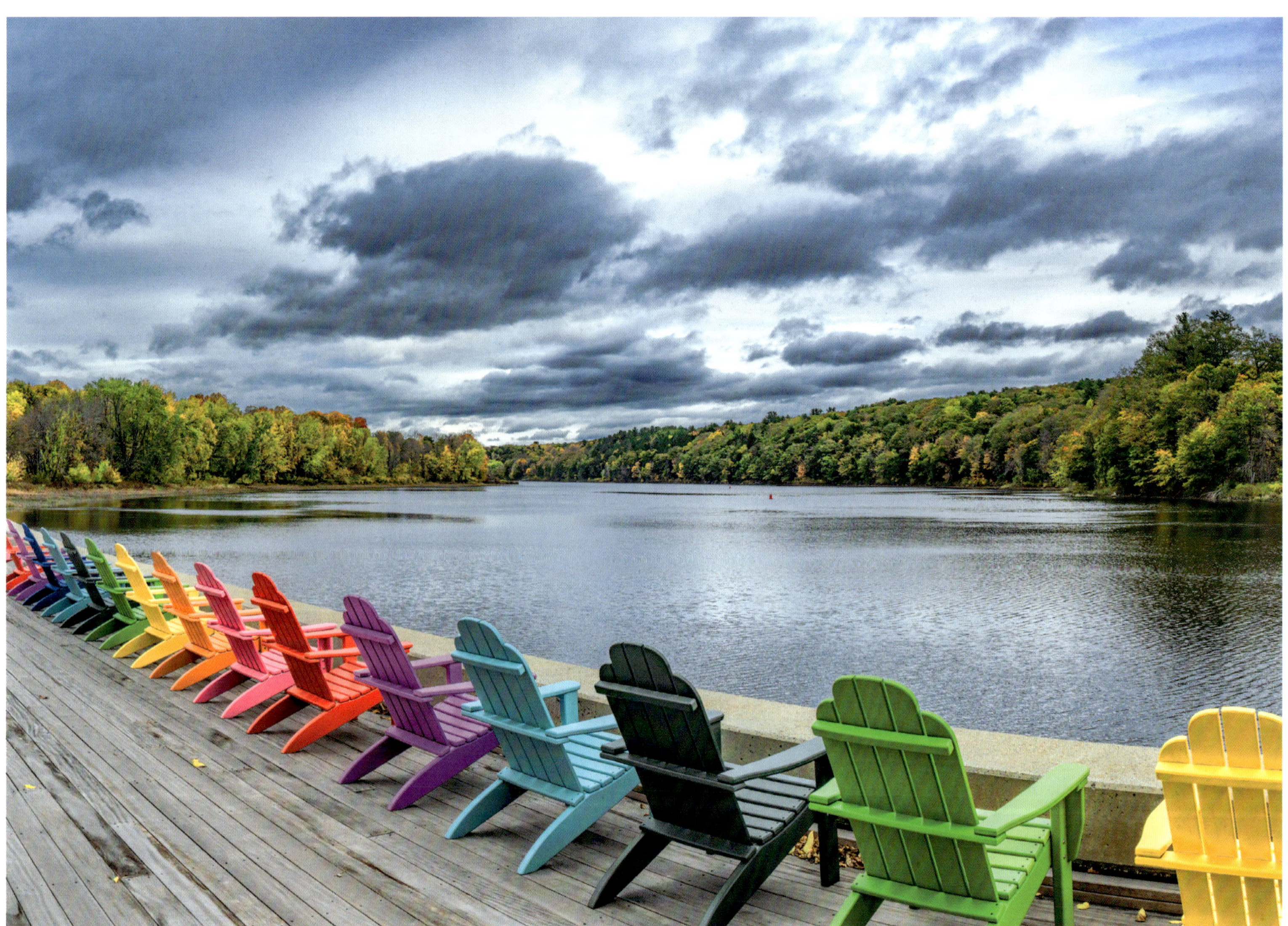

Kennebec River from Granite City Park, Maine

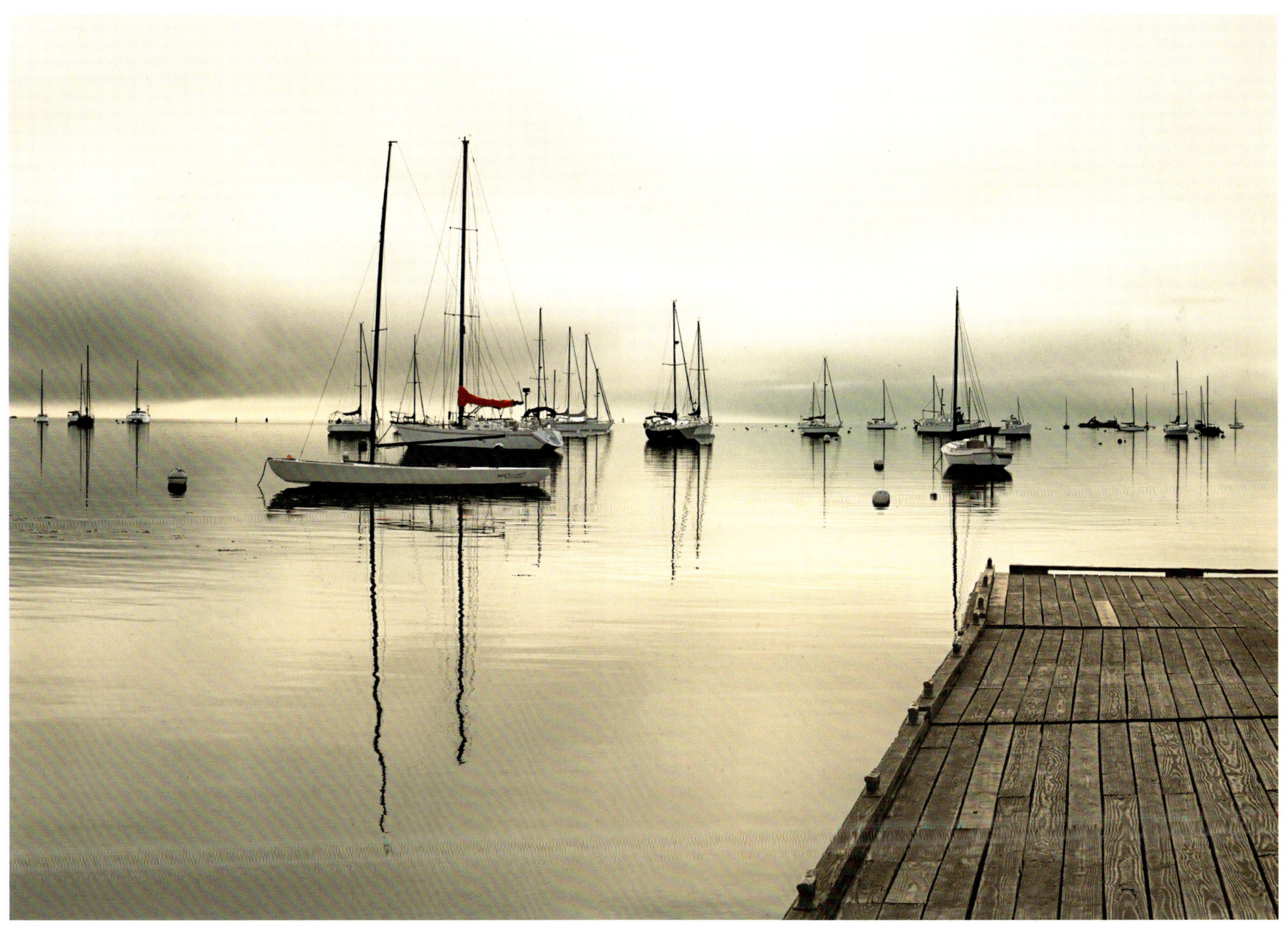

Belfast Harbor, Maine

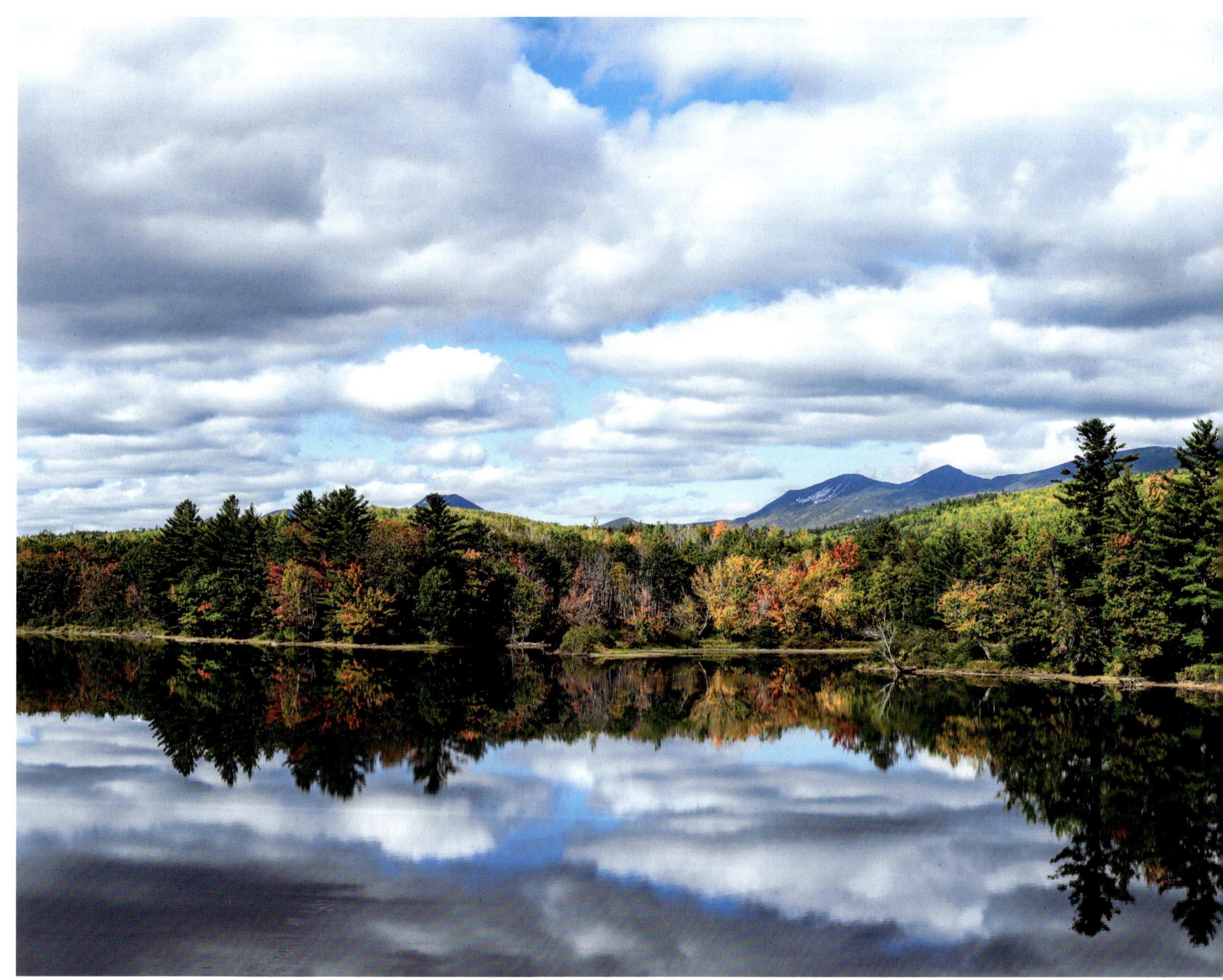

Mount Katahdin and Abol Stream, Maine

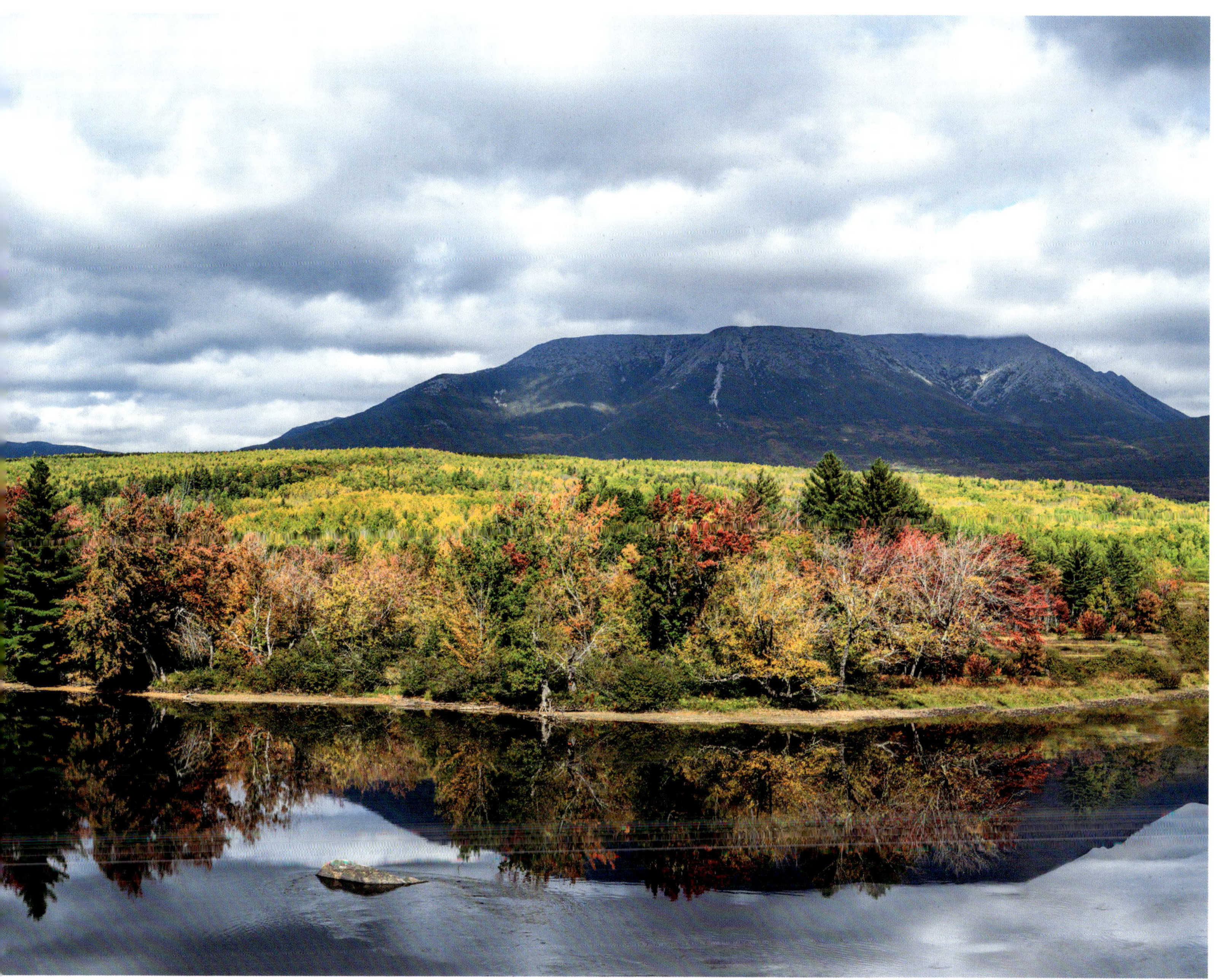

The Penobscot people named this mountain Katahdin, “the Greatest Mountain.” It is the highest mountain in Maine, at 5,269 feet.

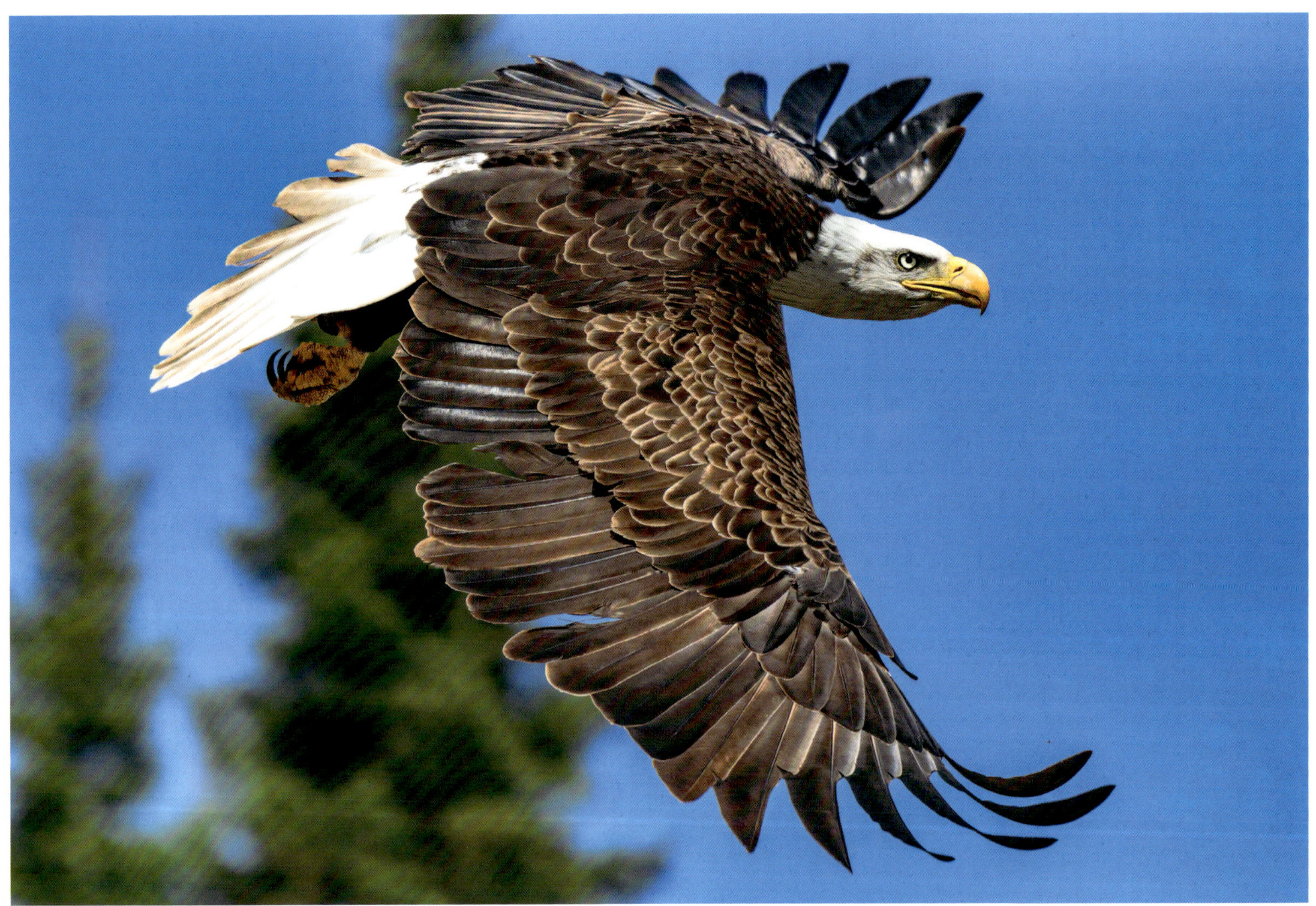

Bald eagle, Deer Isle, Maine

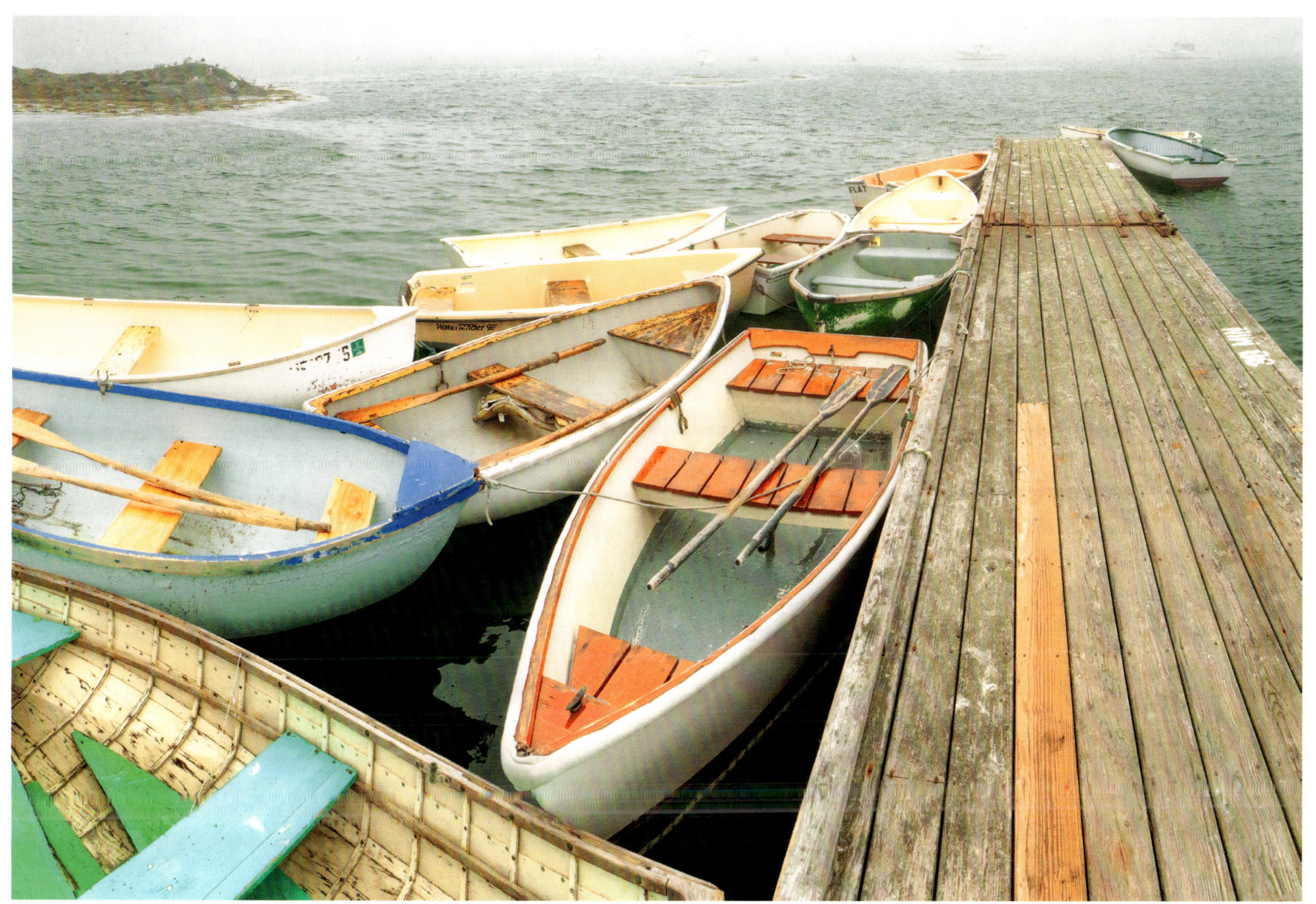

Rowboats, Sorento, Maine

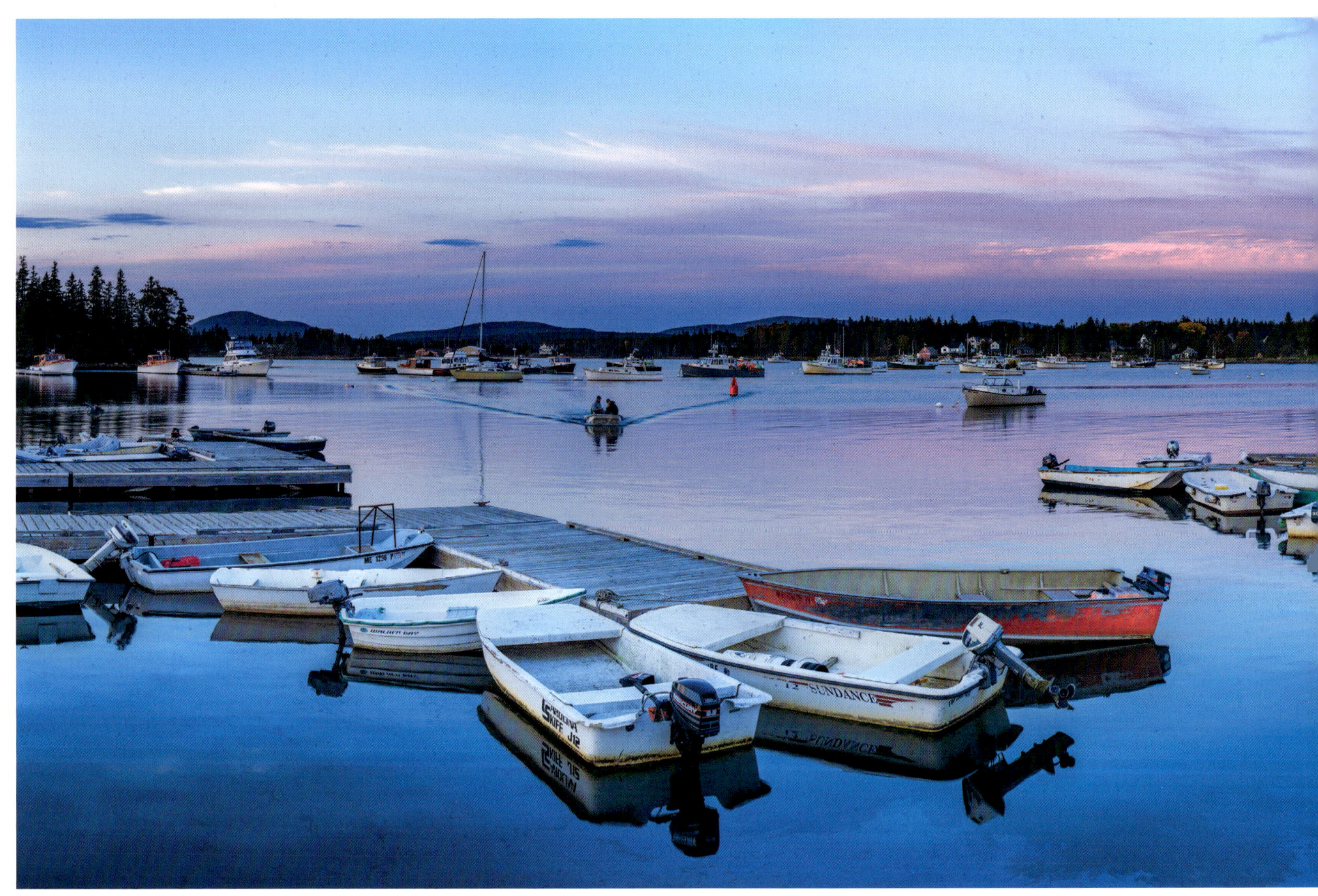

Sunset, Tremont Wharf, Bernard, Maine

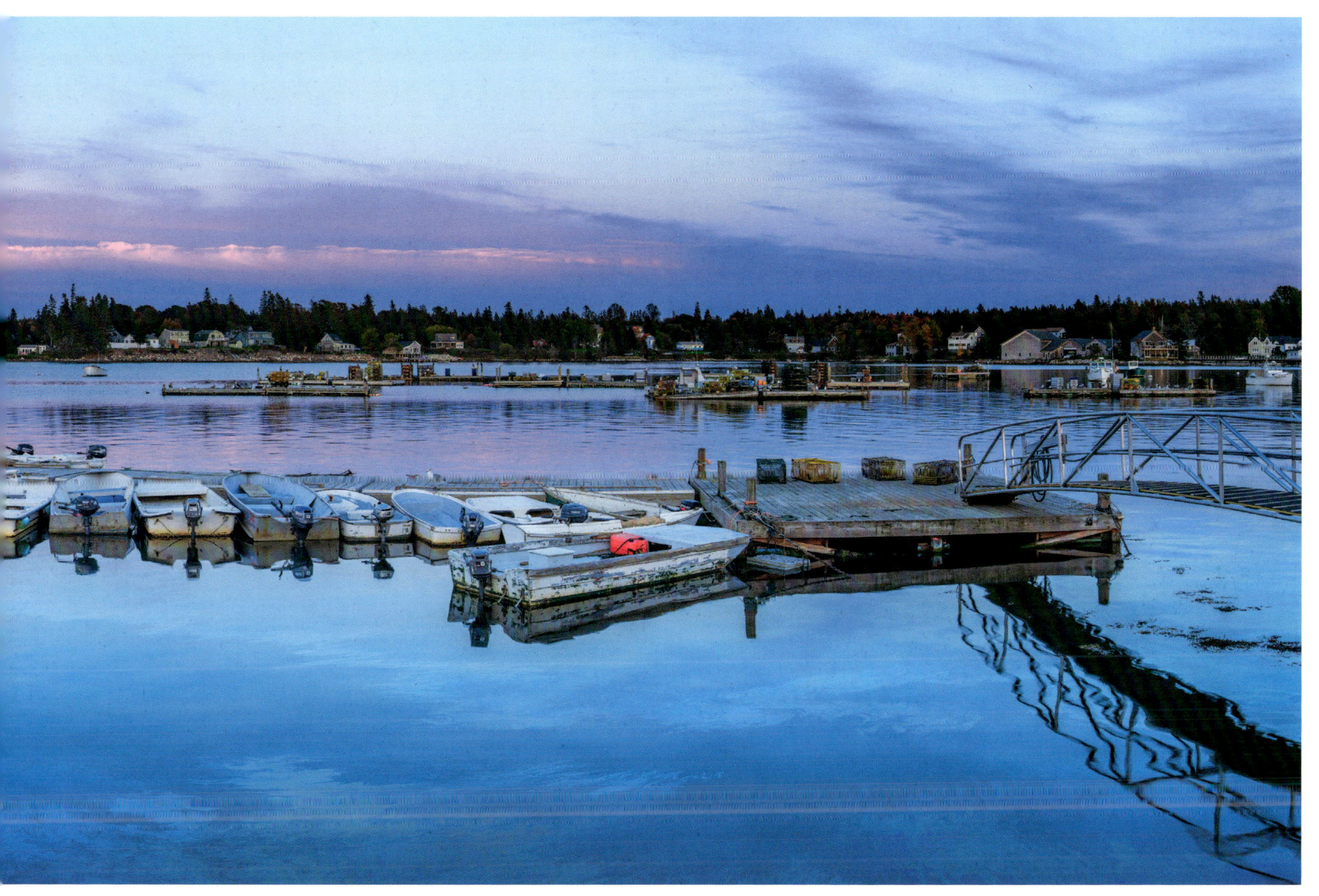

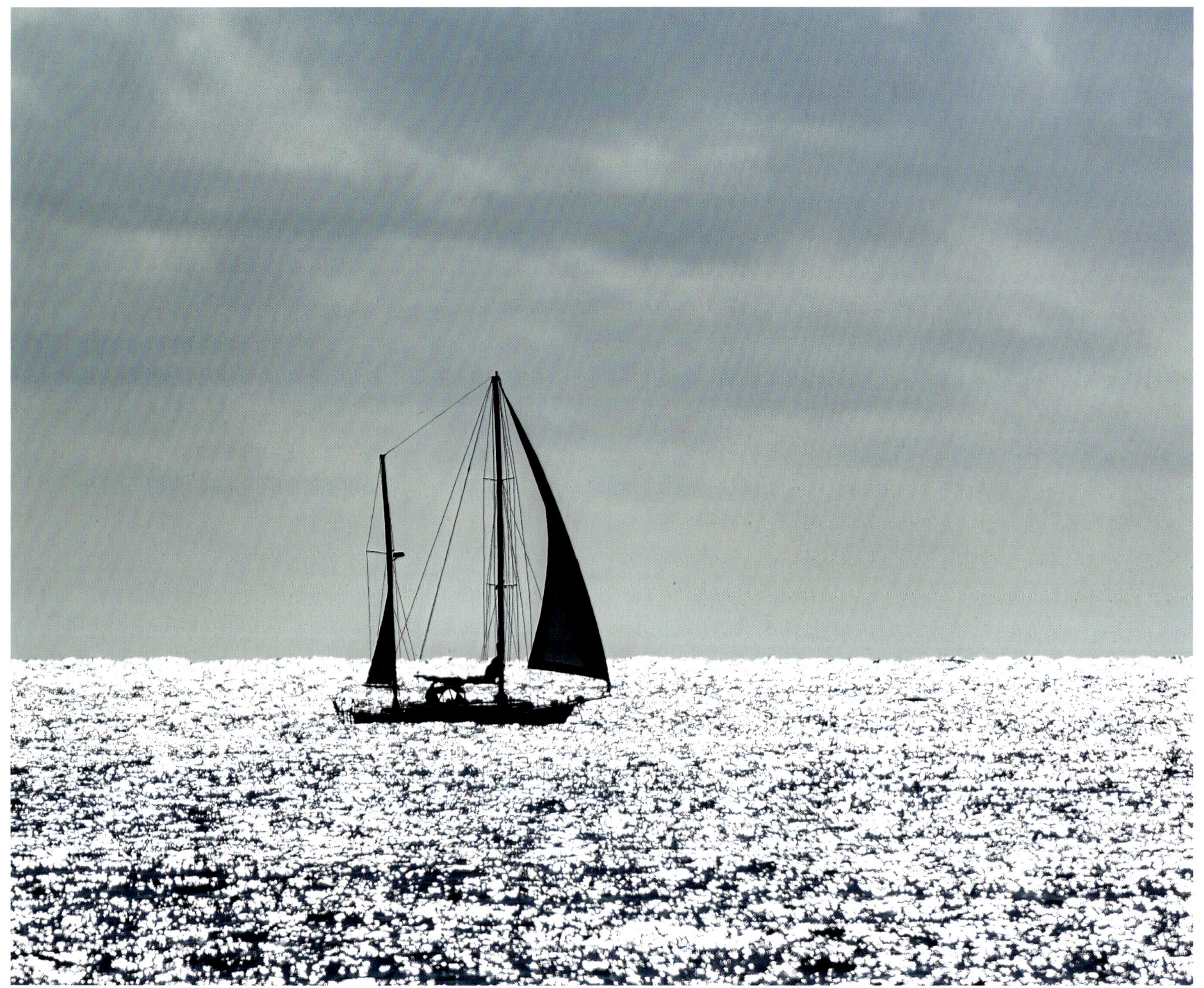

Gulf of Maine

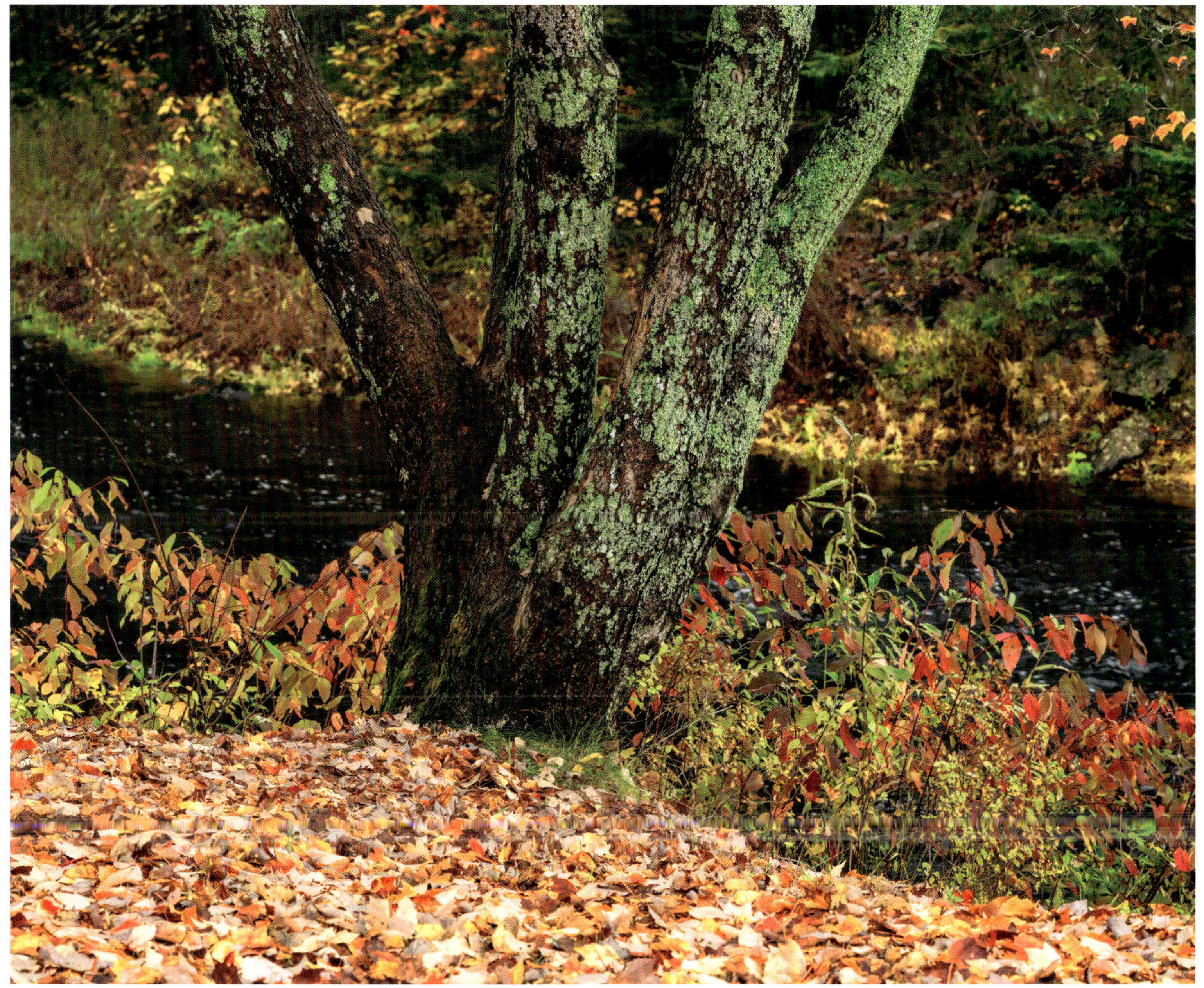

Red maple tree alongside Crawford Stream, Maine

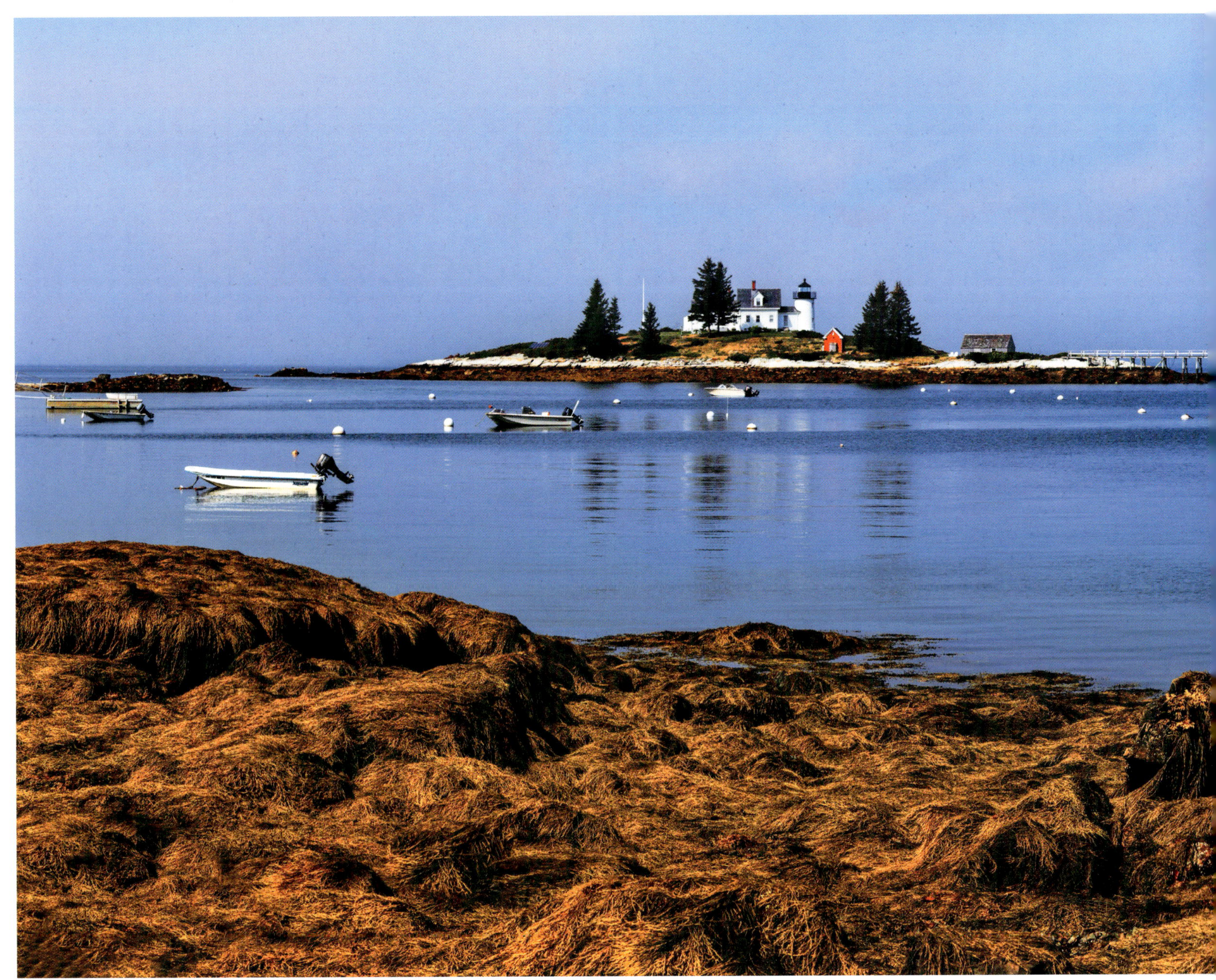

Pumpkin Island Light, Eggamoggin Reach, Maine

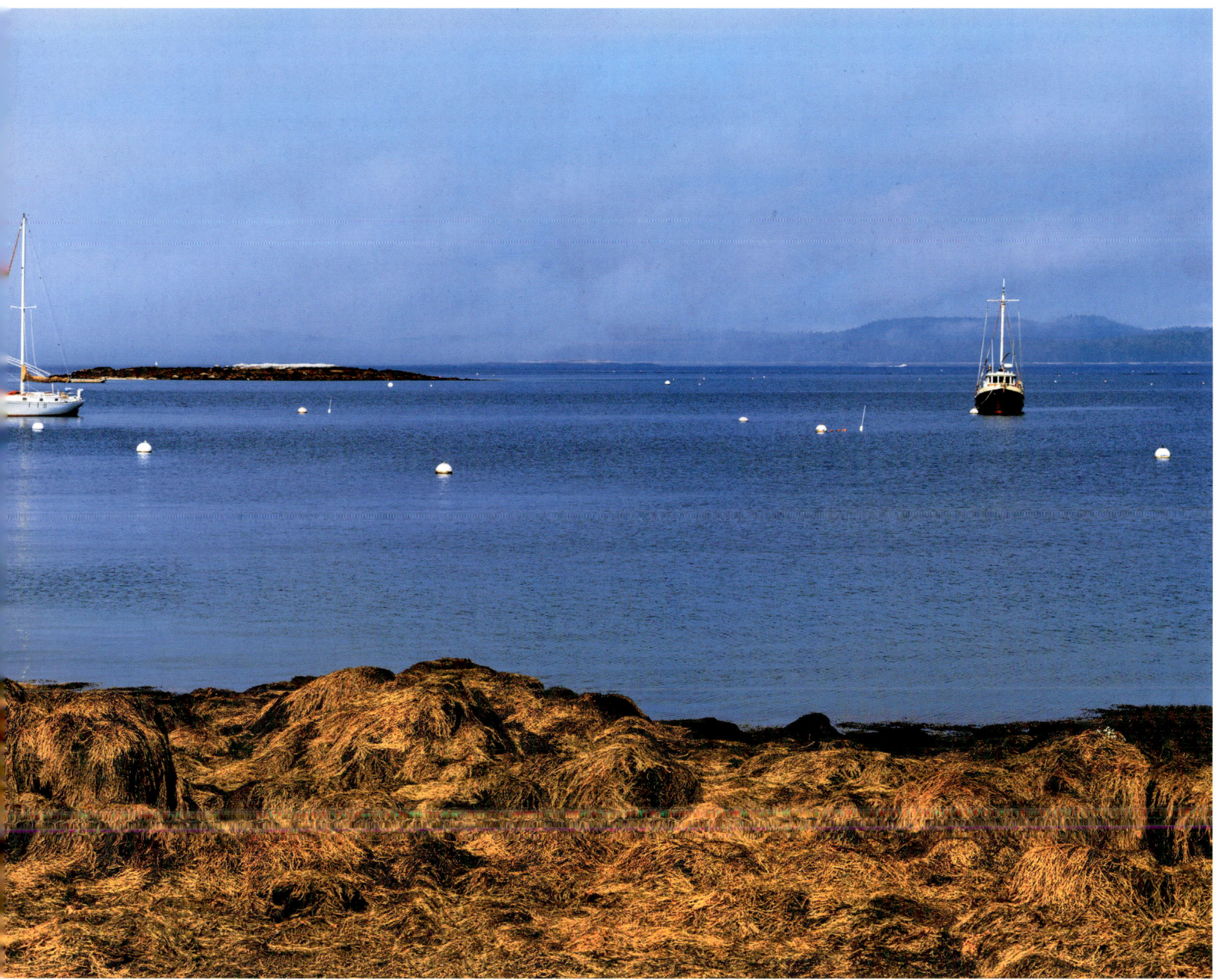

The stuff in the foreground is rock weed. It grows underwater and is visible only when the tide is out.

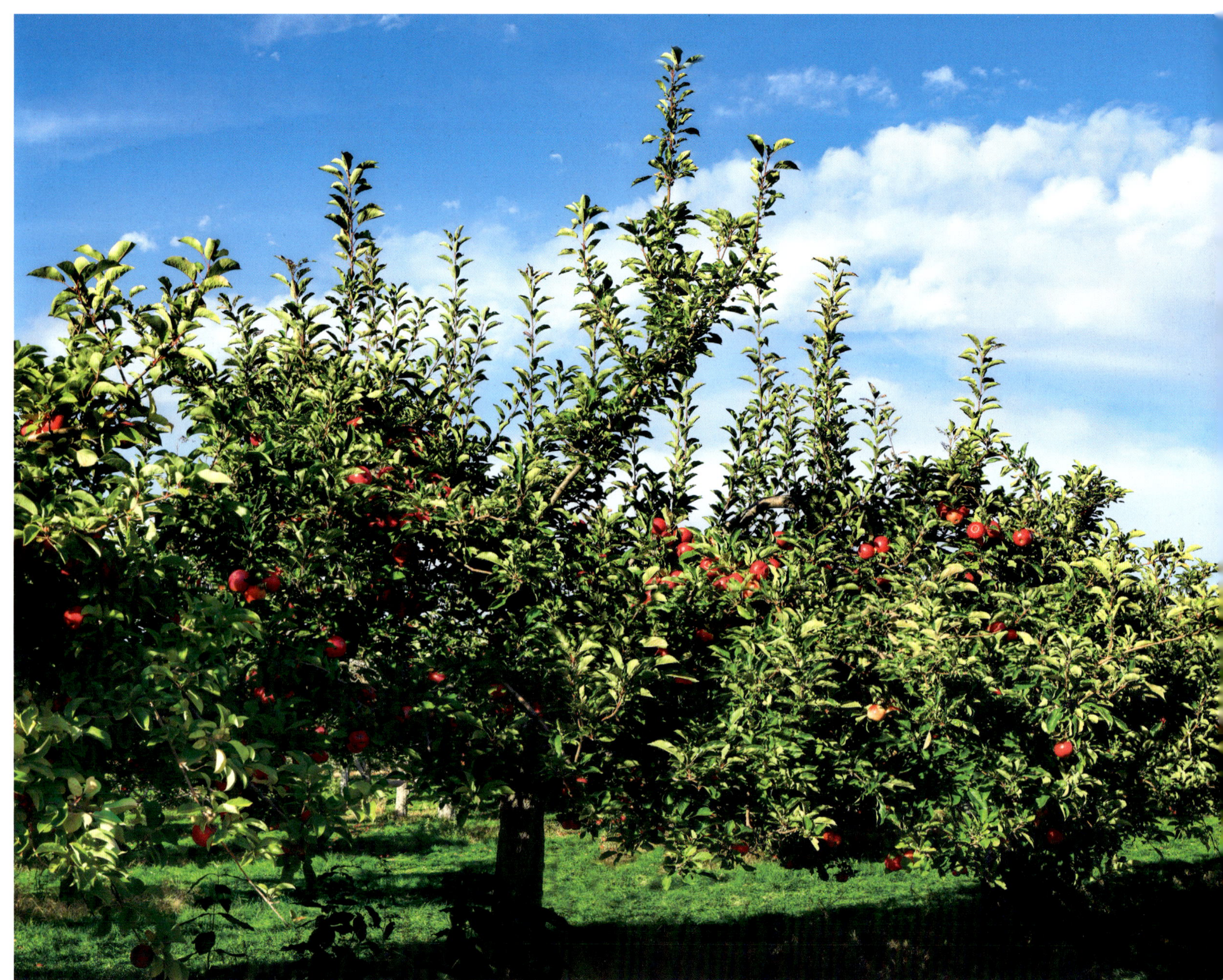

Johnston's Orchard, Ellsworth, Maine

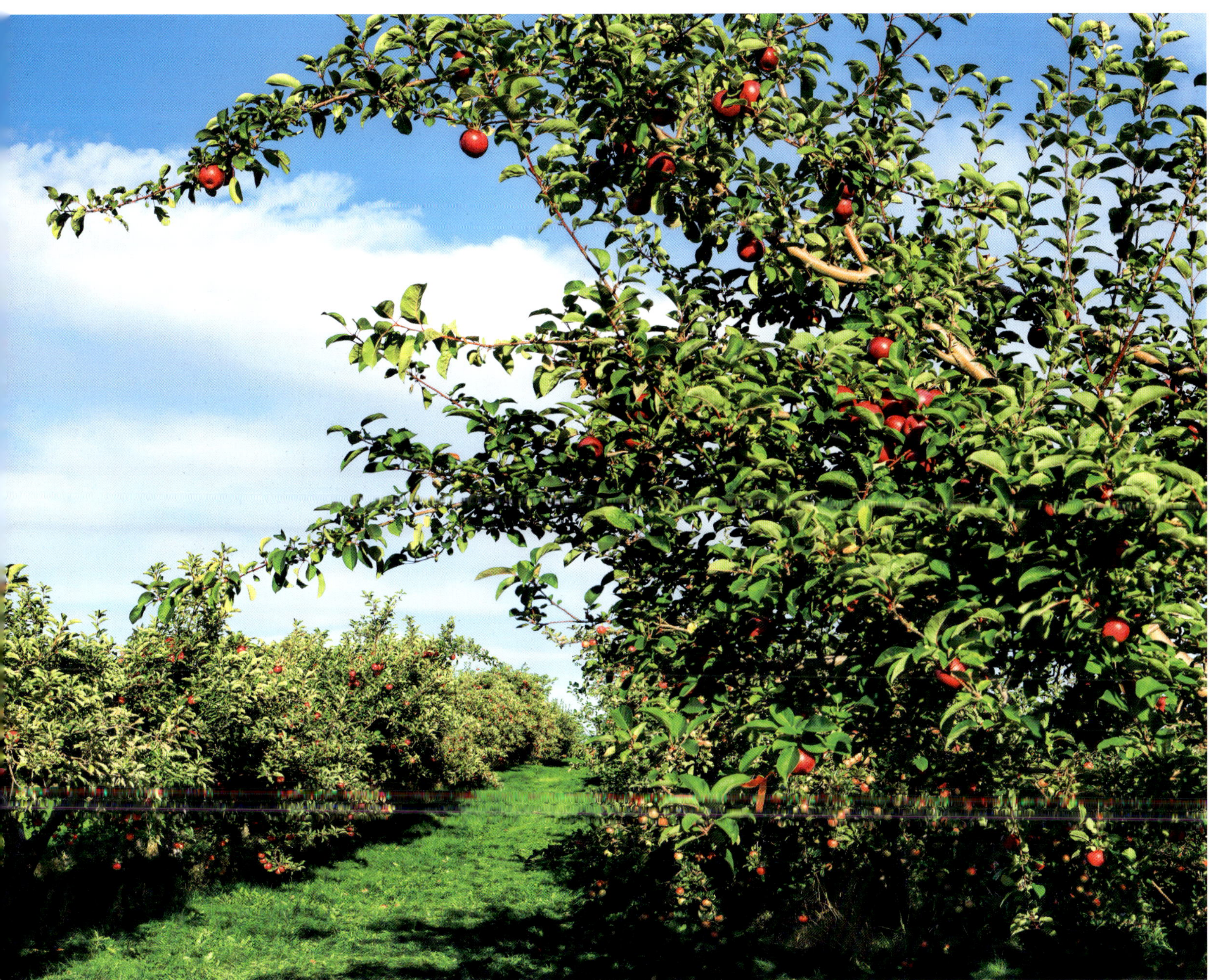

Yup, they were fantastic!

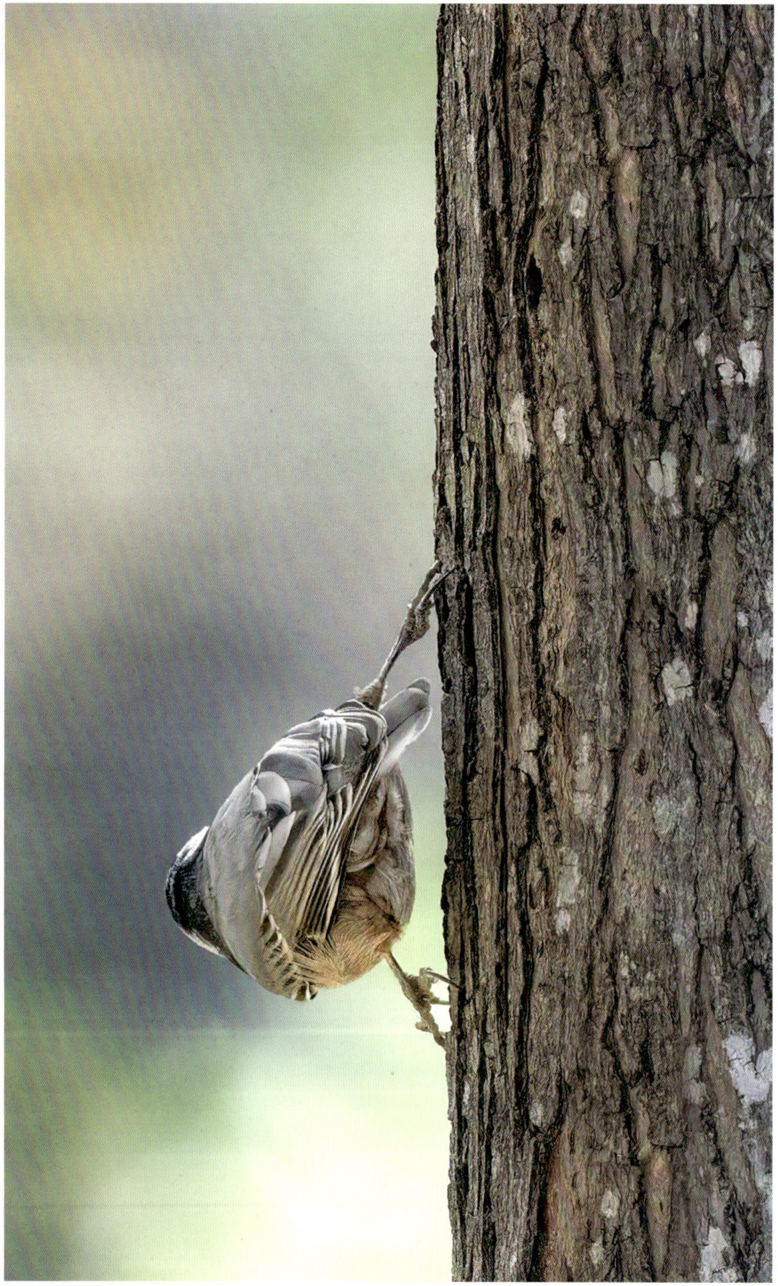

White-breasted nuthatch

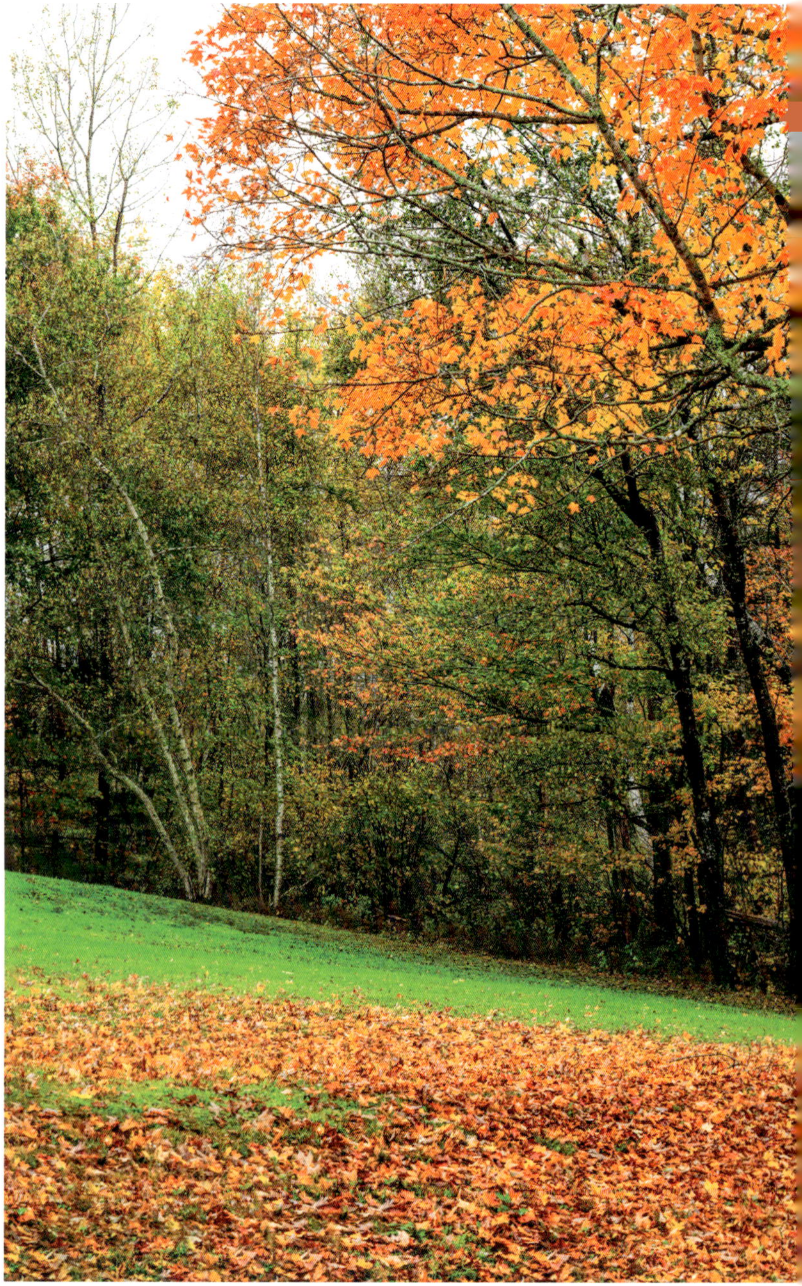

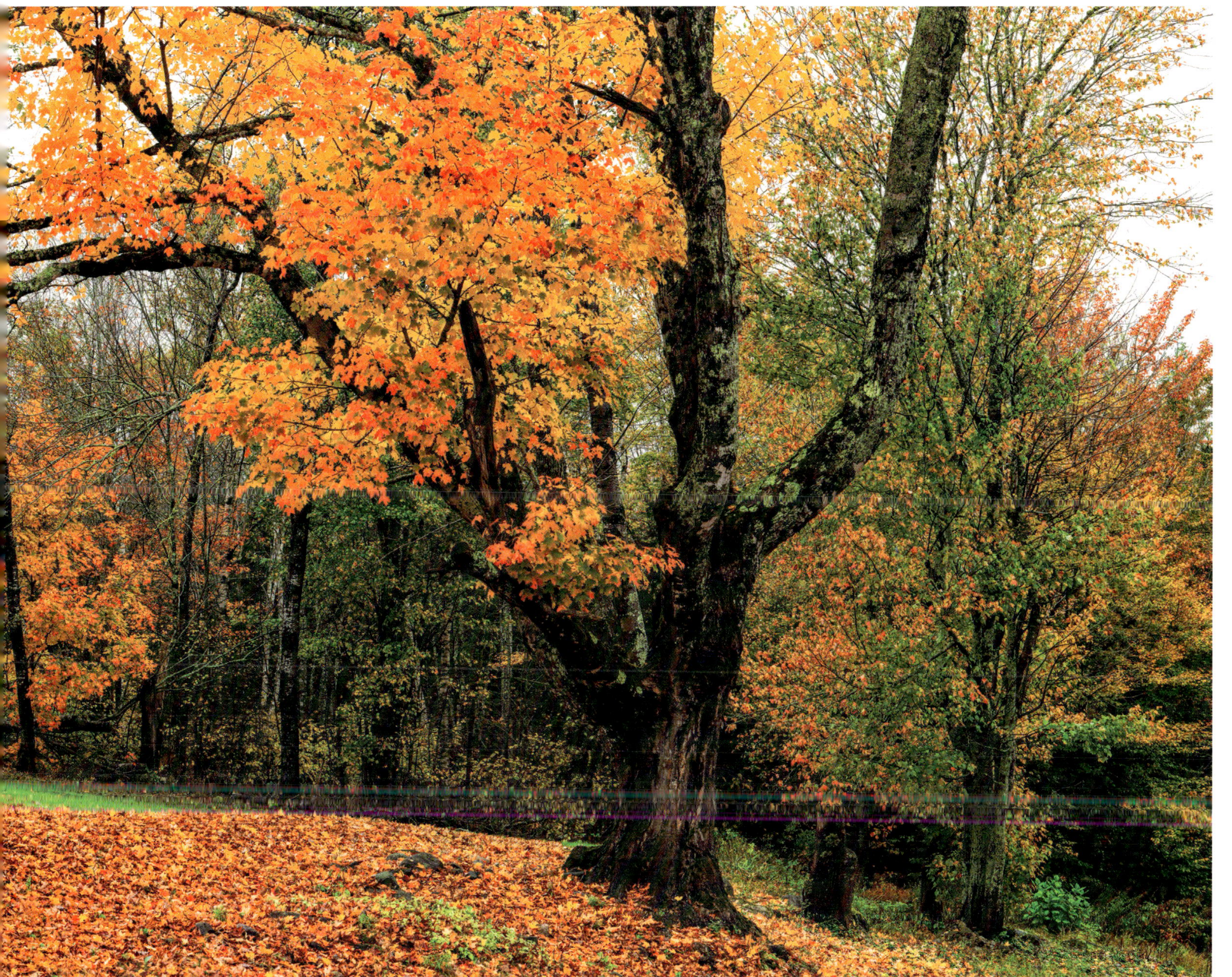

Trees on Maine State Highway 191

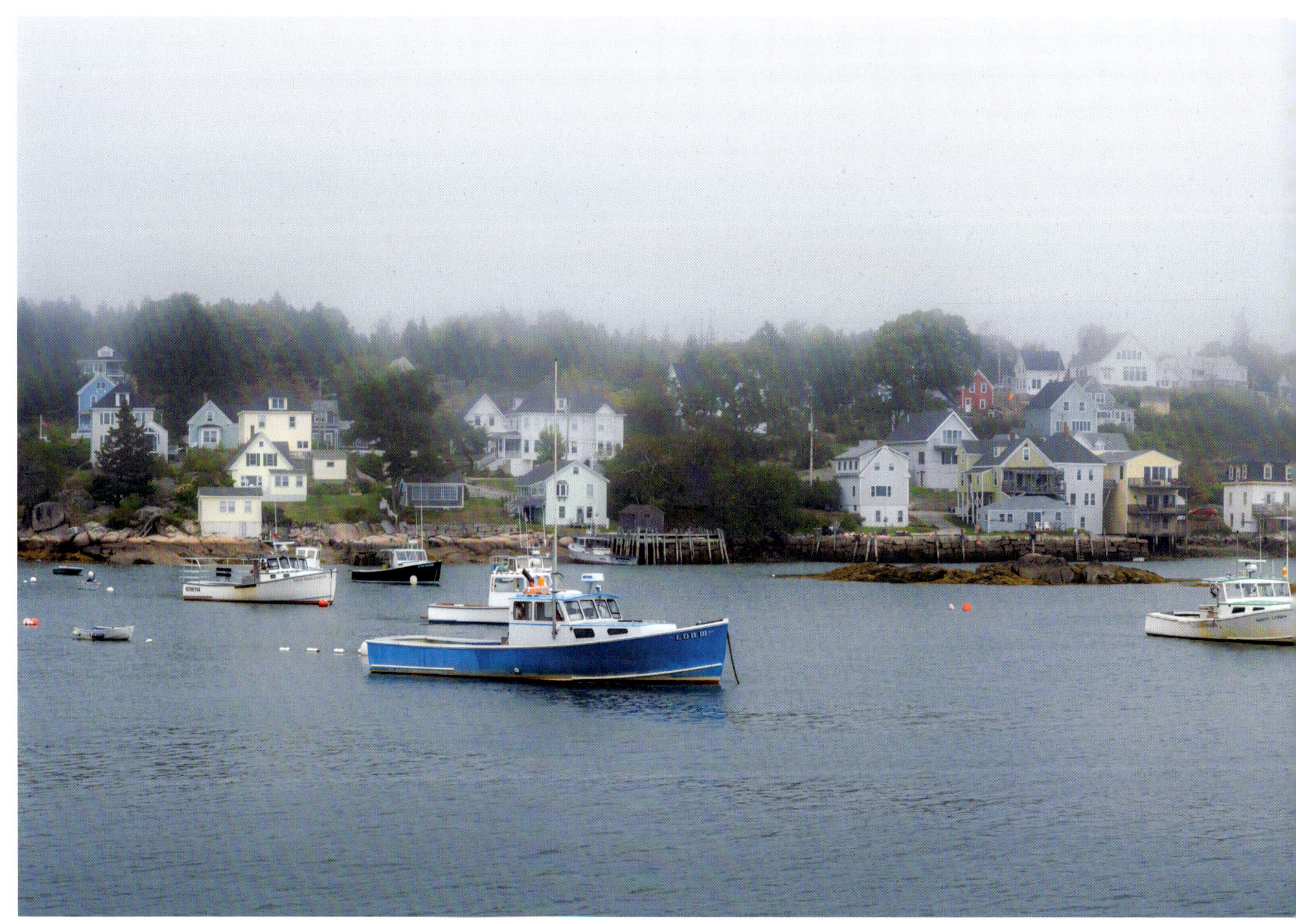

Stonington Harbor, Maine

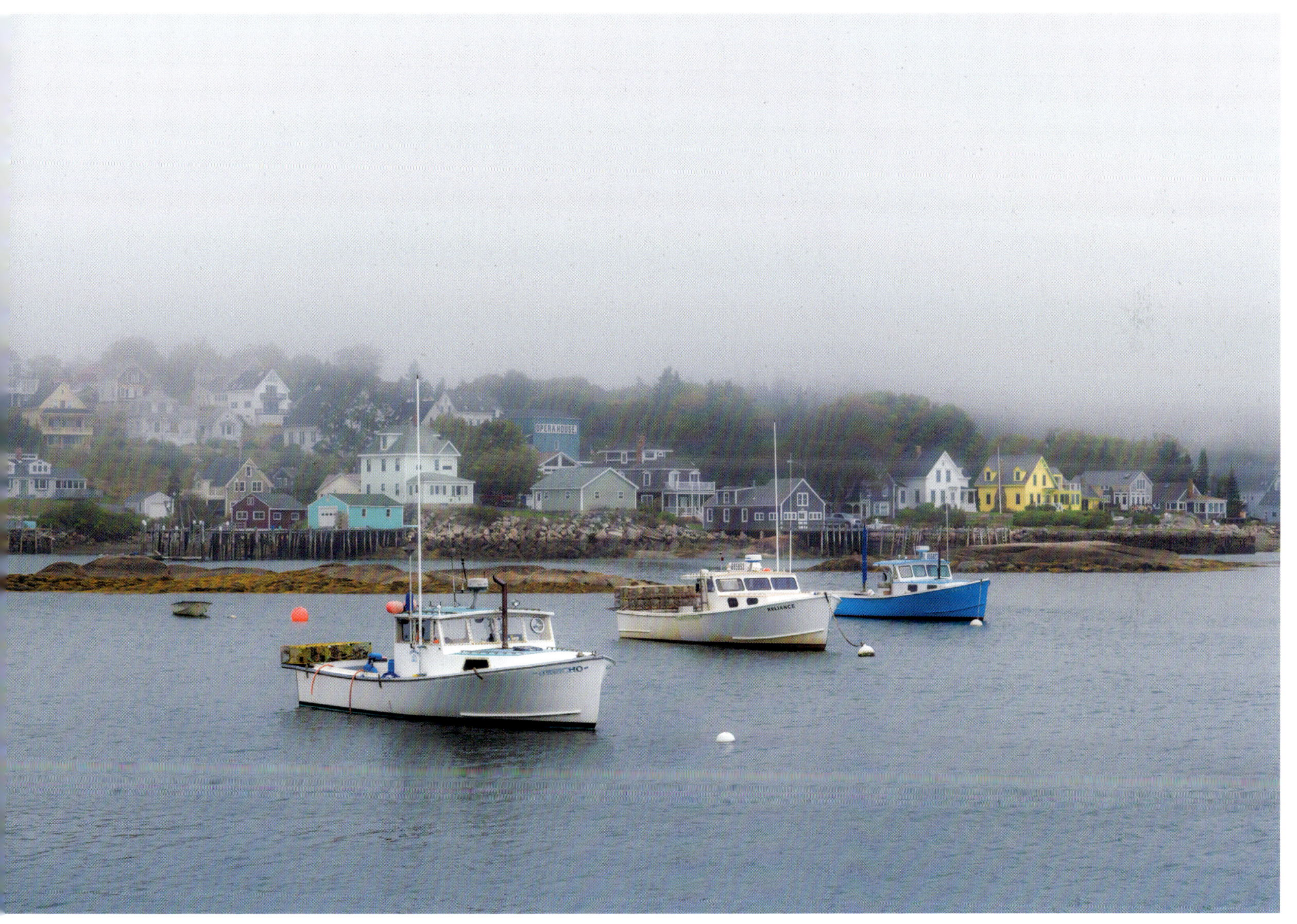
OPERAHOUSE
RELIANCE

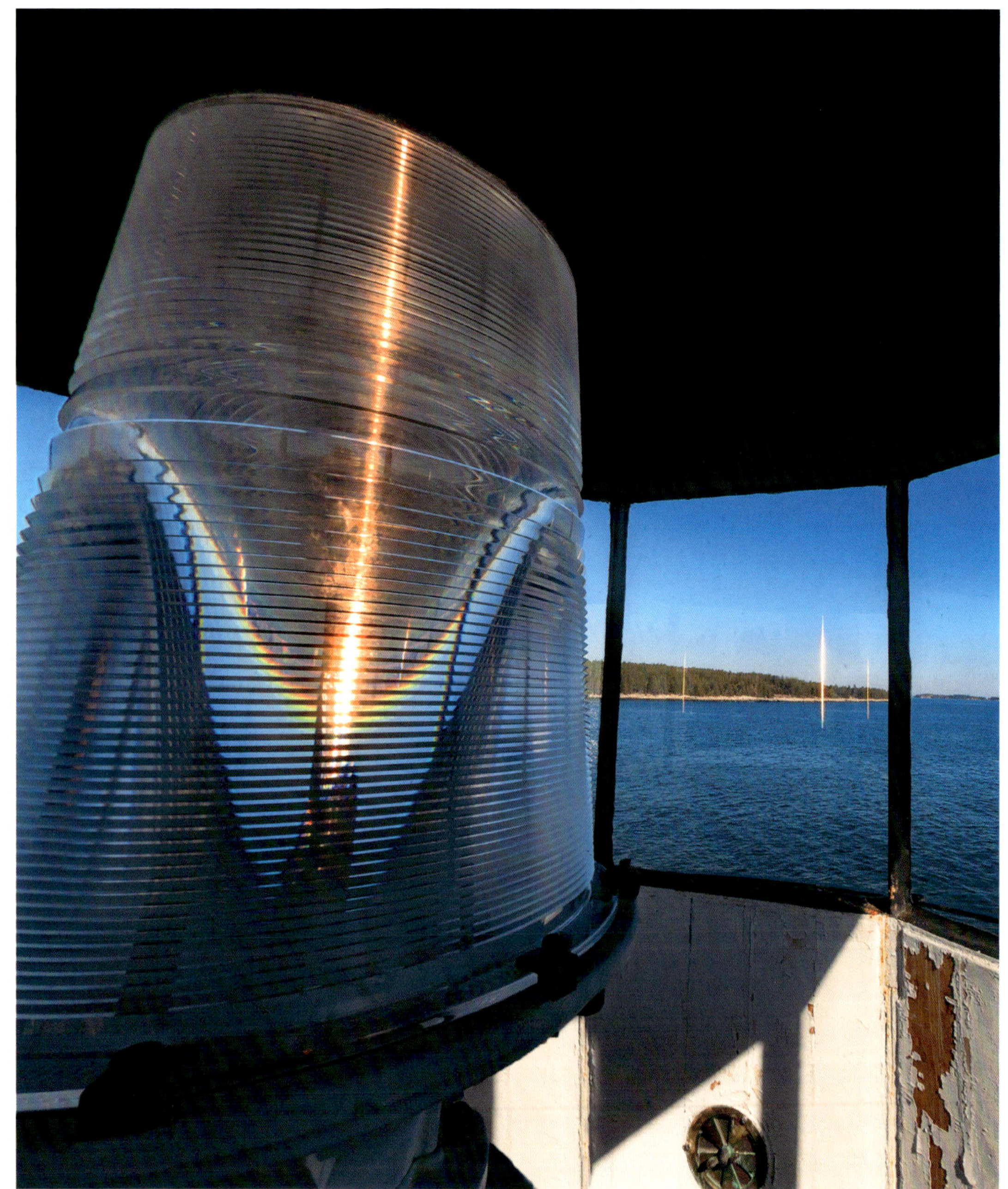

Marshall Point Lighthouse, Maine

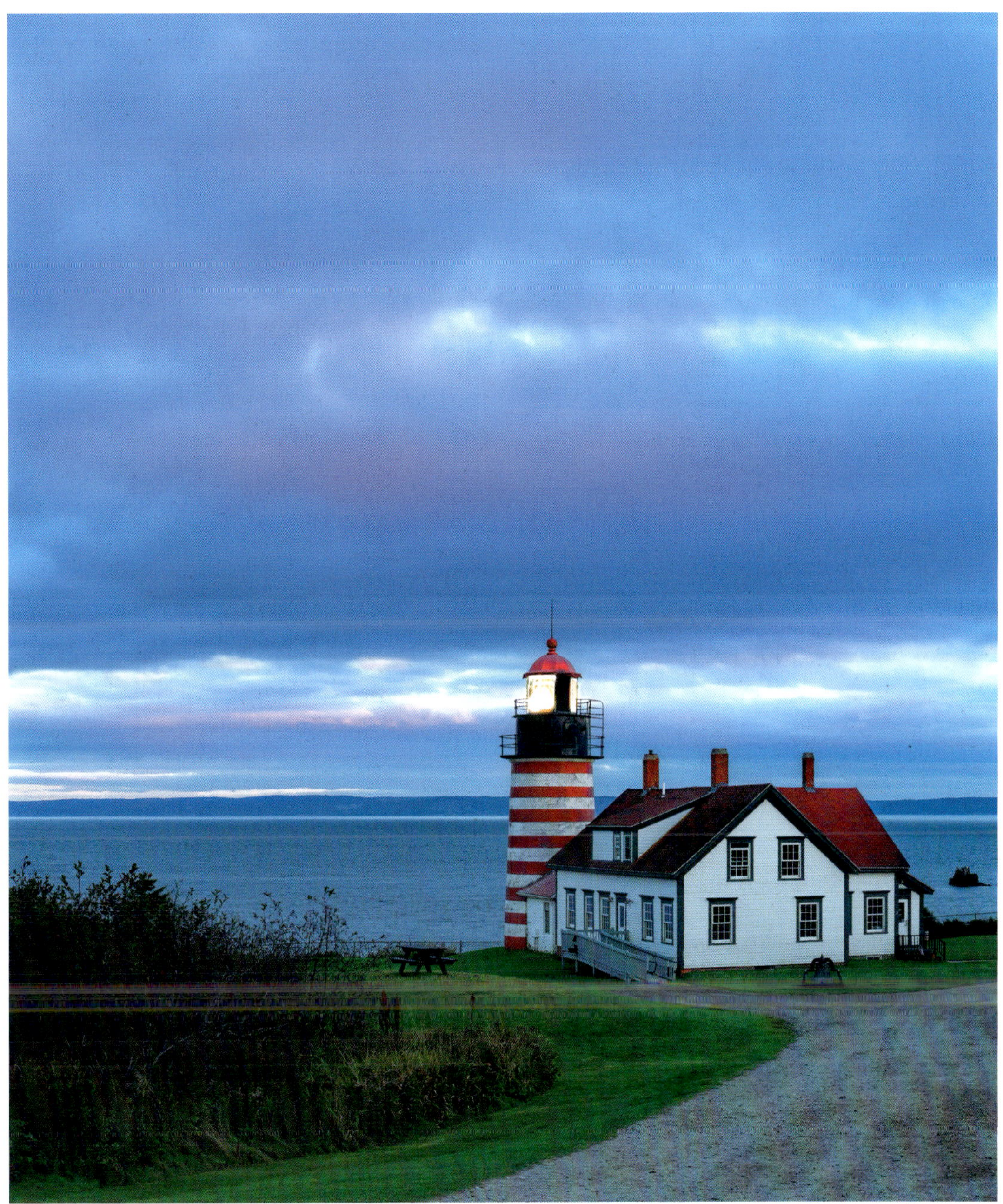

West Quoddy Head, Lubec, Maine

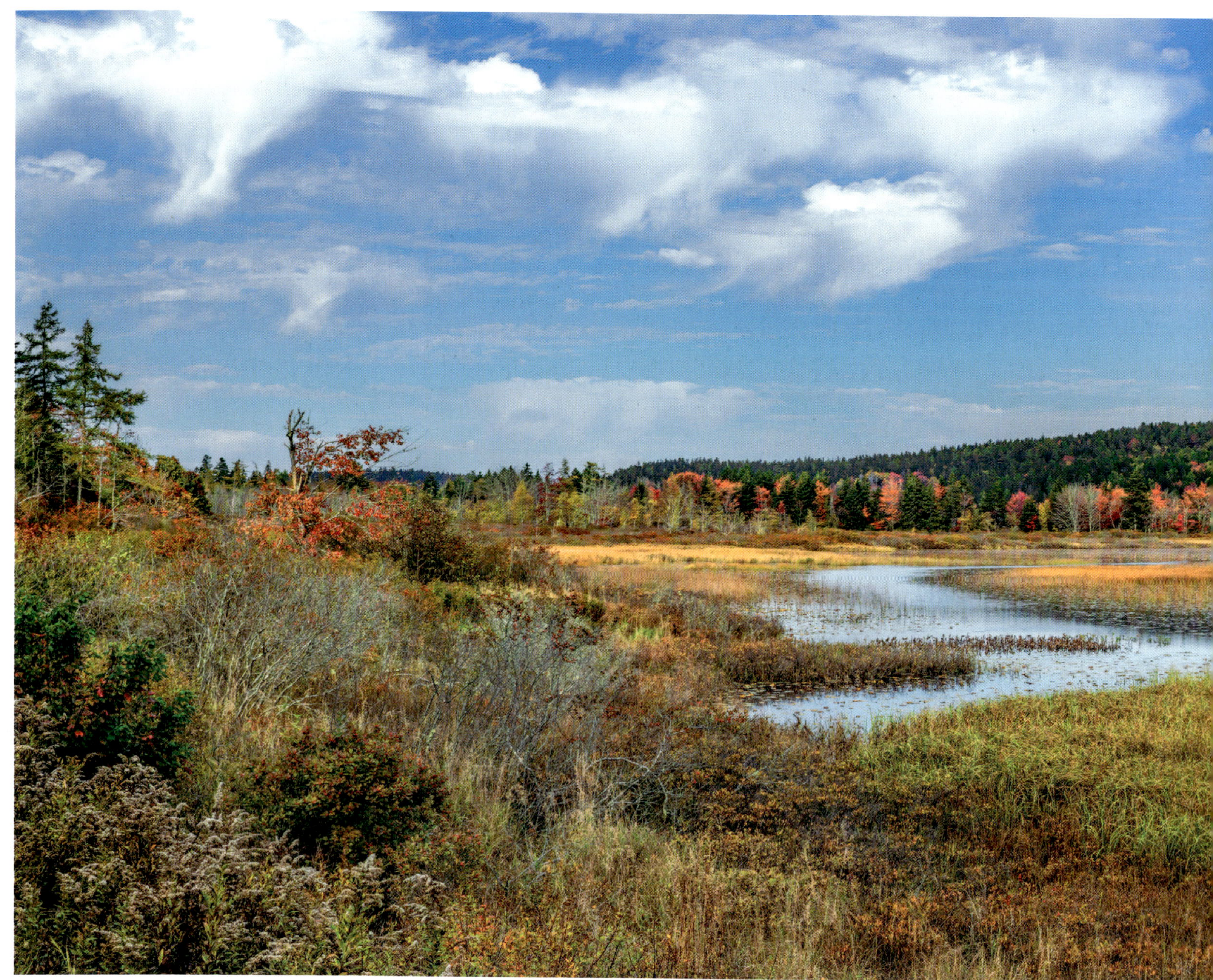

Heath Mill Landing, Maine

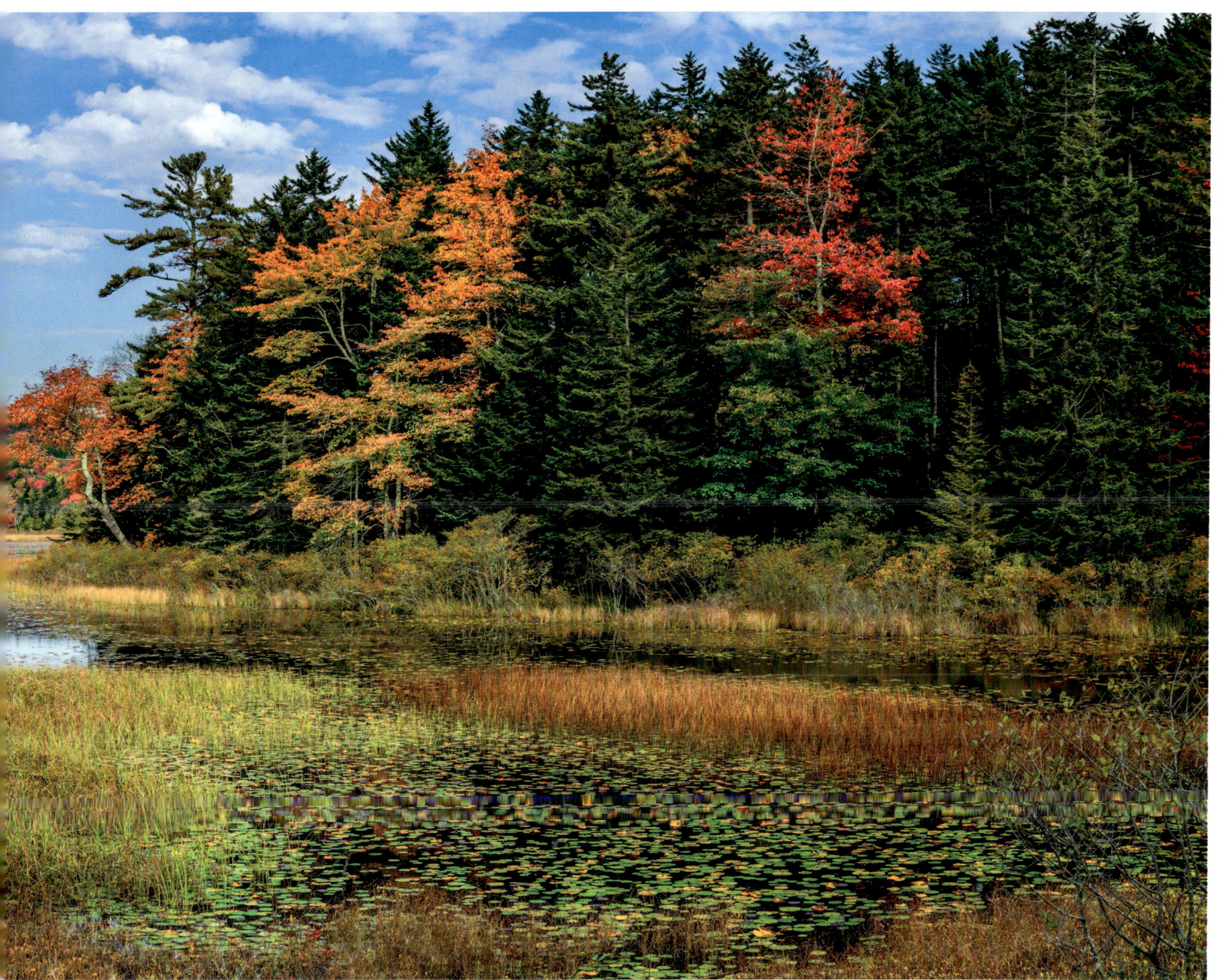

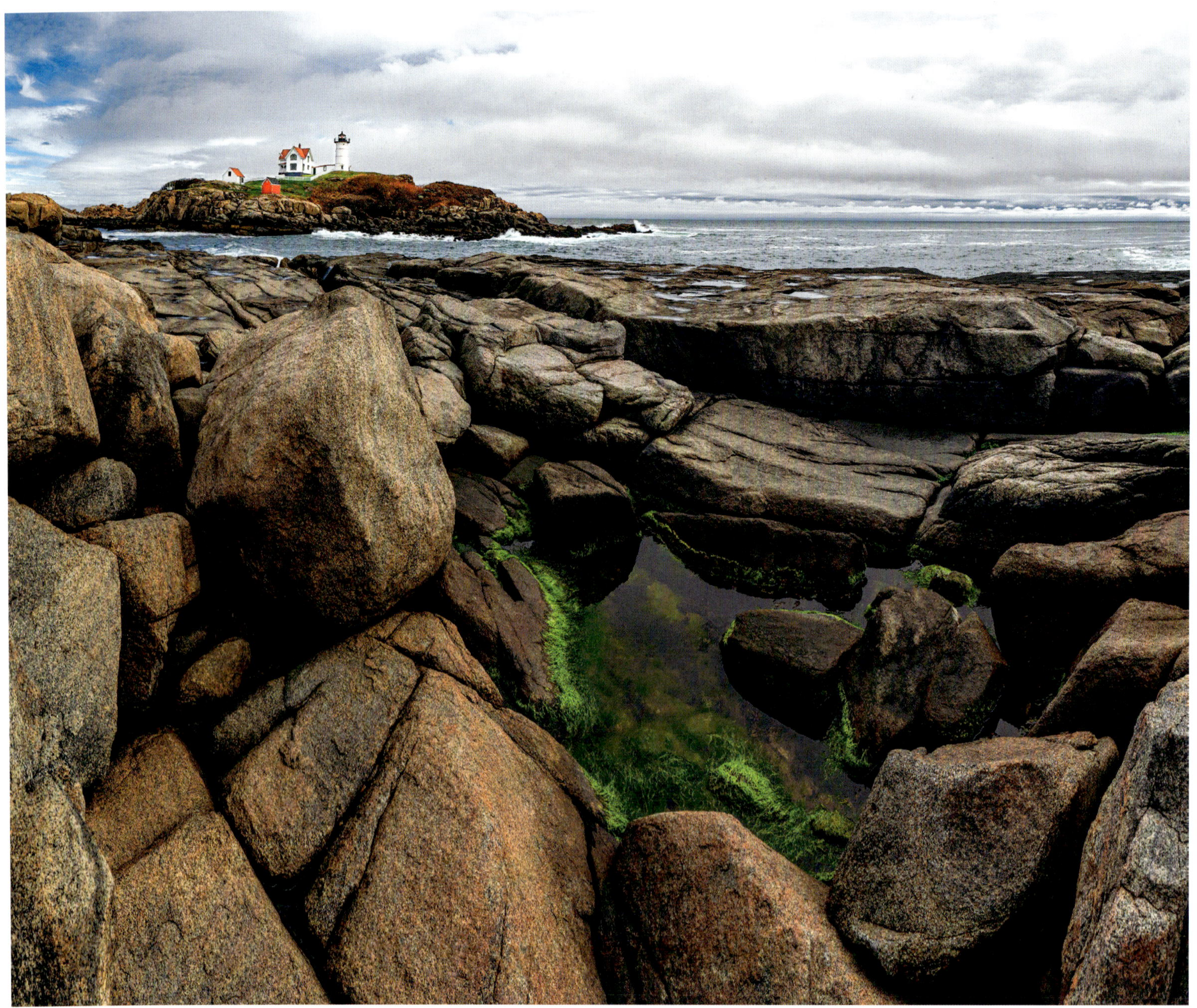

Nubble Light, York Harbor, Maine

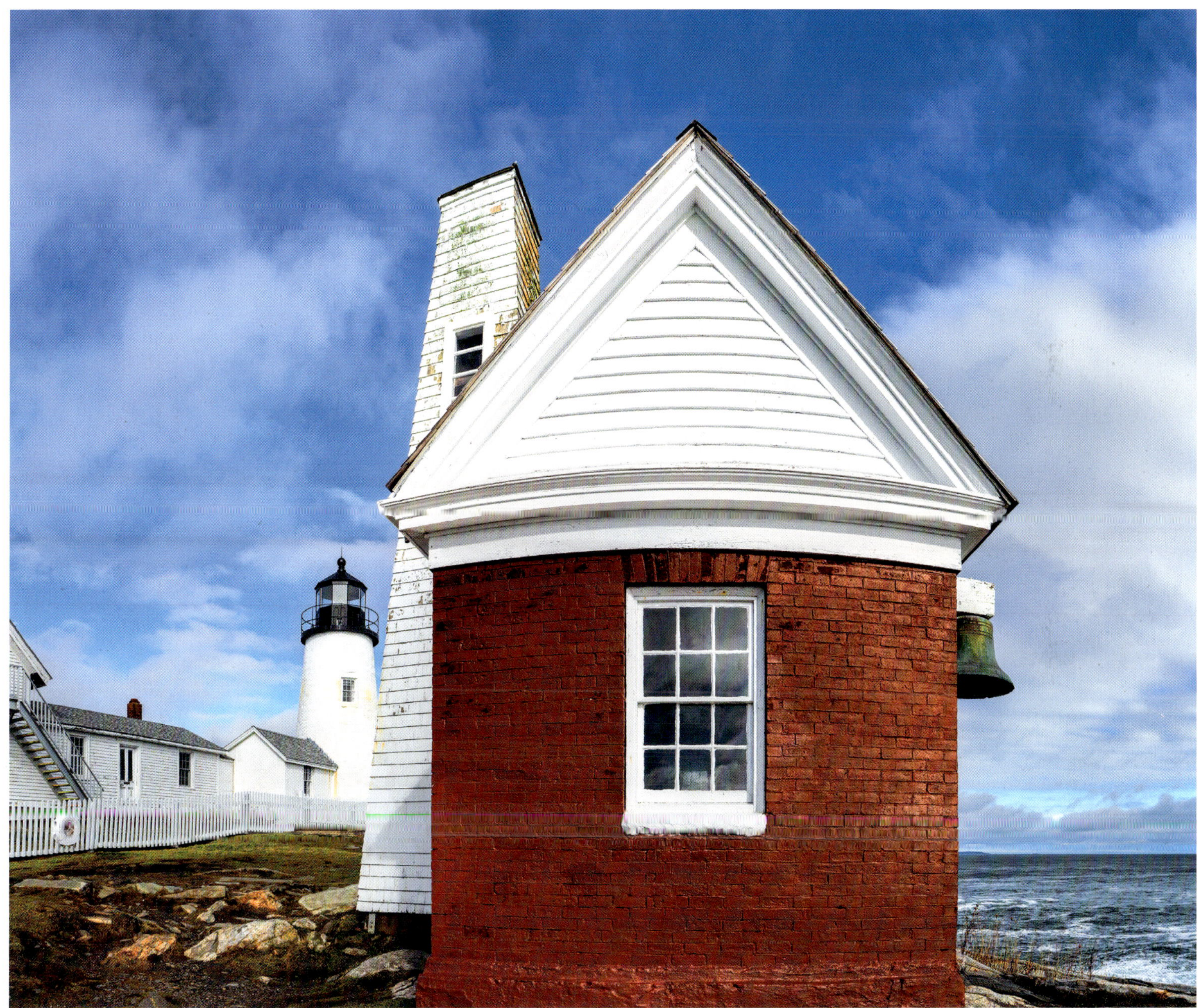

Pemaquid Point, Maine

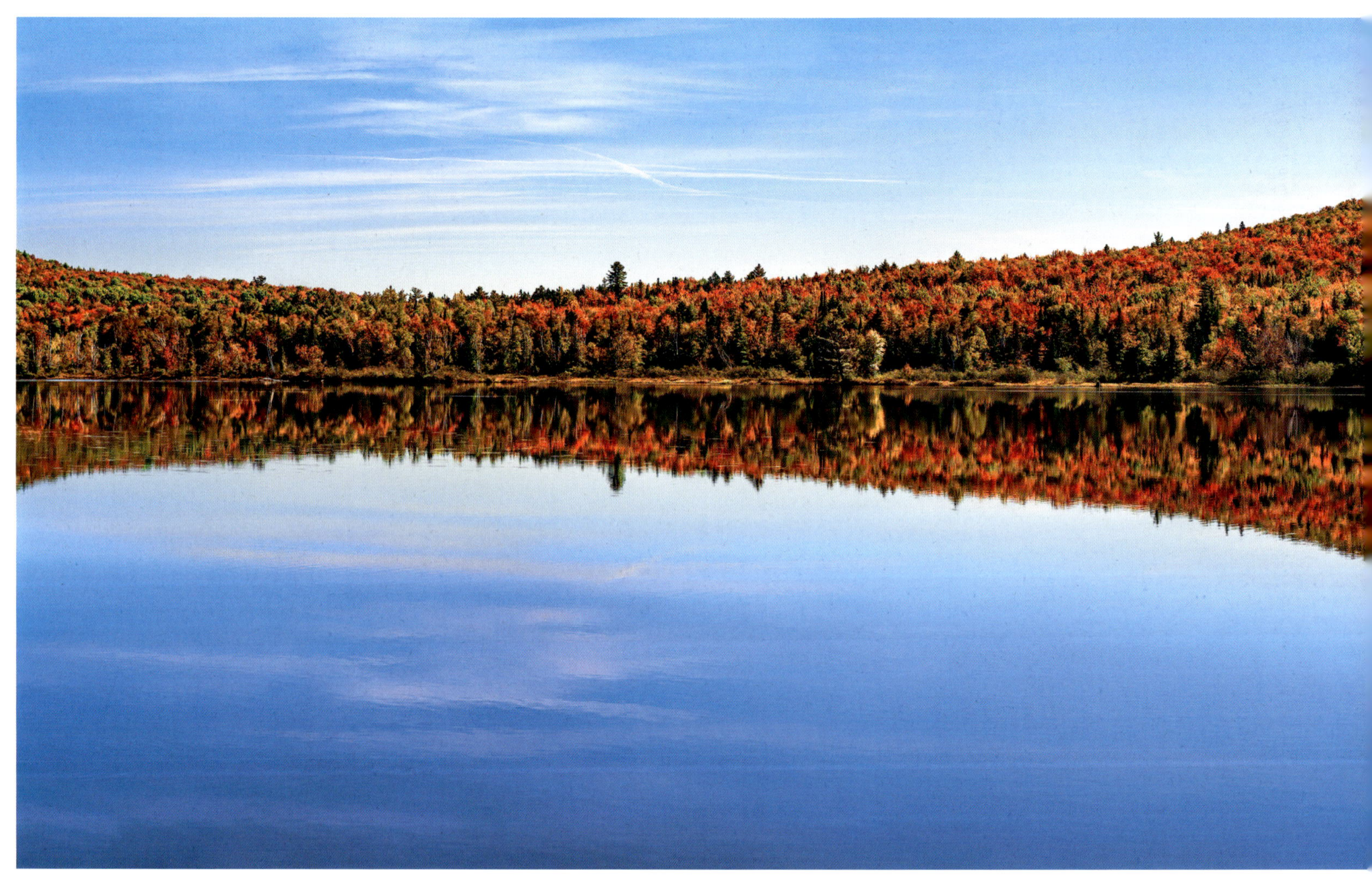

Androscoggin River, New Hampshire

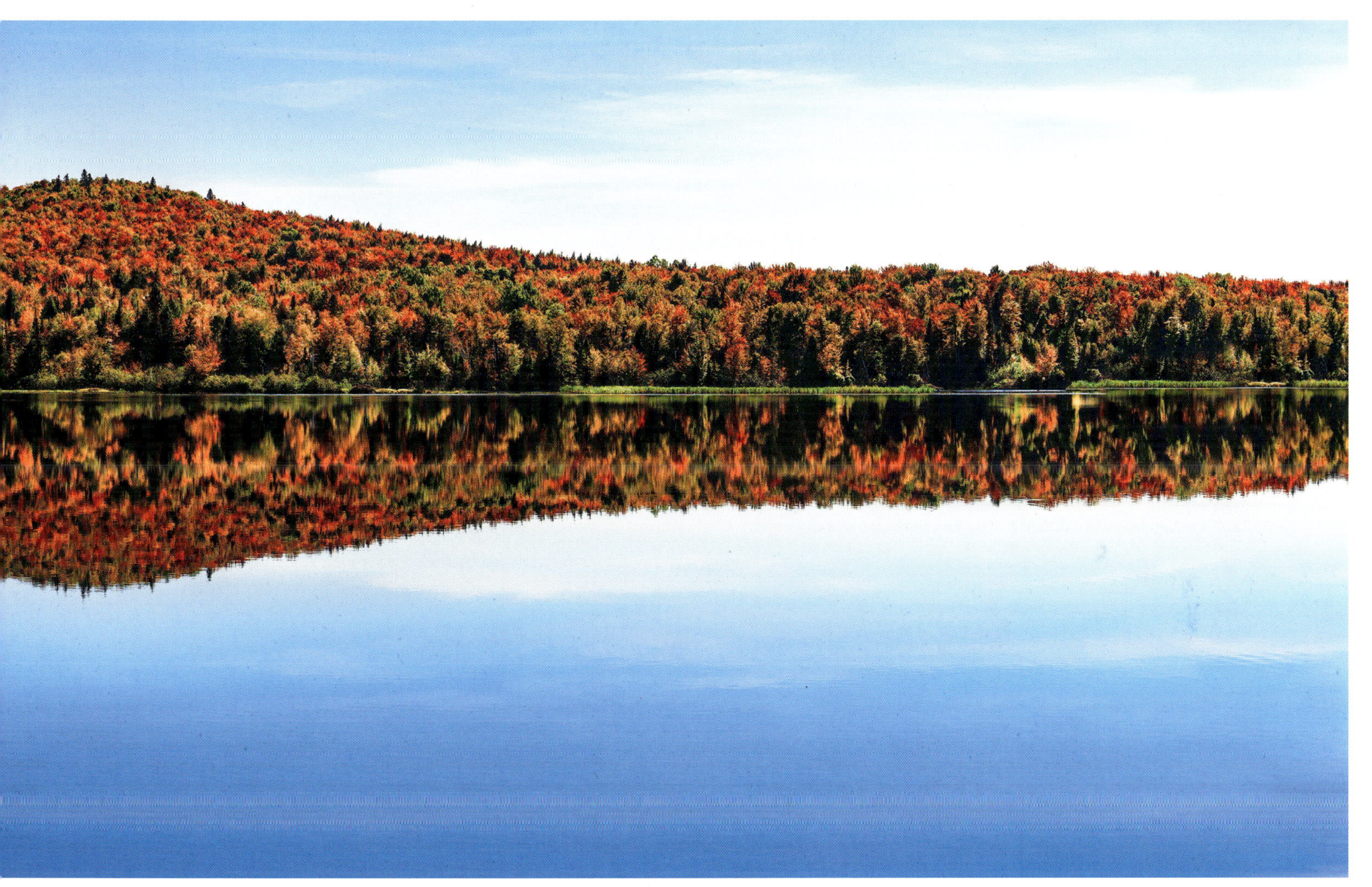

Finding a river this calm is a small miracle.

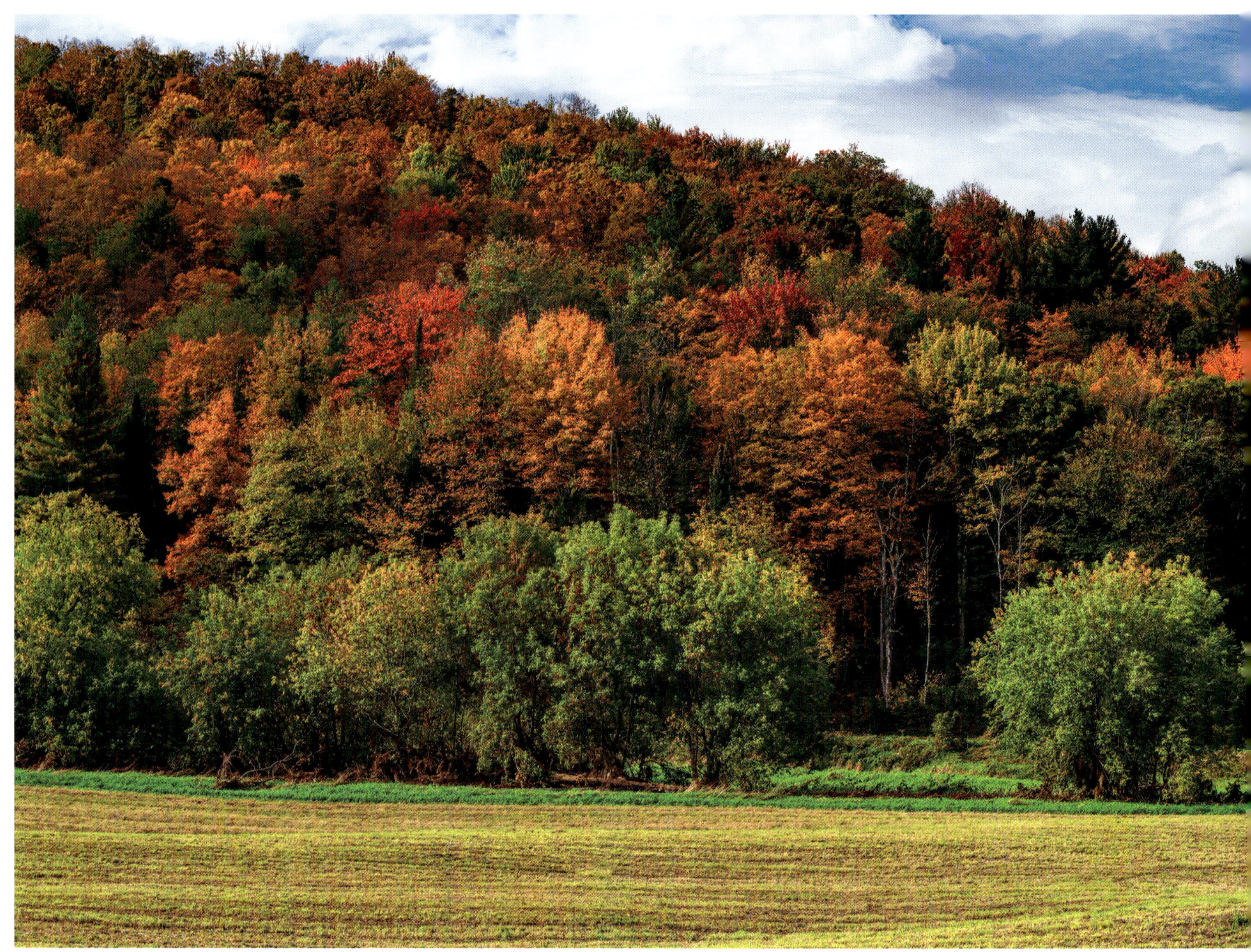

Hay truck along New Hampshire State Highway 16

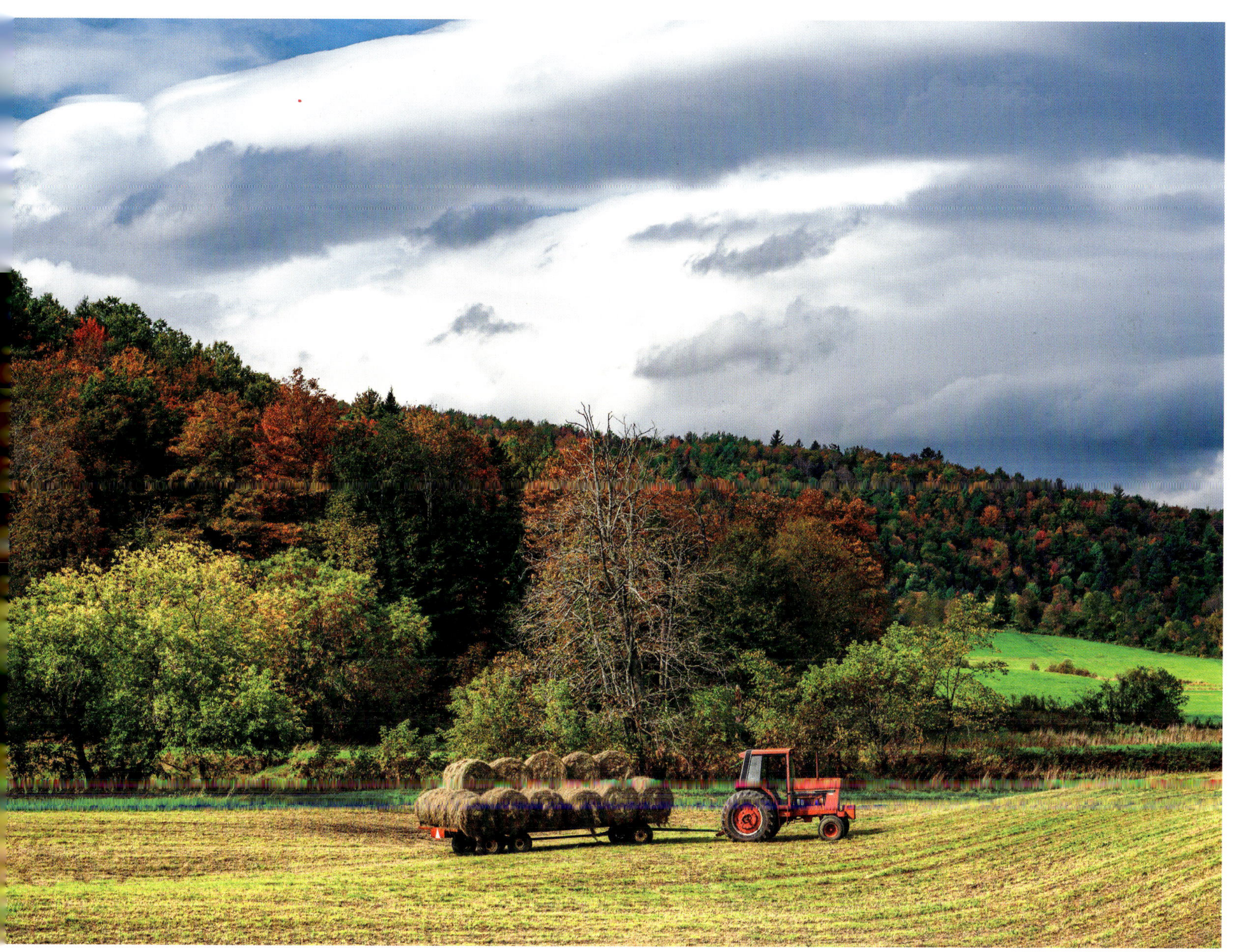

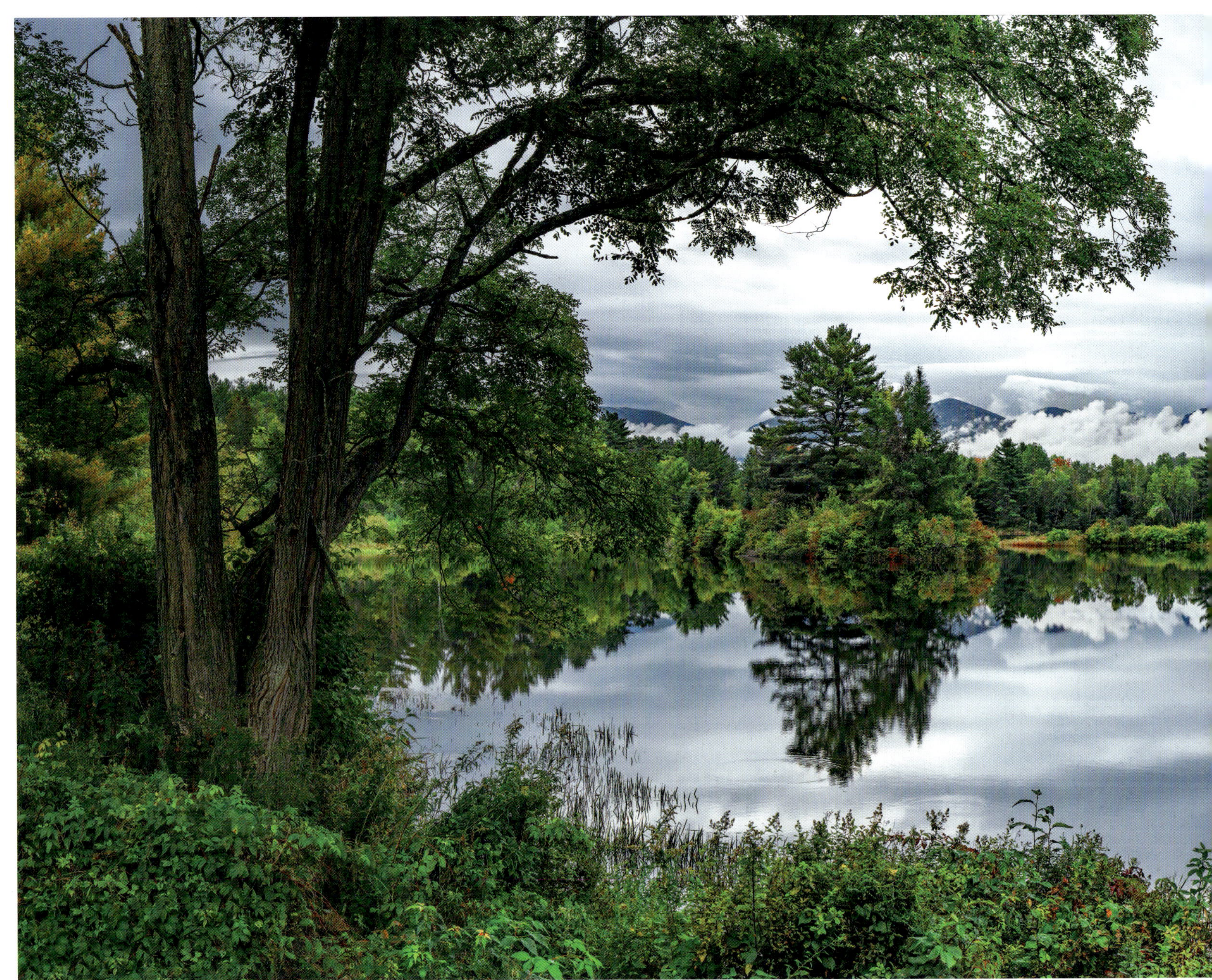

Coffin Pond, New Hampshire

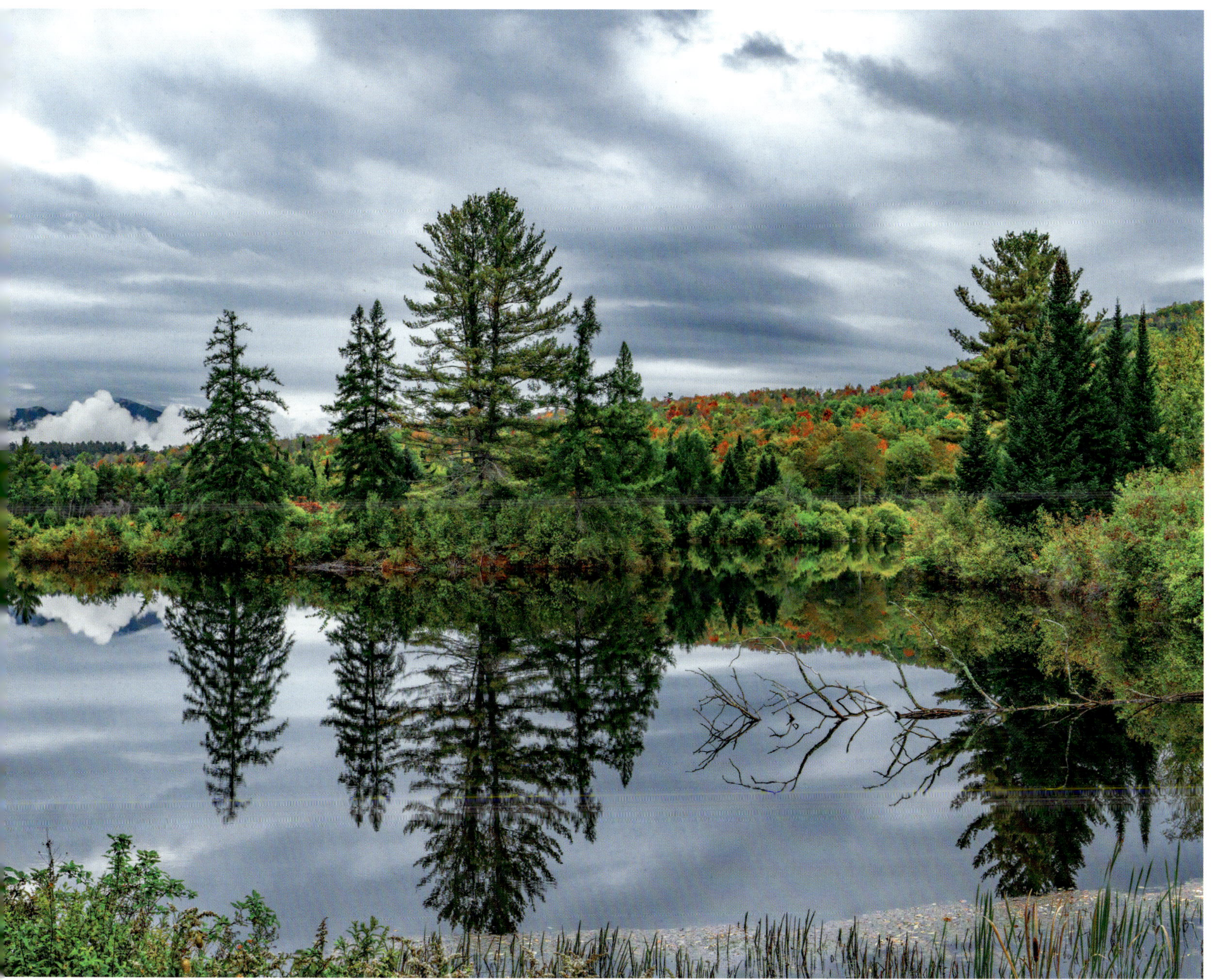

This was one of those times that driving down a road because I had a feeling there might be a shot paid off.

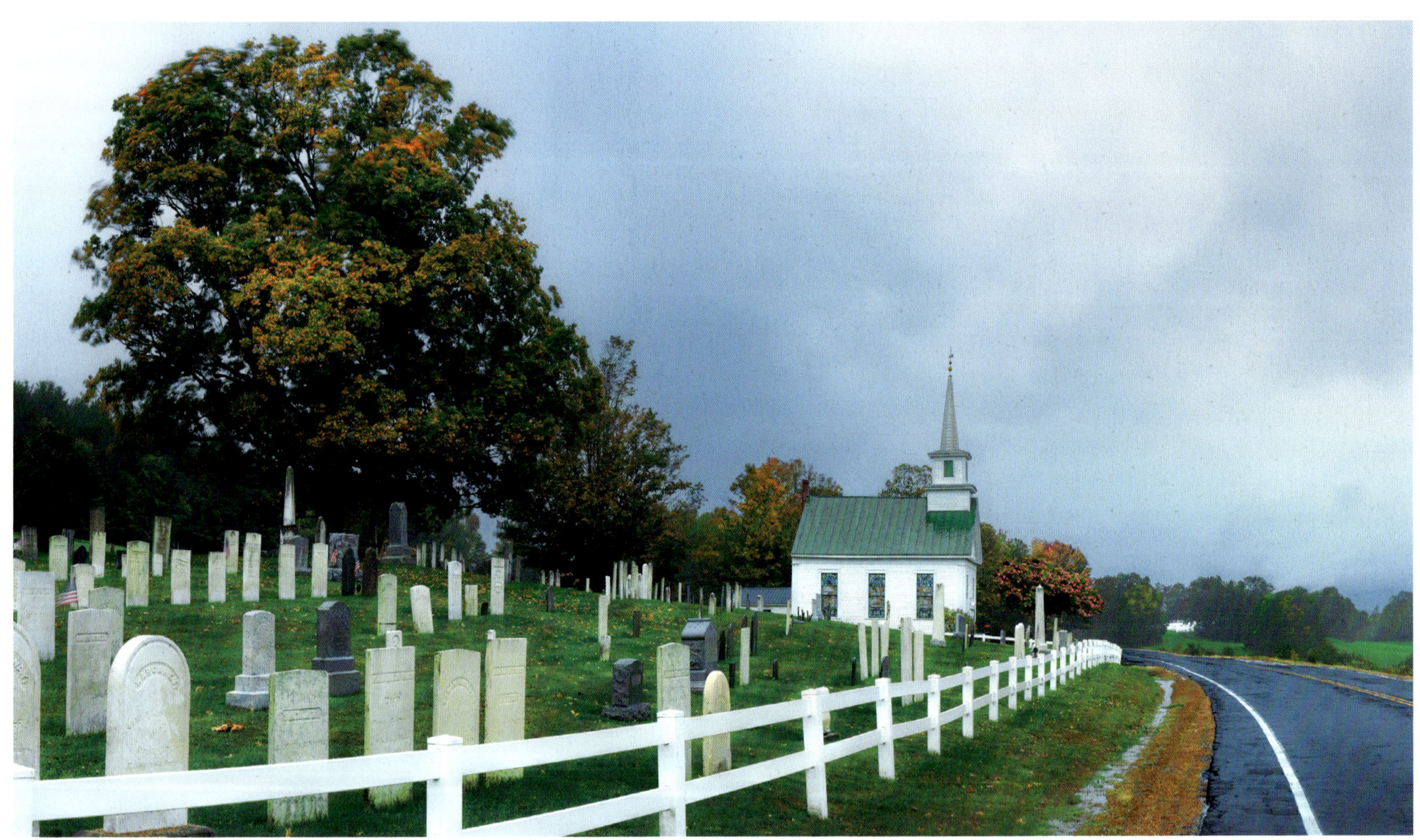

Church in Monroe, New Hampshire, 1854

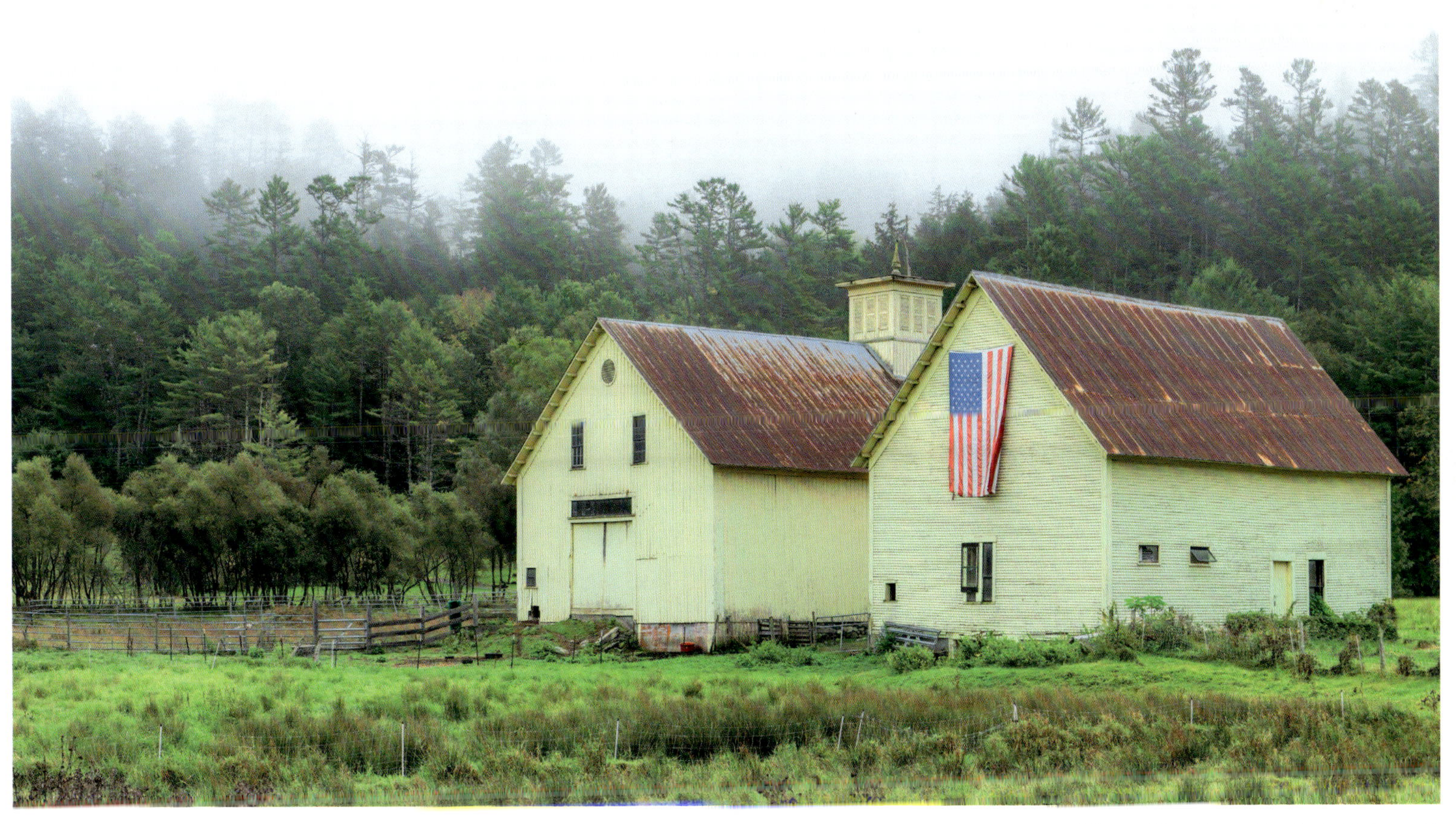

Barn and flag on New Hampshire State Highway 10

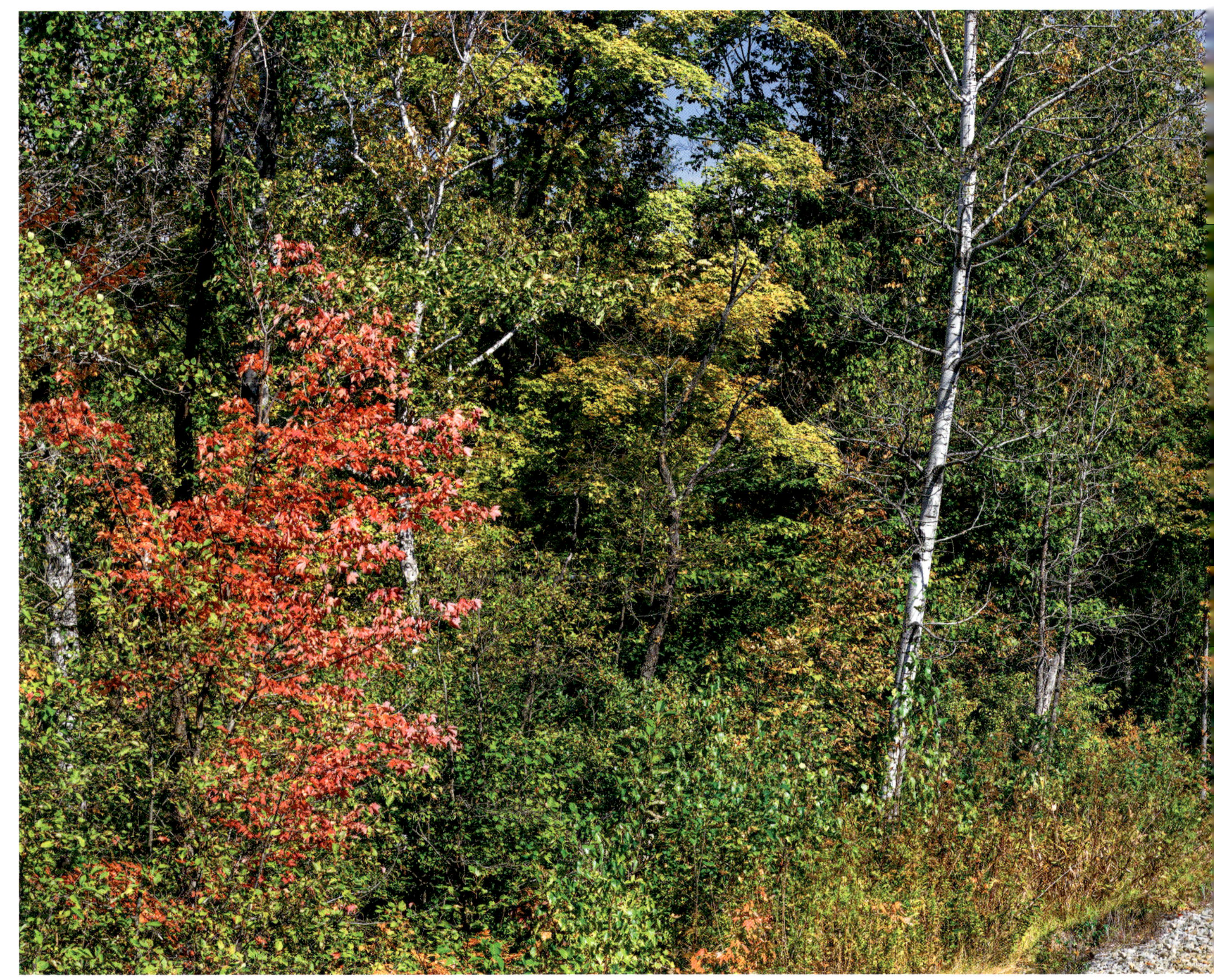

Barker Road railroad crossing, New Hampshire

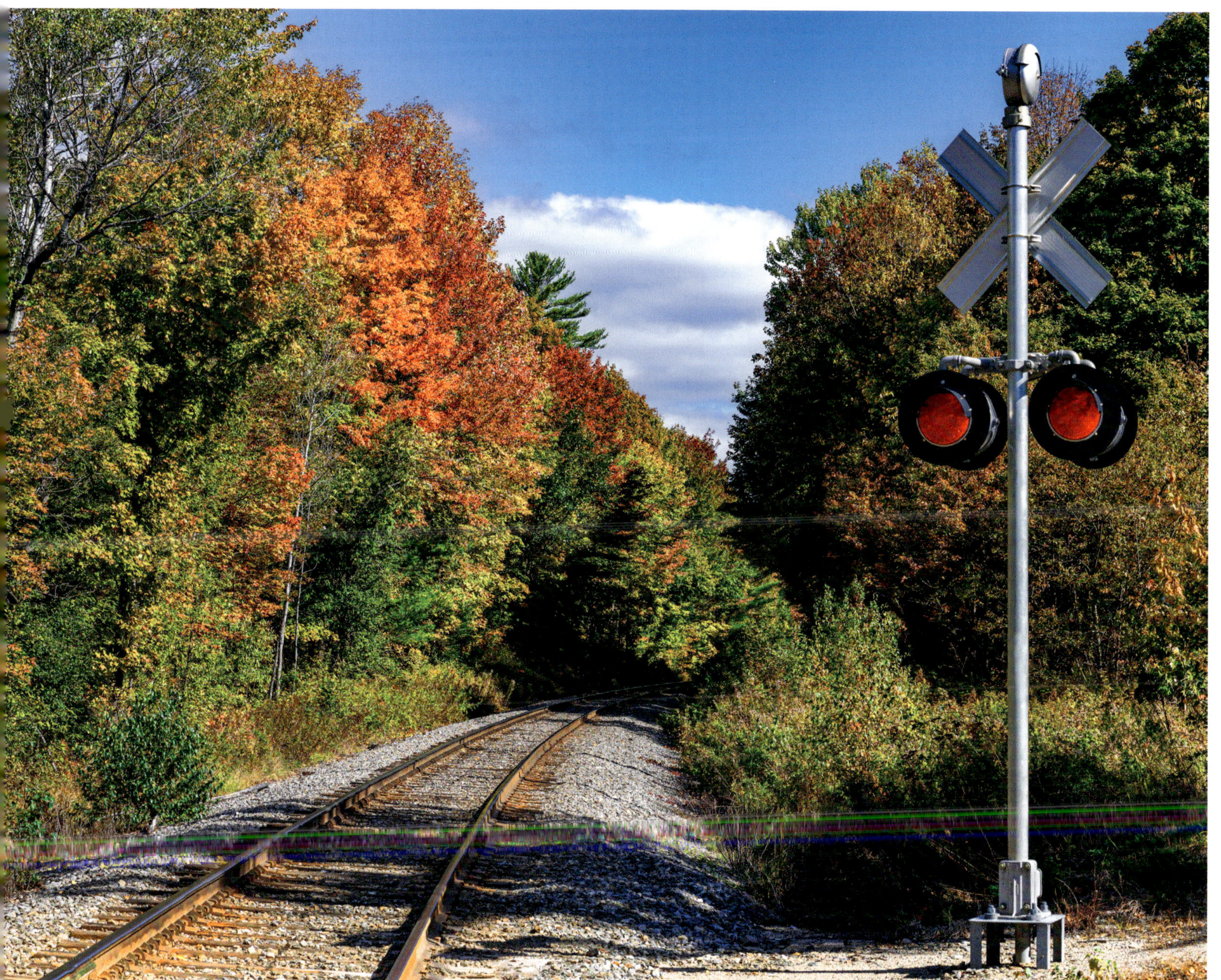

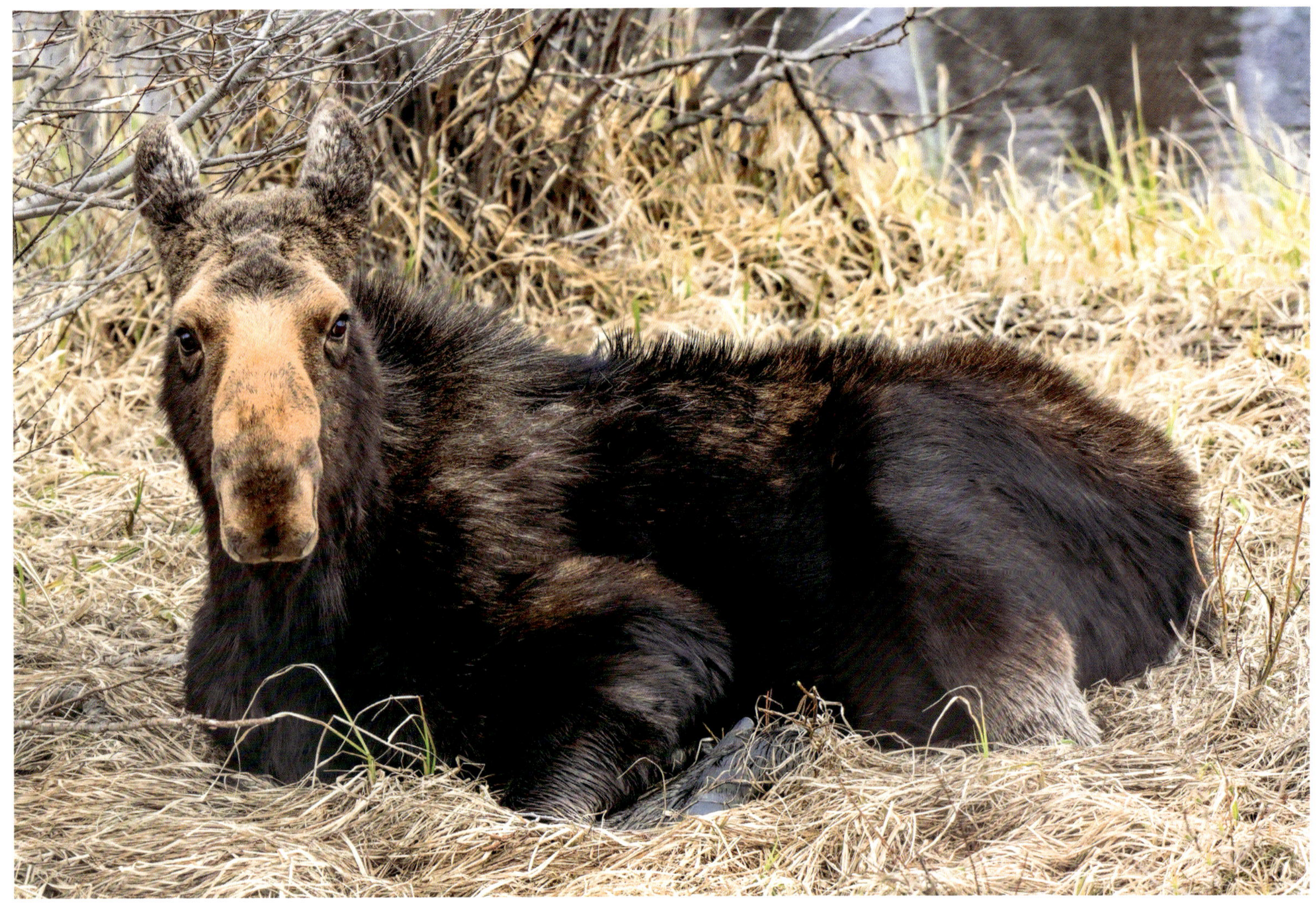

Resting New England moose

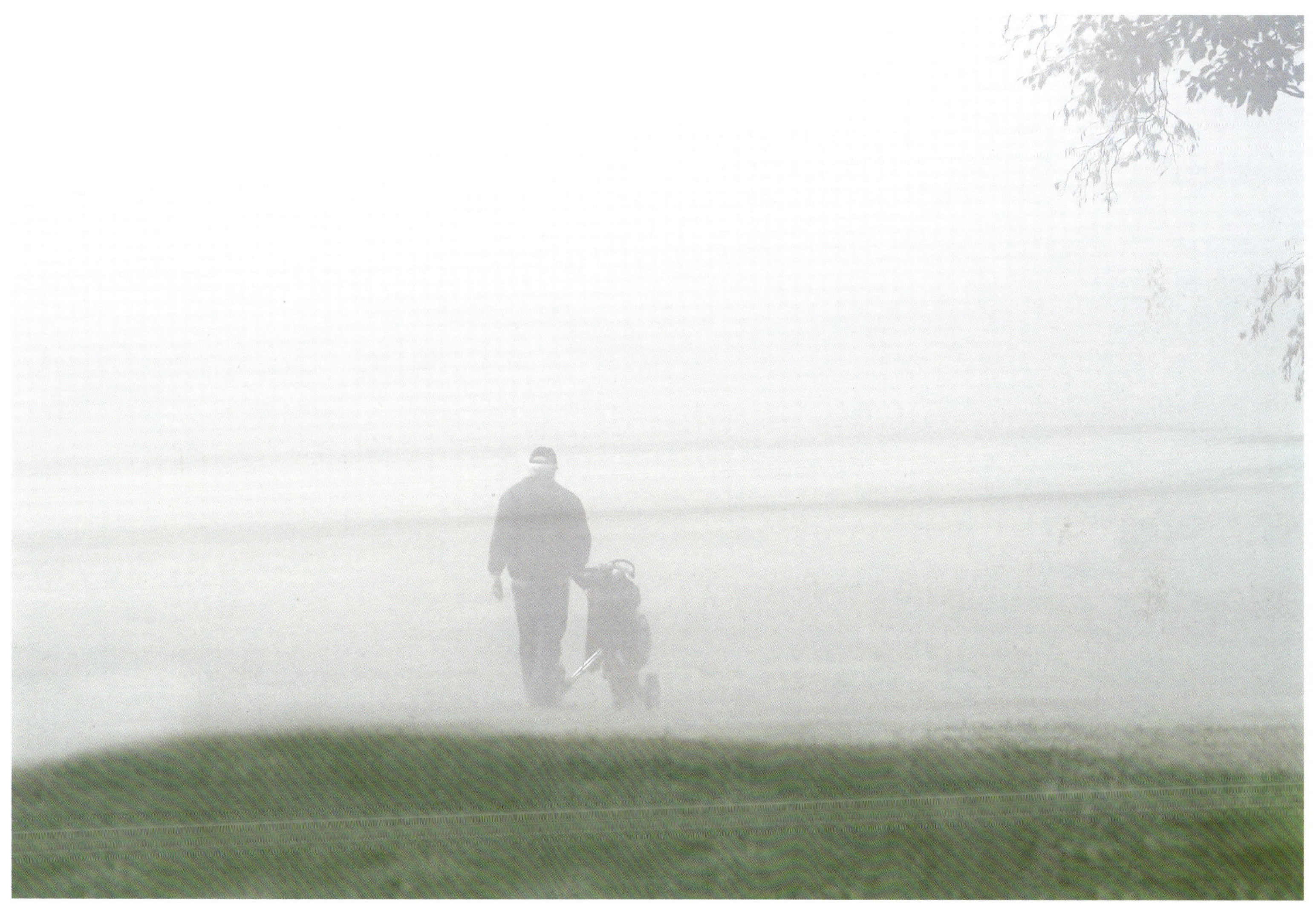

Intrepid golfer, New Hampshire

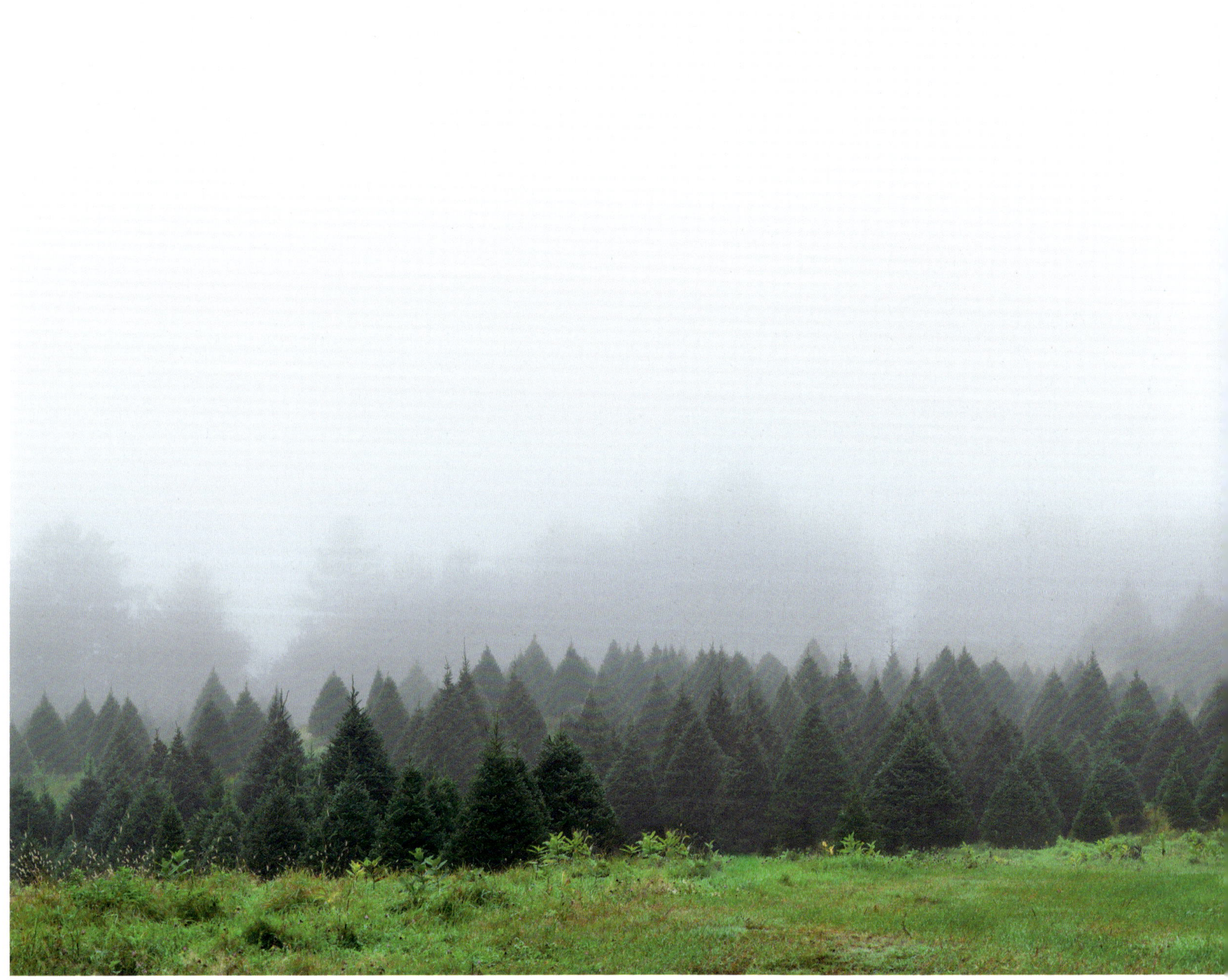

Mountain Star Farms, New Hampshire

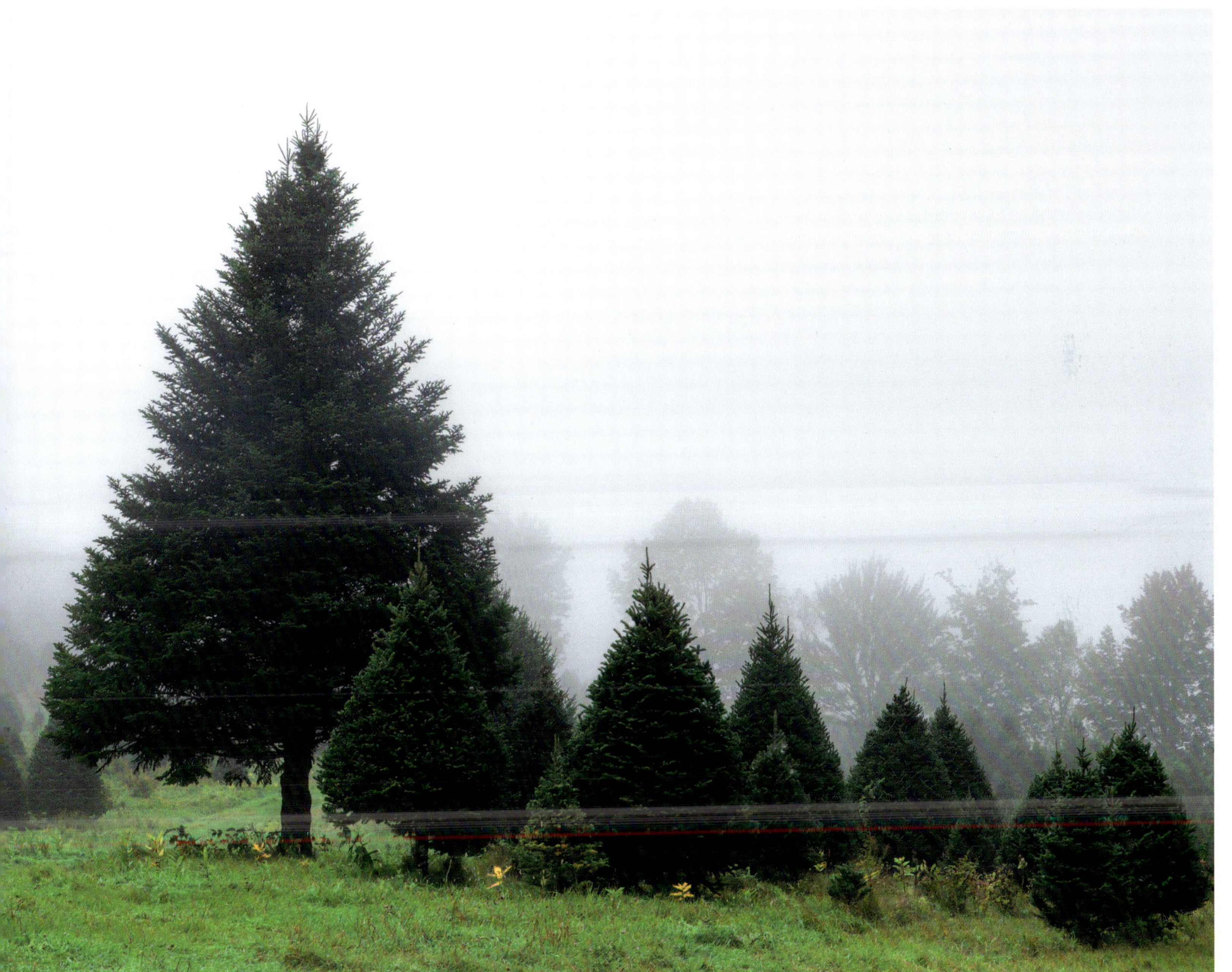

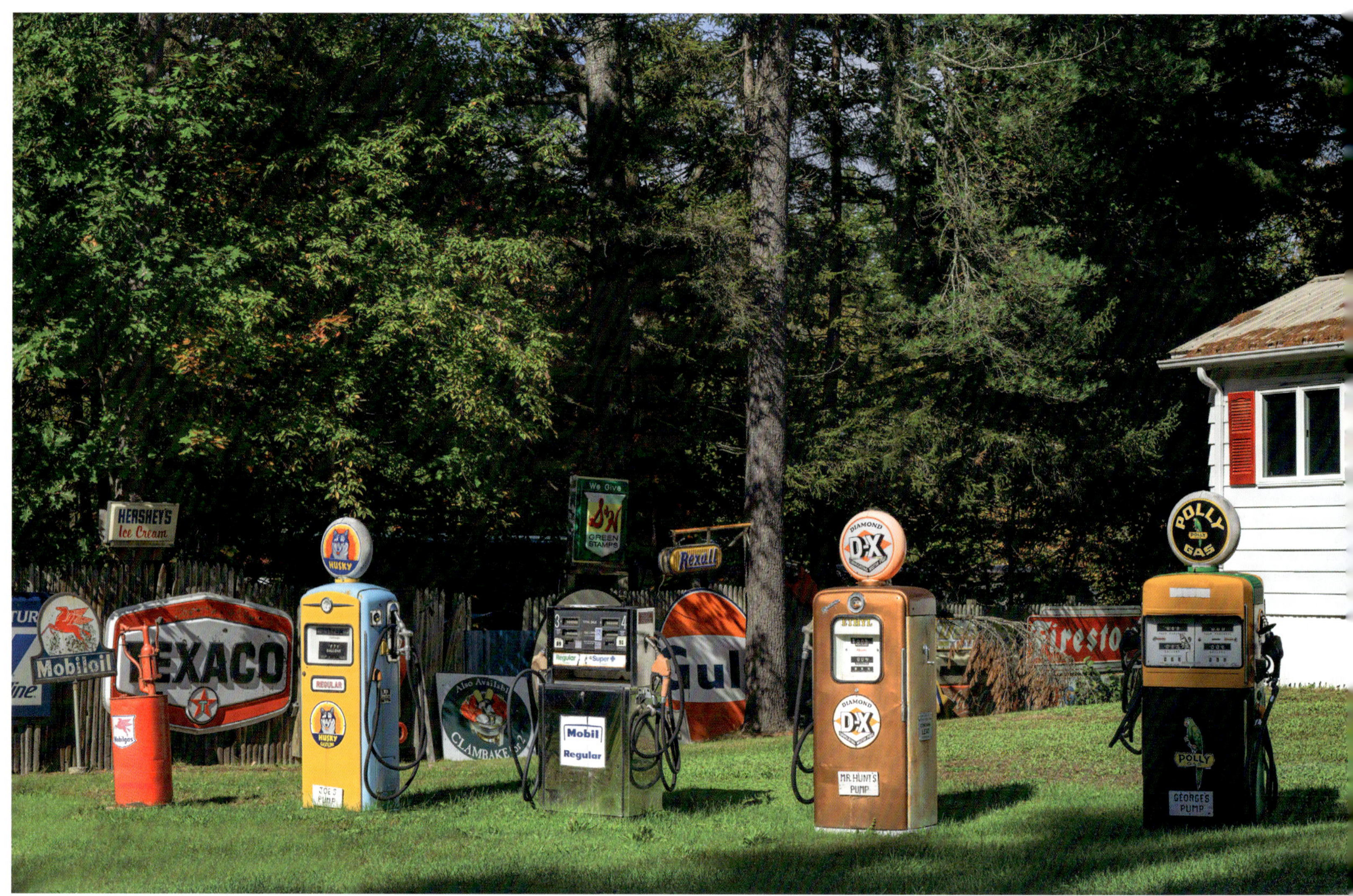

Gas pump collection on Whitefield Road, New Hampshire

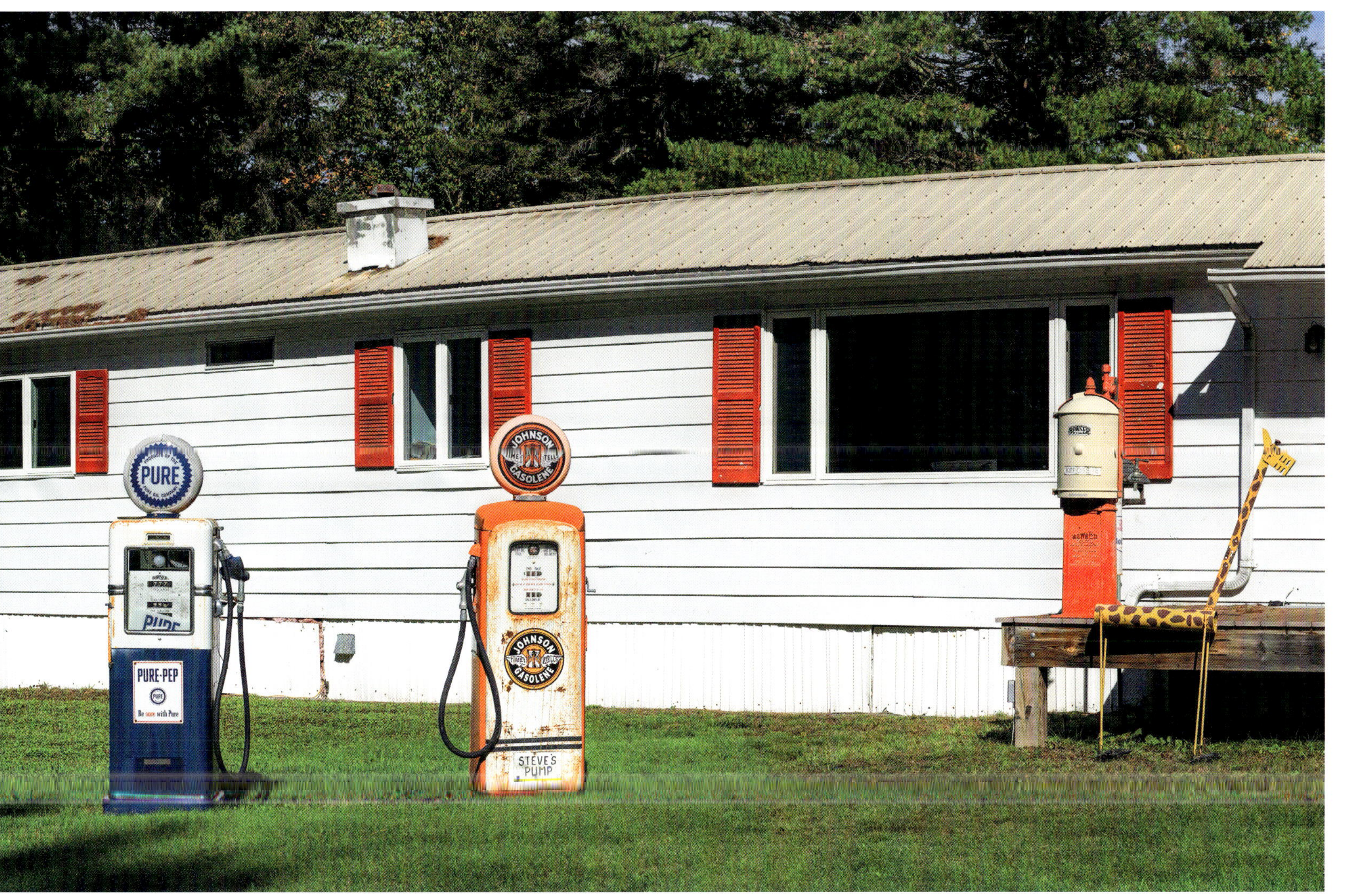

There were more pumps around the side of the house. I liked how these looked like sentries.

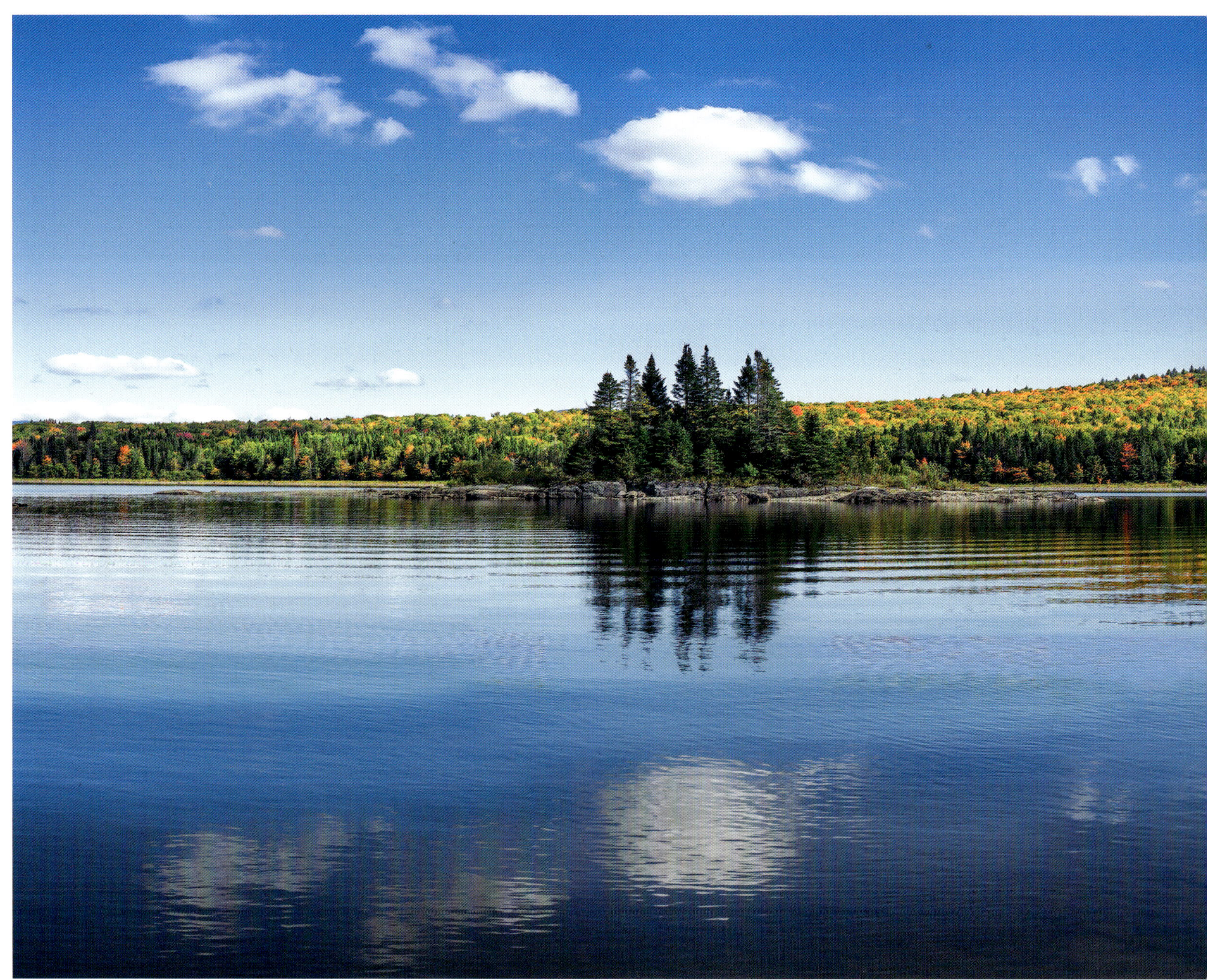

First Connecticut Lake, New Hampshire

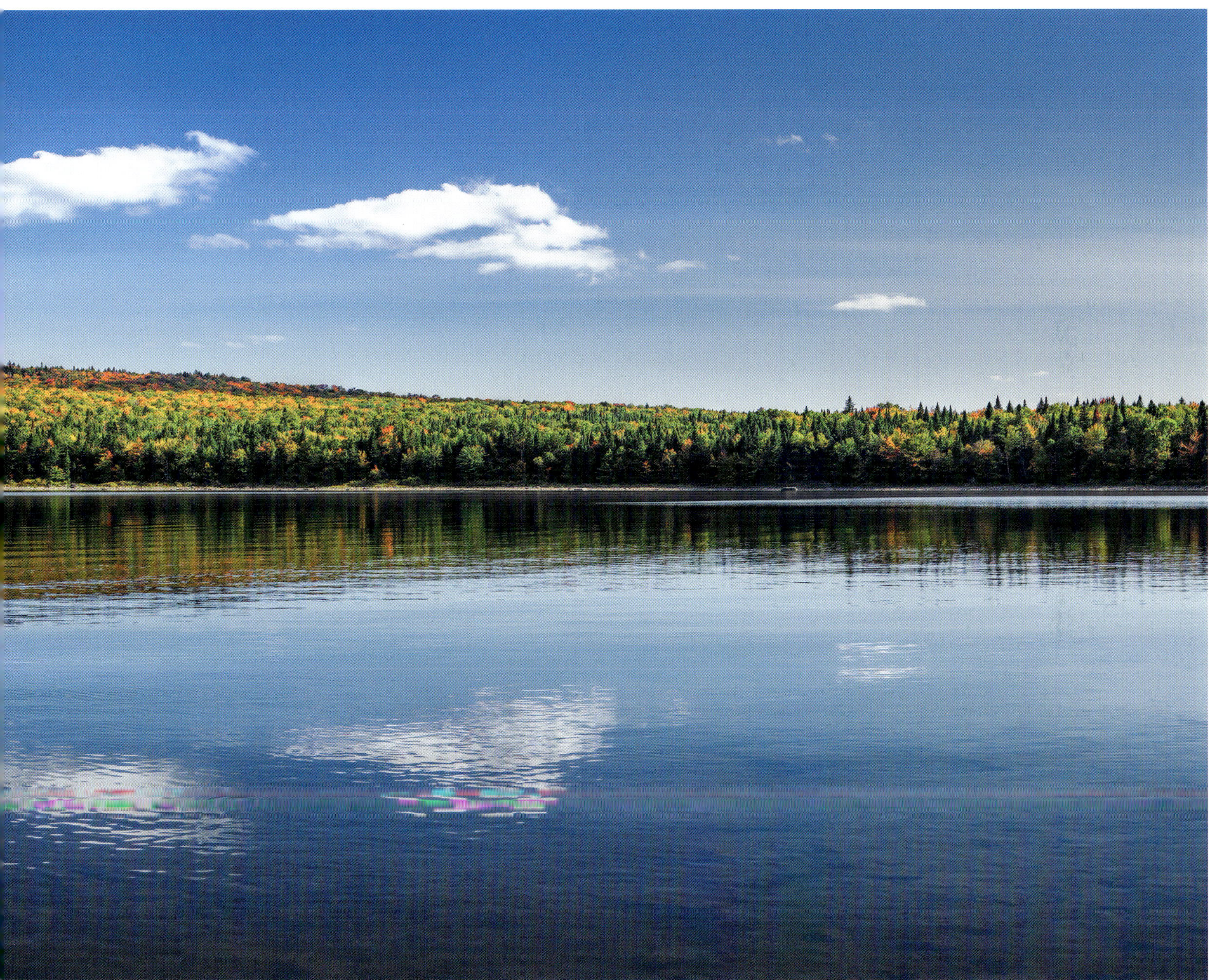

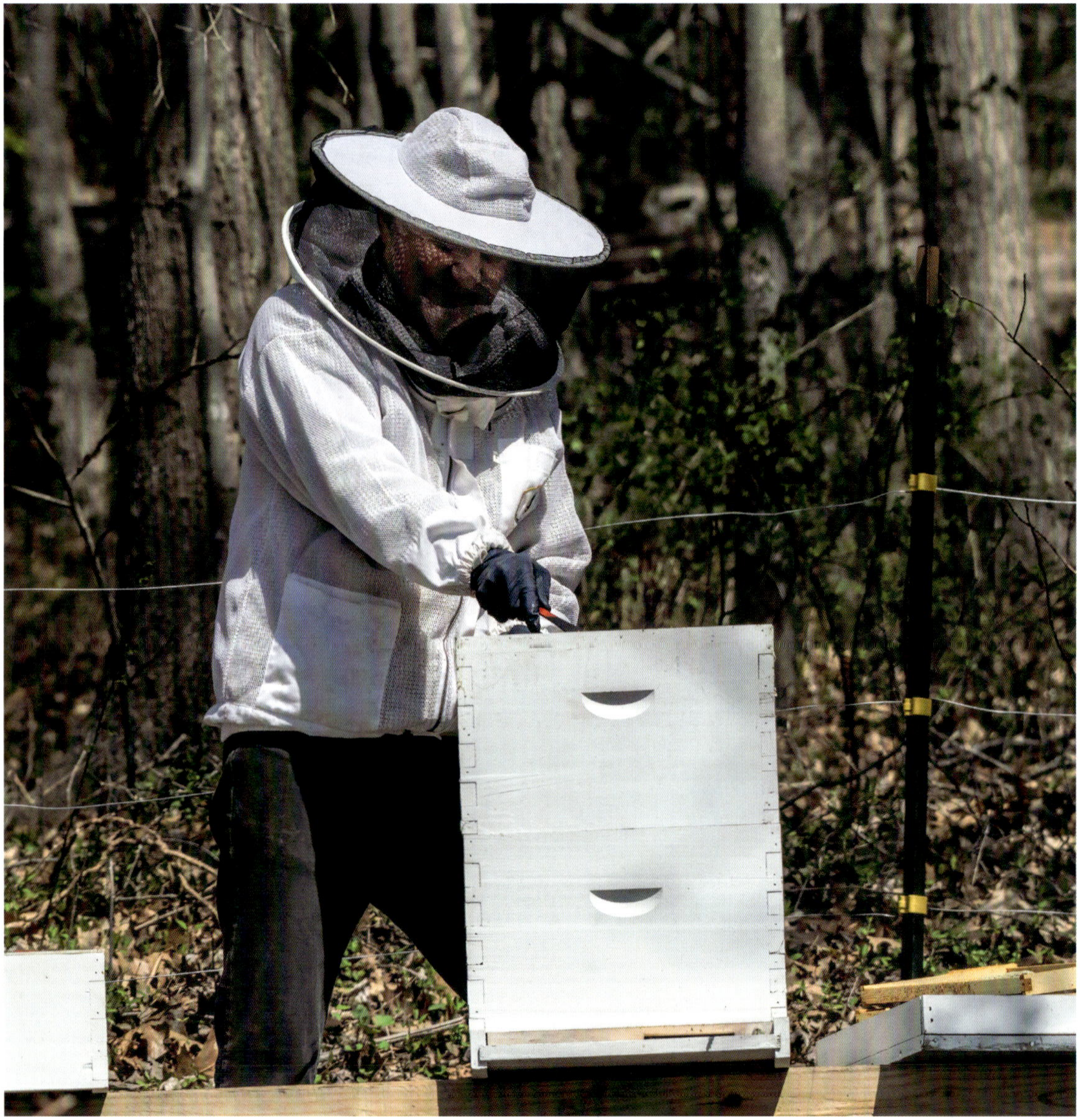

Beekeeper, New Hampshire

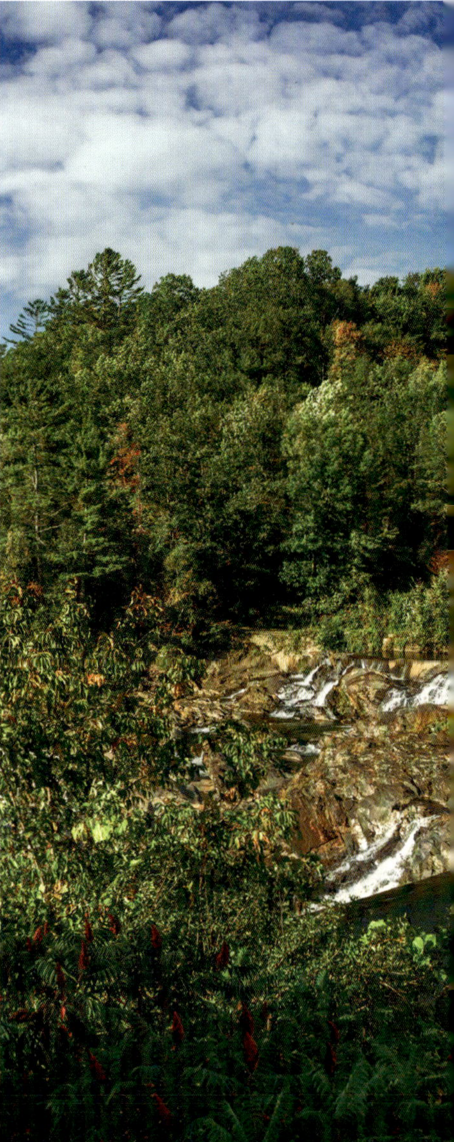

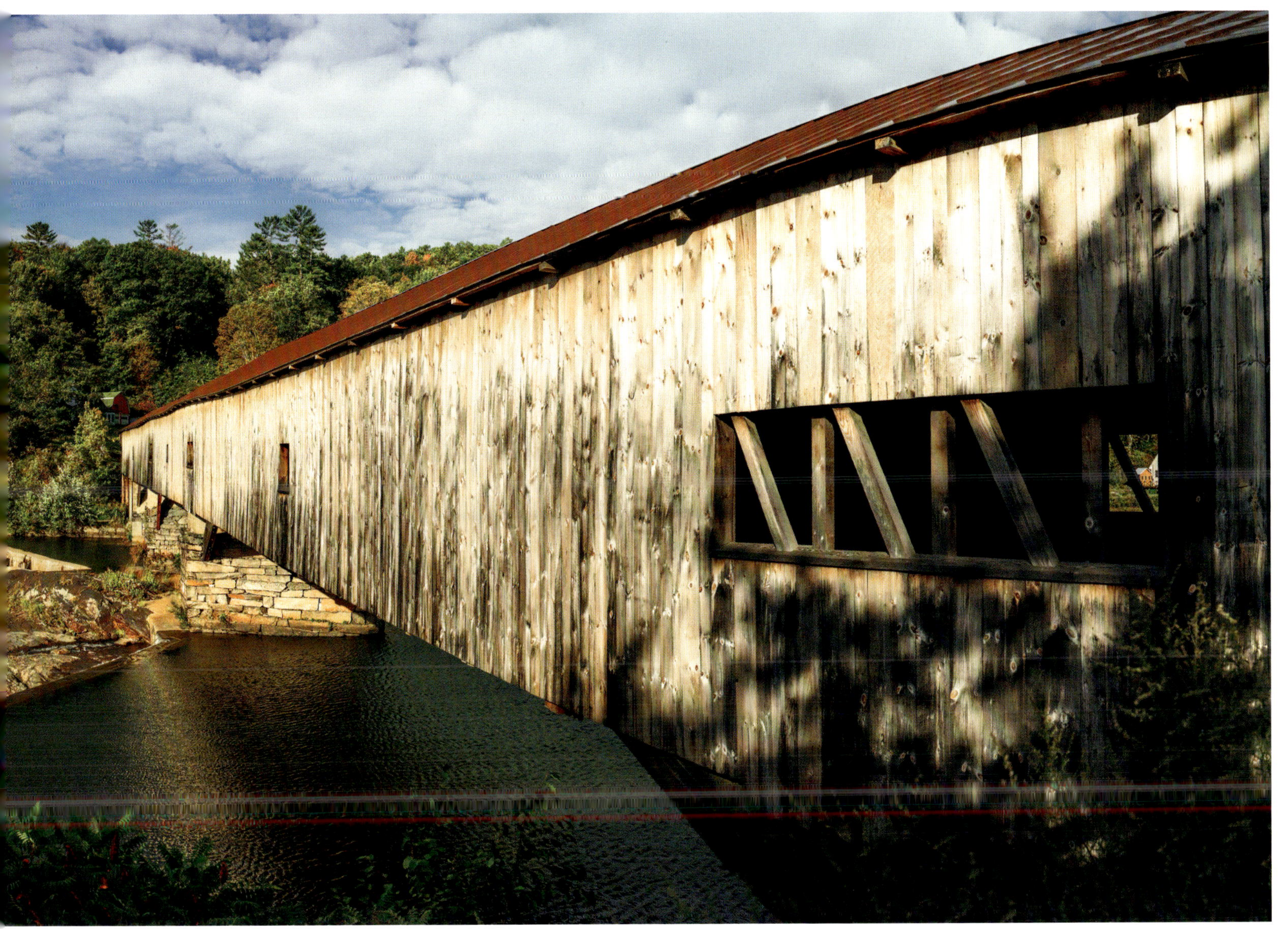

Bath Bridge, New Hampshire, 1832

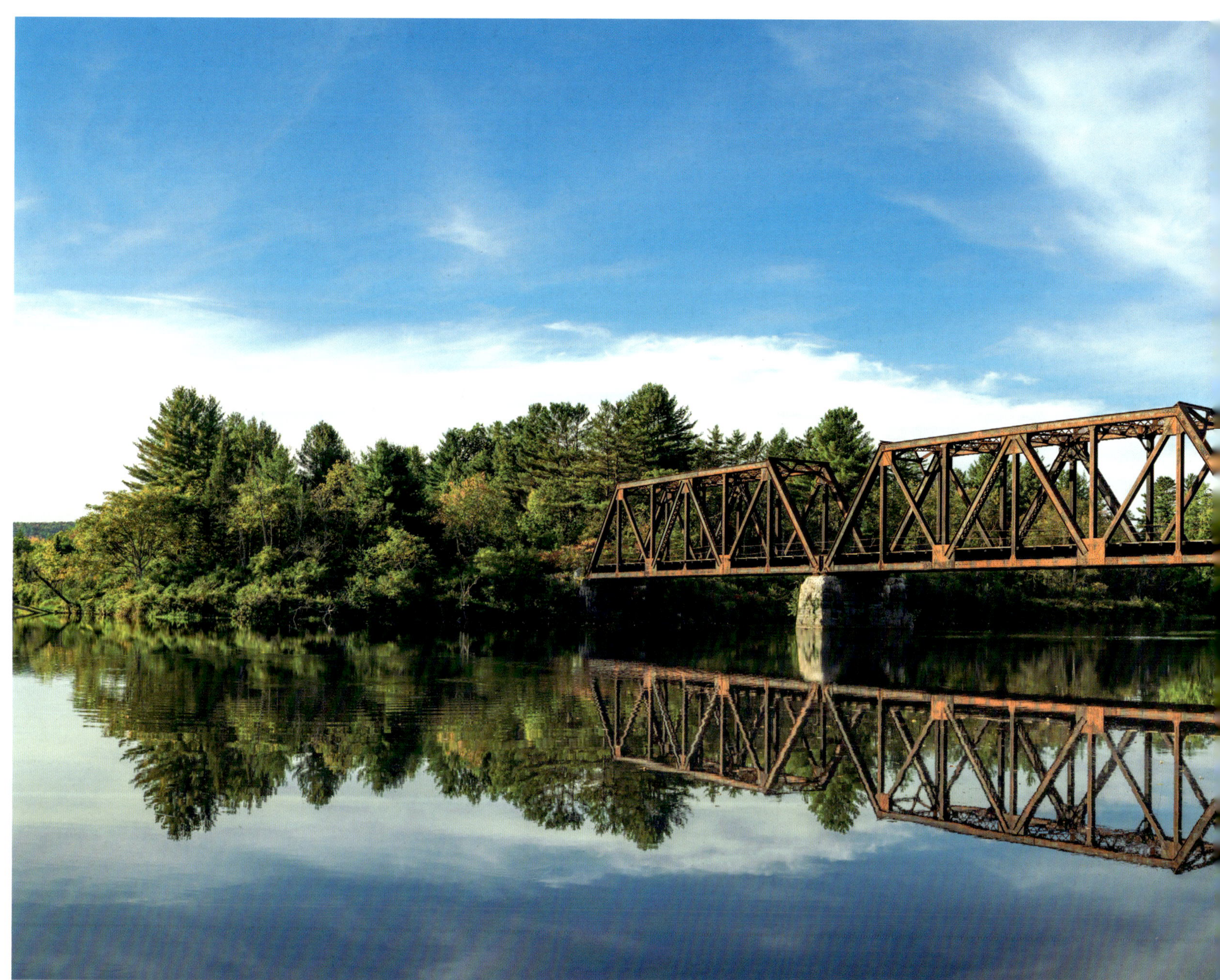

Railroad bridge over Connecticut River, New Hampshire

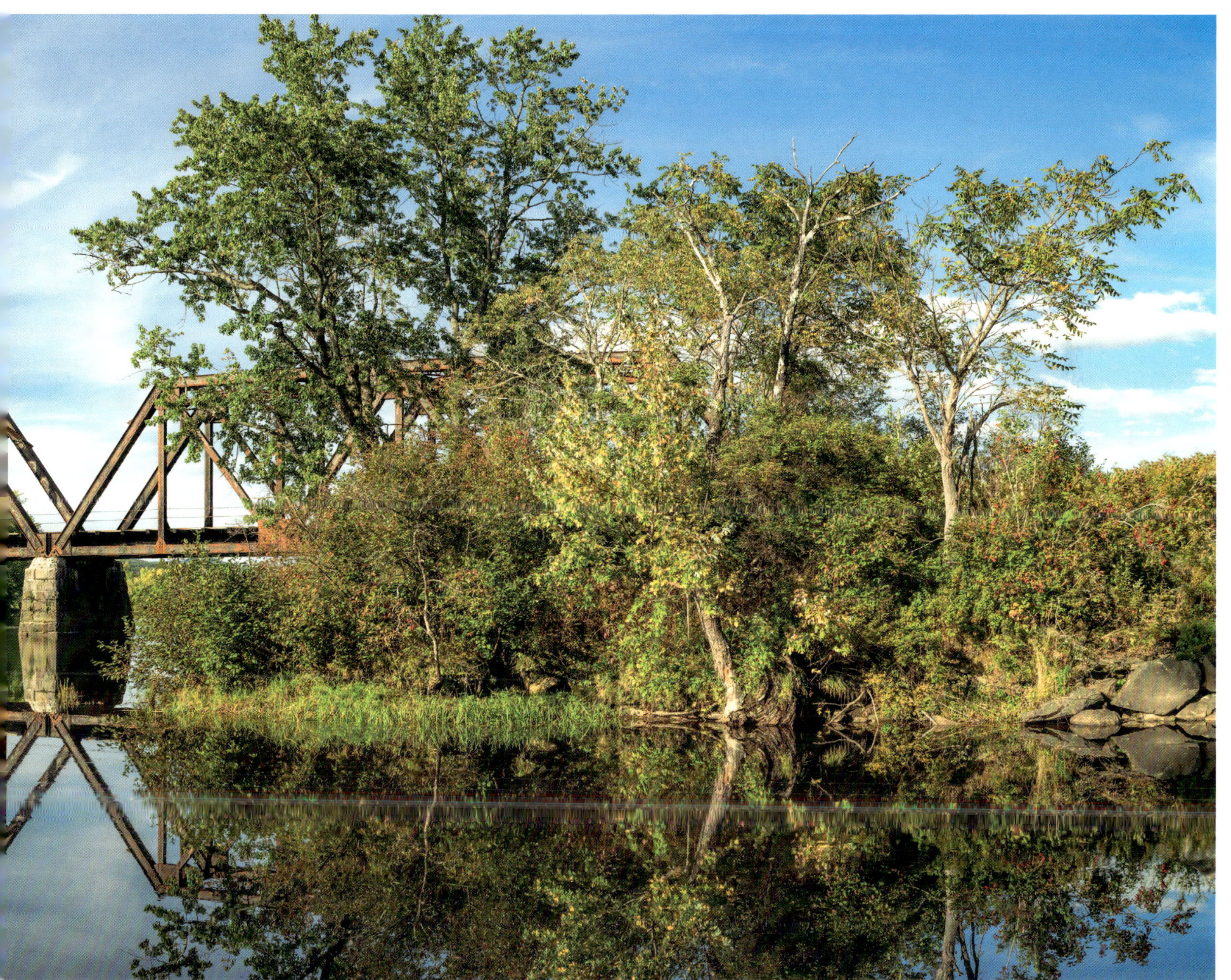

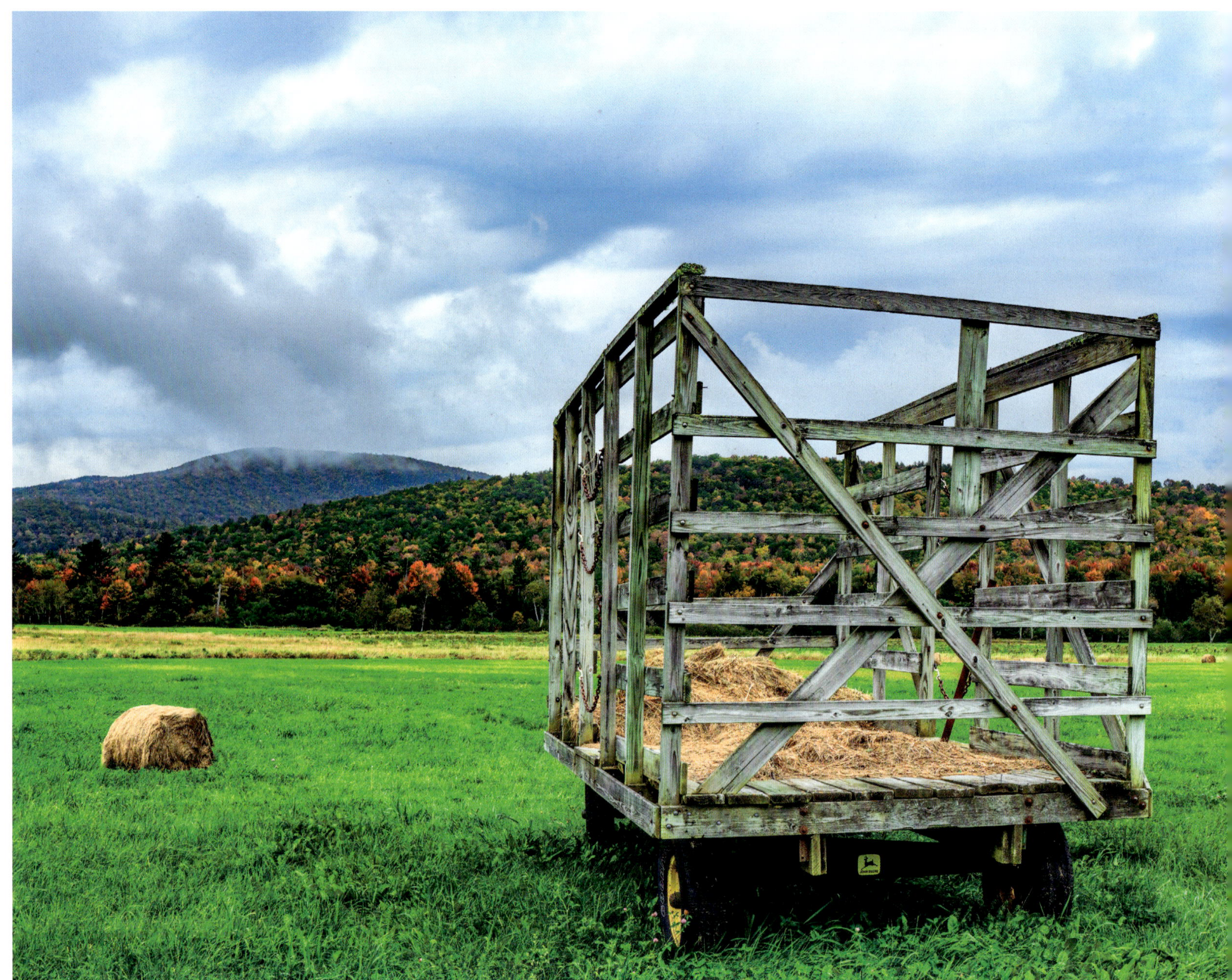

Hay truck along New Hampshire State Highway 116

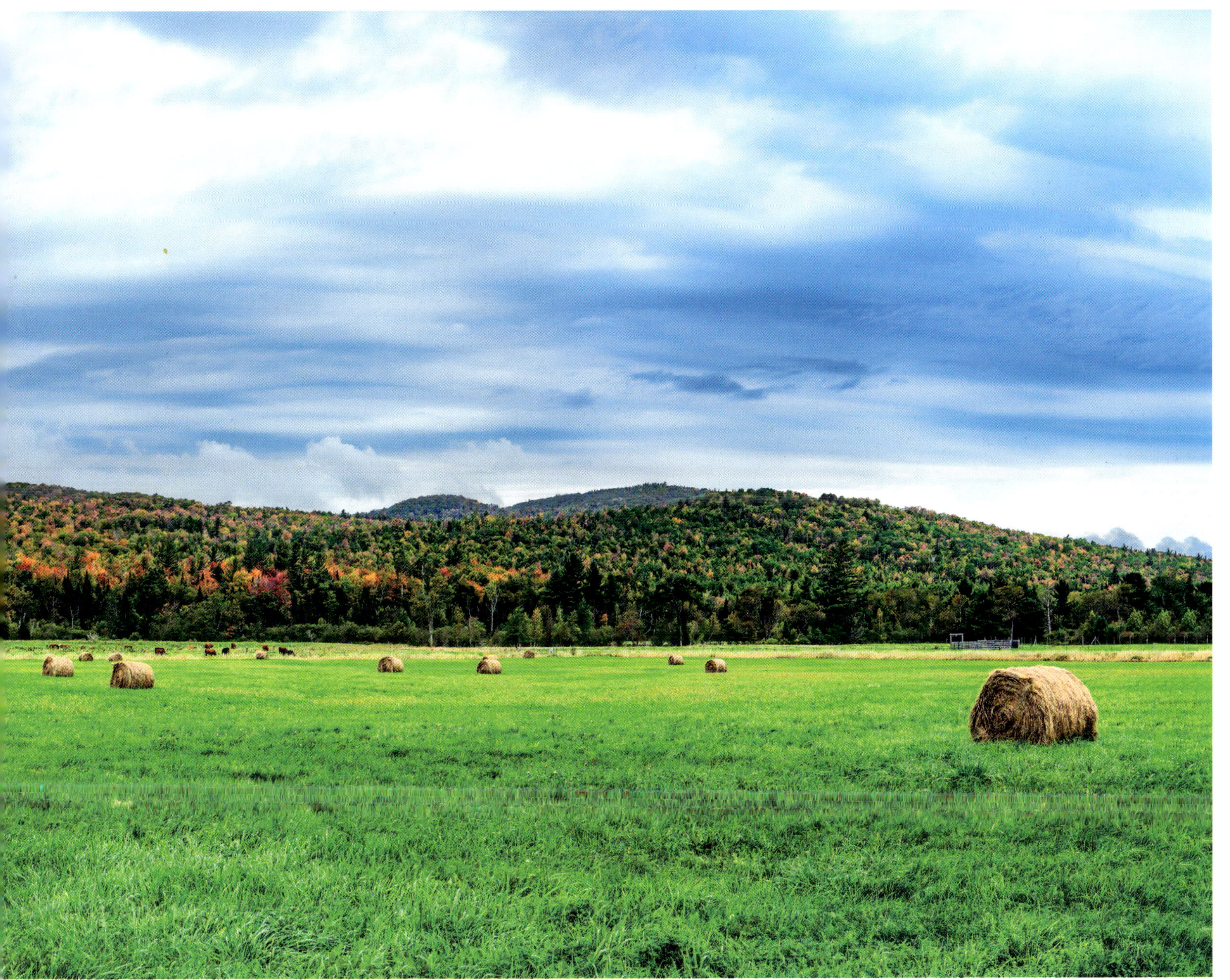

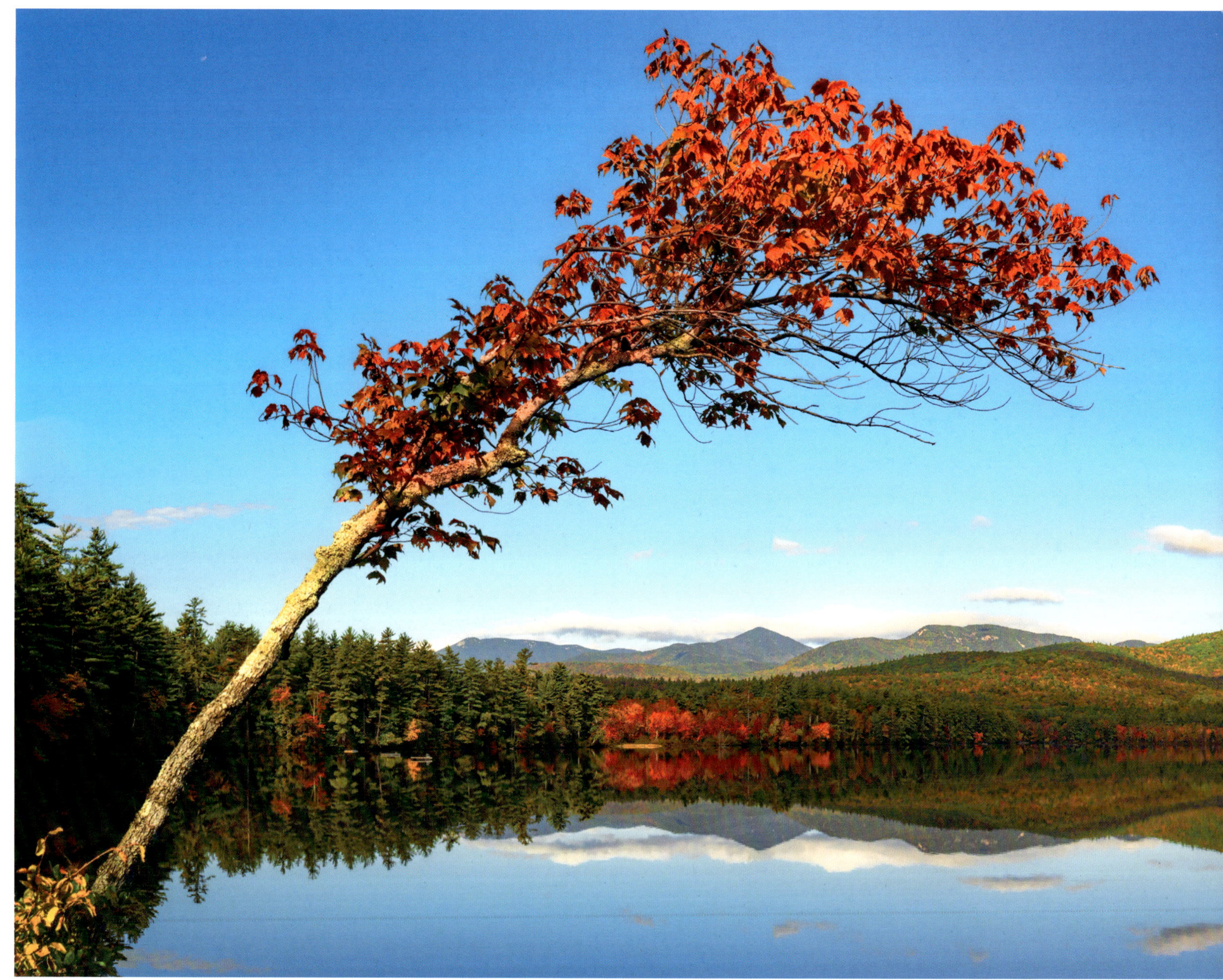

Chocorua Lake, New Hampshire

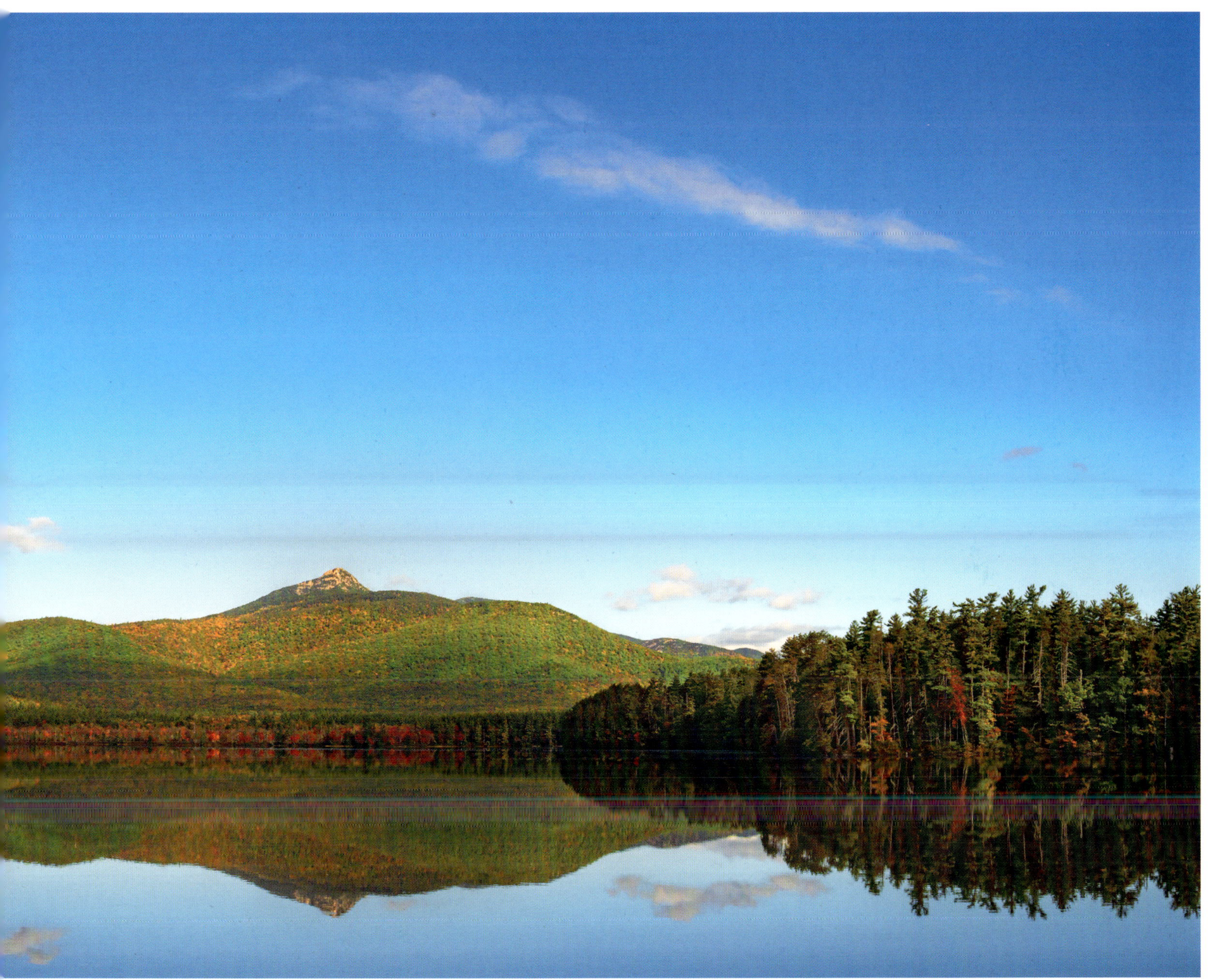

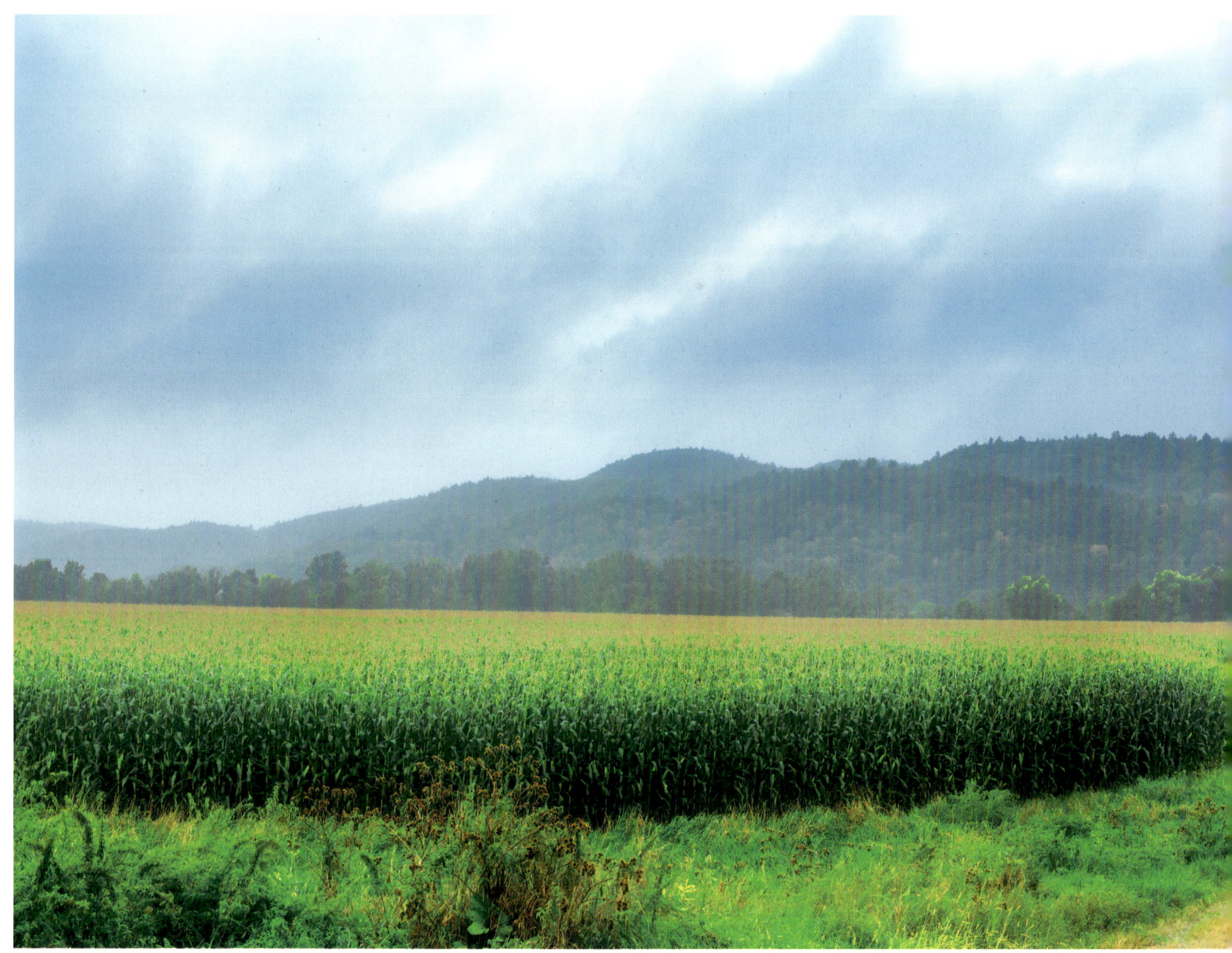

Cornfield in the pouring rain near Woodsville, New Hampshire

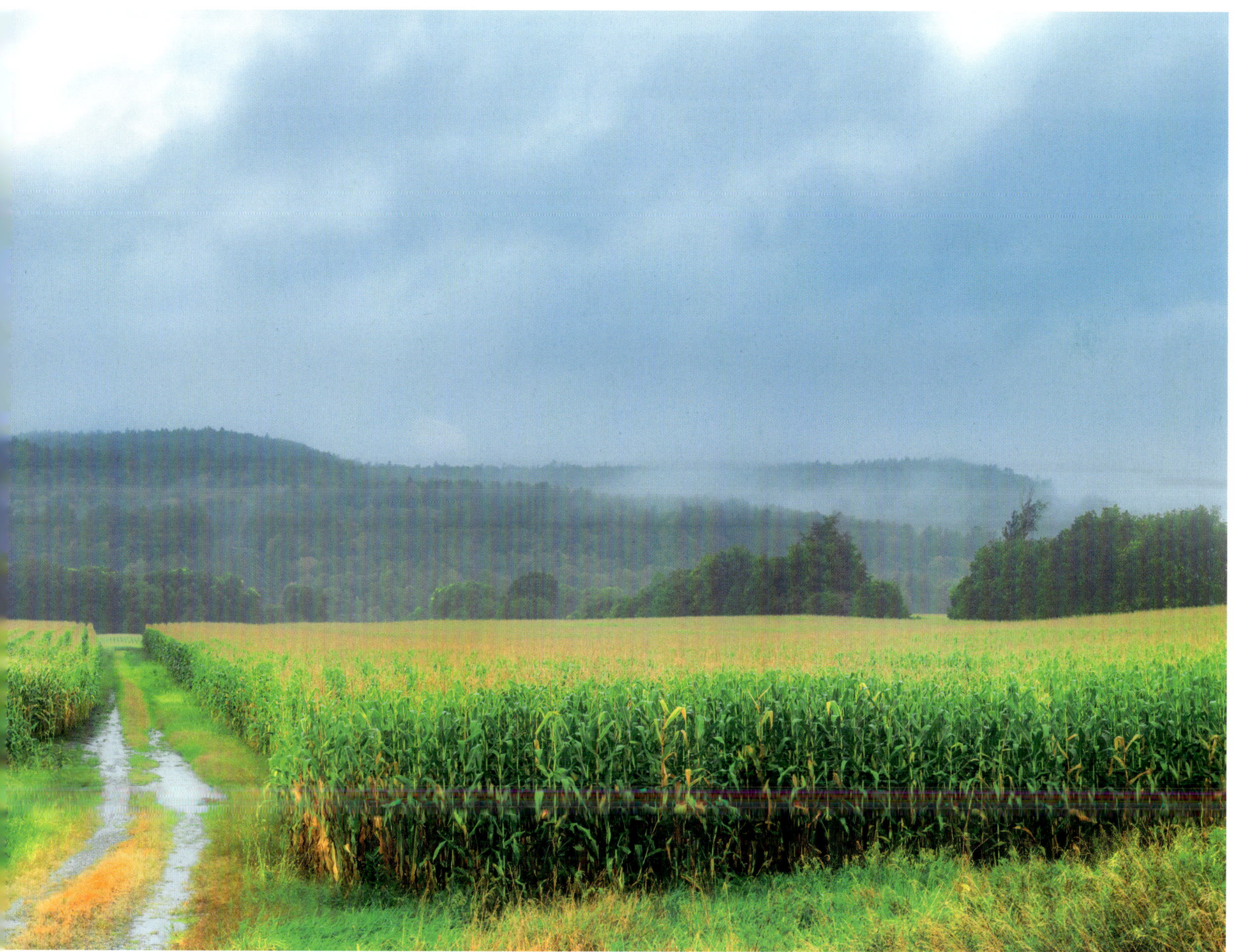

I got completely soaked taking this photo. My camera was dripping (it's okay now). It's a great memory.

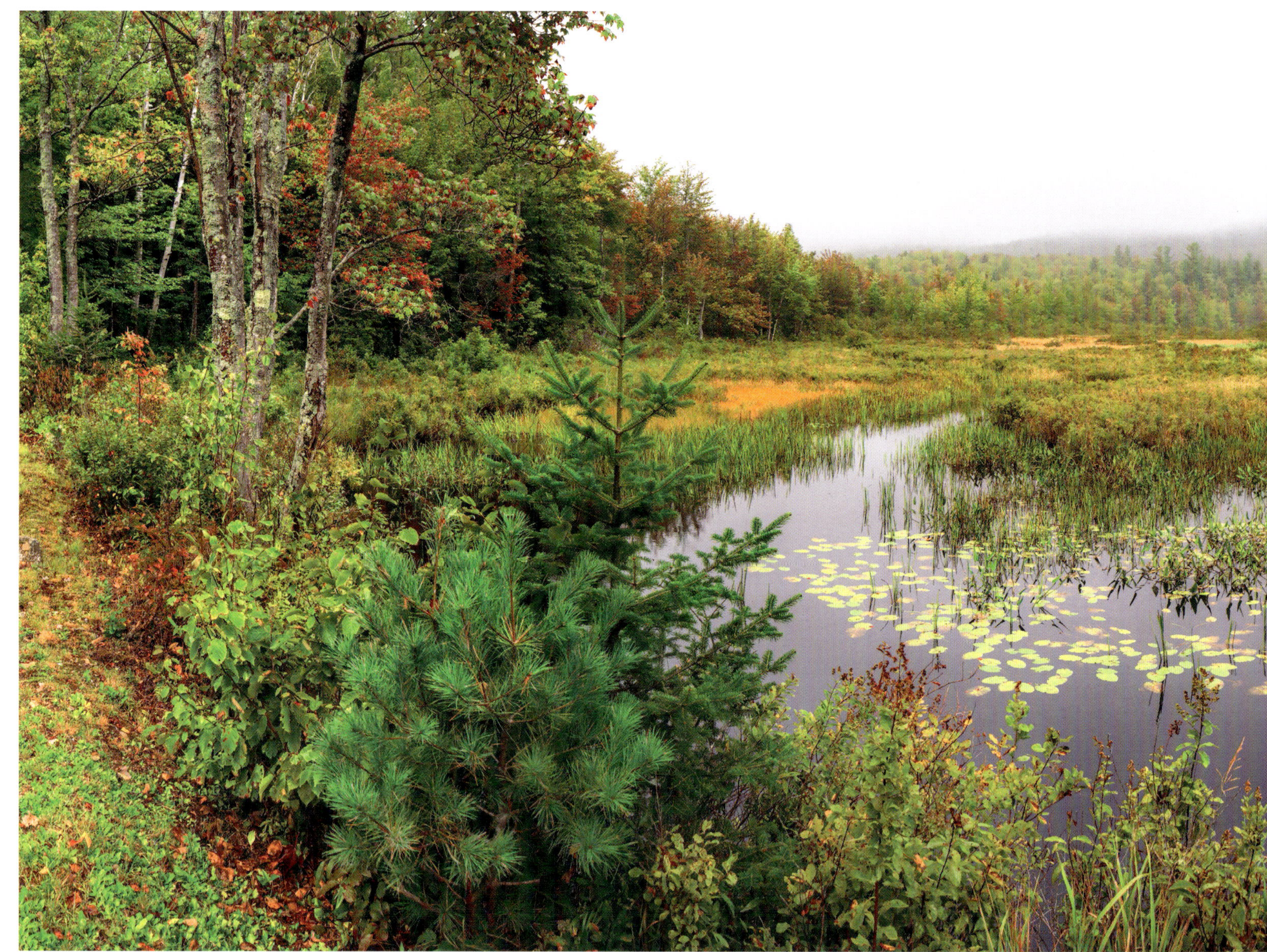

Pillsbury Lake, New Hampshire

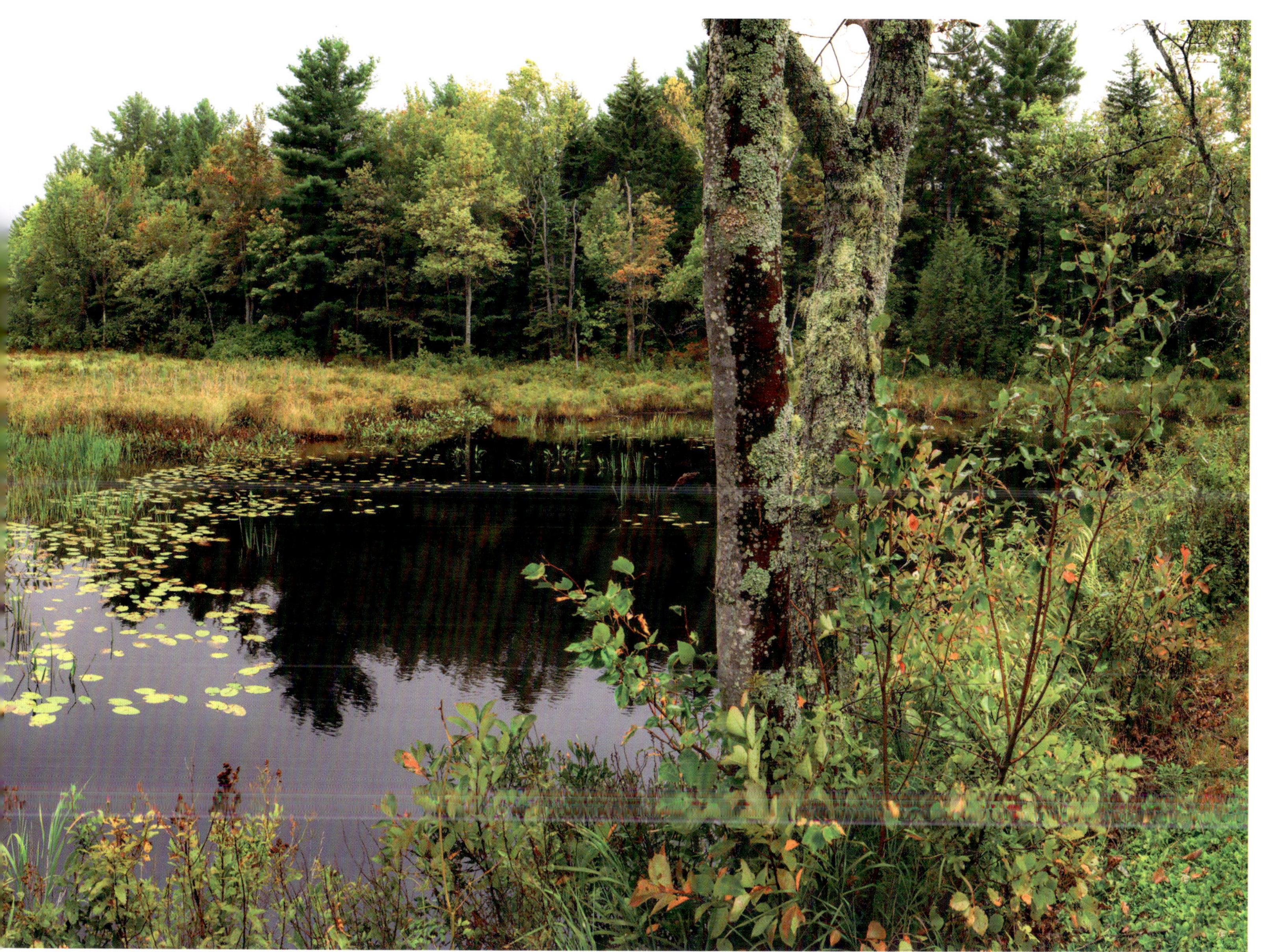

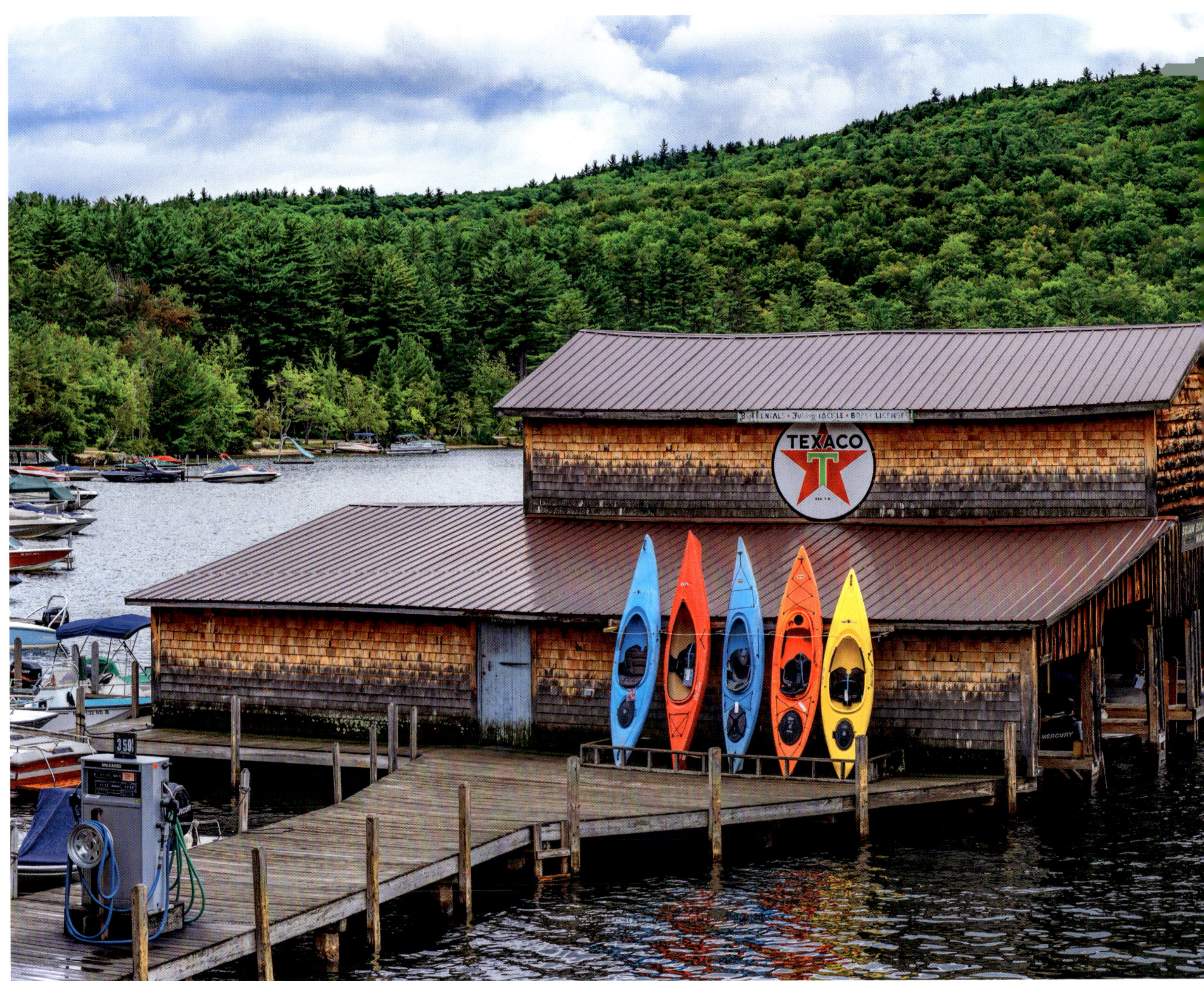

Squam Boats Marina, Squam Lake, New Hampshire

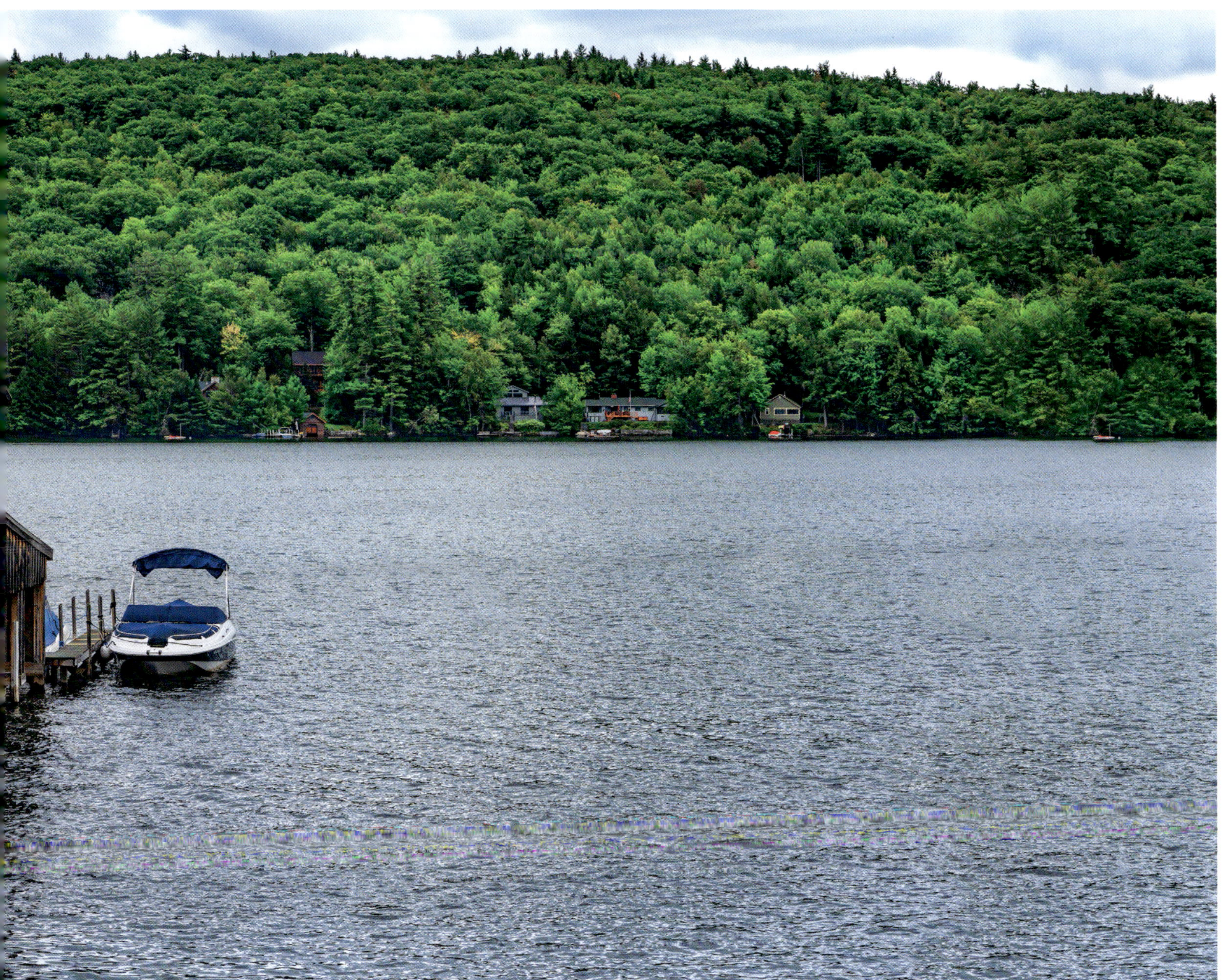

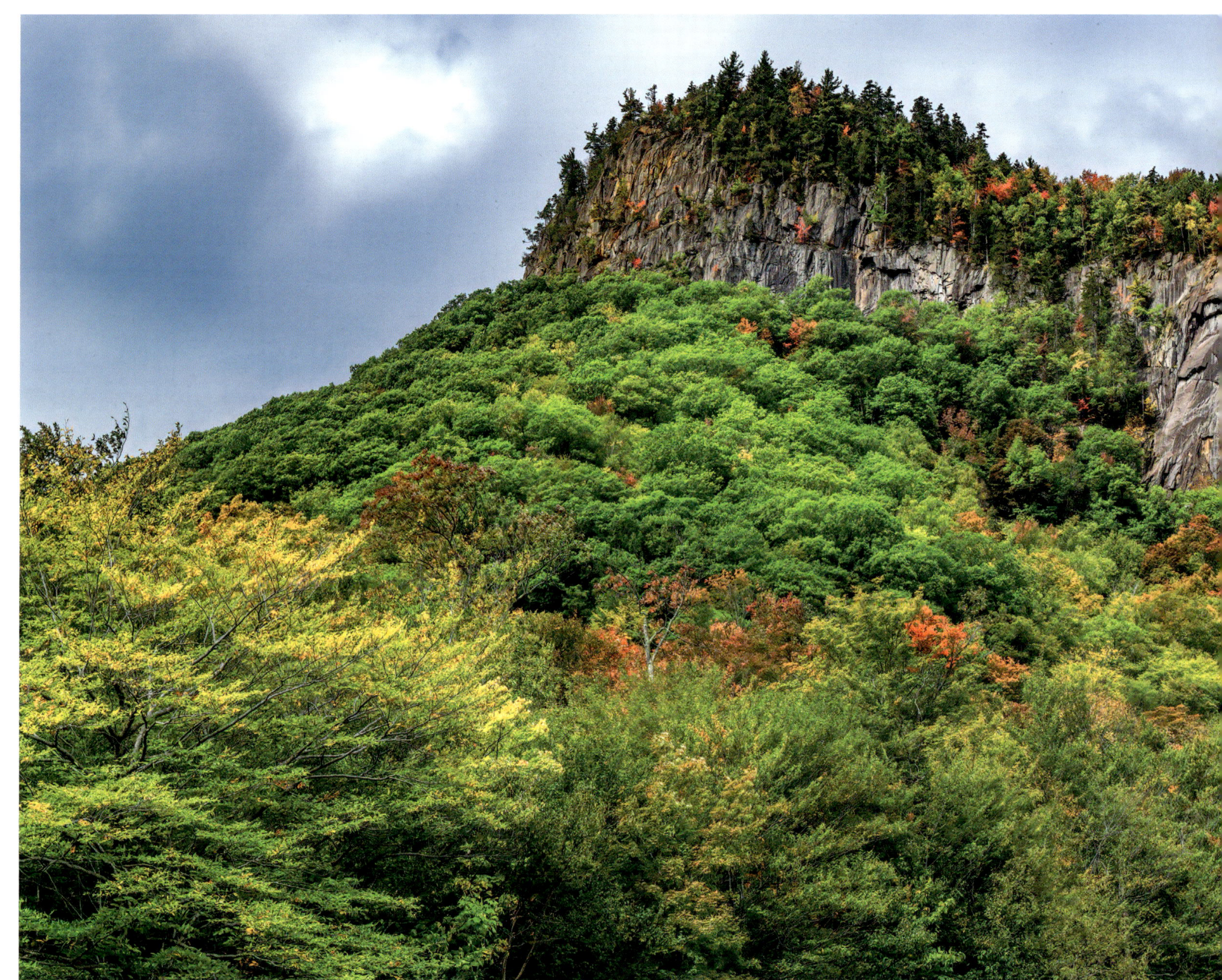

Frankenstein Cliff, White Mountains National Forest, New Hampshire

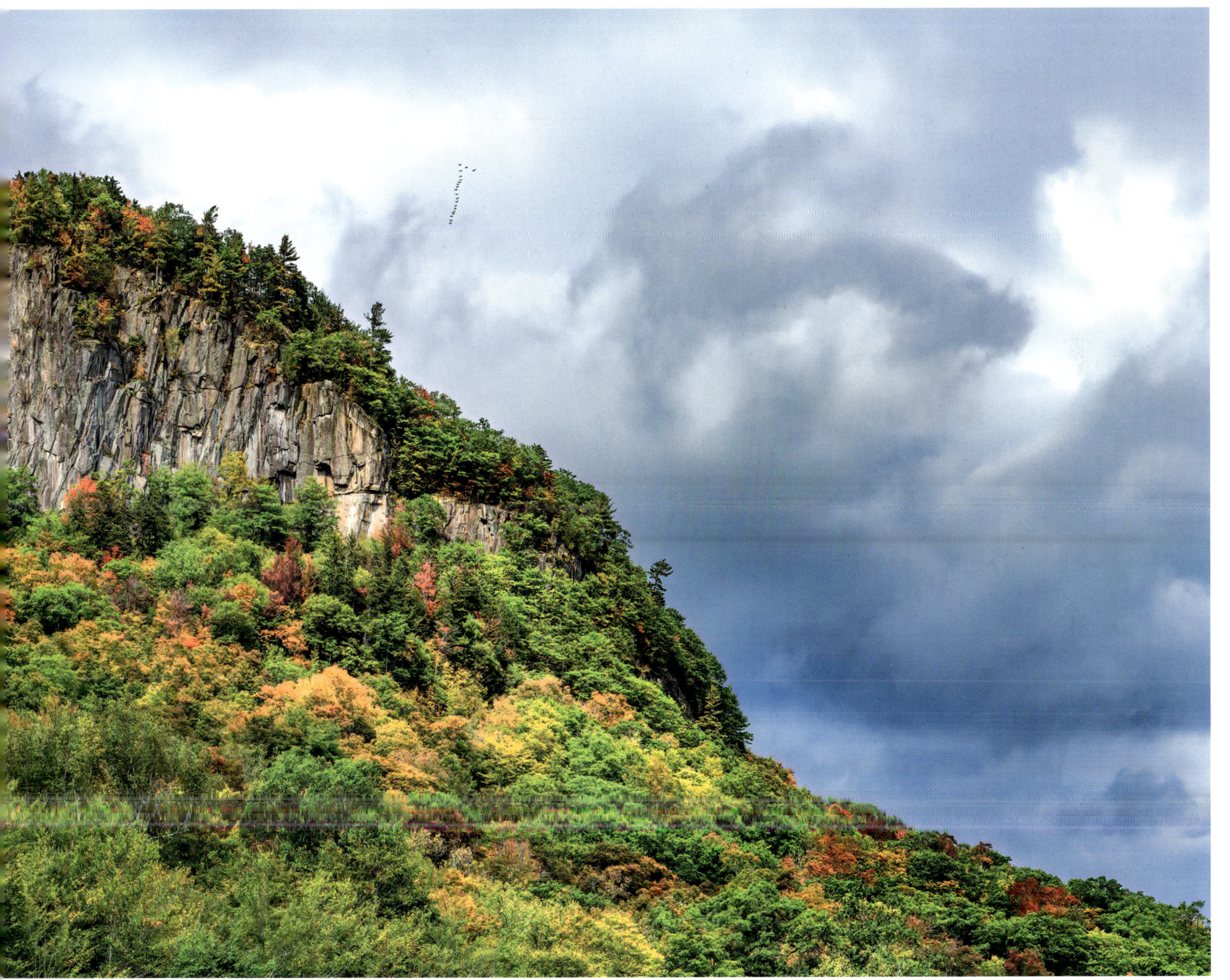

Check out the flock of birds to the right of the mountain. They came by just as I was ready to take the photograph.

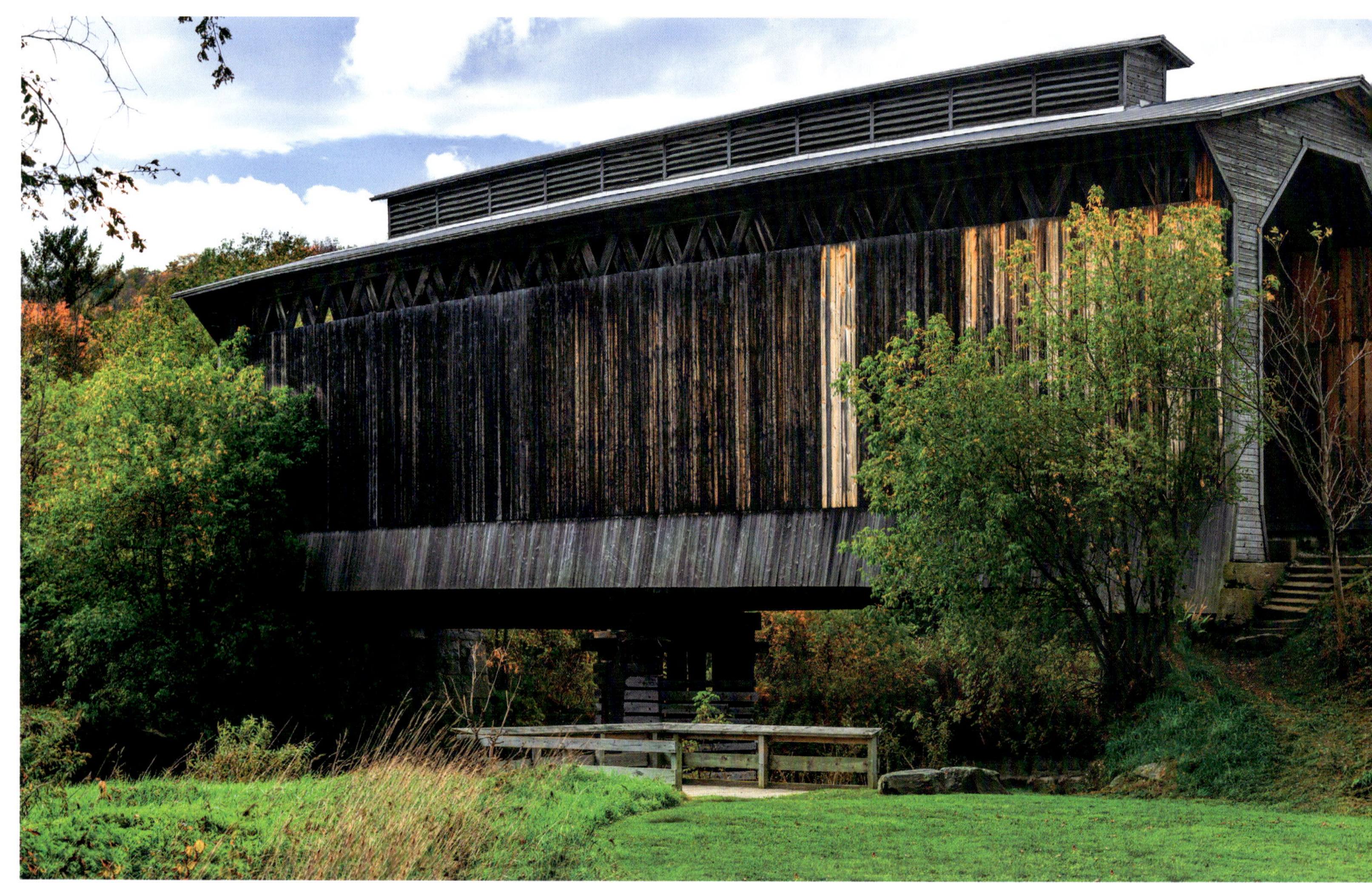

Fisher Bridge, Vermont, 1908

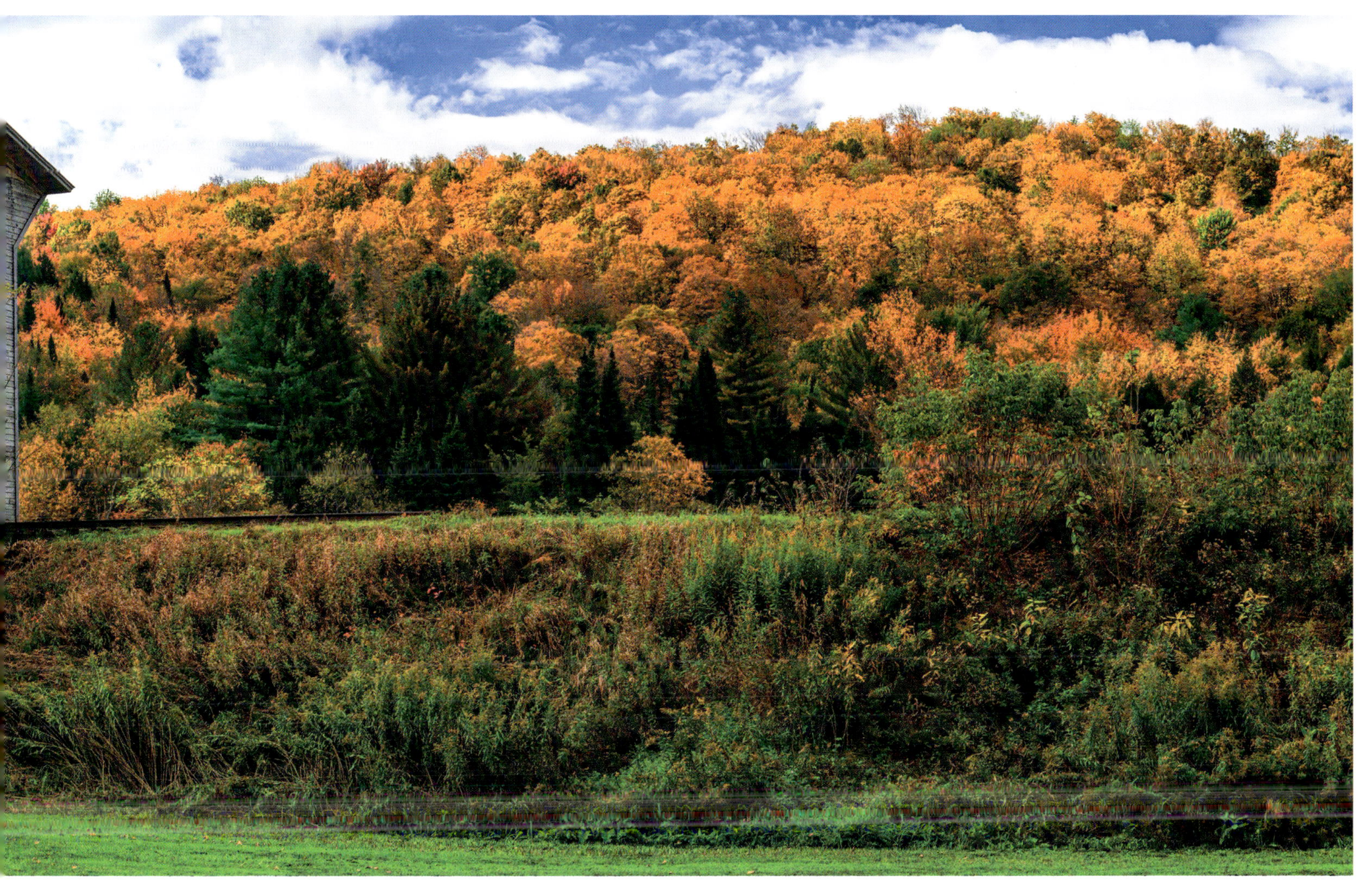

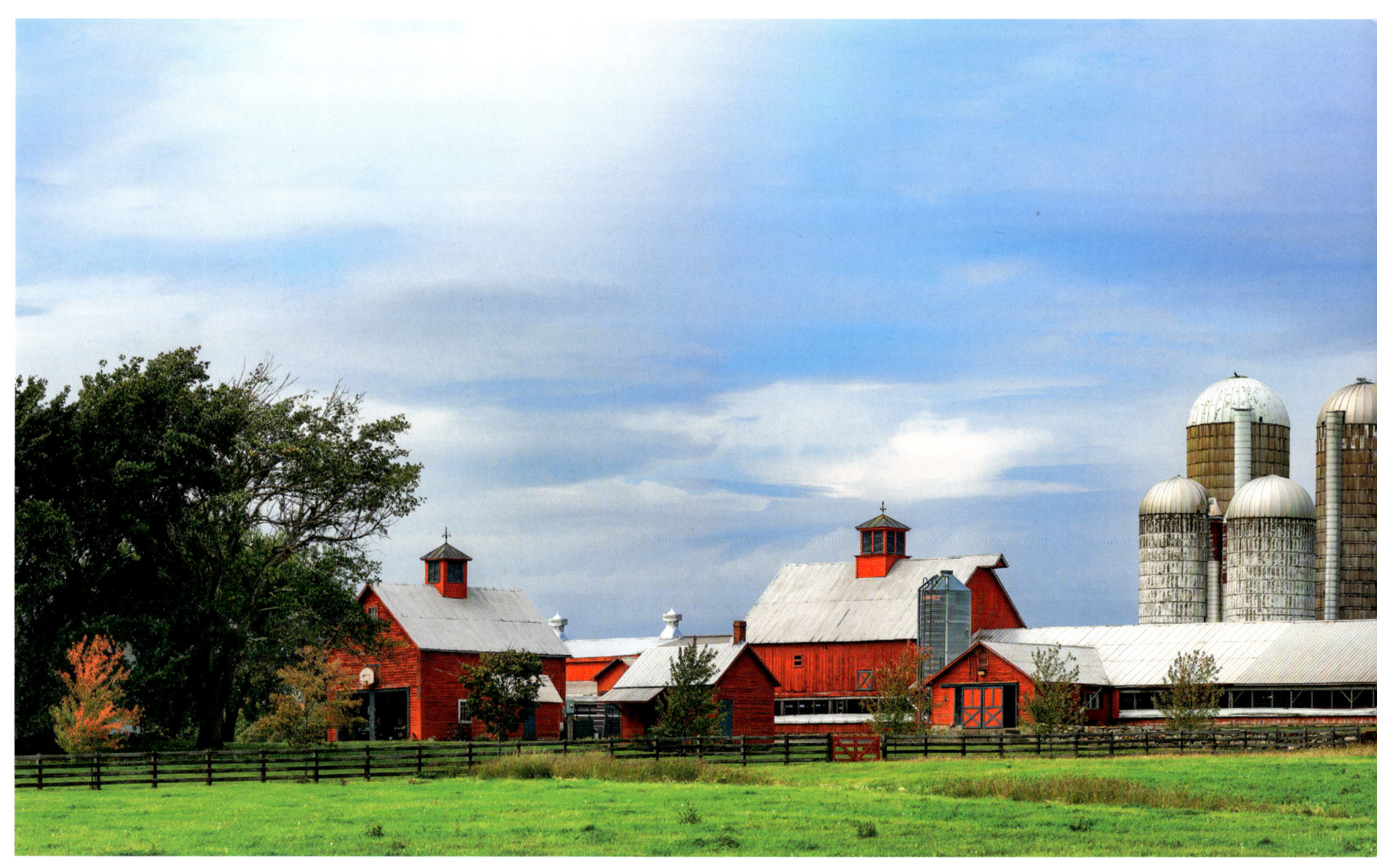

Farm along Vermont State Highway 125

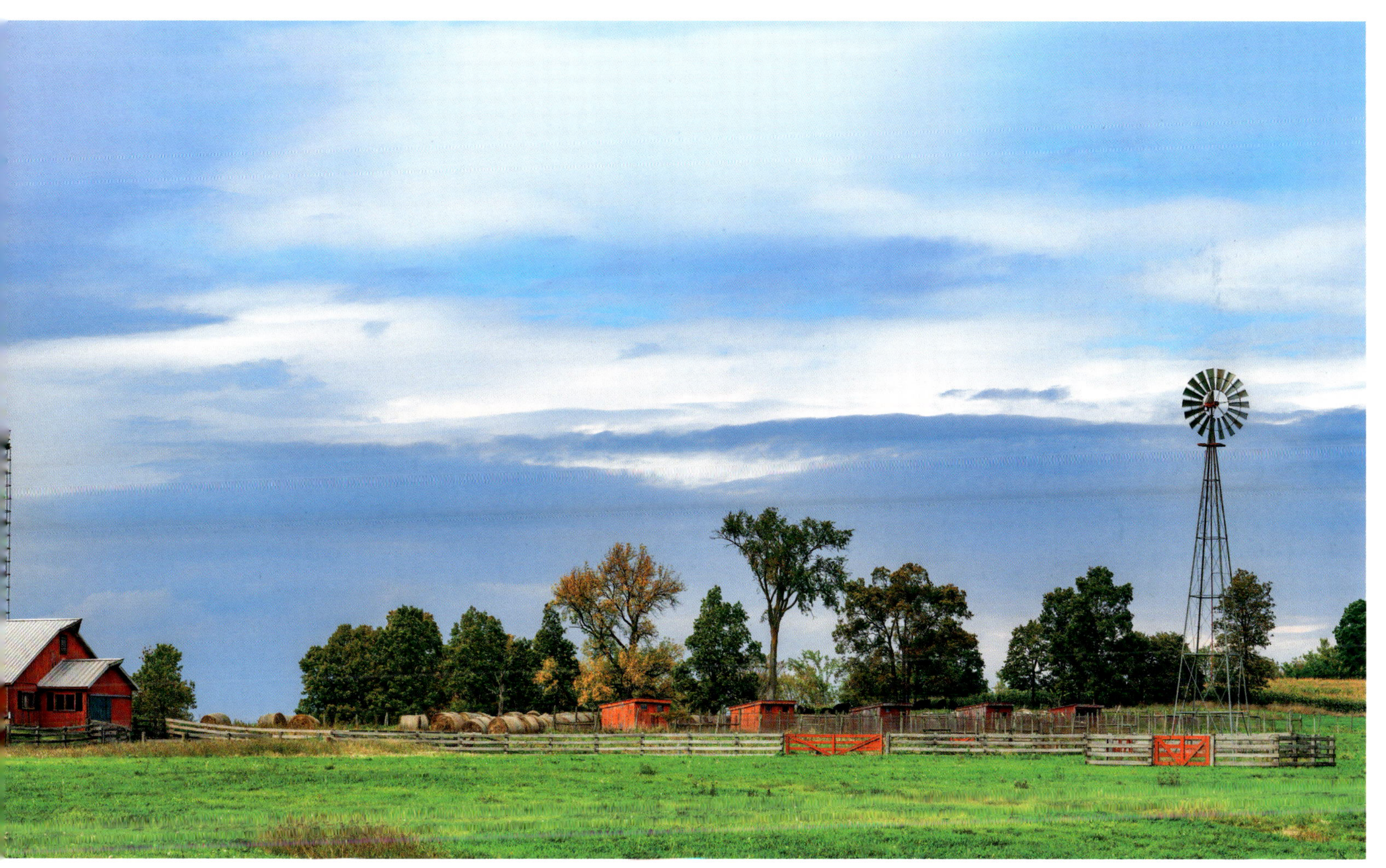

My favorite thing in this photo is the basketball hoop. For me it makes it "home."

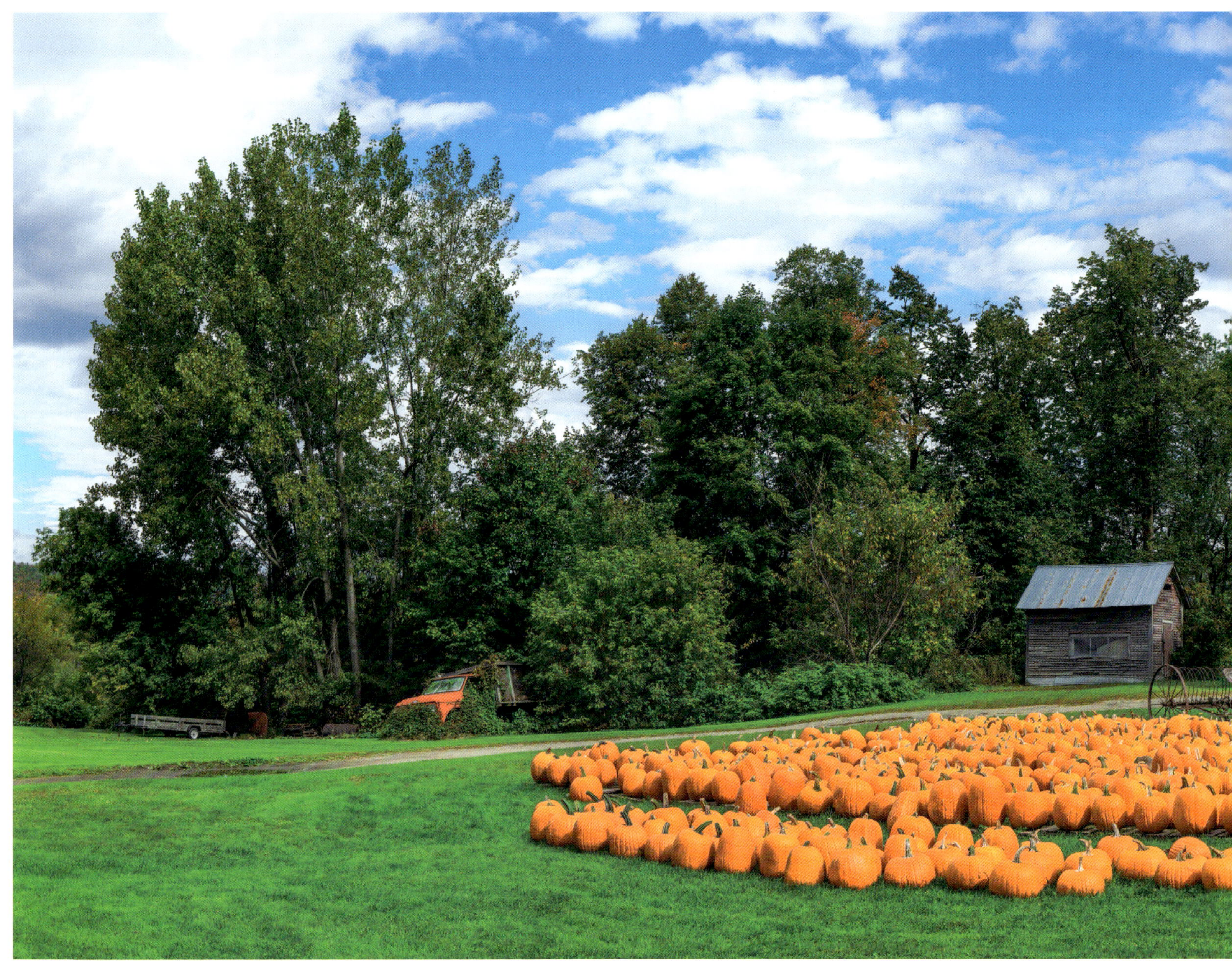

Pumpkin stand, Jeffersonville, Vermont

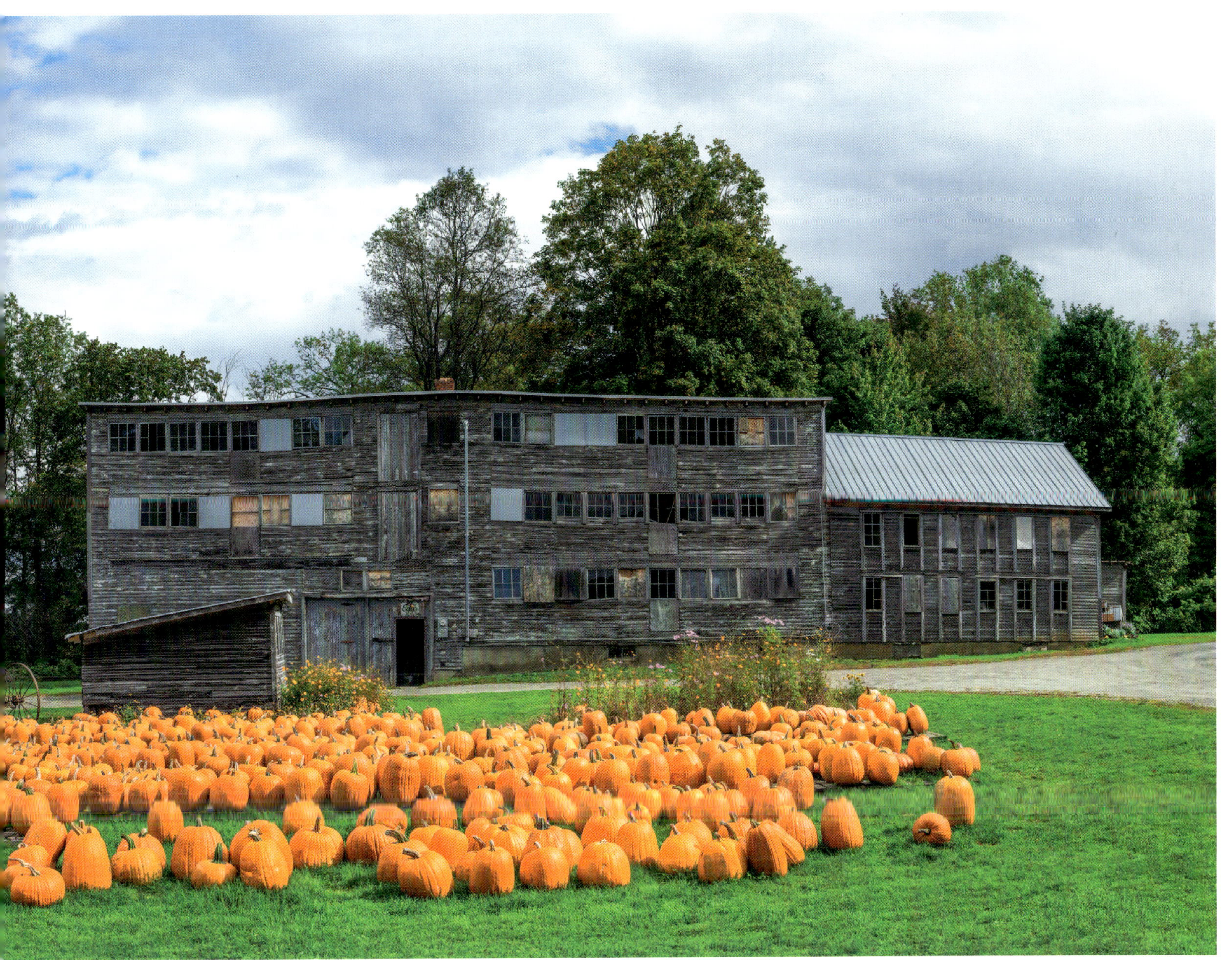

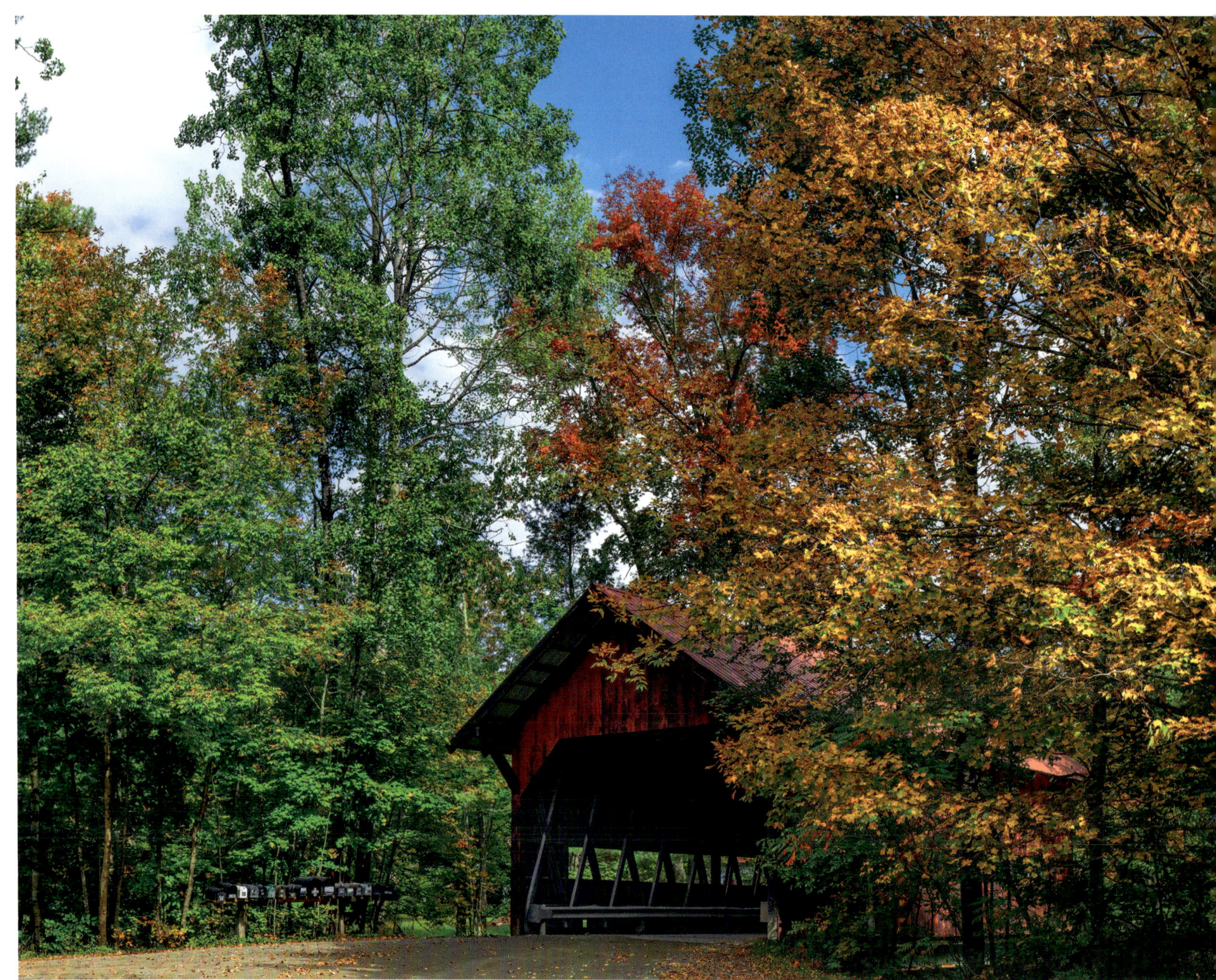

Brookdale Bridge, Stowe, Vermont

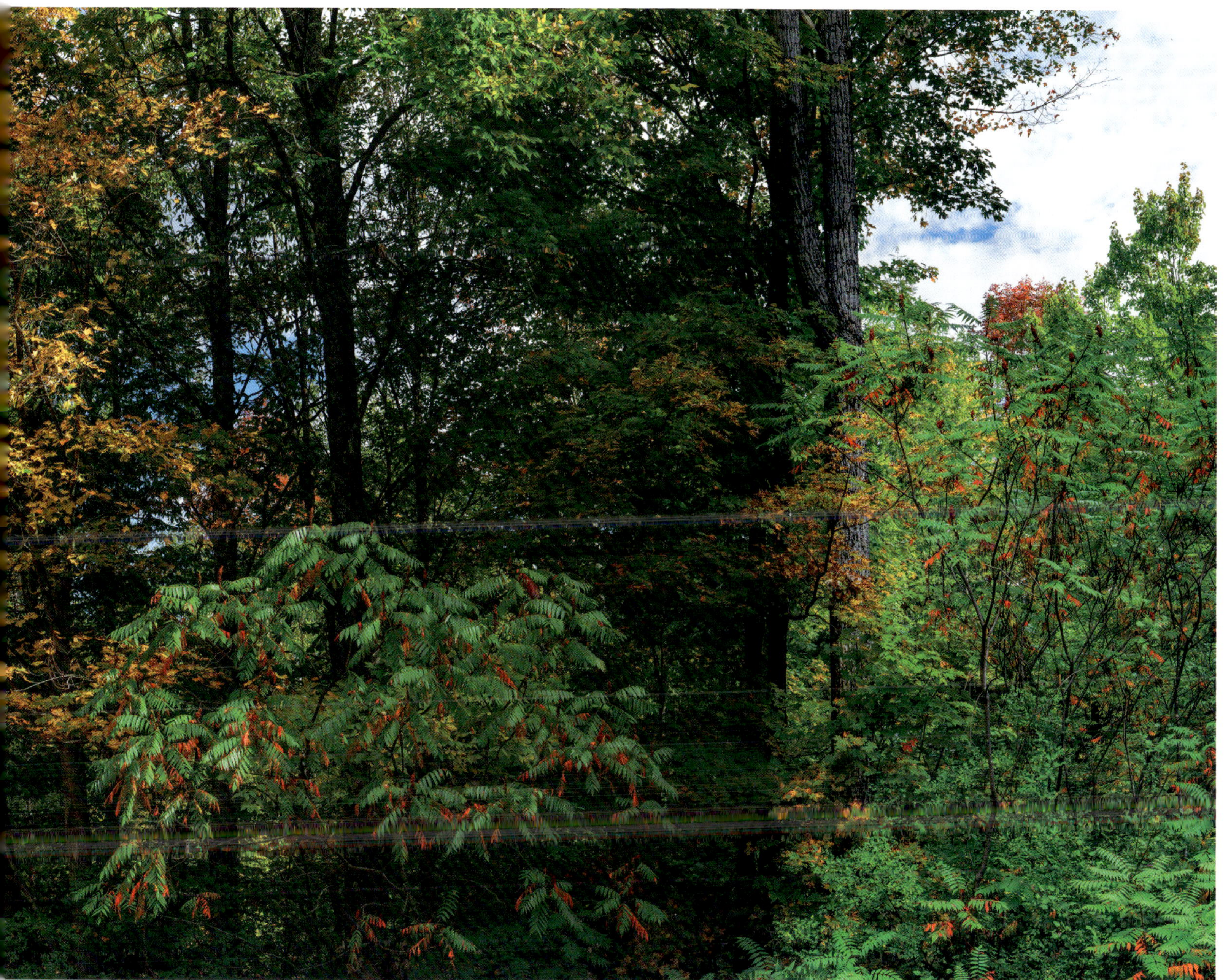

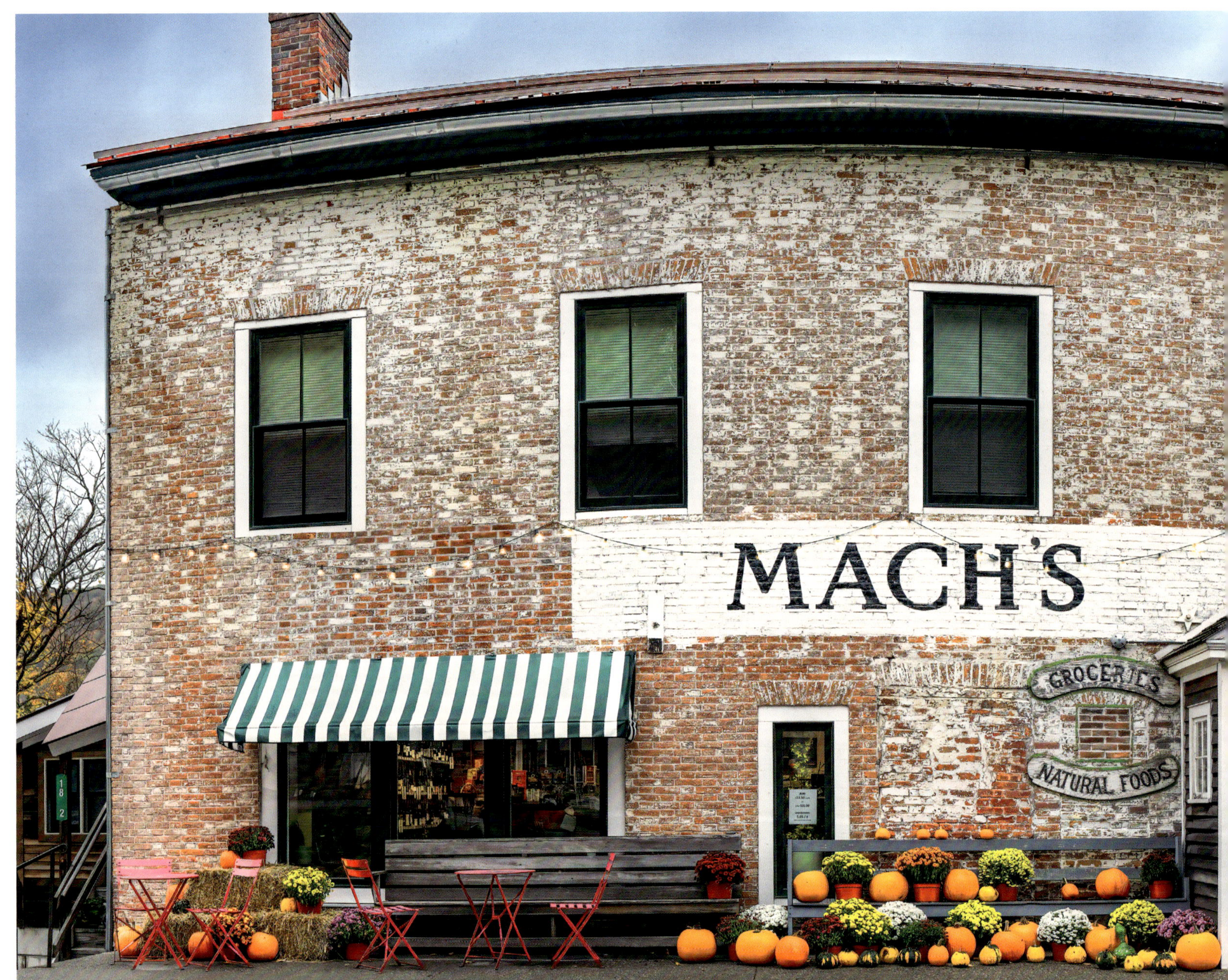

Mach's Market, Pawlet, Vermont

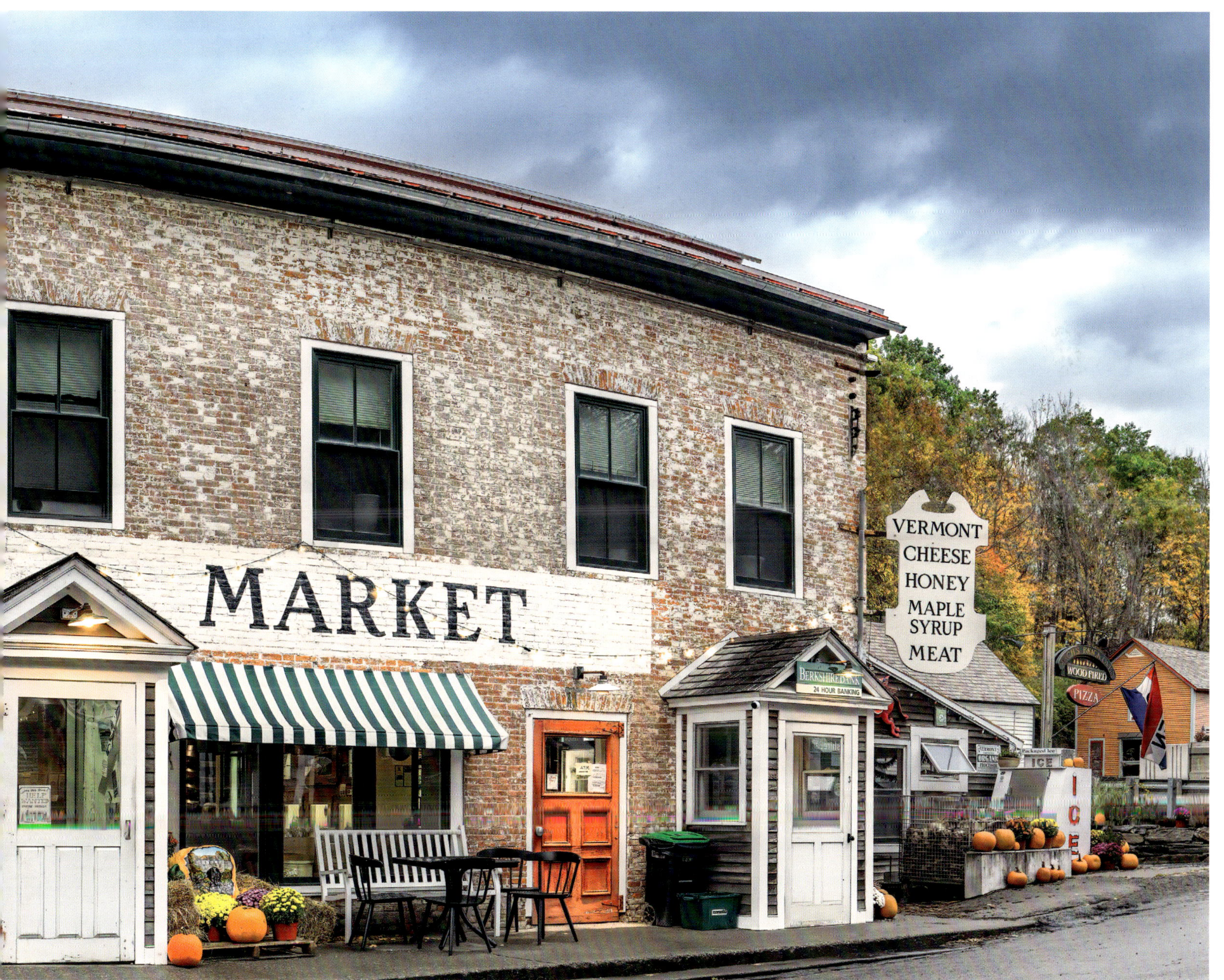

The food here is fantastic! Try the pizza and the crab cakes!

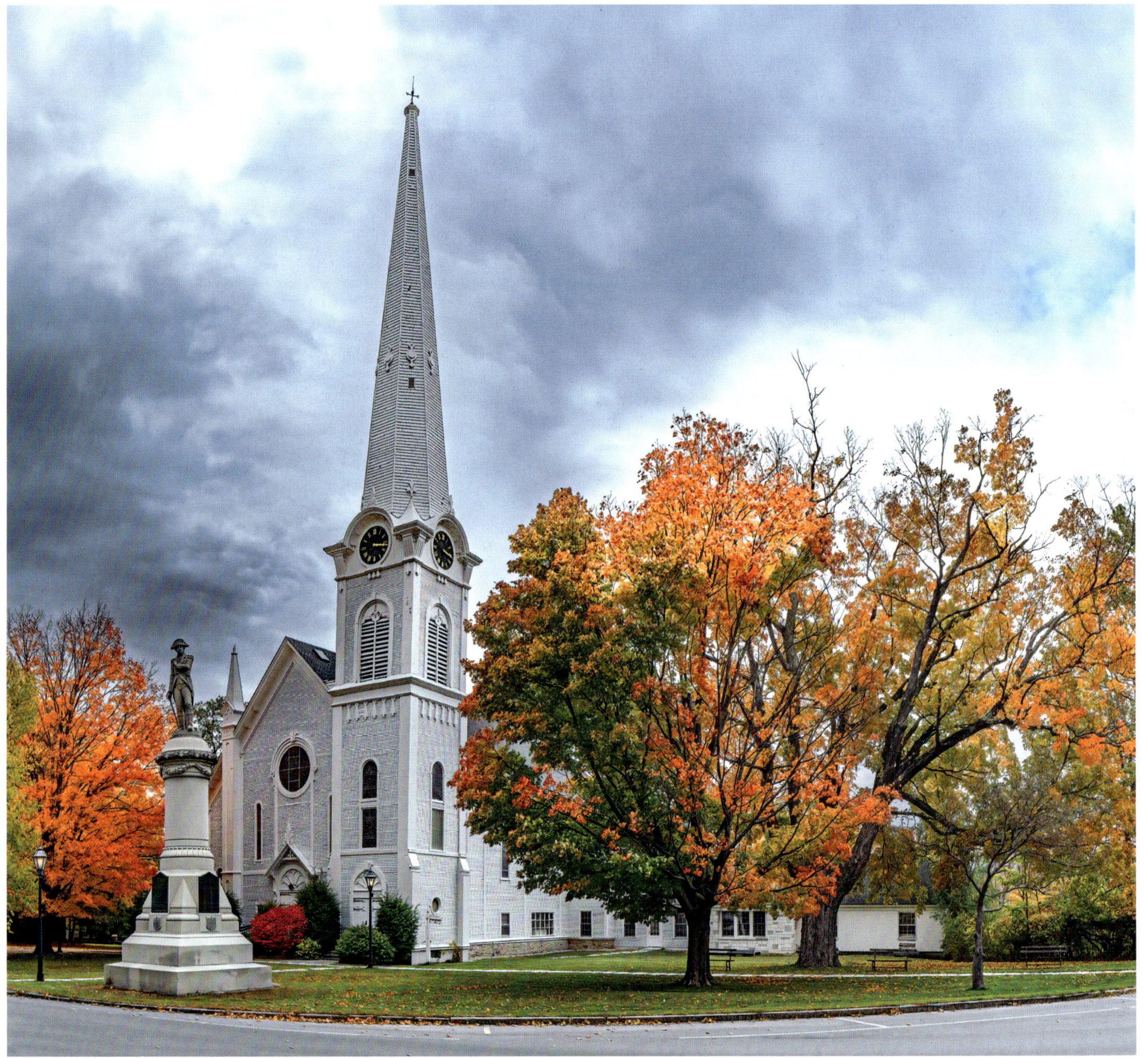

First Congregational Church, Manchester, Vermont

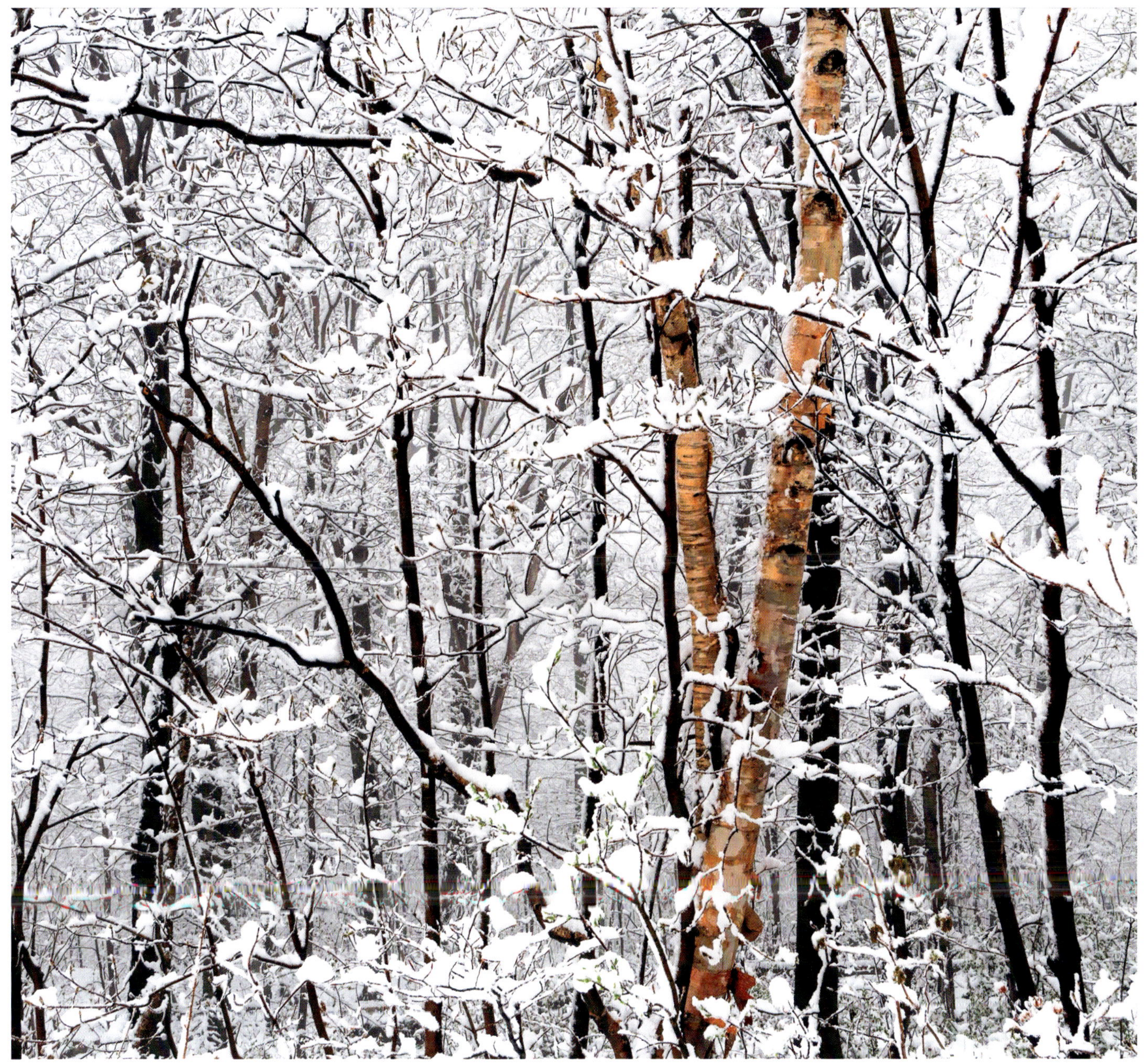

Snowy trees near Swanton, Vermont

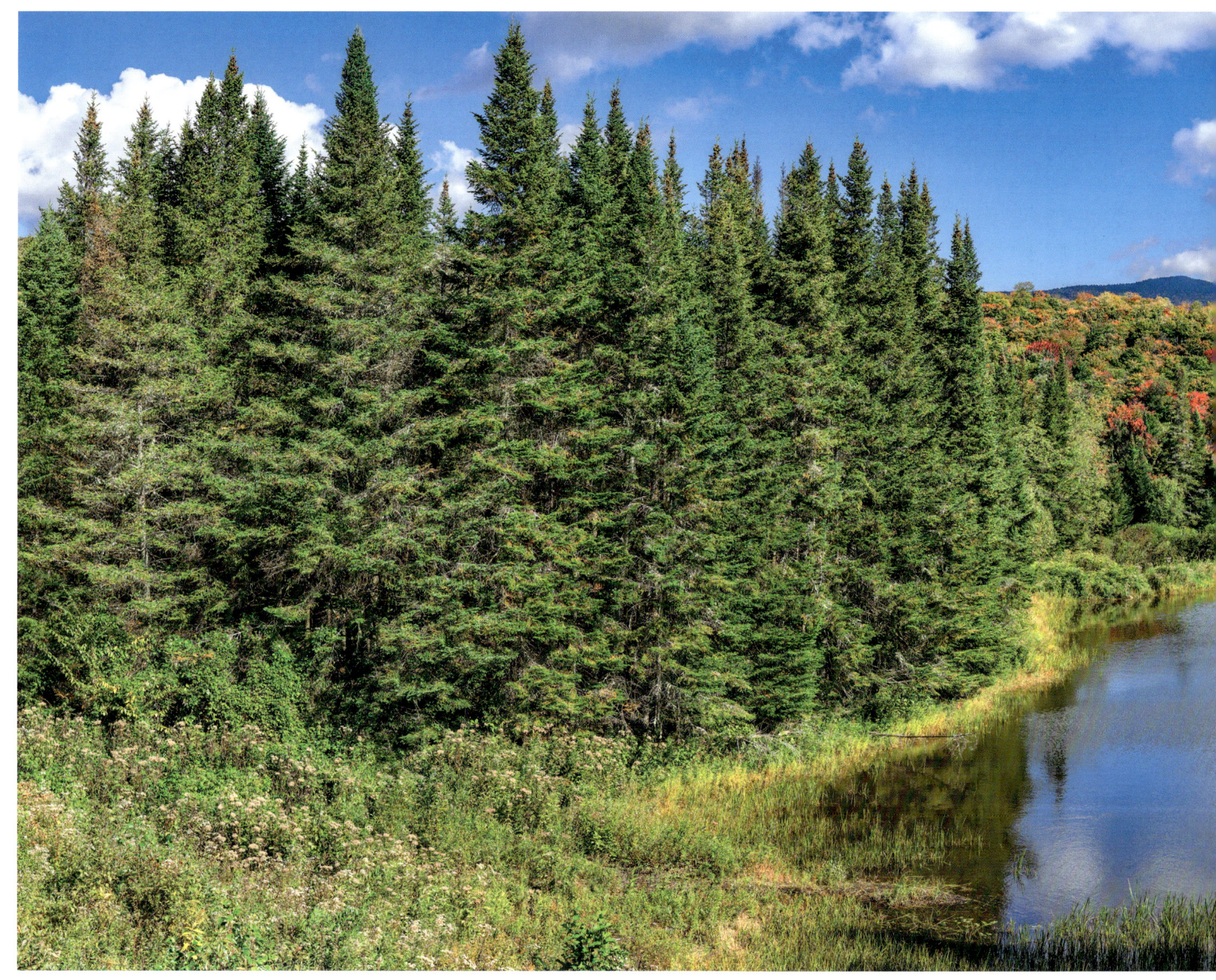

Belvidere Mountain, Vermont

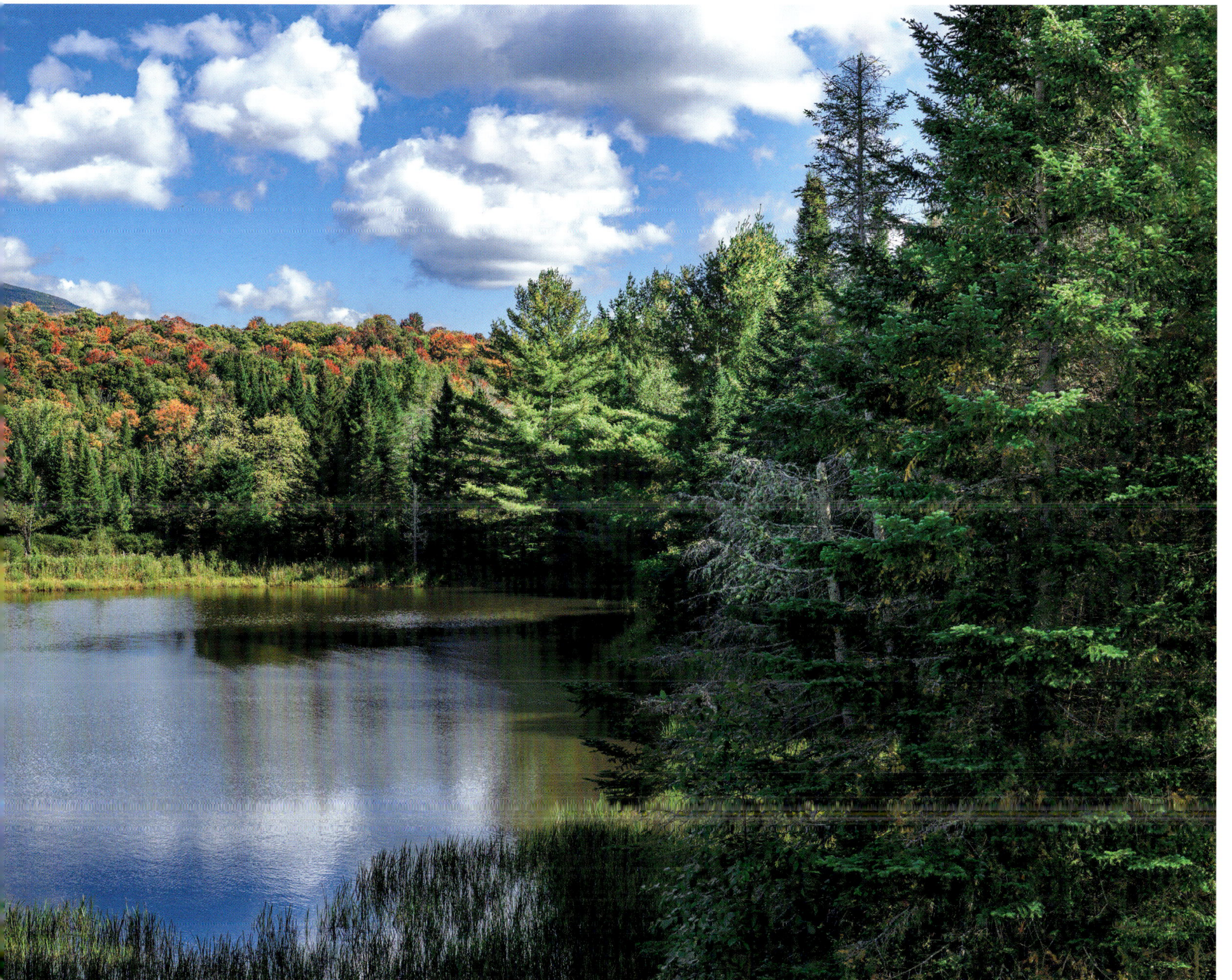

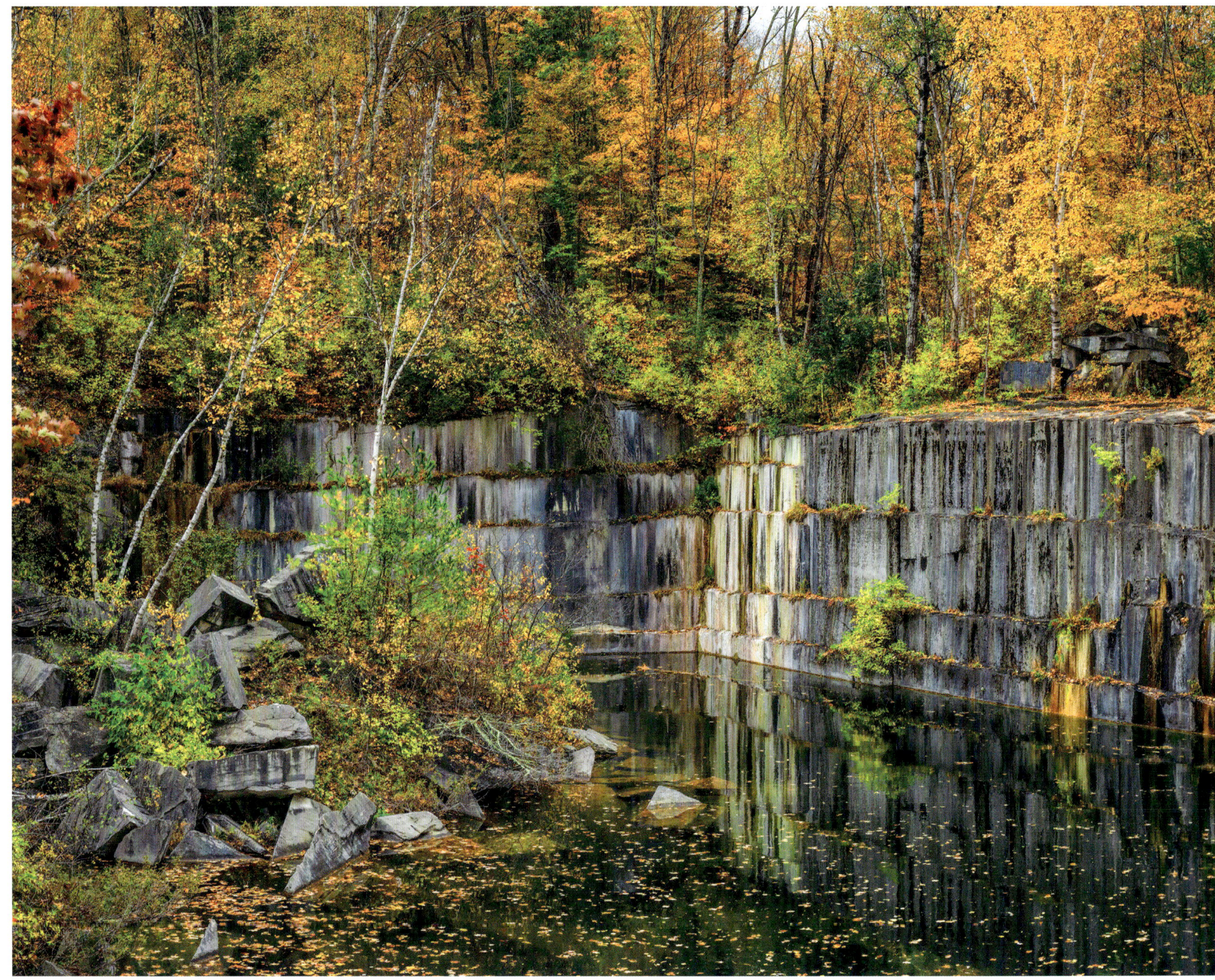

Dorset Marble Quarry, Vermont

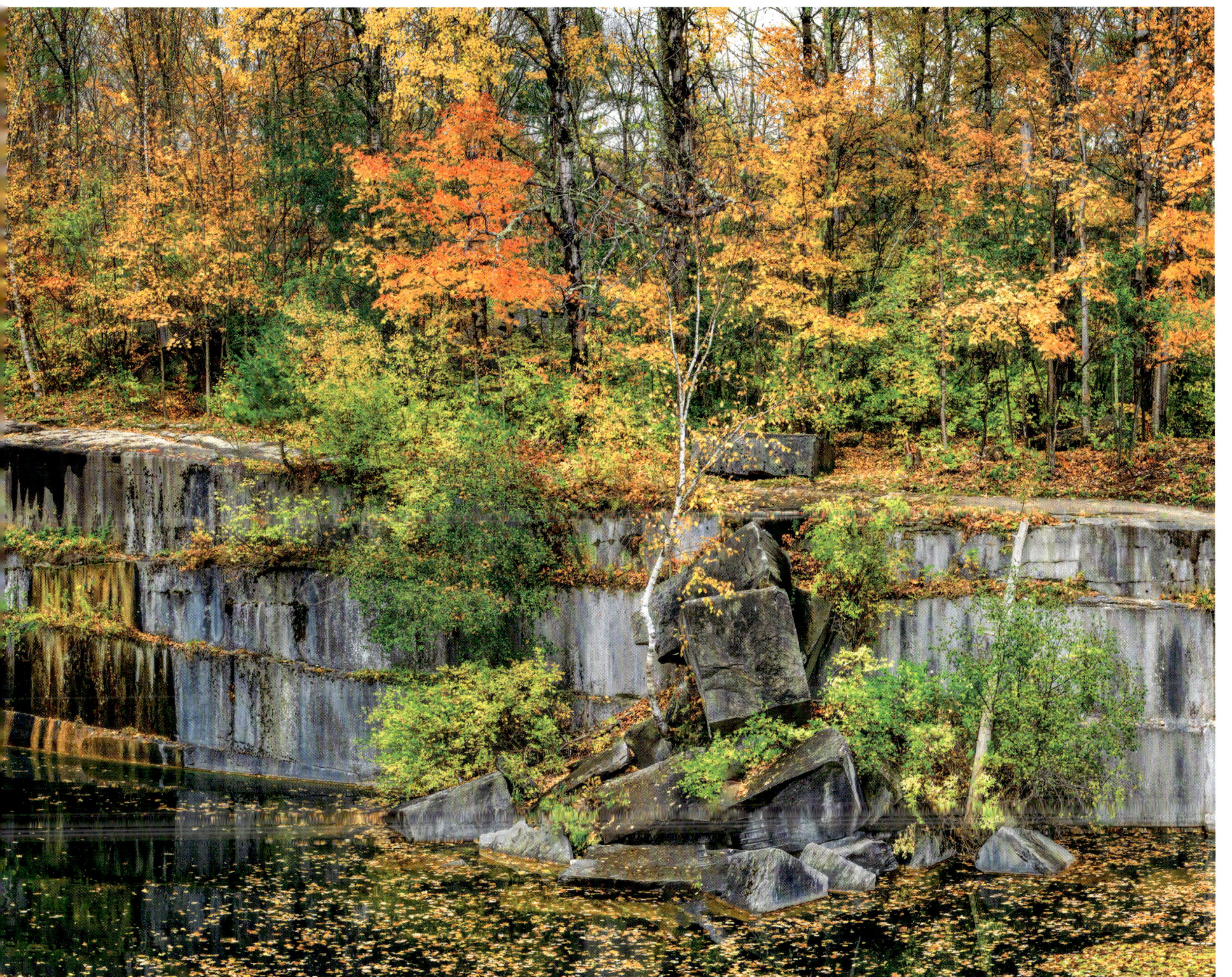

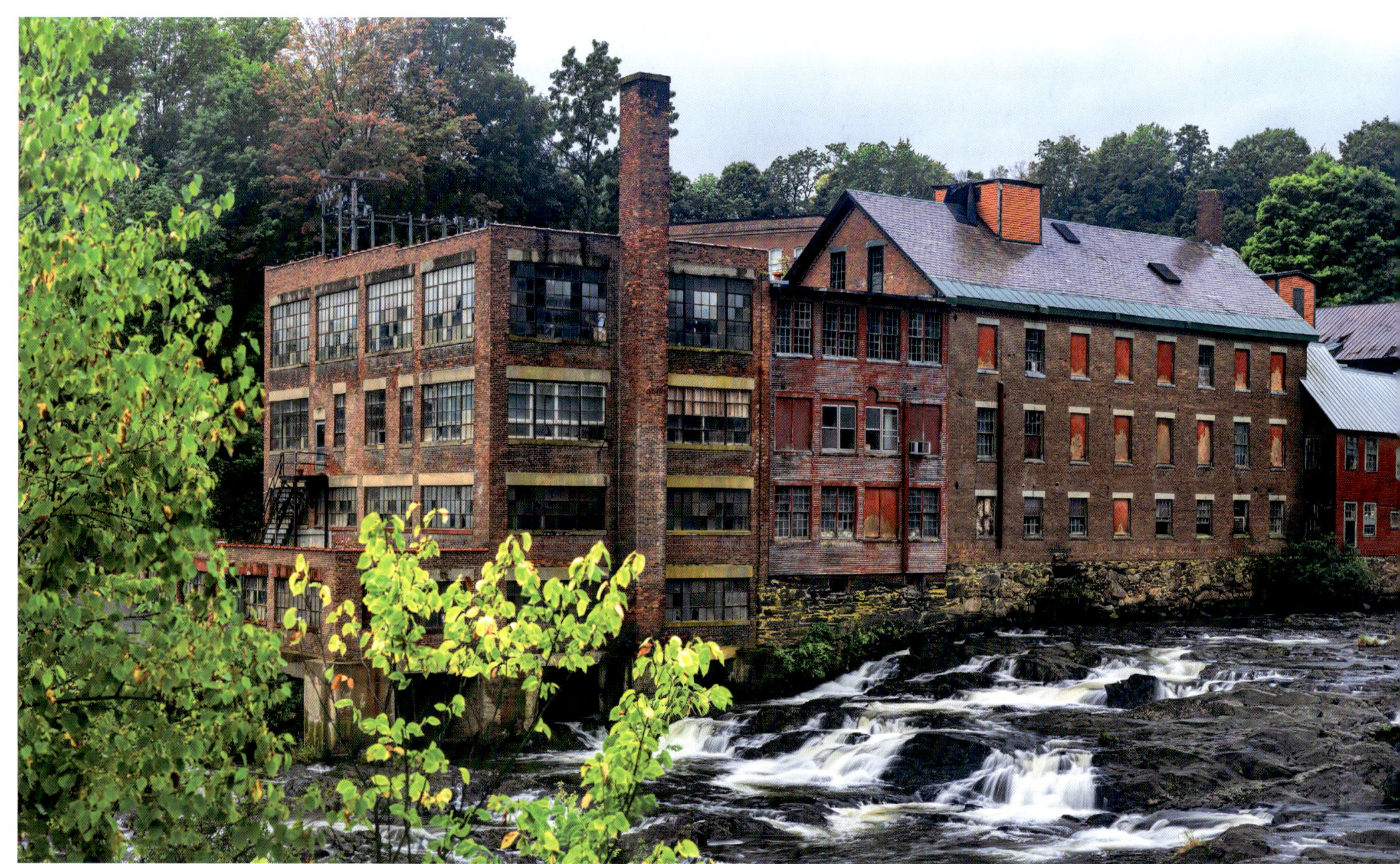

Springfield, Vermont

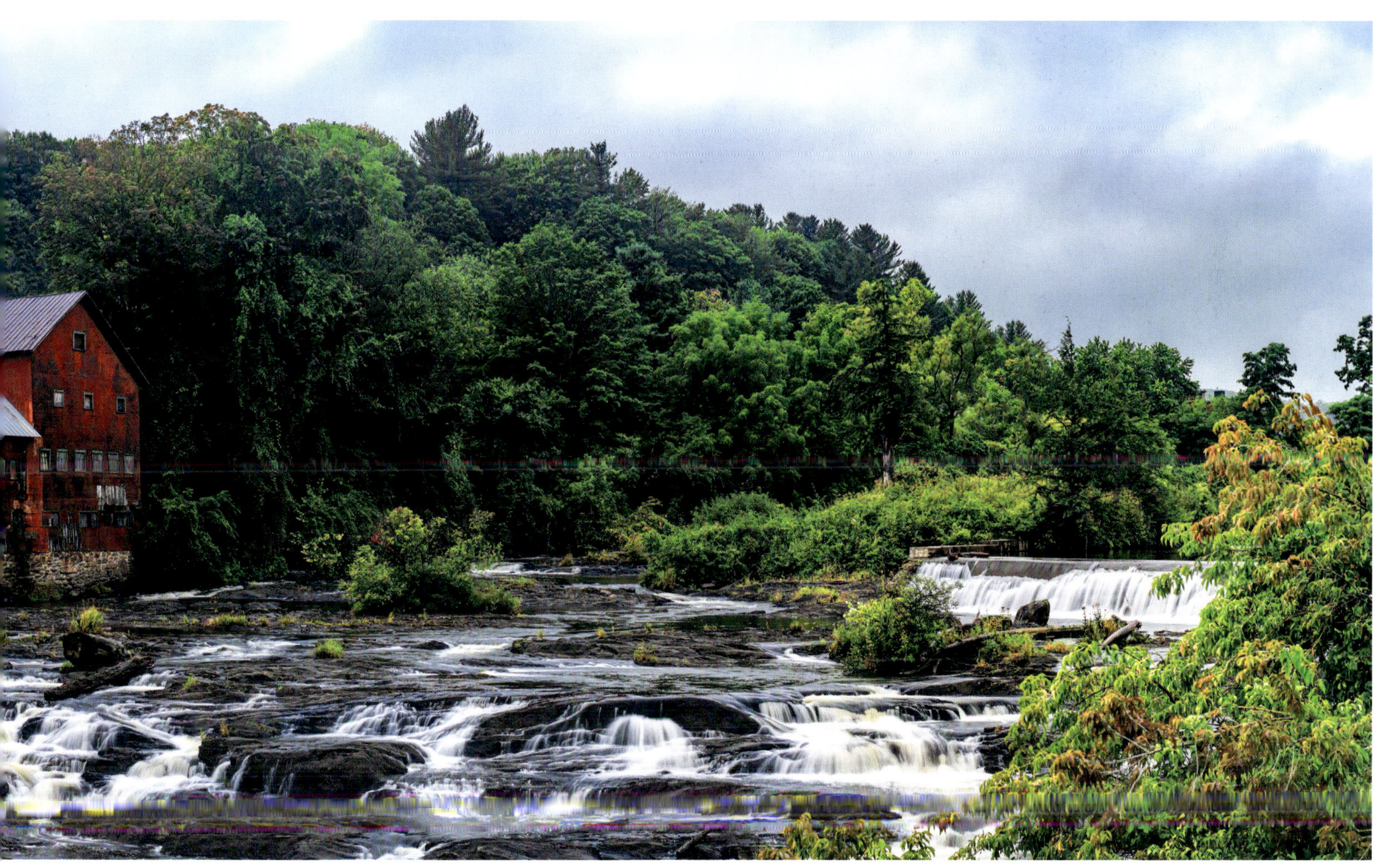

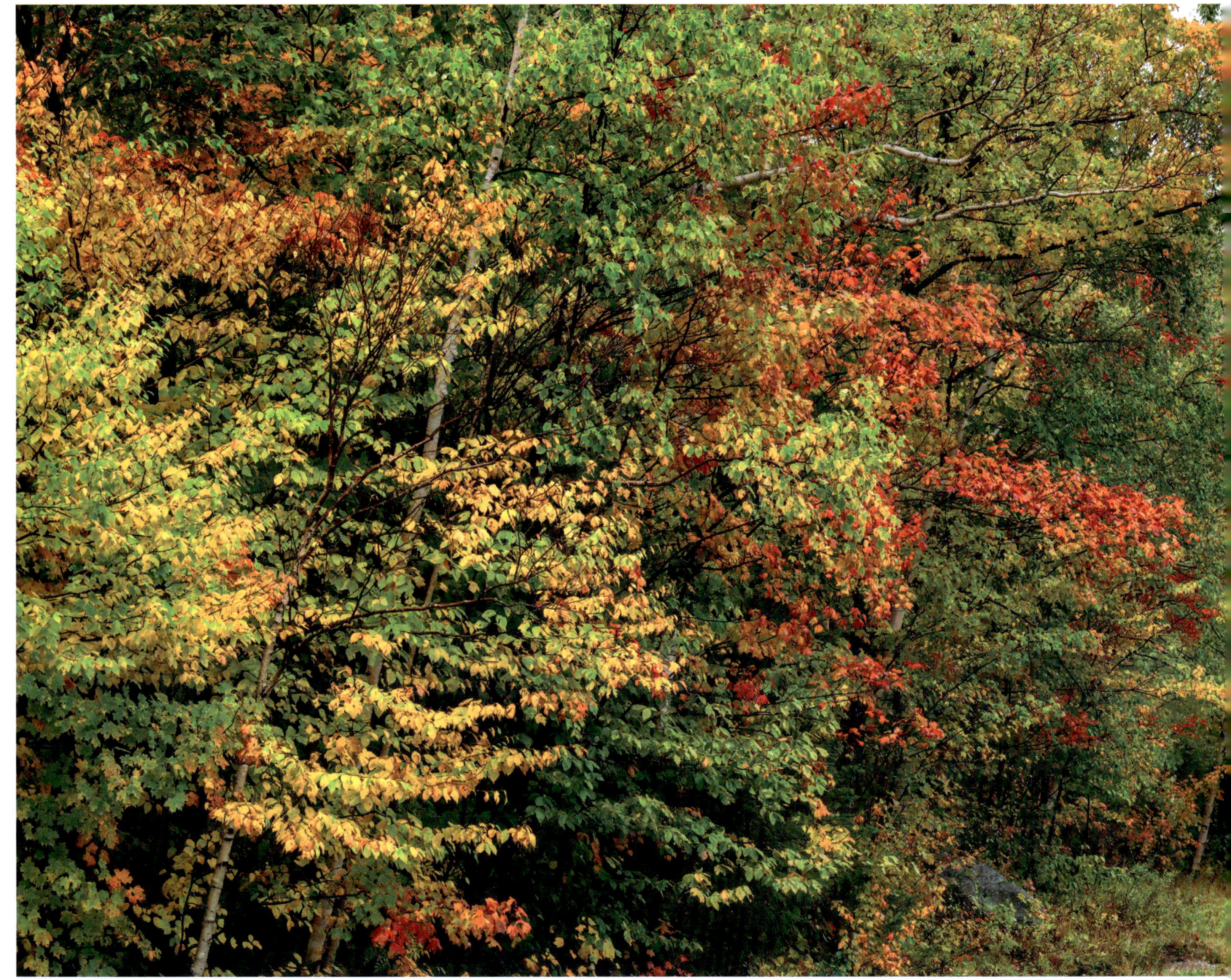

Mount Ellen Ski Area, Vermont

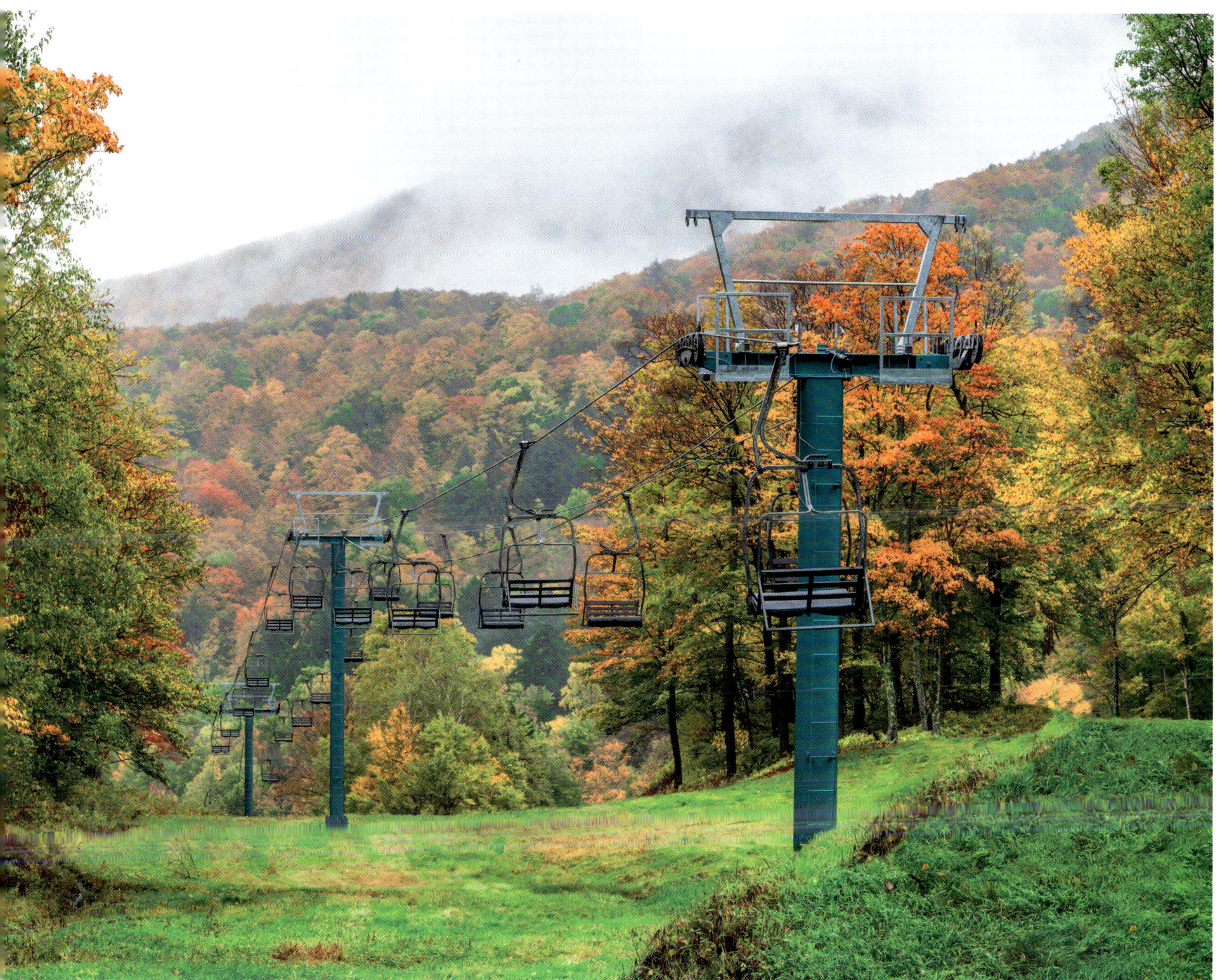

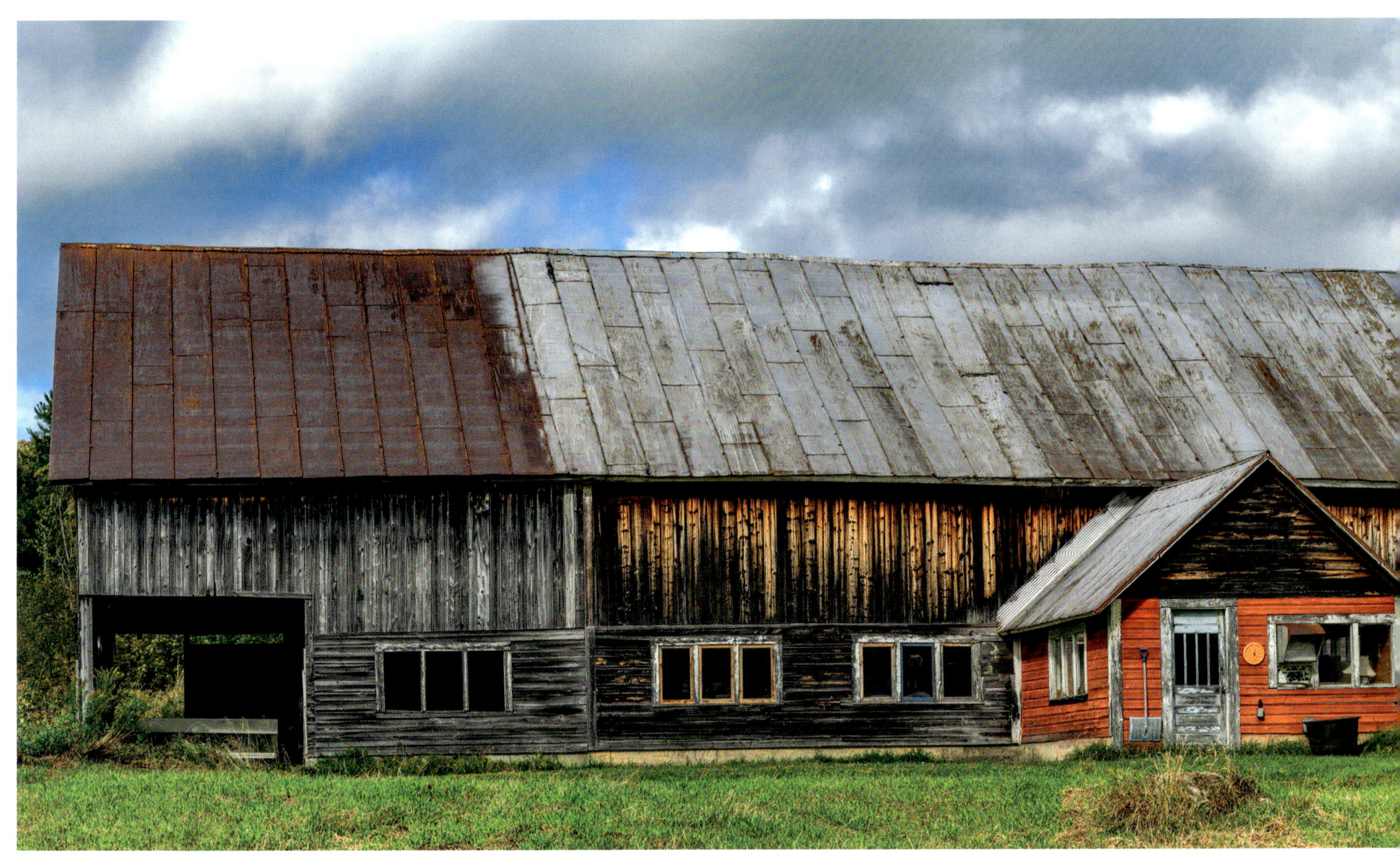

Barn on Seyon Pond Road, Vermont

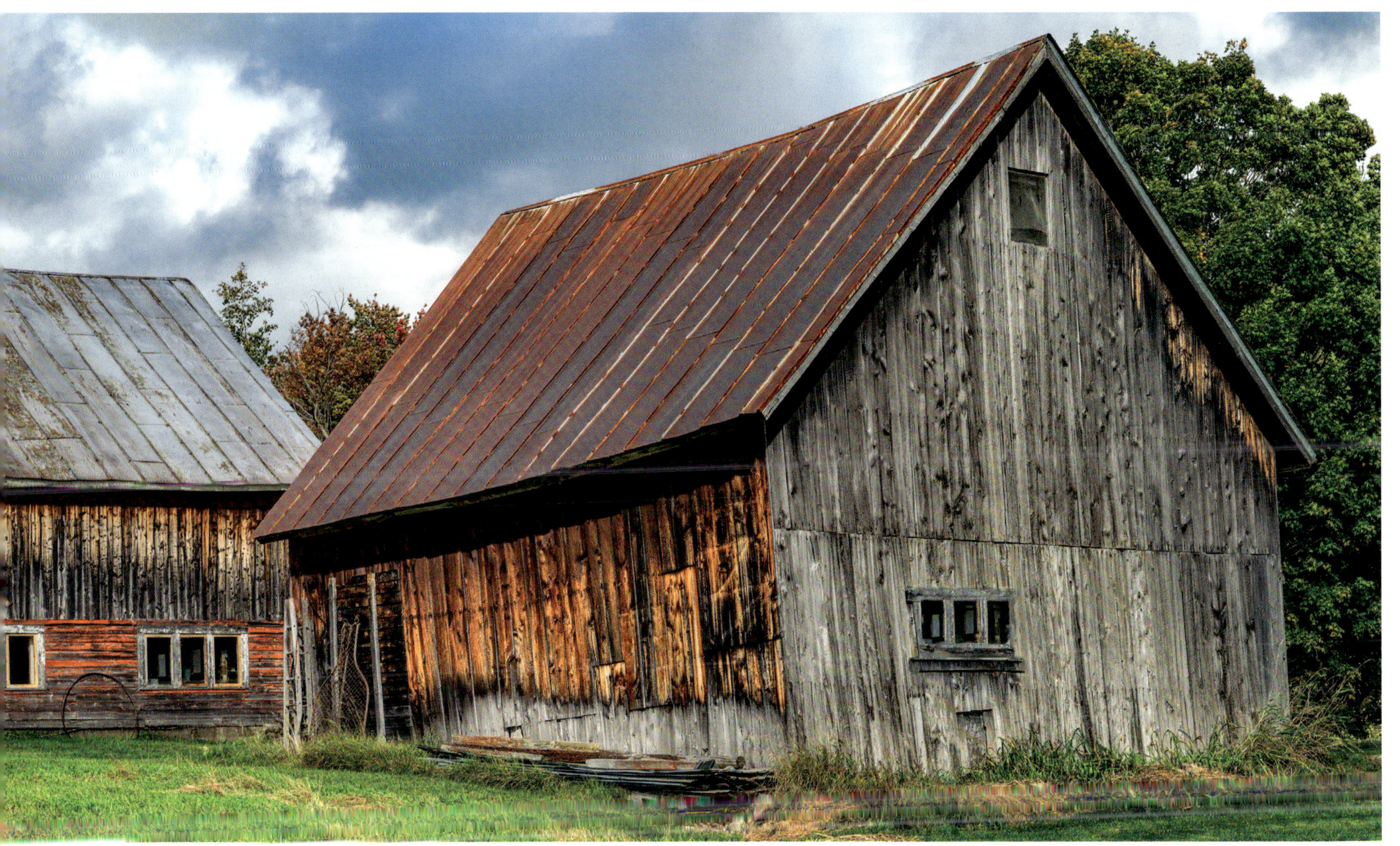

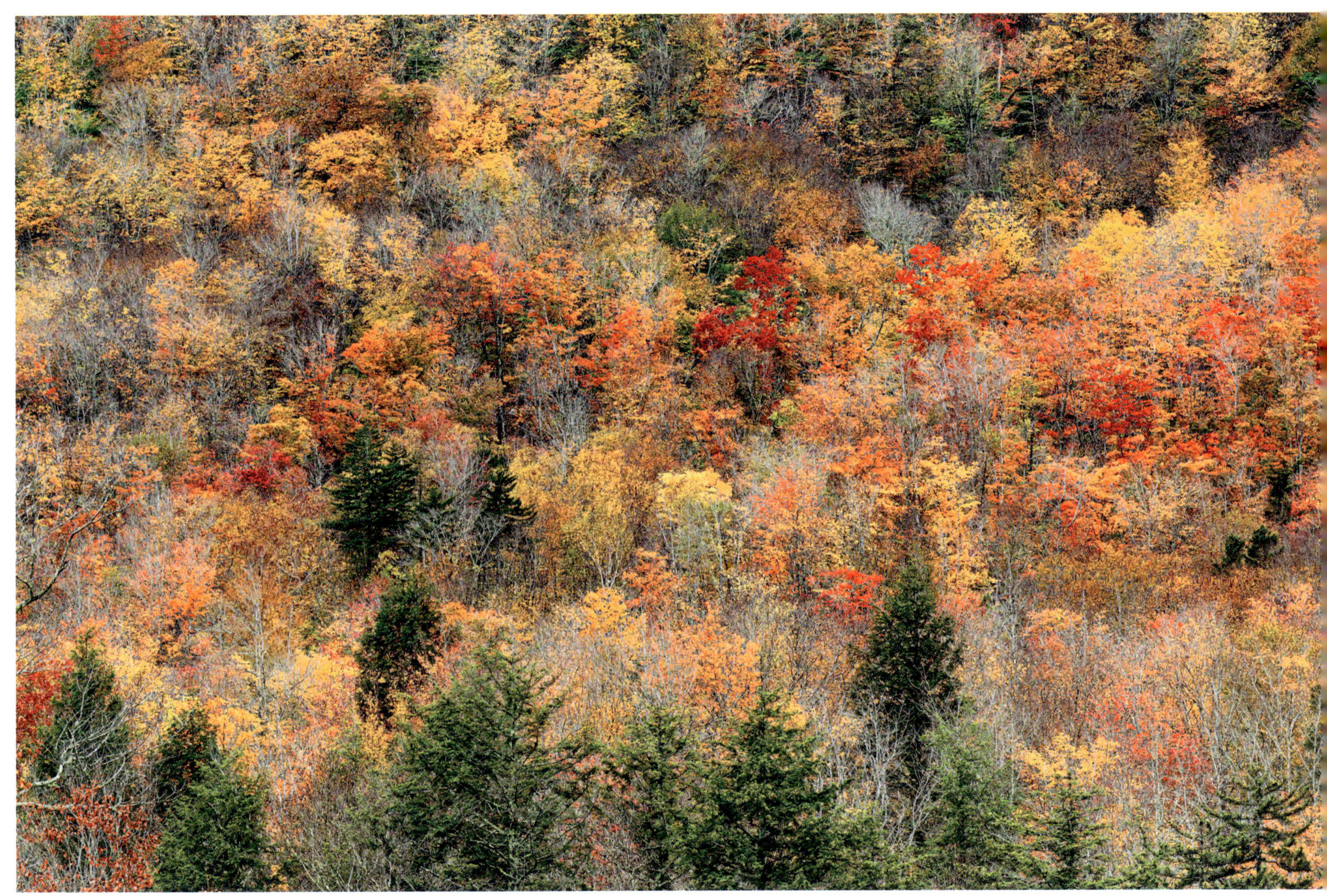

Vermont maple trees

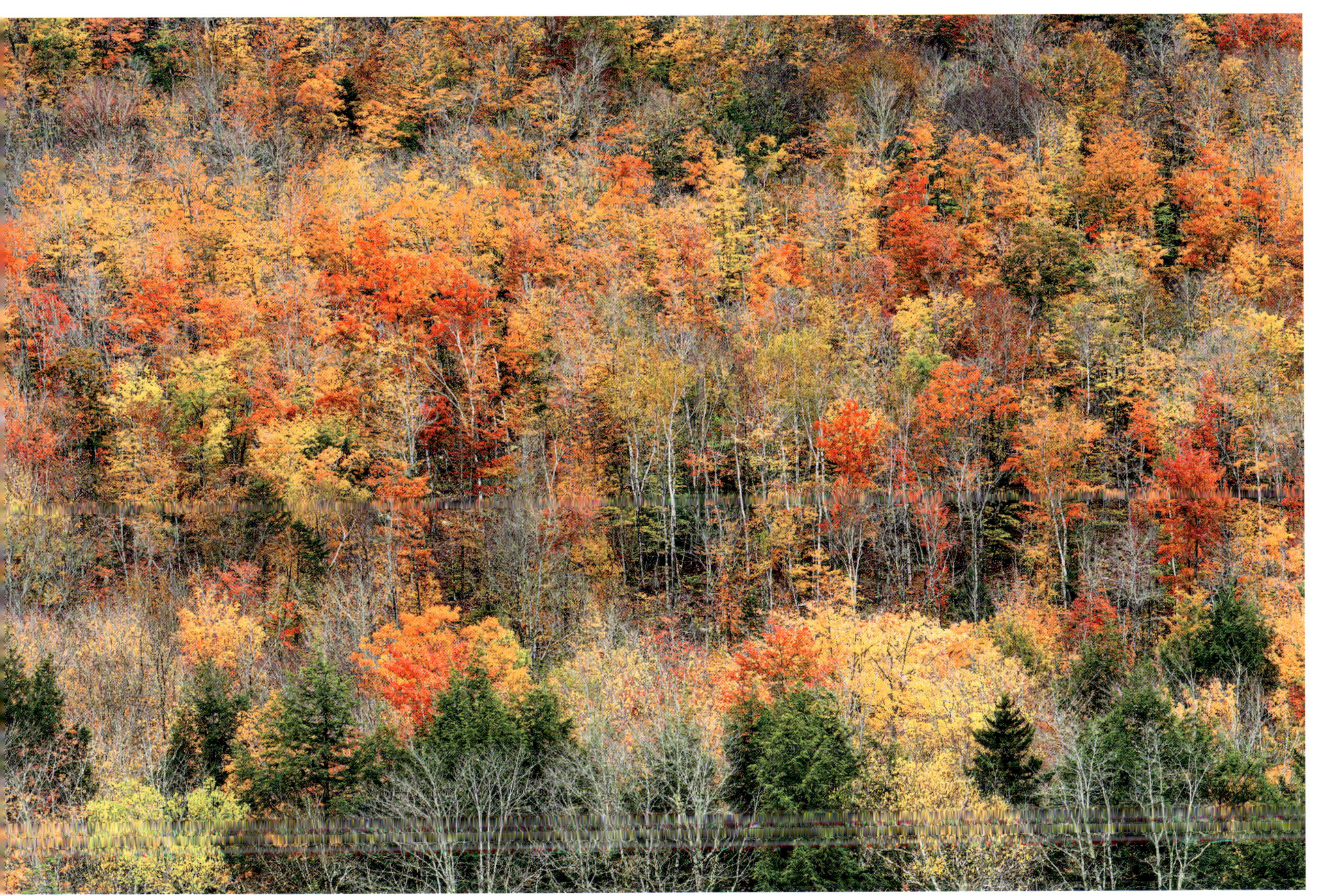

I can think of no better way to say goodbye for now to New England.

APPENDIX

For all the photographers out there who love to have all the tech information, I have included this appendix. May the geeks like me enjoy!

Page	Image Name	Camera	Lens	F-stop	Shutter Speed	ISO	Pano Image Count	Pano Levels	Native Dimensions in Inches
01	Lake McDonough	Nikon D810	Nikkor 85 mm f/1.8	f/10	1/25	64	8	1	61 × 20
02	Taftville, Connecticut	Nikon D850	Nikkor 85 mm f/1.8	f/10	1/30	64	12	1	60 × 22
03	Number 65 with azalea bushes	Nikon D850	Zeiss 135 mm f/2.0	f/10	1/250	64	15	2	47 × 18
04	Kent Falls, Connecticut	Nikon D810	Nikkor 50 mm f/1.4	f/14	1.5″	64	7	1	40 × 16
05	The Marianne, Mystic Seaport, Connecticut	Nikon D850	Nikkor 50 mm f/1.4	f/13	1/200	64	20	2	73 × 25
06A	New England bullfrog	Nikon D300s	Nikkor 300 mm f/5.6	f/5.6	1/1000	3200	n/a	n/a	24 × 16
06B	Gypsy Woods horses	Nikon D500	Nikkor 200–500 mm f/5.6	f/5.6	1/2500	1100	n/a	n/a	24 × 16
07	Sea View Snack Bar, Mystic, Connecticut	Nikon D850	Nikkor 50 mm f/1.4	f/13	1/80	64	10	1	62 × 21
08	50 Farnsworth Street, New London,	Nikon D850	Nikkor 85 mm f/1.8	f/10	1/20	64	18	2	60 × 27
09A	Canada goose on Connecticut coast	Nikon D500	Nikkor 200–500 mm f/5.6	f/7.1	1/6400	2200	n/a	n/a	16 × 24
09B	Old Saybrook Point Lighthouse	Nikon D850	Nikkor 85 mm f/1.8	f/10	1/125	64	6	1	40 × 20
10	Norm's Diner, Groton, Connecticut	Nikon D850	Nikkor 35 mm f/1.4	f/11	1/4	64	26	2	88 × 34
11	The Rough Tide, Thames Shipyards	Nikon D850	Nikkor 85 mm f/1.8	f/10	1/200	64	11	1	49 × 18
12	Gold Star Bridge over the Thames River	Nikon D850	Nikkor 50 mm f/1.4	f/11	1/80	64	28	2	89 × 36
13	Eugene O'Neill Drive, New London	Nikon D850	Nikkor 85 mm f/1.8	f/10	1/160	64	12	1	96 × 24
14	Beach house, Snug Harbor	Nikon D850	Zeiss 135 mm f/2.0	f/13	1/100	64	8	1	66 × 22
15	Claiborne Pell Newport Bridge	Nikon D850	Nikkor 85 mm f/1.8	f/14	1/30	64	7	1	47 × 20
16A	Scituate Reservoir, Rhode Island	Nikon D850	Nikkor 85 mm f/1.8	f/11	1/80	64	5	1	35 × 20
16B	The other side of the road	Nikon D850	Nikkor 85 mm f/1.8	f/11	1/8	64	14	2	50 × 58
17	Bonnet Shores, Wesquage Pond	Nikon D850	Zeiss 135 mm f/2.0	f/9.0	1/200	64	7	1	47 × 18
18	Old New England rock walls	Nikon D700	Nikkor 35 mm f/1.4	f/16	1/8	100	10	1	52 × 22
19	Narragansett, Rhode Island	Nikon D850	Zeiss 135 mm f/2.0	f/9.0	1/200	64	8	1	76 × 22

20A	Great blue heron, Long Pond	Nikon D500	Nikkor 200–500 mm f/5.6	f/8	1/3200	40000	n/a	n/a	24 × 18
20B	Perfect house, Rhode Island	Nikon D850	Nikkor 50 mm f/1.4	f/11	1/160	64	14	2	48 × 36
21	Point Judith Lighthouse, Rhode Island	Nikon D850	Zeiss 135 mm f/2.0	f/9.0	1/200	64	8	1	60 × 22
22A	Picnic spot, Pulaski State Park	Nikon D850	Nikkor 50 mm f/1.4	f/14	1/6	64	20	2	73 × 36
22B	Donkey buddies on Rhode Island farm	Nikon D500	Nikkor 200–500 mm f/5.6	f/7.1	1/3200	2200	n/a	n/a	16 × 24
23	White Mill Pond, Rhode Island	Nikon D850	Nikkor 50 mm f/1.4	f/11	1/80	64	18	2	54 × 22
24	West Greenwich Fire and Rescue, Rhode Island	Nikon D 850	Nikkor 85 mm f/1.8	f/10	1/125	64	9	1	52 × 22
25	Cattle on North Road, Foster, Rhode Island	Nikon D850	Zeiss 135 mm f/2.0	f/8	1/125	64	7	1	47 × 19
26	Town Square, Princeton, Massachusetts	Nikon D850	Nikkor 85 mm f/1.8	f/11	1/8	64	10	1	50 × 18
27	Cemetery, Holden, Massachusetts	Nikon D850	Nikkor 85 mm f/1.8	f/11	1/8	64	8	1	56 × 17
28	Quaboag River crossing, Massachusetts	Nikon D850	Nikkor 85 mm f/1.8	f/11	1/40	64	32	2	114 × 36
29	Day of the Dead display, Massachusetts	Nikon D850	Nikkor 85 mm f/1.8	f/13	1/8	64	10	1	64 × 22
30A	Lone tree, Gilbertville, Massachusetts	Nikon D850	Nikkor 50 mm f/1.4	f/13	1/60	64	12	2	50 × 30
30B	Guinea fowl	Nikon D500	Nikkor 200–500 mm f/5.6	f/5.6	1/2500	640	n/a	n/a	17 × 24
31	Goodnow Farm, Massachusetts	Nikon D850	Nikkor 85 mm f/1.8	f/11	1/20	64	12	1	58 × 21
32A	House near Salem, Massachusetts	Nikon D300	Nikkor 300 mm f/5.6	f/9.0	1/250	200	n/a	n/a	24 × 19
32B	Shelburne Falls, Massachusetts	Nikon D850	Nikkor 50 mm f/1.4	f/10	1/320	64	7	1	48 × 38
33	Major Willard Moore Memorial Park	Nikon D850	Nikkor 85 mm f/1.8	f/13	10″	64	14	2	43 × 16
34	Gilbertville Bridge, Massachusetts	Nikon D850	Nikkor 50 mm f/1.4	f/11	1/80	64	9	1	59 × 23
35A	Sweet, curious New England deer	Nikon D500	Nikkor 200–500 mm f/5.6	f/8	1/3200	22800	n/a	n/a	24 × 22
35B	Halloween week in Massachusetts	Nikon D850	Nikkor 50 mm f/1.4	f/14	1/8	64	16	2	48 × 44
36	Barn near Granby, Massachusetts	Nikon D850	Nikkor 85 mm f/1.8	f/11	1/60	64	20	2	78 × 27
37A	Petersham Memorial Library, 1890	Nikon D850	Nikkor 50 mm f/1.4	f/13	1/60	64	10	2	48 × 38
37B	Rockport, Massachusetts	Nikon D850	Nikkor 50 mm f/1.4	f/11	1/250	200	10	2	40 × 30
38	The Clam Box, Brookfield, Massachusetts	Nikon D850	Nikkor 50 mm f/1.4	f/11	1/5	64	10	1	60 × 21
39	Pigeon Cove, Rockport, Massachusetts	Nikon D850	Nikkor 85 mm f/1.8	f/13	1/125	200	13	1	72 × 22
40	Nobska Lighthouse, Cape Cod	Nikon D850	Nikkor 50 mm f/1.4	f/13	1/160	64	20	2	69 × 28
41	Summer cabins, North Truro	Nikon D850	Nikkor 50 mm f/1.4	f/14	1/80	64	30	2	82 × 33

42	Bracy Cove, Maine	Nikon D810	Nikkor 50 mm f/1.4	f/13	1/15	64	10	1	50 × 20
43	Scarborough Lobster, Maine	Nikon D850	Nikkor 50 mm f/1.4	f/11	1/400	64	9	1	57 × 23
44A	Kennebec River from Granite City Park	Nikon D850	Nikkor 50 mm f/1.4	F16	1/40	64	16	2	40 × 26
44B	Belfast Harbor, Maine	Nikon D700	Nikkor 35 mm f/1.4	f/11	1/100	100	8	1	40 × 26
45	Mount Katahdin and Abol Stream	Nikon D850	Nikkor 50 mm f/1.4	f/11	1/160	64	9	1	50 × 23
46A	Bald eagle, Deer Isle, Maine	Nikon D500	Nikkor 200–500 mm f/5.6	f/5.6	1/2000	160	n/a	n/a	24 × 16
46B	Rowboats, Sorento, Maine	Nikon D700	Nikkor 35 mm f/1.4	f/11	1/200	200	9	1	48 × 32
47	Sunset, Tremont Wharf, Bernard	Nikon D850	Nikkor 50 mm f/1.4	f/9.0	1/4	80	10	1	70 × 22
48A	Gulf of Maine	Nikon D500	Nikkor 200–500 mm f/5.6	f/5.6	1/3200	100	n/a	n/a	24 × 19
48B	Red maple tree, Crawford Stream, Maine	Nikon D850	Zeiss 135 mm f/2.0	f/11	1/40	64	6	1	48 × 38
49	Pumpkin Island Light, Maine	Nikon D750	Nikkor 85 mm f/1.8	f/11	1/250	100	14	2	60 × 23
50	Johnston's Orchard, Maine	Nikon D850	Nikkor 50 mm f/1.4	f/14	1/60	64	9	1	49 × 21
51B	Trees on Maine State Highway 191	Nikon D850	Zeiss 135 mm f/2.0	f/13	1/6	64	18	2	62 × 33
52	Stonington Harbor, Maine	Nikon D750	Nikkor 85 mm f/1.8	f/11	1/400	400	9	1	50 × 17
53A	Marshall Point Lighthouse, Maine	Nikon D300	Nikkor 10.5 mm f/2.8	f/11	1/250	160	n/a	n/a	20 × 24
53B	West Quoddy Head, Lubec, Maine	Nikon D850	Nikkor 50 mm f/2.0	f/11	1/13	64	n/a	n/a	30 × 36
54	Heath Mill Landing, Maine	Nikon D850	Nikkor 50 mm f/1.4	f/13	1/80	64	9	1	41 × 19
55A	Nubble Light, York Harbor, Maine	Nikon D700	Nikkor 35 mm f/1.4	f/16	1/250	100	18	2	48 × 40
55B	Pemaquid Point, Maine	Nikon D810	Nikkor 50 mm f/1.4	f/13	1/80	64	14	2	48 × 40
56	Androscoggin River, New Hampshire	Nikon D700	Nikkor 35 mm f/1.4	f/11	1/320	100	10	1	74 × 22
57	Hay truck	Nikon D700	Nikkor 85 mm f/1.8	f/8	1/500	100	8	1	62 × 23
58	Coffin Pond, New Hampshire	Nikon D850	Nikkor 50 mm f/1.4	f/13	1/50	64	8	1	56 × 22
59A	Church in Monroe, New Hampshire	Nikon D850	Nikkor 50 mm f/1.4	f/13	1/2	64	4	1	48 × 26
59B	Barn and flag	Nikon D850	Nikkor 85 mm f/1.8	f/11	1/15	64	6	1	48 × 26
60	Barker Road railroad crossing	Nikon D750	Nikkor 85 mm f/1.8	f/11	1/125	100	6	1	60 × 23
61A	Resting New England moose	Nikon D500	Nikkor 200–500 mm f/5.6	f/5.6	1/1600	2500	n/a	n/a	24 × 16
61B	Intrepid golfer, New Hampshire	Nikon D500	Nikkor 200–500 mm f/5.6	f/8	1/1200	320	n/a	n/a	24 × 16
62	Mountain Star Farms, New Hampshire	Nikon D850	Nikkor 85 mm f/1.8	f/11	1/40	64	9	1	60 × 22

63	Gas pump collection	Nikon D850	Nikkor 85 mm f/1.8	f/11	1/200	64	10	1	62 × 20
64	First Connecticut Lake	Nikon D850	Nikkor 50 mm f/1.4	f/10	1/100	64	6	1	66 × 27
65A	Beekeeper, New Hampshire	Nikon D500	Nikkor 200–500 mm f/5.6	f/7.1	1/1600	640	n/a	n/a	24 × 24
65B	Bath Bridge, New Hampshire	Nikon D850	Zeiss 135 mm f/2.0	f/11	1/125	64	7	1	41 × 22
66	Railroad bridge	Nikon D850	Zeiss 135 mm f/2.0	f/11	1/100	64	8	1	64 × 30
67	Hay truck along New Hampshire State Highway 116	Nikon D850	Nikkor 50 mm f/1.4	f/13	1/30	64	9	1	56 × 22
68	Chocorua Lake, New Hampshire	Nikon D750	Nikkor 35 mm f/1.4	f/10	1/125	100	9	1	58 × 23
69	Cornfield in the pouring rain	Nikon D850	Nikkor 50 mm f/1.4	f/13	1/10	64	7	1	52 × 19
70	Pillsbury Lake, New Hampshire	Nikon D750	Nikkor 35 mm f/1.4	f/11	1/30	100	10	1	47 × 17
71	Squam Boats Marina, Squam Lake	Nikon D750	Nikkor 85 mm f/1.8	f/10	1/160	100	6	1	35 × 14
72	Frankenstein Cliff, White Mountains	Nikon D850	Nikkor 85 mm f/1.8	f/11	1/125	64	9	1	62 × 24
73	Fisher Bridge, Vermont, 1908	Nikon D700	Nikkor 35 mm f/1.4	f/8	1/500	100	10	1	38 × 12
74	Farm along Vermont State Highway 125	Nikon D700	Nikkor 105 mm f/2.8	f/9.0	1/125	100	12	1	90 × 27
75	Pumpkin stand, Jeffersonville, Vermont	Nikon D850	Nikkor 50 mm f/1.4	f/11	1/100	64	7	1	57 × 21
76	Brookdale Bridge, Stowe, Vermont	Nikon D850	Nikkor 50 mm f/1.4	f/14	1/50	64	8	1	52 × 24
77	Mach's Market, Pawlet, Vermont	Nikon D850	Nikkor 50 mm f/1.4	f/9.0	1/30	64	10	1	51 × 22
78A	First Congregational Church, Manchester, Vermont	Nikon D850	Nikkor 50 mm f/1.4	f/11	1/125	64	14	2	42 × 37
78B	Snowy trees near Swanton, Vermont	Nikon D300	Nikkor 24 mm f/2.0	f/11	1/6	100	n/a	n/a	21 × 18
79	Belvidere Mountain, Vermont	Nikon D850	Nikkor 85 mm f/1.8	f/9.0	1/125	64	5	1	40 × 12
80	Dorset Marble Quarry, Vermont	Nikon D850	Nikkor 50 mm f/1.4	f/11	1/15	64	8	1	48 × 18
81	Springfield, Vermont	Nikon D750	Nikkor 85 mm f/1.8	f/11	1/2	100	9	1	53 × 16
82	Mount Ellen Ski Area, Vermont	Nikon D810	Nikkor 85 mm f/1.8	f/11	1/8	64	6	1	36 × 16
83	Barn on Seyon Pond Road, Vermont	Nikon D850	Zeiss 135 mm f/2.0	f/10	1/125	64	9	1	78 × 23
84	Vermont maple trees	Nikon D850	Zeiss 135 mm f/2.0	f/9.0	1/4	64	5	1	64 × 20

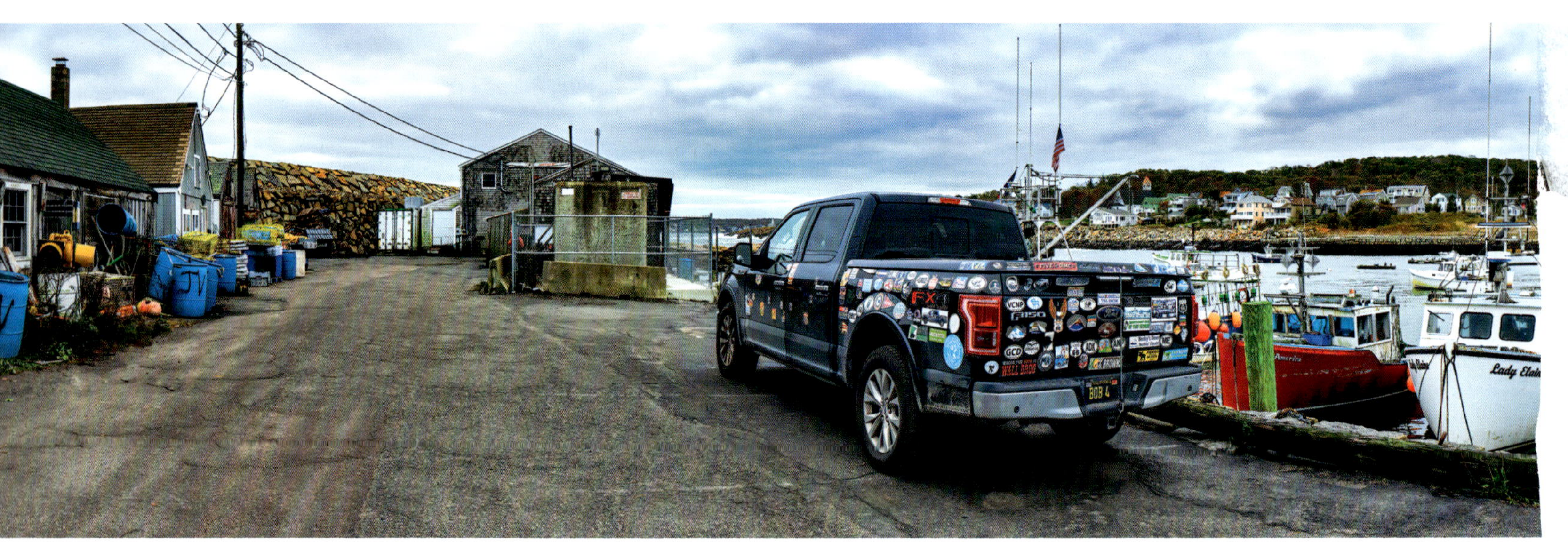

Bob 4 at Pigeon Cove, Massachusetts

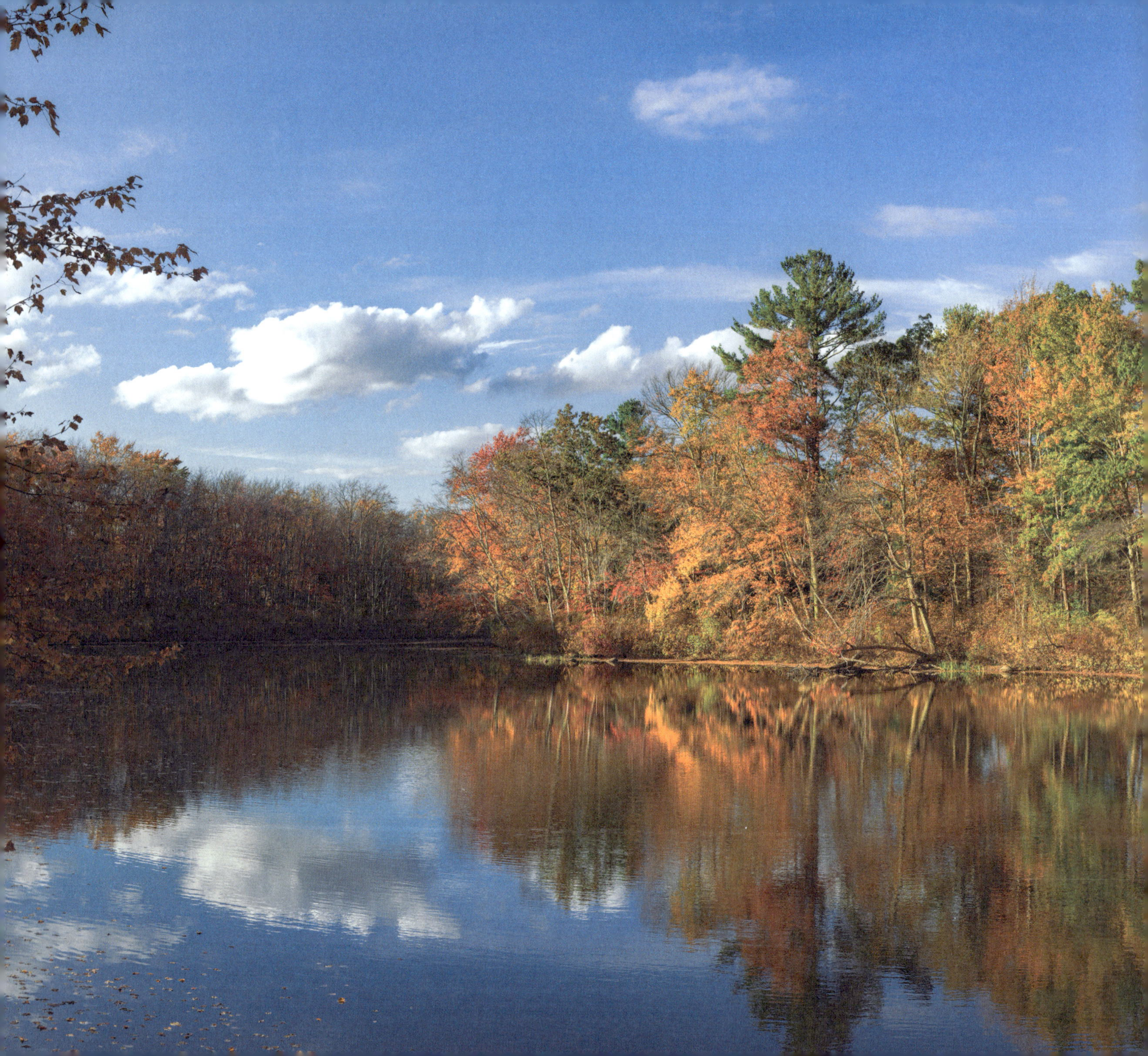